Training and Development in Australia

2nd edition

In Memory of Mollie Hewitt
(1913–1997)

Training and Development in Australia

2nd edition

Andrew Smith
*MA (Camb) MBA (Aston) PhD (Tas)
Associate Professor & Head of School
School of Management
Charles Sturt University*

Butterworths
*Sydney — Adelaide — Brisbane — Canberra
Melbourne — Perth
1998*

AUSTRALIA	LexisNexisButterworths
	Tower 2, 475–495 Victoria Avenue, CHATSWOOD NSW 2067
	On the internet at: www.lexisnexis.com.au
ARGENTINA	Abeledo Perrot, Jurisprudencia Argentina and Depalma, BUENOS AIRES
AUSTRIA	ARD Betriebsdienst and Verlag Orac, VIENNA
CANADA	Butterworths Canada Ltd, MARKHAM, Ontario
CHILE	Publitecsa and Conosur Ltda, SANTIAGO DE CHILE
CZECH REPUBLIC	Orac sro, PRAGUE
FRANCE	Editions du Juris-Classeur SA, PARIS
HONG KONG	Butterworths Asia (Hong Kong), HONG KONG
HUNGARY	Hvg Orac, BUDAPEST
INDIA	Butterworths India, NEW DELHI
IRELAND	Butterworths (Ireland) Ltd, DUBLIN
ITALY	Giuffré, MILAN
MALAYSIA	Malayan Law Journal Sdn Bhd, KUALA LUMPUR
NEW ZEALAND	Butterworths of New Zealand, WELLINGTON
POLAND	Wydawnictwa Prawnicze PWN, WARSAW
SINGAPORE	Butterworths Asia, SINGAPORE
SOUTH AFRICA	Butterworths Publishers (Pty) Ltd, DURBAN
SWITZERLAND	Stämpfli Verlag AG, BERNE
UNITED KINGDOM	Butterworths Tolley, LONDON, EDINBURGH
USA	LexisNexis, DAYTON, Ohio

National Library of Australia Cataloguing-in-Publication entry

---

Smith, Andrew, 1954–
  Training and development in Australia
  2nd edition
  Inclues index
  ISBN 0 409 31177 4
  1. Employees — Training of — Australia. 2. Occupational training — Australia. I. Title.
658.31240994

© 1998 Reed International Books Australia Pty Limited.
Reprinted 2000, 2002.
First edtion 1992. Reprinted 1993, 1995, 1996 and 1997.

This book is copyright. Except as permitted under the Copyright Act 1968 (Cth), no part of this publication may be reproduced by any process, electronic or otherwise, without the specific written permission of the copyright owner. Neither may information be stored electronically in any form whatsoever without such permission.

Inquiries should be addressed to the publishers.

Printed in Australia by Ligare Pty Ltd.

Visit LexisNexis Butterworths at www.lexisnexis.com.au

Contents

Preface	ix
Chapter 1 Training and Development in Australia	**1**
Definitions of Training and Development	1
The Importance of Training and Development	4
Training and Development in Australia	7
The Training and Development Practitioner	11
Summary	16
Discussion Questions	16
Chapter 2 The Australian Training System	**17**
The Need for Change	18
VET in Australia	20
The National Training Reform Agenda	21
Competency-based Training	29
Entry-level Training: Apprenticeships and Traineeships	34
The New Training Providers	37
Summary	39
Discussion Questions	40
Chapter 3 Learners and Learning	**41**
The Passive Learner	42
The Active Learner	48
The Adult Learner	56
The Workplace Learner	69
Summary	74
Discussion Questions	75
Chapter 4 Training and Organisations	**76**
Human Capital Theory	76
Internal Labour Market Theory	81

The OECD/CERI Studies	83
The NIESR Studies	85
The Skills Equilibrium Model	88
Training, Technology and New Working Practices	90
Training and Industrial Relations	97
Training and Human Resource Management	101
Training and Corporate Strategy	104
What Drives Training?	107
Summary	111
Discussion Questions	113

Chapter 5 Analysing Training Needs — 114

Three Level Analysis	115
Analysing Performance Problems	117
Occupational and Competency-based Analysis	119
Methods of Analysis	124
Which Method When?	135
Summary	136
Discussion Questions	137

Chapter 6 Designing Training Programs — 138

The Training System	138
Training Objectives	142
Designing Training Programs	146
Training Strategies	152
The Training Environment	157
Transferring Training to the Workplace	158
Summary	162
Discussion Questions	163

Chapter 7 Delivering Training — 164

The Role of the Trainer	164
Training Methods	166
Training Media	176
Summary	185
Discussion Questions	186

Chapter 8 Assessment and Evaluation in Training — 187

Assessment	188
Evaluation	195
Models of Evaluation	198
Techniques of Evaluation	203

Evaluation Designs	208
Design Validity and Criterion Development	211
Strategic Evaluation	214
Issues in Evaluation	216
Summary	219
Discussion Questions	221

Chapter 9 Management Development — 222

Managers in Australia	222
Models of Management Development	234
Methods of Management Development	240
The Karpin Report	247
The Frontline Manager	250
Summary	253
Discussion Questions	254

Chapter 10 Towards the Learning Organisation — 255

What is Organisational Change?	256
Organisation Development	261
Changing the Corporate Culture	265
The Quality Approach	268
Teamworking	273
The Learning Organisation	276
Summary	281
Discussion Questions	282

Chapter 11 Coaching, Counselling and Consulting — 283

Origins and Practice of Counselling	284
Counselling in the Workplace	286
Coaching	292
Mentoring	295
Consulting	301
Summary	307
Discussion Questions	308

References	309
Index	329

Preface

In the preface to the first edition of *Training and Development in Australia* in 1992, I wrote that a number of forces had acted in the late 1980s and early 1990s to propel issues of training and development onto the agenda of boardrooms in Australia.

In the years since 1992, the importance of training and development has become even more pronounced. Starting under the federal Labor government of 1983–96 and continuing under its Coalition successor, the training system in Australia has been thoroughly reformed to make it more responsive to the needs of industry. Federal, state and territory governments have cooperated in the implementation of competency-based training, the creation of a national framework for training and the introduction of new forms of apprenticeship and traineeship training. These changes have had a major impact on the way training is carried out in Australia. Nor have these changes been limited to the so-called 'supply side' of the training market. The demand for training from industry has also increased dramatically. New approaches to training that embrace all workers, not only managerial and professional employees, have been implemented successfully in many industries and by many companies. The extent and quality of training experienced by the average Australian worker has improved considerably in the last five years.

It is the impact of these changes that has been the principal driving force behind the second edition of this book. Since 1992 *Training and Development in Australia* has been adopted by many universities and colleges throughout Australia as the popularity of training and development as a subject area grows in line with its increasing importance to business and industry. The new edition has been significantly updated and contains two new chapters that reflect the new thinking in the training and development area. Chapter 2 analyses the changes to the vocational education and training system in recent years and Chapter 4 explores the theory of training in the organisational context. I hope that the new edition will serve students of training and development as faithfully as the first.

As always, there is a long list of colleagues whom I would like to thank for their help in the production of the new edition. In particular, however, I would like to thank my wife, Erica Smith, Lecturer in Vocational Education and Training at Charles Sturt University, whose expertise in the area of VET resulted in her making a significant contribution to the new edition, by writing the majority of Chapter 2 on the changes to the Australian training system. And, as always, thanks to my children, Heather, Owen and Sally, who had to put up with yet another paternal absence.

I hope you will find the new edition of *Training and Development in Australia* a stimulating and useful addition to your bookshelf.

Andrew Smith
Faculty of Commerce
Charles Sturt University
1998

Chapter 1

Training and Development in Australia

In recent years, training and development has assumed centre stage in the effort to restructure the Australian economy to meet the demands of global competition. There is a number of reasons for this, including the growing realisation that training and development can play a critical role in improving the international competitiveness of Australian industry (Dawkins, 1989); changes to the industrial relations system that emphasise the importance of training and development at the enterprise level (Teicher and Grauze, 1996); and reforms to the national training system that attempt to improve the provision of training and development for all employees in the Australian economy (Lundberg, 1994). These factors have led to the emergence of a multi-million dollar training industry in Australia and to a significant enhancement of the role of the training and development practitioner in Australian industry.

This chapter begins with a discussion of the various definitions of training and development that are often used interchangeably in the literature. This is followed by an exploration of the state of the art of training and development in Australian organisations and the emerging role of the training and development practitioner.

Definitions of Training and Development

Definitions of training and development are clouded by the variety of terms used to describe the activities normally ascribed to it. 'Training', 'training and development', 'education', 'employee development', 'personnel development' and the much broader 'human resource development' are all terms frequently used in organisations to describe the process of developing the capacities of the work force.

Confusion arises because although the terms tend to be used interchangeably, they also suggest different activities. Thus, training is most commonly associated with the development of job-related skills; education suggests a much broader activity based on the 'holistic' development of individuals; and development implies growth in a non-organisational context as well as in the workplace.

Leonard Nadler, who lays claim to originating the phrase 'human resource development' (usually abbreviated to 'HRD'), regards HRD as an overarching concept that embraces all three activities (Nadler and Nadler, 1989). The core of training and development is, according to Nadler, learning. Nadler defines training and development as:

> organized learning experiences provided by employers within a specified period of time to bring about the possibility of performance improvement and/or personal growth.

Training, education and development are activity areas within HRD, each with a separate focus. Thus, training is learning focused on the present job of the learner; education is learning focused on a future job for the learner; and development is related purely to the growth of the individual without reference to the job of the learner.

Although Nadler's definition of HRD has proved popular, his distinctions between training, education and development remain rather idiosyncratic. More commonly accepted in Australia are definitions which reflect the job/skills orientation of the training and the broader personal growth orientation of education and development. Thus, the United Kingdom Manpower Services Commission (MSC) defined the terms as follows (Manpower Services Commission, 1981):

> **Training:** a planned process to modify attitude, knowledge or skill behaviour through learning experience to achieve effective performance in an activity or range of activities.
>
> **Education:** activities which aim at developing the knowledge, skills, moral values and understanding required in all aspects of life, rather than knowledge and skill relating to only a limited field of activity.
>
> **Development:** the growth or realisation of a person's ability through conscious or unconscious learning.

In contrast to Nadler's view, the MSC definitions stress the broad nature of education and development and the fact that they are not necessarily related to the organisation in which the learner works. Nevertheless, it is also true that training and development activities in organisations are not solely limited to the provision of job-related training. Development activities also take place which may bear no immediate relevance to the job of the learner, yet are considered a worthwhile investment by the organisation.

In this broader sense, training and development can be seen as an important subset of the entire process of the organisation's human resource management (HRM). Studies by the American Society for Training and Development (ASTD) put this relationship into context (McLagan, 1989). In the ASTD study, HRD was defined as:

> ... the process of increasing the capacity of the human resource through development. It is thus a process of adding value to individuals, teams or an organization as a human system.

In the ASTD model reproduced in Figure 1.1 on p 3, HRD constitutes three processes: training and development, organisation development and career development. It is also related closely to other HRM activities such as organisation design, human resource planning, performance management and selection and staffing. The proper development of an organisation's human resources cannot be realised without the meshing of HRD with these other activities.

Figure 1.1— Human resource wheel

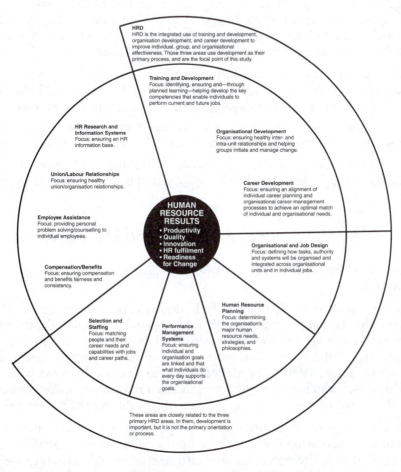

Source: McLagan, P A, *Models for HRD Practice*, ASTD Press, St Paul, Minnesota, 1989, p 3

In the United States, organisational psychologists such as Irwin Goldstein and Ken Wexley have narrowed the definition of training and development. For Goldstein, training is (Goldstein, 1986):

> the systematic acquisition of skills, rules, concepts or attitudes that result in improved performance in another environment.

This is a broad definition that covers a wide variety of training activities. It also covers more than the simple acquisition of skills by referring to concepts and attitudes, and relating training firmly to the improvement of employee performance. However, Goldstein's approach emphasises the acquisition of skills by the trainee, that is, learning, rather than the activities which the enterprise sponsors that facilitate the learning; it is a trainee-centred definition.

Wexley and Latham (1991) adopt the term 'training and development' and define it as:

> ... refer[ring] to a planned effort by the organization to facilitate the learning of job-related behaviour on the part of its employees.

This definition stresses intentionality in the organisation by referring to the planned effort that leads to the acquisition of skills. However, as might be expected from an organisational psychologist, it is concerned only with behaviour which can be observed and measured. It does not embrace the conceptual and attitudinal changes present in the Goldstein definition.

A more comprehensive definition of training and development may be constructed from combining the ideas of Goldstein and Wexley and Latham. In this book, therefore, training and development will be defined as follows:

> Training is an activity, planned by an organisation, to facilitate the acquisition of skills, rules, concepts or attitudes that improve the performance of its employees.

This definition stresses the importance of training and development as an activity consciously planned by the organisation and aimed at performance improvement.

The Importance of Training and Development

Training and development has a positive impact on individuals, organisations and nations.

At the individual level, there is little doubt that training and development increases the earnings and opportunities open to people. Economists have shown how earnings profiles are positively linked to skills, whether acquired through the public education system or through training provided by the employer (Maglen, 1990). The highest wages are earned by those with the highest skills; a fact which many employers use as a reason for making trainees bear some of the cost of their training in lower wages during the training period.

The acquisition of skills also opens up opportunities for career development. Promotion is increasingly determined by the possession of qualifications and skills. In Australia, the processes of award restructuring and enterprise bargaining have created career paths for employees through which progression is determined at least partly by skill (Curtain, 1994a). Training and development has therefore assumed vital importance for individual opportunity.

Investment in training and development also repays the individual in terms of earnings and job security. In times of economic downturn, organisations will tend to lay off their least skilled workers first. It is not in the interest of organisations to risk losing the workers who may be able to make the most contribution to corporate recovery. Skilled and qualified workers also tend to retain their earnings differentials more effectively than non-skilled workers. It has been shown in the United States that high school dropouts saw their average earnings decrease by up to 40 per cent in the 1980s while those with a college degree suffered only an 11 per cent decrease in earnings over the same period (Carnevale, Meltzer and Gainer, 1990).

For organisations, the importance of training and development lies in its links to performance and competitiveness. Although the debate over evaluation in training and development (see Chapter 8) indicates the difficulties of demonstrating the impact of development activities on corporate performance, there is little doubt that training and development is a key ingredient in competitive success. Research in Europe and the United States has shown that training and development plays a critical role in the successful performance of enterprises (Sparrow and Pettigrew, 1985; Bishop, 1994).

Although the mechanisms are not yet entirely clear, it appears that training and development contributes to organisational performance in three key areas. First, training and development has the potential to improve labour productivity. Training in better ways of doing things, whether it be the operation of a machine on the shop floor or the implementation of a corporate plan in the boardroom, increases the output of members of the organisation, that is, their productivity (Steedman, 1993).

Secondly, training and development plays a major role in the improvement of quality. A highly trained work force is not only more productive but also more aware of its responsibility for doing the job properly. Thus, the trained workers realise that the ability of others to do their jobs to a quality standard depends on the standard of their own work. Research in Australia has shown that quality assurance is a major driver of training at the enterprise level (Smith et al, 1995; Hayton et al, 1996). The story of training and development at NEC in Illustration 1.1 shows how the company's commitment to quality improvement was a major driver of training and development.

Finally, training and development improves the ability of the organisation to cope with change. The successful implementation of change, whether technical (new technologies and new products) or organisational (new ways of organising work), relies on the skills of the organisation's employees. Change is, perhaps, the single most important reason why organisations fund training programs (Hayton et al, 1996).

At the national and international level, improving the provision of training has been viewed as a significant element of the policy response to the decline in national competitiveness. In the United States, reports on the competitiveness of American industry and the state of the American work force have consistently highlighted the importance of a national commitment to improved employee training to restore the country's industrial strength (Commission on the Skills of the American Workforce, 1990; United States Congress, 1990). Similar calls have been made in Britain since the mid-1980s (Coopers & Lybrand, 1985) and many commentators have called for the adoption of a national training strategy to match the perceived advantages of countries such as Germany and France that have well-established national training policies (Hyman, 1992).

Illustration 1.1 — Organisational change drives training and development at NEC

A massive investment in employee training has been one of the major drivers behind the success of telecommunications manufacturer NEC Australia. John Ring, national manager training and development, said the decision to invest in people came about with a realisation that, despite NEC's superior technology and substantial market share, profit levels were not meeting expectations. NEC soon realised that it had to focus on customer satisfaction, which could only be realised through boosting the skills and commitment of the work force.

The organisation officially launched 'Improving Quality Together' in April 1991, after several years of working on various productivity and efficiency improvement measures. The next year was spent educating, developing and training the company's 250 managers, from the managing director through to middle management and supervisory levels. John Ring says much of the success of NEC's quality improvement process rested with the level of commitment from the top — hence the full year spent on management training courses to ensure senior management was totally committed to the quality improvement process.

One of the company's most successful initiatives has been to select employees with good leadership and organisation skills for TAFE-accredited train-the-trainer courses. Employees with proven ability from across all sections of the organisation are chosen for the sought-after accreditation, regardless of seniority or job function. Fifty employees have already attained accreditation, including engineers, shop floor people, and staff from the finance and accounting departments. Ring says people are chosen for the course if they have good communication skills, leadership qualities, and have the ability to plan their own work and the work of others. Employees are chosen on the basis of individual annual appraisals, the profitability of work units, and other appraisal methods. Participation is always voluntary.

Another initiative has been the establishment of customised MBAs for a select group of middle managers. NEC's corporate service division spent 18 months developing an MBA program with Monash Mt Eliza Management program. Ring says the program has been designed in a way that is 'totally NEC work related'.

Participants go to a three-day workshop, for example, and develop material which they then use in their own business unit. The first group of 17 managers have just completed their first year of the three-year MBA, attaining the graduate certificate level.

In terms of future goals, Ring says the company is now changing its focus from TQM — with its more common focus on product quality — to TQS, or total quality service, which is customer driven.

Source: Human Resources Report No 92, 8 November 1994

In Australia, the Federal Labor Governments of 1983–96 adopted the improvement of training and development as a major policy platform for the revitalisation of the Australian economy. Based on the findings of the Australian Council of Trade Unions' mission to western Europe in 1986 (Australian Council of Trade Unions/Trade Development Council, 1987), Federal Government training policy in the late 1980s and early 1990s was based on reforming the training system to provide more relevant training to industry and encouraging organisations to improve their own provision of training to their employees through mechanisms such as the training guarantee scheme. These reforms have had a significant influence on the provision of training and development in Australia and are likely to continue to influence the practice of training in Australian organisations.

Clearly, therefore, training and development plays a central role in our experience of work. Individuals, organisations and nations have much to gain from the successful implementation of training and development policies. To what extent is this done in Australia?

Training and Development in Australia

Statistical information on the provision of training in Australia is incomplete and has only been systematically collected since the late 1980s (Smith, 1993). Apart from occasional surveys by employer organisations, the principal source of statistical data on training is the Australian Bureau of Statistics (ABS). Since 1990 the ABS has conducted a number of surveys that have greatly increased our understanding of training and development in Australian organisations. There are three key surveys published by the ABS. The Employer Training Expenditure Survey (ABS, 1990a, 1991, 1994a, 1997) was originally devised as part of the policy development process that led to the Training Guarantee Act and collects figures on how much Australian organisations spend on training their employees. The Training and Education Experience Survey (ABS, 1990b, 1994b) is a census of a sample of the population and collects information on the extent and type of training received by individuals at work. Finally, the Employer Training Practices Survey (ABS, 1994c, 1998) is a survey of organisations and collects information on the type of training that organisations provide to their employees and their reasons for doing so.

Training expenditure in Australian organisations

The Training Expenditure Survey is the most significant of the ABS surveys and provides a series on training expenditure from 1989 to 1996. The most recent survey reveals that in 1996 only 18 per cent of Australian organisations surveyed reported some training expenditure. This represents a significant decrease from the 1993 figure of 25 per cent. The average expenditure on training per employee was $186 over the July–September quarter, representing an annual rate of approximately $744. Employees received an average of 4.9 hours of training over the quarter (19.6 hours or less than three working days per annum). Australian organisations spent an average of 2.5 per cent of payroll on training. Thus, whilst the level of training activity appears to have increased since 1989, there has been a significant decrease since 1993. This, perhaps, reflects the suspension of the Training Guarantee Scheme in 1994 and its subsequent abolition in 1996.

Figure 1.2 — Employer training expenditure (July–September 1989–96)

	1989	1990	1993	1996	% Change 1989–96
% Employers reporting training expenditure	22	24	25	18	-18
% Payroll spent					
Private sector	1.7	2.2	2.6	2.3	+35
Public sector	3.3	3.2	3.4	3.2	-3
Total	2.2	2.6	2.9	2.5	+14
Average expenditure per employee (A$)	133	163	191	186	+40
Average training hours per employee	5.5	5.9	5.6	4.9	-11

Source: Australian Bureau of Statistics (1990a, 1991, 1994a, 1997)

Spending on training also varies considerably by sector and industry. In 1996 public sector organisations spent 3.2 per cent of payroll compared with their private sector counterparts, who spent 2.3 per cent. However, the increase from 1989 is almost entirely accounted for by the private sector, which improved its performance by over 30 per cent, while public sector spending as a percentage of payroll remained fairly static. Variation across industry sectors is even more apparent, with air transport, mining and communications spending well over the average, while manufacturing, retail and recreation and personal services spent considerably less than the average. These figures therefore present a picture of generally modest expenditure on training activities, but with a trend improvement, particularly in the private sector.

Distribution of training and development

The Training and Education Experience Survey and its forerunner (How Workers Get Their Training) reveal the extent and distribution of training within the Australian work force. The survey showed that in 1993, 86 per cent of workers received some form of training. On-the-job training was the most common form of training, with 82 per cent of workers receiving it. The incidence of in-house training in organisations was far less, with only 31 per cent of workers receiving it. About one-fifth of the work force (19 per cent) was studying for an educational qualification. However, like the figures on training expenditure, there was considerable variation between industries in the type of training received by employees. Employees in the utilities, communications or service industries were more likely to receive training than those in transport, manufacturing or agriculture. Part-time workers were consistently less likely to receive training than full-time workers (Baker and Wooden, 1992).

There were also considerable differences in training experiences between employees in different occupations. Thus, professional and para-professional workers were considerably more likely than unskilled and semi-skilled workers to receive training. Females, although slightly more likely to receive training than males overall, were less likely to receive training in sub-professional occupations, particularly in blue-collar occupations. Further analysis of the statistics highlighted the gender difference more clearly. Of those who participated in training in 1990, females received 46 hours of training, compared to 66 hours for males. A number of factors appear to impact on the likelihood of workers receiving training (McKenzie and Long, 1995):

- the incidence of training rises with the number of hours worked;
- the incidence of training rises with the educational level of the worker;
- the incidence of training rises with the skill level of the worker;
- the incidence of formal (off-the-job) training rises with the size of the organisation.

The available statistical evidence therefore shows a highly differentiated pattern of training provision in Australian organisations, with the incidence of training skewed toward the more privileged end of the labour market (full-time professional workers in large organisations). The large numbers of unskilled or semi-skilled workers in small to medium organisations appear not to be benefiting so much from the provision of training (Baker and Wooden, 1995).

Training and development practices in Australian organisations

The Training Practices Survey gathers data on the type and extent of training provision within organisations, using the same sample frame as the Training Expenditure Survey. Figure 1.3 on p 10 gives a summary of some of the key findings from this survey. The survey confirms that the major reason for investment in training was the improvement of employee work performance. However, the organisation of training was rather ad hoc and unsystematic. Formal needs analysis methods are not often used, written training plans are not used frequently and most enterprises do not employ qualified trainers. Training expenditure, however, appeared to be increasing, driven by processes of organisational change — investments in new technology, implementation of quality assurance programs and new management practices.

The ABS data is supported by case study research into why Australian organisations provide training to their employees (Smith et al, 1995; Hayton et al, 1996). This study shows that although the level of systematic training provision is low in Australian enterprises, there is a growing awareness amongst managers of the need to train which is being driven by the necessity to improve quality, invest in new technology and the demands of work reorganisation.

Figure 1.3 — Enterprise training practices in Australia

Training Practices	% Employers Reporting Structured Training
Reason for training:	
• Improve work performance	91
• Respond to new technology	61
• Improve quality	60
Methods to determine training needs:	
• Skills audit/TNA	22
• Informal methods	47
• None	9
Existence of written training plan:	22
Employ a qualified trainer:	33
Changes in training expenditure (last 12 months):	
• Increased	51
• Decreased	9
• No change	40
Factors for increasing training expenditure:	
• Technological change	32
• New management practices	25
• Quality assurance	21

Source: ABS (1998)

International comparisons

Many of the reforms to the training system instigated by the Federal Government since the late 1980s have been explicitly based on the assumption that Australia's training effort lags well behind that of competitor countries, especially within the Organisation for Economic Cooperation and Development (OECD) (Dawkins, 1988; 1989). Yet, international comparisons of training statistics are notoriously difficult to interpret (Ryan, 1991). Countries do not collect comparable figures, and definitions of what constitutes training, particularly at the organisational level, vary significantly, reflecting the diversity of training systems that exist in the developed world. Nevertheless, figures collected by the Bureau of Industry Economics appear to indicate that total Australian expenditure on training is not so far behind Australia's competitors as policy-makers might assume (Figure 1.4).

Figure 1.4 suggests that comparisons of firm and individual spending on training are not favourable to Australia, which spends only 1.2 per cent of gross domestic product (GDP) on education and training compared to Japan's 5.6 per cent and Germany's 2.1 per cent on training. Evidence from the United States (Lynch, 1994) and the United Kingdom (Training Agency, 1989) indicates that Australia fits into the pattern of training provision common in the English-speaking world; that of low quality enterprise training with the emphasis on the government's role in supplying trained workers through the provision of schools, tertiary institutions and labour market training programs (Finegold and Soskice, 1988).

Figure 1.4 — Estimates of expenditure on education and training (percentage of GDP, 1980)

	Australia	USA	Japan	West Germany	France
Government • Education • Labour market training programs	5.9 0.07	6.8 0.3	5.9 na	4.7 0.5	na na
Firms	0.9	0.4 – 1.2	5.0	2.0	0.4
Individuals	0.3	0.5	0.6	0.1	na
Totals	7.2	8.0	11.5	7.3	na

Source: Bureau of Industry Economics (1990)

International comparisons of training activities can, however, be misleading. Sloan (1994) has shown that statistics used to justify the Federal Government's introduction of the Training Guarantee Scheme (which appeared to demonstrate that Australia's private investment in training is lower than that of the United States, Germany and Japan) were outdated and flawed. Alternative statistics quoted by Sloan seem to indicate that Australian investment in training may be comparable to other OECD countries, in particular to other English-speaking countries such as the United Kingdom, Canada and the United States.

However, the comparative evidence is difficult to interpret as Sloan, for example, relies on indirect indicators such as average length of tenure in jobs, which she takes as a proxy measure for training activity. There is a variety of other factors which could influence such measures and, contrary to Sloan's assertions, there is no compelling evidence that Australia is a 'high training' country. Thus, the available figures suggest that Australia is a low to middle ranking country in terms of investment in training and development.

The Training and Development Practitioner

The role of the training and development practitioner has not been thoroughly researched. The confusion surrounding the terms which was discussed earlier extends to the activities of the practitioner. Does the training and development specialist instruct others, administer others who instruct, design learning opportunities in which others instruct, perform a non-instructional role as part of a broader HRM team or perform a combination of these tasks?

Illustration 1.2 — A new standard for training and development

> A new education and training standard is set to revolutionise company training practices in Australia. The Australian Institute of Management is trialling the new scheme, Investors in People, which promises to be easier to administer than the unwieldy ISO 9000 quality standard. IiP is a UK-developed standard — similar to ISO 9000 — which ties training directly to the company's business plan, so the investment can be measured against pre-ordained benchmarks such as profitability or absenteeism.
>
> The program has four stages with 24 indicators. The stages are:
> 1. Ensuring the commitment of management to the program's success;
> 2. Reviewing of individual and collective responsibility for tasks and the ability of individuals to perform them;
> 3. Assessing the action taken, such as meeting training needs;
> 4. Evaluating the assessment processes.
>
> In the UK IiP has been adopted for 23 per cent of the work force since 1992 when it was launched. There are around 50 case studies which relate IiP directly to improvements in the bottom line.

Source: HR Report No 123

The American Society of Training and Development (ASTD) study of the HRD practitioner in the United States focused on the question of the roles and skills required of the HRD practitioner (ASTD, 1997). The ASTD identified six areas of competence for the HRD practitioner and four universal competencies. These are illustrated in Figure 1.5.

The six areas of competence are:
1. Providing performance support services;
2. Using technology for delivery support and using new technology-based performance tools;
3. Managing human performance systems;
4. Promoting continuous learning at the individual, team and organisational level;
5. Managing change processes;
6. Providing services from a decentralised position using outside support.

The four universal competencies that underpin each of these areas are:
1. **Awareness of the industry or corporation.** Trainers will need to understand the vision, strategy, goals and culture of the organisation and how to link to their organisation's goals.
2. **Management skills.** These include leadership skills, understanding customer focus and project management skills.
3. **Interpersonal skills.** These include traditional coaching, facilitation, communication, questioning and listening skills.
4. **Personal technology skills.** Being able to utilise different forms of software and understand performance support systems.

Figure 1.5 — HRD competencies

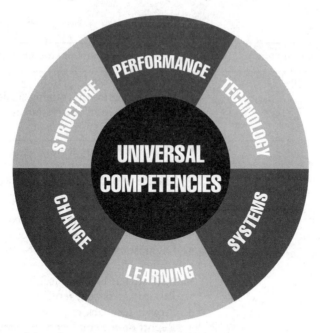

Source: Training and Development in Australia, July 1996

These competencies are very broad in scope. They cover not only the traditional skills of the training practitioner but also encompass a broad understanding of the business issues to which HRD is closely related and the organisational skills needed to ensure that the function retains a high profile in the organisation.

In Australia, a set of workplace trainer competencies has been developed as part of the push to establish national competency standards for all occupations: see Chapter 2. However, by contrast with the ASTD core competencies, the Australian standards are very narrow indeed and really only relate to delivery of training programs. At the time of writing the competency standards were under revision. Figure 1.6 presents the draft workplace trainer and assessor competencies released in 1998.

Figure 1.6 — Workplace assessor and trainer competency standards (draft)

Category 1

Units of Competency	Elements of Competency
Prepare for Training	• Confirm the need for training • Plan and document training session • Arrange location and resources • Notify trainee(s)
Deliver Training	• Introduce training session • Deliver training session • Provide opportunities for practice • Confirm trainee is ready for assessment
Conduct assessment in accordance with established procedures	• Identify and explain the context of assessment • Plan evidence gathering opportunities • Organise assessment • Gather evidence • Make the assessment decision • Record assessment results • Provide feedback to person(s) being assessed • Report on the conduct of the assessment
Review training	• Evaluate training session • Record training • Provide information on training

Category 2

Units of Competency	Elements of Competency
Plan training program	• Confirm the need for training • Define training program requirements • Develop training programs • Develop training session • Prepare training materials • Arrange program resources
Deliver training	• Prepare trainees • Present training session • Provide opportunities for practice and feedback • Review delivery of training session
Review and promote training	• Evaluate training • Record training data • Report on training • Promote training

Units of Competency	Elements of Competency
Plan and establish assessment procedures	• Establish evidence required • Establish suitable assessment method(s) • Identify appropriate assessment tools • Modify assessment tools • Establish assessment procedures
Review assessment	• Review the assessment procedures • Review the evidence and competency decision • Report review findings

Again, the Australian competency standards are very narrow, and reflect the approach of the National Training Board which oversaw the establishment of the process for determining national competency standards: see Chapter 2. However, the competencies tell us very little about the role of the training and development practitioner in contemporary Australian organisations.

Here the results from Australian research examining the role of enterprise training carried out by researchers from the Group for Research in Employment and Training at Charles Sturt University and the University of Technology, Sydney, paint a picture of an underdeveloped and rather powerless function (Smith et al, 1995; Hayton et al, 1996). This research, which is explored in more detail in Chapter 4, shows that:

- training activities are not carried out in a systematic way in most Australian organisations;
- only the larger organisations support a training specialist or training department;
- training is being increasingly devolved away from training specialists and towards line managers;
- training specialists are largely brokers of training rather than direct trainers;
- training has very little connection to the business strategy of Australian organisations.

This evidence highlights the rather lowly position of the training practitioner in modern Australian organisations. This is also borne out internationally, as similar work in the United Kingdom has drawn equally pessimistic conclusions about the role and importance of training professionals (Rainbird, 1994).

Despite its close links to the broader function of human resource management in organisations, training and development practitioners are becoming increasingly professional in their outlook (Moy, 1991). The professional training and development body in Australia, the Australian Institute for Training and Development (AITD), was formed from the National Conference on Training organised by the Commonwealth Government in 1971. Since that time, the AITD has grown quickly and established strong branch representation in each of the states and territories, and organises an annual conference of training and development practitioners in Australia. In 1993 the Training and Development

Council of Australia was formed to allow consultation between governments and the major stakeholders in the training system.

Summary

This chapter has examined the concept and practice of training and development in Australia. Definitions of training and development are rendered obscure by the overlapping nature of the terms used in the field. In particular, the distinctions between training, education, development and HRD are the subject of much, often dry, debate in the field. In general, training is distinguished from the longer-term processes of education and development by its short-term, job-related focus. HRD embraces the wider activities of career development and organisational development as well as training and development activities.

Individuals invest in their own development by undertaking training and becoming more valuable in the labour market. For organisations, training and development offers a means of capitalising on human resources to improve competitiveness and cope with change. Nationally, training and development of the work force is viewed by governments as an important means of improving economic competitiveness.

Research on training and development in Australia shows that employers spend an average of 2.5 per cent of payroll on training activities. However, the pattern of expenditure varies considerably between industry and occupational groupings. It appears that training expenditure is biased in favour of professionals and those employed in service industries and/or the public sector. International comparisons are difficult to interpret, but many influential groups are convinced that Australia's performance in training and development lags behind that of our competitors.

American and Australian research into the roles and competencies of the HRD practitioner has shown how wide the brief of the trainer can be. The successful practitioner seems to require an array of technical, business, interpersonal and intellectual skills to perform well. This wide competency base may well be a major reason behind the growing demand for professional recognition by practitioners.

Discussion Questions

1. What is training and development, and how does it differ from HRD?
2. How does the training practitioner differ from other professionals in the field of human resource management?
3. Does training make any difference to the performance of a business? If so, how?
4. What evidence is there that the level of training activity is increasing in Australia?

Chapter 2

The Australian Training System

In the last chapter, it was noted that training and development is important not only at an individual and organisational level, but also at a national level. Improving the skills of the work force is one way to increase Australia's competitiveness, and from the mid-1980s onwards, Australian governments have devoted considerable attention and resources to training and development.

It is difficult for governments to regulate how organisations train their workers, although most developed countries do have some form of government intervention. Australia's training policies over the last 15 years have included some direct interventions, but the main focus of attention has been on developing a coherent vocational education and training (VET) system for the country. VET in Australia is provided mainly by Technical and Further Education (TAFE) through the state training authorities. This has led to a very fragmented system of training developing in Australia. Much of the development in training policy in recent years has been aimed at reducing the effect of this fragmentation and encouraging the growth of a national system of training.

Organisations participate in the training system in four ways:
- as employers of graduates of courses run by providers of vocational education and training (VET);
- as purchasers of training from VET providers;
- directly, by themselves becoming registered providers of VET courses which fit into the national training system;
- by using training processes or products such as competency-based training or national modules.

This chapter explains the background to recent changes in Australia's training system, and the implementation of what has become known as the National Training Reform Agenda. It sketches the framework within which VET now operates in Australia and some of the major principles of the VET system. Particular attention is paid to the growing number of providers of training, to the changes to 'entry-level training', and to competency-based training, which is the method of training, design and delivery now used by most training providers and by many enterprises for their own training.

The Need for Change

There were a number of factors behind the changes to Australia's training system which have occurred since the mid-1980s.

First, there was a perception that Australia's comparative economic decline was in part due to its poor performance in expenditure on training. This perception was not necessarily supported by the evidence but, nevertheless, the perception was strongly held by policy-makers: see Chapter 1. It was reinforced by the publication in 1987 of a report of an overseas fact-finding mission by the Australian Council of Trade Unions and the Trade Development Council. This report, 'Australia Reconstructed', (ACTU/TDC, 1987) drew unfavourable comparisons between Australia's skills base and that of other OECD countries, and recommended that increased attention needed to be paid to employment policies, and particularly to training.

Secondly, there was considerable concern about rising youth unemployment. From the mid-1970s to the mid-1980s, unemployment amongst teenagers rose from around 5 per cent to around 20 per cent, as shown by Figure 2.1. By the late 1990s, the rate had settled to around 25 per cent of the 15–19 years age group.

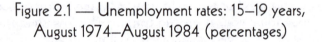

Figure 2.1 — Unemployment rates: 15–19 years, August 1974–August 1984 (percentages)

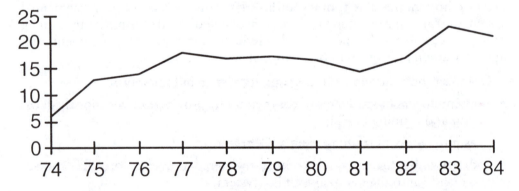

Source: Smith and Keating (1997:23)

The rise in youth unemployment was not necessarily related to the economic cycle, but appeared to be structural; that is, jobs young people traditionally did when they entered the labour force, such as low-level clerical work or unskilled factory work, appeared to be disappearing. Some types of jobs were growing, notably in fast food and hospitality, but these jobs were part-time or casual and were usually held by young people still at school. Policy-makers believed that a reform of vocational education was necessary to equip young people with the skills they needed for the new, more sophisticated economy.

From the early 1980s onwards, as a response to youth unemployment, retention rates at school began to rise: Figure 2.2. It was not until 1992 that the rates began to level off and, finally, to fall. Although the high retention rates decreased the number of young people who were officially unemployed, they created further difficulties in that many young people remained at school who were perhaps not so interested in the traditional academic curriculum designed for Years 11 and 12 to prepare young people for university. Additionally, they led to a decline in participation in TAFE programs between 1983 and 1993 of 8 per cent for 16- and 17-year-olds and 5 per cent for 18- and 19-year-olds (Sweet, 1994). In 1992 only about 25 per cent of 16–18-year-olds in Australia were participating in vocational education (at school, TAFE or at work), whereas in Germany the figure was nearly 80 per cent (OECD, 1995).

Figure 2.2 — Year 12 retention rates as a percentage of Year 7 enrolments

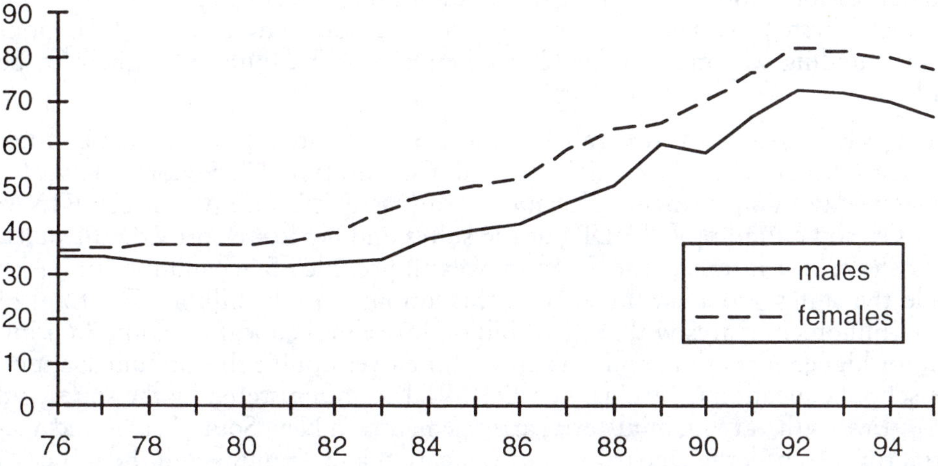

Source: ABS 1984–95, Cat No 4221.0

Thirdly, Australia's economic plight led to a number of initiatives designed to restructure industry. During the late 1980s, many industries, such as the waterfront, dramatically reformed the way they operated, removing a number of restrictive practices including demarcations between trades. Simultaneously, industrial relations reforms were proceeding in most Australian industries: see Chapter 3. Award restructuring simplified the traditionally complicated, industrial awards, and later, enterprise bargaining devolved responsibility for industrial relations to the enterprise. The significance for training was that the restructured awards often contained links between training, skills and wages. They also placed emphasis on multiskilling, which meant that it was no longer sufficient for workers to learn only one trade or skill.

Finally, the nature of work and jobs was changing. Traditional industries such as manufacturing and primary industry were either in decline or employing fewer people to do the same work; the 'tertiary' or service industries were expanding their share of the economy, with tertiary industry expected to account for over 60 per cent of Australia's gross domestic product by the year 2000 (Dunphy and Stace, 1990). Within all industries, technology and changes in work organisation had led to a decline in what Reich (1991) has described as 'routine production services' and to an increase in jobs involving higher-level skills and, particularly, communication skills. It was believed that these changes could not be served by the training system as configured in the mid-1980s.

VET in Australia

Traditionally, VET has been given very little attention in comparison with school and higher education sectors. TAFE colleges grew out of such disparate institutions as mechanics institutes in the capital cities and schools of mines in the goldfields of Victoria. In addition, some secondary schools were set up as technical schools. Although extra resources were put into VET in times of war and depression (Goozee, 1995), it was not until the Kangan Report of 1975 that the TAFE system as it is today was established and that sufficient Commonwealth funding was made available to enable proper capital investment to be made.

The VET system in Australia is more complicated than in some other countries because of Australia's federal Constitution. The Commonwealth Department of Employment, Education, Training and Youth Affairs (DEETYA) provides some funding for VET but the states and territories provide the most. In 1989–90, for instance, the Commonwealth provided $440 million for TAFE while the states provided three times this amount: $1.47 billion. The total of $1.91 billion compares with $10.18 billion for school education and $3.64 billion for higher education, and was only a little over double the amount spent on pre-school education (Marginson, 1993). VET is administered by the states and territories, with varying ministerial arrangements. In New South Wales and Victoria, for instance, the Department of Education and Training and the Office of Training and Further Education, respectively, oversee VET as well as school education.

The involvement of Commonwealth and state governments in VET has often created tensions, as the governments do not necessarily agree on policies. During the Hawke–Keating Federal Labor Governments of 1983–96, the Commonwealth was centralist in its policies, and VET was no exception. In 1992 the Commonwealth Government proposed that it should take over the VET sector while diminishing its role in the school sector. This was not accepted by state governments, but as a compromise the Australian National Training Authority (ANTA) was established, to coordinate a national VET approach. ANTA is governed by a ministerial council (MINCO) which includes the ministers for VET from all the states and territories and their Commonwealth counterpart. As well as balancing state and federal interests, VET policy-makers have needed to take into account other major stakeholders. Trade unions have always had a strong interest in training, and during the period of the Labor Federal Government a tripartite approach to VET was taken, involving governments, unions and business. Since the election of the Federal Coalition Government in early 1996, however, this tripartite approach has not continued.

Much of Australia's VET effort has been directed towards providing apprenticeship training. Apprenticeships and traineeships together accounted for 24 per cent of TAFE courses in 1994 (Smith et al, 1996). Apprenticeships were imported from Europe during the colonial period in Australia, having been firmly established in Europe since the Middle Ages. In Australia, apprenticeships have become entrenched in the industrial landscape. Government regulations cover the licensing of apprenticed trades, industrial awards prescribe pay levels for apprentice training, and contractual arrangements (indentures) between the employer and the apprentice ensure continuity of employment for apprentices throughout their period of training, which is normally four years. Apprenticeships are common in traditional industries such as metals and construction, and are found mainly in trades dominated by men, hairdressing being the notable exception.

Although Australia's VET system had provided Australian industry with skilled workers for many years, it was becoming increasingly obvious by the mid-1980s that the system was unable to respond to the challenges presented by restructuring and the changes to the nature of work discussed earlier. Amongst the many criticisms made of the training system at this time, the most important were:

- VET arrangements for emerging industries were inadequate;
- TAFE was not flexible enough to meet industry's needs;
- qualifications were frequently not portable across state boundaries;
- there were not enough linkages between education providers, such as between schools and TAFE;
- apprenticeship training was old-fashioned and too dependent on time served rather than skills gained;
- training which took place within companies was not recognised elsewhere;
- training was not always equally accessible to people from minority or equity groups: women, Aboriginal people and people from non-English-speaking backgrounds (NESB).

It was concerns over the inflexibility of the training system and the poor performance of Australian employers in providing training to their employees that persuaded the Federal Labor Government to undertake the reform of the training system which has come to be known as the National Training Reform Agenda.

The National Training Reform Agenda

The National Training Reform Agenda is not, as the name implies, a coherent set of interlocking reforms (Allen Consulting Group, 1994). Rather, it is the term given to a series of decisions on training reform taken by Commonwealth, state and territory governments from the mid-1980s to the early 1990s. The 'agenda' culminated in the establishment of ANTA, which formally began operations in January 1994, although it had been operating informally before then. ANTA is located in Brisbane, and represents a compromise between the states and territories on the one hand and the Commonwealth on the other. Its dimensions are that the Commonwealth is willing to invest extra funding through the state training systems, provided that the states and territories support a nationally consistent approach to VET and that they 'maintain their own effort' in VET. Part of the agreement with the states has been the establishment of a ministerial council (ANTA MINCO) which has overall responsibility for all national policy in VET.

Illustration 2.1 — Workskill Australia and the Skill Olympics

Workskill Australia Foundation conducts regional and national skill competitions and one of its most exciting roles is participating in the International Youth Skill Olympics. Over the last decade Workskill has developed a nationwide system of skill competitions which recognise competency attainments at regional, national and international levels in 44 occupations. Overall, 30,000 young Australians have had the chance to benchmark their skills against demanding standards since Workskill was first established. Workskill is more than a training provider. It has pioneered new ways of assessing and promoting skill competency. It has also become a member of the International Vocational Training Organisation, enabling it to pioneer a number of new technology competition categories in the Skill Olympics.

Australia's national skill competitions are linked to the International Youth Skill Olympics. This event occurs every two years and involves 28 nations including countries such as Germany, Austria, Korea, Japan and Taiwan. These countries are recognised as leaders in the field of skill formation. The idea for the Skill Olympics originated in Spain. In 1950, Spaniards involved in vocational training invited neighbouring Portugal to compete in a new and exciting skills competition. Almost 40 years later, the competition has developed as a way of promoting vocational training standards. It has also grown into a major international event, with Australia leading the development of such new skill categories as mechatronics, computer-aided draughting and information technology.

Year	1st	2nd	3rd	Australia
1985	Korea	Taiwan	Japan	5th
1987	Korea	Taiwan	Australia	3rd
1989	Korea	Taiwan	Austria	6th
1991	Korea	Taiwan	Japan	8th
1993	Taiwan	Korea	Brazil	10th
1995	Austria	Korea	China	10th
1997	Austria	Korea	Taiwan	6th

Skill Olympics Country Rankings 1985–97

Source: Australian Training Review No 25

The national training system remains dynamic, with important changes continuing to be made. There is no official starting point for the reforms, nor were they necessarily developed in a sequential and cohesive manner. Decisions were made through national committees and ministerial councils, but in some cases the Commonwealth initiated developments without the agreement of the states and territories. A good example of this has been the large number of labour market programs for unemployed people, which have had an impact upon the level of VET activity.

The training guarantee

The reform measure of most relevance to Australian organisations was the Training Guarantee. The Training Guarantee was a uniform levy which required organisations with payrolls in excess of A$200,000 to spend at least 1.5 per cent of payroll on eligible training per year. Organisations spending less were required to pay the shortfall to the Taxation Office. Eligible training was defined as structured and employment-related. Specifically, this meant that training must be part of a recognisable program which was employment-related. Both on-the-job and off-the-job training were eligible under the scheme. The Training Guarantee attempted to ensure that the skills developed through training were related directly to the workplace and led to productivity growth.

The arguments for the Training Guarantee emphasised the need for a highly trained work force in the restructuring of Australian industry and that governments had a role to play in encouraging training to take place in organisations. The Federal Labor Government subscribed to this point of view during the consultations that preceded the introduction of the Training Guarantee (Dawkins, 1988). Overseas examples were used to illustrate how government intervention was considered necessary to build and maintain a national skills base; in particular, the high growth Asian 'Tigers' of Singapore, Hong Kong and Korea were quoted as examples of the efficacy of such intervention. However, a number of major criticisms have been made of the Training Guarantee and its impact.

A key criticism made by employer groups was that the compliance costs of the training guarantee were excessive. Research by Velten (1990) showed that many enterprises considered that the costs of keeping records and ensuring all eligible training was reported outweighed the cost of paying the levy. Small businesses, in particular, expressed this view and there was a widespread belief that many small enterprises simply paid the levy rather than incur the costs associated with training (Business Council of Australia, 1990). A refinement of this criticism is that the imposition of a minimum level of expenditure on training led some enterprises to reduce their training expenditure to this minimum level, particularly in a time of economic recession (Pollock, 1991). However, there is little evidence to support the contention that the training guarantee had the effect of depressing training expenditure in this way. The training guarantee was also attacked for its focus on the quantity rather than the quality of training (Noone, 1991) and for providing a regime based on punishing non-compliance rather than rewarding enterprises which increased their commitment to training.

Nevertheless, advocates of the Training Guarantee were able to demonstrate some positive effects. Teicher (1995) identifies three such effects. First, the requirement to record the training that took place in the enterprise led to a greater level of accountability for managers in providing the requisite training for employees. Secondly, the availability of more information on training activities in the enterprise allowed managers to evaluate the effectiveness of training more closely. Finally, the Training Guarantee raised the status of training within enterprises, so that managers were able to take a more strategic approach to the linking of training activities with the business needs of the enterprise. However, there is little firm evidence that the Training Guarantee played a significant role in the increase in training expenditure noted in Chapter 1 (Baker, 1994) and the scheme was suspended in 1994 and finally abolished soon after the election of the Federal Coalition Government in 1996.

Report driven reform

The development of the training reform agenda was significantly influenced by four key reports commissioned by the Federal Labor Government between 1989 and 1993.

A major early milestone in the training reform agenda was that established through the Commonwealth Review of the Training Costs of Award Restructuring (Training Costs Review Committee, 1991), chaired by former CEO of Nissan Australia, Ivan Deveson. This committee was established to examine the funding of training, and arose from consideration of the likely costs of implementing award restructuring. The impact of the training costs review was to establish the concept of the 'open training market' through a recognition of the considerable amount of training that takes place outside of TAFE colleges and of the need to encourage greater diversity and competition in the training market.

The view also emerged, within government, that VET in Australia had been too provider driven and, in particular, that the state TAFE systems which had developed throughout the 1970s and 1980s were not sufficiently responsive to client needs, and, in particular, to the needs of industry clients. In other words, the level of VET activity was seen to depend on what TAFE chose to offer, rather than on what industry needed. It was necessary therefore to make the system more client, or industry, driven.

A committee chaired by Brian Finn, then CEO of IBM Australia, provided a report to the Australian Educational Council in 1991 on Young People's Participation in Post-compulsory Education and Training (Australian Education Council Review, 1991). The Finn Review focused on the relationship between school education and the VET system. In particular, the review drew a distinction between general and vocational education, highlighting the need for more vocational preparation in schools and more general education in TAFE. Finn set a number of targets for the VET system which were to be achieved by the year 2001:

- 95 per cent of people by age 19 should have completed Year 12 or an equivalent post-school qualification, or be participating in education or training;
- almost all young people by age 20 should attain a vocational qualification recognised by the National Training Board as a Level 2 in the Australian

Standards Framework or be progressing towards a higher-level qualification;
- 60 per cent of young people by age 22 should attain a vocational qualification recognised by the National Training Board as a Level 3 in the Australian Standards Framework, or a higher-level qualification.

Upon the recommendations of the Finn Review, a working party was appointed under former business executive Eric Mayer (the Mayer Committee). The 'Mayer Report' defined a set of seven key competencies including communication, working with others in teams, solving problems and using technology (AEC/MOVEET, 1993). Mayer recommended that the key competencies should be incorporated into education and training credentials.

The Finn and Mayer reports represented, amongst other things, a very tentative step towards extending some of the principles of training reform into the education sectors, particularly the school sector. As Sweet (1993) has pointed out, however, this was a very guarded step, and there were no overt recommendations that schools should become active participants in VET.

In 1992 the Employment Skills Formation Council issued a report on the Australian Vocational Certificate Training System (AVCTS). The report, known as the Carmichael Report (Employment and Skills Formation Council, 1992), recommended changes to the system of entry-level training in Australia, including the consolidation of apprenticeships and traineeships into a single system of entry-level training. In the same year, the Commonwealth Government announced funds for a number of pilot programs for the new program, and at the same time announced the introduction of Career Start Traineeships, which were intended as a more flexible form of traineeships.

The outcomes of the Carmichael Report and the pilots were twofold:
- They led to the agreement by education and training ministers in 1995 to a set of principles for entry-level training, around what became known as the Australian Vocational Training System (AVTS).
- They also led to a tacit acceptance of a greater role for the school sector in VET in Australia, including in entry-level training. Much to the surprise of most education and training officials, schools had been very active in the pilot programs supported by the Commonwealth funds.

Key developments in the National Training Reform Agenda

Central to the training reforms has been the use of competency-based training (CBT). CBT provides a common standard for all training programs that operate under the new training arrangements. Thus, Carmichael's recommendations for the new apprenticeship and traineeship system included, as an important element, that all the programs would be competency-based in the future. The concept of CBT emerged in Australia and some overseas countries during the late 1980s. It had its origins both in education theory and in the principle of a more industry-led training system. It has been argued that specified learning outcomes provide both for better teaching practices and for more legitimate forms of assessment. Although CBT had been practised for many years by some TAFE colleges (for example, Candy and Harris, 1990), it was not common.

The emergence of competency-based approaches to training within the state and territory training systems led training ministers to agree to the development of national industry competency standards. In order to facilitate this, the Commonwealth Government, with the agreement of the states and territories, established the National Training Board in 1990 to supervise the development of industry competency standards and to endorse these standards once they had gained the approval of the relevant industry bodies. It also provided funds for the development of the standards and for the development of a national training curriculum through the Australian Committee for Training Curriculum (ACTRAC).

One of the results of the fragmented nature of Australia's training system has been the lack of portability of qualifications between states. Training courses developed or qualifications awarded in one state or by one college were often not recognised in another state or another college. In order to introduce greater consistency in the recognition of training courses and qualifications, in 1992 the training ministers endorsed a National Framework for the Recognition of Training (NFROT).

The framework was an agreement on a set of 10 principles, including providing 'for national principles in the recognition of accredited courses, training programs, training providers and competencies held by individuals'. It also provided sets of principles for competency-based assessment and the recognition of prior learning. The basic principle behind the operation of NFROT was that training providers could be accredited by state and territory accreditation bodies and, once accredited, they would be nationally recognised. NFROT had been regarded as the foundation for the national training system. It has not been as successful as was originally hoped, however, and has been subject to different interpretations across the country. This has led the ministers (ANTA MINCO) to design a new approach, the National Training Framework: see below.

By 1991 the two education and training ministerial councils, the Australian Education Council (AEC) and the ministers for employment, education and training (MOVEET) began holding joint meetings in which to discuss the broader implications of training reform for all three sectors of education and training. In 1994 a decision was made to combine the two councils into the Ministerial Council on Education, Employment, Training and Youth Affairs (MCEETYA). To a large extent, this was an acknowledgment of the need to consider post-compulsory education and training as a whole, as well as within the context of the major changes that have occurred to the labour market and employment. Following the precedent of the New Zealand qualifications framework and the recommendations of the Rumsey Report (1992), MCEETYA endorsed the Australian Qualifications Framework (AQF) in 1994. The framework was a further, if belated, acknowledgment of the need to view education and training in a more integrated manner than has occurred in the past. The framework (Figure 2.3) integrates and codifies qualifications across the different education sectors.

Figure 2.3 — The Australian qualifications framework

Secondary Schools	Vocational Education and Training	Higher Education
Senior Secondary Certificate of Education	Advanced Diploma Diploma Certificate IV Certificate III Certificate II Certificate I	Higher degrees Degrees Advanced Diploma Diploma

More recently, some other major changes have followed the change of Federal Government in March 1996. The Coalition Government has convinced the states and territories to accept the principles of a more flexible and industry-led entry-level training system, which it originally called the Modern Australian Apprenticeship and Traineeship System (MAATS). More recently, the official title 'MAATS' has been discontinued, with the more loosely defined term 'new apprenticeships and traineeships' being adopted. An explicit part of the rhetoric of new apprenticeships and traineeships, is the role of schools, including the possibility of students beginning apprenticeships while they are at school (Kemp, 1996).

Reviews of the National Training Reform Agenda, (Allen Consulting Group, 1994) and of the operation of ANTA (Taylor, 1996) have resulted in the development of the National Training Framework, which includes significant changes to the recognition system and the development of training packages. The new National Training Framework reflects dissatisfaction with NFROT and other aspects of accreditation of courses. NFROT has not as much as was hoped led to portability of qualifications between states, and, in addition, training providers have complained that accreditation processes (managed by a separate body in each state and territory) have been very complex and burdensome. Under the new framework, instead of courses being accredited, training packages will be recognised. Training packages will be based directly on industry competency standards, and will consist of competency standards, assessment guidelines, and a statement of qualification level and title. The new National Training Framework will contain three components. The endorsed elements of the training packages, such as the industry competency standards, the assessment guidelines and the recommended qualifications and level, will form the basis of nationally recognised qualifications which will be issued by nationally recognised training organisations. Because training and qualifications will be based directly on competency standards, it is hoped that enterprises will be able to negotiate better, more focused training with providers of VET. Noonan illustrates how the new process will work with an example from the small business sector (Noonan, 1996).

Noonan describes how a small business wants a training program for a number of its employees which is relevant to its needs. The program needs to be able to provide nationally recognised qualifications. The business approaches two or three registered VET providers and after responses from them, decides to discuss its training needs with one. The provider has access to the relevant training packages and proposes a training program utilising the packages that will deliver the relevant qualification. The provider uses some of the learning materials in the packages but is able to adapt some of its own. The business and the provider discuss a range of delivery options, including the delivery of training of part of the programs at the worksite. It is possible for staff with relevant experience to be trained as workplace assessors and to assess some elements of the program. The program is then delivered as agreed. The participants are assessed against the competency standards and the provider issues the relevant qualification (Noonan, 1996).

In the new system, industry provides the foundation and its interests are represented through government funded state and national industry training advisory bodies (ITABs). The ITABs have existed for a number of years and are tripartite bodies involving representatives from employers, unions and governments. They are established on an industry basis and are responsible for drawing up the training plans for their industry sector each year. These training plans are then submitted to the state training authorities for funding.

The system is also firmly based on CBT. National industry competency standards are developed by or through industry (in most cases, the national ITABs), and provide the basis for training packages endorsed by the National Training Framework Committee, which operates under the auspices of ANTA. Training packages which consist of the competency standards, assessment requirements and the qualifications, are developed by industry, and endorsed by the ANTA National Training Framework Committee. They are used by training providers (TAFE colleges, private providers, industry) to deliver training programs to students and trainees. After assessment against the standards, qualifications are issued by the registered providers.

The new training system

The current and proposed training arrangements are represented in Figure 2.4 on the following page.

There are now many training providers operating in what has become known as the 'training market'. Apart from TAFE, there is a growing number of private providers. Providers are registered by the state and territory training recognition authorities, which are usually a part of the state training authorities. The final training qualifications trainees receive are issued upon the basis of national agreed policy on the recognition of competencies.

Finally, national policy on VET in Australia is determined through the ANTA Ministerial Council (MINCO), which is made up of the Commonwealth and state and territory training ministers.

Although the system described in Figure 2.4 on p 29 looks very precise and organised, it is important to remember that the VET system is continually changing.

Figure 2.4 — The new Australian training system

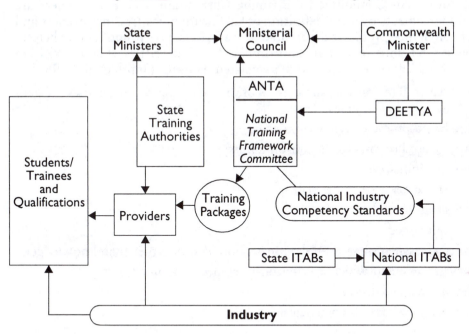

Competency-based Training

The introduction of CBT on a large scale was one of the key features of the National Training Reform Agenda. In a sense, CBT is the foundation stone of training reform, and many of the institutional changes were introduced to support CBT as a training system. However, definitions of what constitutes CBT can vary significantly. Two of the more commonly accepted definitions of CBT are provided by the Australian Chamber of Commerce and Industry and Vocational Education and Employment Training Advisory Committee (VEETAC).

> A way of approaching (vocational) training that places primary emphasis on what a person can do as a result of training (the outcome), and as such represents a shift away from an emphasis on the process involved in training (the inputs). It is concerned with training to industry specific standards rather than an individual's achievement relative to others in the group (Australian Chamber of Commerce and Industry, 1992).

> Training geared to the attainment and demonstration of skills to meet industry-specified standards rather than to an individual's achievement relative to that of others in a group (VEETAC, 1992: 5–8).

The key points in both these definitions are:
- the focus of the training is on the outcome of the training;
- the outcome is measured against specified standards, not against other students;
- the standards relate to industry.

These definitions of CBT are widely used, and the latter definition is that used by the Australian Committee for Training Curriculum (ACTRAC). There are some disagreements over the definition of CBT, with providers and teachers and trainers often interpreting it differently. Some writers have found it more helpful to divide CBT into 'essential' and 'implied' characteristics (Elam, 1971, in Tuxworth, 1989) or 'essential' and 'associated' features (Smith et al, 1996).

In the Australian context, some or all of the following characteristics are generally found in CBT courses. They:
- are based on competency standards;
- are focused on outcomes, not on inputs;
- involve industry;
- recognise prior learning (RPL);
- are modularised;
- are self-paced;
- have assessment based on demonstration of skill rather than knowledge;
- have assessment which is criterion-referenced and ungraded;
- have flexible delivery;
- widely recognise competencies.

Features of CBT

Industry competency standards describe the competencies which a worker in that industry should possess. The standards consist of units of competency, each of which is divided into elements of competency with performance criteria. The National Training Board was set up in 1989 to facilitate the development of competency standards by approved competency standards bodies (often the industry training advisory bodies). In 1995 the NTB was amalgamated with ACTRAC, the curriculum body, to form the Standards and Curriculum Council, part of ANTA, to enable a closer link between standards and curriculum. In 1996 the council was replaced by ANTA's National Training Framework Committee. Despite all these changes, competency standards remain the base for competency-based curricula. By January 1997, ANTA's figures showed that about 78 per cent of Australian industry was covered by competency standards. Competency standards vary greatly in quality and nature. Those developed early in the training reform period tend to be more prescriptive and narrow. Those developed later have had the benefit of others' experience and tend to be more holistic. Some competency standards are cross-industry (such as 'clerical/administrative functions in the private sector'); some are enterprise specific (such as 'McDonald's Crew' or 'Qantas Cabin Crew'). Where an industry has no competency standards, CBT has to be based on other standards, but is always related to industry requirements.

CBT is always concerned with what the student or trainee will be able to do at the end of the training. There is less concern with what the inputs are or how the trainee has completed the training. So long as the trainees achieve the listed competencies, it does not matter who instructs them, how or when the training takes place, what resources are used or the content of the program. The new 'training packages' take this concept to its logical extreme in which only the standards and the assessment are of interest.

The aim of CBT is to provide employees who are able to perform in industry, which is therefore involved at several stages in the training process. Industry is involved in drawing up the competency standards and in monitoring CBT courses. In an ideal CBT situation, at least some of the training is delivered in the workplace on the job, and some of the assessment takes place in the workplace under 'real life' conditions. Of course, CBT is also utilised by enterprises who choose to provide their own training rather than contracting it out to outside providers. In these cases, CBT takes place actually within the workplace, sometimes in a training room, sometimes on the job.

Because the focus of CBT is on outcomes and not on inputs, it does not matter where trainees gained their learning. The trainee may have learned a skill in a previous job or at home, but never had that skill recognised officially. For instance, many people teach themselves word processing to help them study or to improve their efficiency at work; many young people who grow up on farms are proficient at welding. If people enrol in a course for which they already have many of the skills, it is inefficient and wasteful for them to repeat those parts of the course. They can therefore apply to the training provider for Recognition of Prior Learning (RPL). This form of RPL is different from the credit transfer which TAFE and other training providers have always given, where trainees are exempted for certificated academic study they have previously undertaken. RPL is also used in industry to help place people on appropriate pay levels.

Because CBT is aimed at producing people with specific competencies, courses can be divided into distinct modules. Each module has its own competencies or learning outcomes, and can be studied in a relatively short period (typically between 18 and 60 hours). This makes it easy for people who do not want to study a whole course to select those modules in which they are interested. It also makes the process of RPL easy, as people only need to show proficiency in a limited number of competencies to be exempted from a module. Many modules are included in a range of courses. The National Communication Modules, for example, are included in most entry-level CBT courses. If a trainee has successfully completed one of these modules, he or she need not repeat it if it is included in another course in which he or she enrols.

Although CBT can be delivered in a variety of ways, many training practitioners believe that true CBT must be self-paced. If the aim is for the trainee to reach a certain level of competence, there is not much point in tying the trainee down to a fixed length course. Ideally, the trainee should be able to move on to further modules as soon as he or she has reached competence. In self-pacing, trainers are unlikely to instruct in a group situation; the trainees are likely to work through modules by themselves, whether the modules are print-based or computer-based, with the trainer providing assistance where required. The trainees can then ask to be assessed whenever they are ready, or at one of a choice of pre-arranged assessment times. Employers are likely to approve of self-pacing since employees undertaking a course, whether in the workplace or with a VET provider, will be able to return to their jobs as soon as they have achieved the required competencies.

Although vocational education has always been concerned with the attainment of skill, CBT places a greater emphasis on skill as compared with knowledge. Assessment, whether based on competency standards or on other learning outcomes, relates to the trainee being able to do something, rather than knowing things. This has meant that many of the written tests which used to be given to students in TAFE colleges and other VET providers have been replaced with skills tests. Since each student has to be observed separately, these tests often take up a lot of class time. A major advantage, however, is that the tests are more valid; they assess competence itself rather than assessing, for instance, how well students can do written tests. Since assessment in CBT is based on demonstration, an objective standard tends to be used. Norm-referenced assessment awards students results according to their performance compared with other students taking the course. A student who performs well may not get a high grade if everyone else does well. The TER (Tertiary Entrance Ranking) for university entrance is an example of norm-referencing. In CBT, on the other hand, assessment is against certain clearly-laid down criteria. If a student achieves these criteria, he or she will 'pass' or be judged competent. It is of no importance how other students in the course perform.

CBT is often associated with what is known as 'flexible delivery', meaning training that can be delivered in a variety of ways to meet the diverse needs of clients. Students enrolled in the same module may be studying it in a number of different modes. Flexible delivery generally involves:

- more flexible access;
- choices of modes of study (full-time/part-time, external/face to face, etc);
- choices of ways of learning, some of which often involve communication technology (video, interactive CD ROM, audiographics, etc);
- student choice of timing and manner of assessment.

There is thus some overlap with self-paced learning.

It is a feature of CBT that trainees' competencies are clearly described. Sometimes, the trainee's certificate from the training provider will give not only the module title but also the learning outcomes of each module. Job applicants can then show a prospective employer exactly what they are able to do. The employer can be assured that the applicant is trained to current industry requirements, consistent with national standards. In some cases, proof of competence may determine where on a pay scale the applicant is placed. The trainee can use the certification of competencies to get RPL in another course, and may be exempted from complete modules and also from individual learning outcomes within further modules. Because CBT is generally related to endorsed competency standards, competencies are usually the same all over Australia.

The implementation of CBT in Australia

Ministers for VET approved the introduction of CBT into Australian VET courses in 1990, with substantial implementation expected by the end of 1993. A survey of 1994 courses, however (Smith et al, 1996), indicated that this target had not been achieved, as only 29 per cent of TAFE courses and 39 per cent of a sample of non-TAFE courses were competency-based at that time. The survey found that some industry areas had still not had competency standards approved and this was creating a barrier to the implementation of CBT; it also found that some state systems had policies which encouraged certain CBT features and discouraged others. CBT is rapidly becoming the standard, however, though it is used differently in different places. A recent study of CBT and teaching and learning found that while TAFE colleges tended to try to implement all features of CBT, industry and enterprise providers were more likely just to utilise those features which they saw as helpful for their trainees (Smith et al, 1997).

Many arguments have been advanced against competency-based training. Some critics (for example, Collins, 1993b) consider that CBT is too behaviourist in its orientation. They believe that CBT will only teach specific skills, and will not help trainees gain underlying knowledge or understanding. This is sometimes seen to be at odds with the generic skills needed to cope with the more complex jobs offered by today's industry. In a similar vein, Field and Ford (1995) have argued that CBT is not compatible with organisational learning: see Chapter 10.

It has also been argued that CBT, because of its fixed outcomes, does not incorporate adult learning principles. Advocates of CBT maintain otherwise because CBT is often offered in a self-paced and flexible manner, and trainees may be able to determine what they learn and how and when they learn it. Self-pacing, however, because it usually involves working with print materials or computers, requires a certain level of literacy, making it difficult for people with low levels of literacy or from a non-English-speaking background. CBT has also been shown not to suit many young people, being more appropriate for mature trainees and workers (Smith et al, 1997). Finally, many people argue that CBT is expensive to implement, because it requires trainees to demonstrate competence and therefore they all need access to appropriate equipment. Where CBT is self-paced, however, this is not a difficulty, as all students will not need access to equipment at the same time.

Despite these arguments, CBT is becoming increasingly widely used, by enterprises as well as by VET providers. As competency standards become more widely available, CBT is becoming easier to implement. In the early 1990s, courses tended to be based on learning outcomes which were not always the same as competency standards. However, training packages will relate training directly to competency standards. It is hoped that this will make CBT easier to understand for trainers and trainees alike. It has been argued, however, that in learning outcomes, training providers were able to add in some of the underlying knowledge and understanding which were missing from standards. The quality of the competency standards is of paramount importance here. All standards are now supposed to incorporate the seven key competencies, and so should allow for development of generic skills.

Illustration 2.2 — Competency-based training in BHP

> In BHP at Wollongong, trades training is provided as part of the Graded Tradesperson Scheme by the Technical Training Department. There are six levels of training, each of which attracts a pay increase when satisfactorily completed. BHP has been using CBT for over ten years, and most training is self-paced. In most cases, the products made during training are used within the BHP plant. Each level of training involves completion of a number of modules, all of which are accredited under the national metals curriculum. When workers already think they have the skills for a particular module, they may apply for RPL (known in BHP as Recognition of Current Competency). They are encouraged to apply as there are cost savings for the company in not providing unnecessary training. There are appeal mechanisms in place if a worker is not granted RCC.

Source: Lowrie, 1997

Entry-level Training: Apprenticeships and Traineeships

Entry-level training has been a major focus for training reform. There have been many criticisms made of the apprenticeship system. Some of the key criticisms raised include (Smith, 1997):

- they are too inflexible: young people wishing to attain certain occupational skills are forced to undertake a major commitment and cannot learn these skills and have them recognised in any other way;
- they are confined to young people: until recently, adults have not been allowed access to either apprenticeships or traineeships;
- they are based on time served: even if apprentices learn their skills quickly, they still have to serve their time as apprentice workers. This is clearly at odds with the principles of competency-based training;
- they depend on a four-year commitment by the employer. In uncertain economic times, employers may be unwilling to make this commitment. Thus, apprenticeship commencements always fall during periods of recession, sometimes leading to skills shortages during times of recovery four years later;
- they offer restricted access: apprenticeships are generally in traditionally male trades, and do not exist in the newer industries such as information technology or tourism.

Attempts have been made to deal with some of these criticisms. Following the Kirby Report in 1985, the Commonwealth Government supported the establishment of a system of traineeships called the Australian Traineeship System. These are employment-based, entry-level training contracts, like apprenticeships, but generally only run for one year, and they offer better access for equity groups and more opportunities for training in emerging industries. Career Start

Traineeships provided similar access for people of all ages, and NETTFORCE was set up in the 1994 'Working Nation' White Paper (Keating, 1994) in an attempt to increase traineeship numbers. As with apprenticeships, employers are offered a subsidy to encourage them to take on trainees. The apprenticeship subsidy (known as the CRAFT subsidy) was, however, withdrawn in 1996 for larger companies.

Figure 2.5 illustrates the gradual growth in traineeships compared with apprenticeships since 1985. Apprenticeship figures have remained fairly constant, and the Australian situation contrasts with that in other countries, like Britain, where apprenticeships have declined rapidly (Gospel 1994, 1995). Generally, their survival is attributed to the relationship they have in Australia with industrial awards.

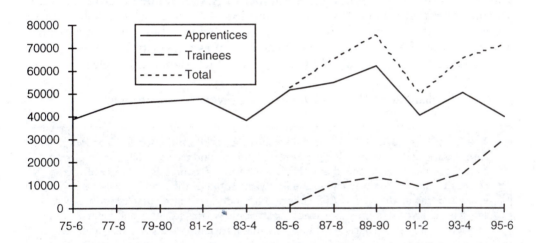

Figure 2.5 — Training commencements: 1975–96

Source: Australian National Training Authority, unpublished data, October 1996

Group Training Companies have been established to ensure a steady supply of apprentices. Group Training Companies employ apprentices and trainees, taking the risk away from individual employers, and send the apprentices and trainees out to different employers for their on-the-job training.

Apprenticeships have proved surprisingly resilient. AVTS and MAATS both attempted to remove the apprenticeship as an individual form of entry-level training, and subsume it under a general umbrella of entry-level training. Much of its resilience has been attributed to its relationship with industrial relations matters and with regulation of industries. By 1997 every state except New South Wales had abolished the list of declared trades which forms the basis of deciding which trades had to have apprentice training, yet apprenticeships continue to survive, and the 'new apprenticeships and traineeships' system appears to accept that the two forms of entry-level training will continue.

The resilience of apprenticeships and the gradual growth of traineeships suggest that their combination of off-the-job and on-the-job training may be particularly advantageous. Both of these forms of entry-level training provide for a certain number of days of off-the-job training; in apprenticeships, this has been enshrined in legislation. Traditionally, this training has been provided by TAFE for apprenticeships. Trainees have been more likely to receive their off-the-job training at non-TAFE providers, as traineeship training has been contracted out. In some cases, traineeships can be provided totally on-the-job; for example, the Coles–Myer traineeship.

The Federal Coalition Government is proposing to introduce reforms into entry-level training through user-choice principles. User-choice will enable organisations to choose the provider to whom they will send their apprentices and trainees for off-the-job training. It will also enable organisations to negotiate with their existing provider to improve the flexibility and quality of training arrangements. A certain amount of funding (calculated on a 'unit-cost' basis) will flow to the chosen provider. A number of ANTA-funded user-choice pilot schemes operated around Australia during 1996–97 to see what would happen under this system. Some companies changed providers, but not always from a TAFE to a non-TAFE provider. For instance, a Western Australian mining company changed from its local TAFE college to a Victorian TAFE college.

Illustration 2.3 — On-the-job delivery — Cherbourg

The Certificate Level 3 in fit-out and finish is delivered on-the job in Cherbourg, a rural Aboriginal community in Queensland. Students and trainers alike are employed by the town's council, and the TAFE funding for the course is transferred to the council to pay for the training. In the first year, some of the teaching was delivered in classrooms at the local TAFE college, Nurunderi, but after that everything was site-based. Two huts on-site provide classrooms where students and trainers can discuss theory at appropriate times. The students are involved in building and maintaining a number of houses in the community and a motel. Aboriginal apprentices had traditionally found it hard to attend block release at TAFE in Brisbane, and on-the-job delivery has proved successful in retaining students. It is hoped that when the students complete their apprenticeship, some will be employed permanently by the council, reducing the need for the council to employ sub-contractors in the building trade in future years.

This scheme has proved very successful in retaining the Aboriginal apprentices to the end of their time, and also in developing high levels of competence. However, there were some difficulties. Production demands by the Council reduced the time available for training, and also the trainers found it hard to teach skills which were not needed for the current jobs in hand. Finally, the trainers felt that the apprentices would have benefited from more role models such as might have been found in a range of TAFE teachers.

Source: Smith & Keating, 1997

Other companies negotiated changes to curriculum. For instance, a group of Chinese restaurateurs persuaded a provider to adapt the traditional traineeship for Chinese cuisine. Despite the success of the pilots, however, misgivings have been expressed about adoption of user-choice nationally. The New South Wales Government, for instance, will only adopt it initially for first-year apprentices, and is concerned about what will happen in 'thin markets' where there are few providers and not many apprentices and trainees. In Western Australia, a preferred supplier arrangement will be used for some trades because of the low numbers of apprentices. State governments are also, naturally, concerned about possible effects on their TAFE systems, particularly in country areas. Many TAFE colleges are highly dependent upon apprenticeship and traineeship courses for their survival.

One option open to organisations under user-choice will be to provide the off-the-job training for their apprentices and trainees themselves. While this may seem an ideal way to integrate on-the-job and off-the-job training, there are some concerns that apprentices and trainees might lose the big picture of their occupation or trade, and also that training might be neglected if production pressures are too great (Smith, 1997). There are already some on-the-job apprenticeships operating. The example described in Illustration 2.3 involves building apprentices at Cherbourg Council in Queensland.

The New Training Providers

A key element of the National Training Reform Agenda was to create a more open training market that would allow private training providers to compete with the established state training systems, particularly with TAFE. It was felt that this would provide more options for organisations and individuals, would keep costs down, would encourage TAFE to have more of a customer focus and would enable enterprises to access government funding for their own training, where appropriate. This policy was also in line with the Hilmer Report (Independent Committee of Inquiry, 1993), which advocated competition in every aspect of government services.

TAFE provides about 85 per cent of VET activity at present, although there have always been other training providers, such as business colleges or hospitality schools. These providers have traditionally, however, operated on a fee-for-service basis; that is, students or enterprises buy training at the commercial rate. Several policies have encouraged the entry of more providers into the training market:

- the tendering out of some labour market programs (for unemployed people), of traineeships, and since the early 1990s, of ANTA growth funding;
- the introduction of NFROT, which allowed courses by any provider to be accredited;
- registration processes, also under NFROT, for non-TAFE providers, giving assurances to purchasers of training (individuals and companies) that providers were approved;
- the introduction of user-choice for apprenticeships and traineeships from 1998.

Illustration 2.4 — Examples of training providers in each category

---

Commercial: Metropolitan Business College

This college, established in Canberra for over thirty years, had 120 full-time and 50 part-time students in 1996. Most students were fee-paying but some were funded by the government on labour market programs. All courses offered were in the business area, including marketing and graphic design, many of their courses being 'bought in' from other providers. They also offered tailor-made training to various government departments and other clients.

Community: Mission Employment, Wagga Wagga

In 1996, nearly twenty full-time teaching staff worked at this large Skillshare in a country town. Most of its courses used government funding to teach a wide range of unemployed students. The course included computing, Internet, retail, welding, forklift licence, hospitality, first aid, job-seeking. A few courses, such as Internet training, were offered on a commercial basis to local companies, and to fee-paying students.

Enterprise: BHP Port Kembla

The technical training department in BHP Port Kembla employed 26 staff in 1996, servicing a company of 9000 employees. The department had four main areas of training: first year training (electrical and mechanical apprentices), administrative systems, trades and safety. Around 60 apprentices went through first-year training each year, with most of the items produced by the apprentices being used for production in one of the company's plants. The trades courses offered by the department provided BHP employees with a chance to further their skills, with wage rises dependent upon each of the six levels of tradesperson within the company.

Industry: Australian Chamber of Manufactures (ACM)

The ACM Training Centre is an industry training provider owned and operated by the Australian Chamber of Manufactures in Richmond, Victoria. By the late 1990s, the ACM Training Centre, providing apprentice training for several manufacturing companies in Victoria, had also diversified its activities into the provision of management and professional training and a Group Training Scheme dealing principally with traineeships. Traineeships had become an important part of the centre's activities.

Source: Smith and Keating, 1997

Under tendering and user-choice arrangements, government money flows to non-TAFE providers. Companies can also register as training providers and access government funding in this way.

There are four generally recognised types of providers of VET besides TAFE:

1. **Commercial providers** — providing courses to industry and individuals for profit (for example, business colleges, beauty schools, flying schools);
2. **Community providers** — non-profit organisations, funded by government or community sponsors (for example, community colleges, Skillshares);
3. **Enterprise providers** — companies or other organisations providing training mainly for their own employees (for example, large firms, local councils);

4. **Industry providers** — organisations providing training to enterprises across an industry (for example, state pharmacy guilds, training centres operated by associations of manufacturers).

The above categories are not clearly defined and some providers offer a range of commercial and government-funded courses, making them difficult to classify. Enterprises are generally only recognised as being part of the training market when they provide accredited training and are registered providers. It is difficult to estimate the exact number of non-TAFE training providers. In 1995 there were just under 1000 registered training providers (Smith et al, 1996), with, perhaps, double that number of unregistered providers. However, they share some common characteristics. Generally, non-TAFE training providers are concentrated in a relatively small number of areas of training, particularly in business administration and hospitality. Most of the non-TAFE providers offer only a very small number of courses and much training is not accredited. As non-TAFE providers are often involved in many other activities, training may be only one of the provider's activities. Illustration 2.4 provides some examples of non-TAFE training providers in each of the categories.

Summary

Since the mid-1980s, the Australian training system has been undergoing major change. The federal nature of the Australian Constitution has meant that the training system has been fragmented and slow to change in response to developments in the business environment. The former Federal Labor Government made training reform a central policy after the report of the ACTU/TDC Mission to Western Europe in 1987.

A number of reports paved the way for the changes to the training system which became known collectively as the National Training Reform Agenda. The Deveson, Finn, Mayer and Carmichael Reports advocated the opening up of the training system to market forces and the use of competency-based training to reform the system so that a more unified, national system would emerge.

One of the first reforms implemented was the Training Guarantee Scheme in 1990. This stipulated that employers with payrolls in excess of $200,000 per annum had to spend up to 1.5 per cent of their payroll costs on training their employees. The scheme, however, drew much criticism and was suspended in 1994, and finally abolished by the new Coalition Federal Government in 1996.

The major elements of the National Training Reform Agenda included:
- the use of CBT as the basis for all accredited training in Australia;
- the establishment of industry competency standards for all occupations;
- the establishment of the Australian National Training Authority to oversee the funding of training and to develop training policy;
- the establishment of a framework for the recognition of training at a national level to ensure the portability of qualifications from one state to another;

- the reform of entry-level, apprenticeship and traineeship training.

CBT has become the widely accepted standard for the delivery of training in Australia. However, the interpretation of what constitutes CBT can vary widely. In general, CBT uses industry competency standards to frame training design and is concerned with the maximisation of the flexibility of training through the involvement of industry in program design, the use of self-pacing, modularisation and giving recognition for prior learning.

Entry-level training has been a major focus for reform. Both Labor and Coalition Federal Governments have produced proposals for the subsuming of apprenticeships and traineeships into a single system based on CBT. However, the apprenticeship has proved remarkably resilient to reform and is likely to continue for the foreseeable future. Recently, proposals to free the market for the off-the-job component of apprenticeship and traineeship training have been floated under the title of user-choice.

A key feature of the training reforms has been the creation of a more open training market. This would allow private training providers to compete more effectively with traditional public providers such as TAFE and so drive down the costs of training and make training more responsive to the needs of industry. As a result, the numbers of private providers have been growing and are likely to increase in the future.

Discussion Questions

1. To what extent can reforms to the training system improve Australia's competitive position in the world?
2. How can improvements to the training system help to overcome the problem of youth unemployment?
3. Why is the Australian training system so fragmented?
4. What were the principal measures taken under the National Training Reform Agenda?
5. What is competency-based training and how does it differ from orthodox approaches to training?
6. Why have apprenticeships survived so long in Australia?

Chapter 3

Learners and Learning

Discussions of the role of training and development in the workplace have become increasingly focused on the role of the learner rather than the role of the trainer (Ford, 1997). These discussions have emphasised the importance of how people learn at work, rather than the training activities that employers use to create learning opportunities. In a study of the basic skills requirements of the American work force, Carnevale detailed 13 basic skills that employers appear to require. Top of the list was the ability 'to learn how to learn' (Carnevale et al, 1990). After the ability to learn how to learn, employers wanted the traditional job-related skills that might be expected. However, it was clear from this study that employers regarded learning as an essential activity for their employees if they were to improve the performance of their organisations.

This chapter will examine the theory on which learning in the workplace is based. This body of literature is not, however, coherent within itself. The early studies of learning were, in fact, concerned not so much with the processes of learning in humans as with the outcomes of that learning. The behavioural studies of Watson, Thorndike and Pavlov focused only on the externally observable results of the learning process, that is, behaviour. This behavioural orientation has set the agenda for much of the research carried out in the twentieth century in the area of learning, particularly the work of B F Skinner, regarded by many as the giant of learning theory in this century. From the 1930s, educational psychologists became increasingly dissatisfied with the inability of the behaviourists to explain exactly how humans learn. Bruner, Ausubel and others were concerned with exploring the cognitive processes that occur within the mind to effect learning.

This cognitive orientation in learning theory, and its modern manifestation in the form of information processing theories, has come to dominate the debates about learning in the latter part of the century. Other educational theorists are concerned not so much with explaining behaviour or learning processes, as with developing better ways of teaching so that theory can lead to improvements in the way we learn. Many of the so-called 'humanistic' theorists, such as Rogers and Knowles, write about the practice of teaching (pedagogy/andragogy) rather than the ways in which we learn.

This chapter will take the point of view of the learner. Thus, behaviourism emphasises the passive role of the learner, whose behaviour is largely shaped by the environment. Cognitive theorists stress the importance of the active participation of the learner in the learning process. The section on adult learning will examine the claims of the humanist and radical theorists to have found ways of improving the provision of education through better teaching. Finally, a section on workplace learning will draw together the theories of learning, and examine how these can be carried out to improve the practice of training and development.

The Passive Learner

The term 'behaviourism' was coined by the American psychologist John B Watson in the early twentieth century. For Watson, the exploration of the inner workings of the human mind were a distraction from what should be the real object of scientific inquiry for psychologists, namely, observable behaviour:

> The time seems to have come when psychology must discard all reference to consciousness; when it need no longer delude itself into thinking that it is making mental states the object of observation. (Watson, 1915)

This focus on the scientifically observable and measurable has become the hallmark of the behaviourist school. From this perspective, the learner is a passive subject who emits responses to certain stimuli in the environment. As a result, laws can be derived which will predict the response to be expected given the presence of certain stimuli in the environment. There are strict causal chains which govern human behaviour.

In this section, three forms of behavioural learning theory will be examined: the classical conditioning of Pavlov, Skinner's operant conditioning and the most recent manifestation of behaviourism in the training and development field, Bandura's social learning theory.

Classical conditioning

The name that is most often associated with studies of stimulus response (SR) behaviour is that of the Russian physiologist Ivan Pavlov (1839–1936). Pavlov's dog has become synonymous with the concept of conditioning. Pavlov's famous experiments examined the response of a dog to the presence of a stimulus (meat powder) in the environment. The presence of the meat powder caused the dog to salivate. Pavlov described this process as the unconditioned response (salivation) to an unconditioned stimulus (meat powder). Pavlov then proceeded to show that the sound of a bell followed closely on a large number of occasions by the presence of the meat powder would result in a situation where the dog would salivate at the sound of the bell alone. In this case, the dog had become conditioned to salivate at the sound of a bell. Pavlov called the sound of the bell the 'conditioned stimulus' and the following salivation, the 'conditioned response'. Figure 3.1 on p 43 shows the classical conditioning process.

Figure 3.1 — Representation of the classical conditioning process

STEP 1 UNCONDITIONED STIMULUS ⟶ UNCONDITIONED RESPONSE
        (Meat powder)   (Salivation)

STEP 2 CONDITIONED STIMULUS ⟶ UNCONDITIONED RESPONSE
        (Buzzer, followed closely in time,   (Salivation)
        over many trials, by the *uncondi-
        tioned stimulus*)

STEP 3 CONDITIONED STIMULUS ⟶ CONDITIONED RESPONSE
                                     (Salivation)

Source: Camp, R R, Blanchard, P N & Huszczo, G E (1986) *Toward a More Organisationally Effective Training Strategy and Practice*, Prentice-Hall, Englewood Cliffs, New Jersey, p 65

A conditioned response could be extinguished by reversing the process, that is, presenting the conditioned stimulus (the sound of the bell) continuously without the unconditioned stimulus (the meat powder) until the dog ceased to salivate at the sound of the bell alone. There are, however, certain differences between the conditioned and the unconditioned responses. First, the conditioned response is weaker than the unconditioned response; the dog salivates less at the sound of the bell than at the presence of the meat powder. Secondly, the conditioned response can be generalised to other similar stimuli, for example, the ringing of a buzzer rather than a bell in the same situation.

While classical conditioning is a fairly narrow form of learning, it is nevertheless true that many of our basic behaviour patterns are learned in this way. It has been demonstrated that the adverse response of a trainer to poor performance by the trainee may lead the trainee to experience feelings of anxiety and nervousness when working on similar problems in the future. This classically conditioned behaviour may also be difficult for trainers to extinguish unless they control their responses to the trainee performance very carefully in the future to ensure the conditioned response is fully extinguished. It is possible that the creation of favourable learning climates by the trainer may condition trainees to return to that person for further training in the future (Lovell, 1980).

Operant conditioning

B F Skinner developed the work of the early behaviourists into a theory of how humans modify their behaviour, called operant conditioning. He built upon Thorndike's (1874–1949) law of effect, which states that individuals will select those behaviours which are followed by desirable consequences. According to Skinner, these consequences can be consciously manipulated by others to modify the behaviour of the individual in a desirable direction. Skinner was an extreme behaviourist; he had no time for the investigation of the internal processes of the mind which result in learning or changes in behaviour. He believed it is enough to analyse the behaviour itself, because it is capable of observation and measurement, and predict how an organism will behave in a given set of circumstances:

> A science of behaviour will be needed for both theoretical and practical purposes even when the behaving organism is fully understood at another level, just as much of chemistry remains useful even though a detailed account of a single instance may be given at the level of molecular or atomic forces. (Skinner, 1975)

Needless to say, Skinner did not think it important to wait for science to explain behaviour at that level.

Central to operant conditioning are the rewards and punishments that follow behaviour in order to change it. Desired behaviour can be encouraged through reinforcement. Reinforcement may be positive, that is, pleasant consequences for the individual, or it may be negative, that is, the removal of unpleasant consequences. Undesirable behaviour can be discouraged by the use of punishment. Figure 3.2 shows the relationship of reinforcement or punishment and behaviour.

Figure 3.2 — Reinforcement of punishment stimulus

Contingency \ Consequence of	Pleasant Rewarding (desirable)	Noxious Aversive (undesirable)
Applied — after a response	Positive Reinforcement (1)	Punishment (2)
Withdrawn — after a response	Punishment (3)	Negative Reinforcement (4)

Source: Woolmer, B (1988) *Introduction to the Human Learner* (Course notes), Riverina-Murray Institute of Higher Education, p 44

Everyday observation of the workplace shows that operant conditioning is a very common phenomenon. Workers on piece rates will maximise their output in order to collect the highest bonus at the end of the pay period. The bonus acts as a positive reinforcer (1) encouraging workers to continue to work at the highest performance level. Workers who are late for work may lose a percentage of their pay as a result of non-attendance. Docking pay in this way acts as a punishment (3) to deter future lateness. A persistent latecomer to work may eventually be disciplined or sacked in order to stop the behaviour once and for all (2). Finally, workers who have been disciplined in the past may have that record removed from their files as a reward for good behaviour later on. This acts as a negative reinforcer (4) for good industrial conduct.

Effective modification of behaviour depends on the frequency with which reinforcement or punishment follows responses. Generally, Skinner did not view punishment as an effective means of altering behaviour. While punishment may inhibit an undesirable behaviour very effectively, it does not reinforce the correct behaviour. It may even act as a positive reinforcer to the punisher, who observes that the punishment stops the undesirable behaviour and is therefore inclined to use punishment on subsequent occasions. Thus, behaviour modification depends on the frequency of the application of reinforcers. There are various schedules for reinforcement, ranging from continuous, in which the reinforcement is delivered immediately after every manifestation of the desired behaviour, through fixed interval schedules (reinforcement at certain periods); fixed ratio (reinforcement after a predetermined number of behaviours) to intermittent schedules, in which reinforcement is delivered after an uncertain and constantly changing number of behaviours.

Skinner found that an intermittent schedule of reinforcement was the most powerful in terms of prolonging the duration of the responses, that is, if people are uncertain when the reward for a particular behaviour will appear, they will tend to continue to display the behaviour for a considerable period after the reward has been withdrawn, in the hope that it will reappear. Intermittent reinforcement may be given unwittingly with potentially adverse consequences. Supervisors who often 'rise to the bait' on the shop floor may actually be encouraging this behaviour in their employees through intermittently reinforcing it.

Operant conditioning techniques are often used in training situations without the trainer being aware of the technique itself. Thus, the instructor who is training a machine operator in a complex series of tasks will often coach the trainee by praising any actions which come near the desired sequence of behaviour. As the operator becomes more competent, however, the instructor will only praise those actions that are precisely correct until the trainee has mastered the tasks completely. This technique, known as 'shaping', is the basis for sports coaching (Lovell, 1980).

Shaping and the other behaviourist techniques emphasise the role of the environment in conditioning the behaviour of individuals. As such, the stimuli most commonly associated with the behaviourist school are extrinsic, that is, they impinge on the individual from outside. Praise or reproach from the instructor, paycheques or disciplinary interviews are examples of extrinsic stimuli to which the individual responds. However, stimuli can also be intrinsic, originating within the individual. What motivates craftspeople to produce high quality work if not an intrinsic pride in their skill? Individuals will set their own goals and standards and will therefore experience a sense of satisfaction if they achieve them (positive reinforcement) or a sense of dissatisfaction if they fail (punishment). In this sense, reinforcement and punishment become an important component in individual motivation.

Skinner, however, would dissociate himself from the notion of intrinsic reinforcement. His concern was with the stimulus, which he regarded as essentially external to the individual. The craftsperson's pride may be the desire for (external) social approval. It is also important to note that human beings possess the ability to resist even the most powerful conditioning, as the gaols of Australia so painfully remind us.

Behaviourism has not been without its critics. The major criticisms of this approach may be summarised under the headings of 'determinism' and 'epiphenomenalism' (Locke, 1977). Behaviourism is accused of being determinist because it overstates the effect of the environment in conditioning the behaviour of individuals and dismisses the concept of a free will by which people have the ability to resist the promptings of the environmental stimulus and choose their own responses. Epiphenomenalism refers to the behaviourists' refusal to recognise the workings of the mind in the learning process because they cannot be subjected to rigorous scientific measurement and evaluation. Behaviourists claim that only behaviour is observable; anything else is intangible and of marginal relevance to human learning. To prove the behaviourists' claim that human learning is solely the product of environmental influence is clearly impossible, as it would involve the creation of a control group for which there is no environment (Latham and Saari, 1979).

Despite the controversy surrounding the work of Skinner and the claims of the behaviourists, there is no doubt that the concept of operant conditioning has been one of the major milestones in the development of learning theory in this century and exerts great influence in the design of training programs in industry and commerce. The recent debates about competency-based training have been partly based on the claims by critics of this approach that competency-based training is based solely on behaviourism and does not allow trainees to learn anything other than strictly job-related skills (Collins, 1993b).

Social learning

Bandura elaborated a theory of learning which, while retaining many of the essentials of the behaviourist school, posited a much greater role for the cognitive mental processes of individuals (Bandura, 1969). Bandura's research showed that in a stimulus-response (SR) situation, the stimulus can have an effect beyond the individual subject experiencing it. People can learn by observing others in an SR situation and later reproduce the behaviour they have learned while observing. Thus, social learning theory emphasises the importance of having a role model on which to base one's own behaviour.

In strict terms, the modelling process is not a conventional SR situation. The individual is observing the model and imitating the actions in order to gain the reward or avoid punishment. It is, in fact, the model that is reinforced rather than the individual. Social learning theory also attempts to explain the cognitive processes that occur in the subject's mind, thus avoiding the charges of determinism brought against the behaviourist school. Figure 3.3 on p 47 shows the processes that occur during the social learning situation.

According to Bandura, the subject's cognitive processes are engaged through attention to the environment. The subject observes the SR learning situation and learns from the activities of the model which behaviours result in reinforcement and which in punishment. This information is then retained and rehearsed by the subject, perhaps without any behaviour occurring. The subject reproduces the observed behaviour when required. Social learning theory has been applied most directly in workplace learning situations through the development of behaviour modelling: see Chapter 8. In behaviour modelling, trainees learn by observing and imitating the actions of a role model. The technique is most often used in management training programs where managers are being trained to deal with complex social situations such as dealing with employee grievances.

Figure 3.3 — Graphic representation of the social learning processes

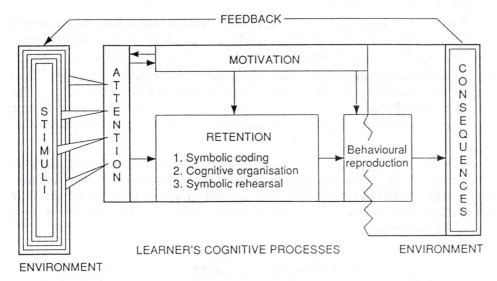

Source: Camp, R R, Blanchard, P N & Huszczo, G E (1986) *Toward a More Organisationally Effective Training Strategy and Practice*, Prentice-Hall, Englewood Cliffs, New Jersey, p 76

Although springing from the behaviourist tradition in terms of its emphasis on SR leaning, Bandura later tried to differentiate his theory of social learning from the behaviourists and named it 'social cognitive theory'. Some writers have claimed that Bandura's work spans the gulf between the positions of the behaviourists and the cognitivists because it attempts to explain the processes by which an individual learns in an SR situation. The theory of social learning seems, however, to share more in common with the behaviourist position in its concern to explain behavioural outcomes and its emphasis on the, albeit vicarious, response of the individual to stimuli.

Conclusion

The behaviourist school has had a significant impact on the conduct of training and development programs. Despite the criticisms made of its assumptions and methodology, behaviourism remains very popular within industrial and organisational psychology circles (Latham, 1989). There is a number of implications for training and development practitioners arising from the research findings of the behaviourists.

1. **People respond to reinforcement.** Organisations need to reinforce trainees in order to motivate them to enter training programs and to perform adequately during the programs.

2. **Responses to stimuli are individual.** As a result, instruction needs to be oriented towards the individual. Blanket training programs involving groups of trainees are likely to be less than effective, as they ignore the individuality of response and group dynamics may interfere with the natural responses of trainees.

3. **The effectiveness of rewards is similarly individually determined.** Status may appeal to some while money alone appeals to others. Uniform policies of reward for training may not achieve consistent results.

4. **Training programs should proceed from the simple to the complex.** This is so whether the program involves the learning of skills or concepts. The notion of shaping, demands that each step in the program be well-defined and that successful performance be accompanied by progressive reinforcement.

Many training techniques have been developed using behaviourist principles of learning. These include programmed instruction (PI) and its modern counterpart, computer-based training, behaviour modelling and training programs in self-management and self-organisation. These techniques are covered in more depth in Chapter 8.

The Active Learner

Alongside the researches of the behaviourists, other psychologists have taken a different approach to the problem of human learning. For these researchers, behaviourism is an inadequate theory to explain the process of learning. The exclusive concern of Skinner and his colleagues with the observable behaviour of learners, while it may be scientifically rigorous, does not further our understanding of what happens inside the mind of the learner. Cognitive psychology is concerned precisely with the investigation of these mental or cognitive processes. For the cognitivists, the learner is active rather than passive. Learning occurs as a result of the participation of the learner and is therefore dependent on the motivation of the individual. True learning cannot come about as a result of the passive response of the learner to stimuli presented in the environment. This view of the active learner has come to dominate research and theory about human learning in the latter half of the twentieth century.

This section examines the principal streams in cognitive thinking about the learning process. The origins of cognitive theory in the development of Gestalt psychology in the late nineteenth century are discussed, followed by an examination of the work of the leading cognitive learning theorists of the twentieth century, including Bruner, Ausubel and Gagne. The section concludes with a discussion of the modern cognitive approach: information processing theory.

Gestalt

Derived from the German word meaning 'pattern', the Gestalt psychologists of the early part of the twentieth century were concerned with the phenomenon of perception. As the name of the school implies, Gestaltists took the view that human perception is organised on the basis of finding patterns in the objects observed. Max Wertheimer (1886–1943) formulated four laws which govern perception in this way. According to Wertheimer's laws, we will tend to group objects perceived on the basis of their similarity to each other and their physical proximity. Further, we will also tend to fill in the gaps in the information presented visually by supplying the missing information (closure) or by projecting lines on the basis of the pattern we perceive (continuation). Together these laws form the principle of Pragnanz, which governs the Gestalt view of perception (Wertheimer, 1961).

Wolfgang Kohler (1887–1967) demonstrated in his work with primates how Gestalt psychology is relevant to the learning process (Kohler, 1925). In one famous experiment, Kohler suspended a banana over a cage containing some apes. In a far corner of the cage he placed a chair. At first, the apes attempted to reach the banana by jumping but without success. Suddenly, one of the apes, who did not appear to have been thinking about the problem in any way, walked over to the chair, brought it over to the point at which the banana was suspended, climbed onto it and grasped the banana. Kohler interpreted the result of this and similar experiments as an example of 'insightful learning'. The ape has a flash of inspiration which enables it to solve the problem without going through the laborious trial and error sequences of the behaviourists.

This notion of insightful learning, in which problems are solved through a conceptual leap, stood in sharp contrast to the behaviourist notion of stimulus response learning. Wertheimer replicated Kohler's work with groups of schoolchildren to demonstrate that Gestalt principles also apply to human learning. Despite the appeal of the concept of insightful learning, other researchers subsequently showed that this type of learning relied on previous exposure to the type of problem concerned, often in a structured situation, that is, the individual is already half aware of the solution to the problem before the flash of inspiration takes place. Nevertheless, the contribution of the Gestaltists to our understanding of the processes of learning is undeniable.

Cognitive learning

Gestaltists were concerned with the phenomenon of perception. However, perception itself cannot account for the learning process, which obviously involves many more cognitive processes than the initial perception. Nor is it the case that insightful learning is the most usual form of learning; much of our learning takes place in a far more sequential and organised fashion, for example, classroom learning or the acquisition of manual skills. For many cognitive psychologists, part of the answer to this problem of human learning lay in the ways in which we organise the information presented in the learning situation. It seems that we learn and retain information by ordering not only our perceptions but the knowledge we absorb in the learning situation.

Jerome Bruner was a cognitive psychologist in the 1950s who later used his ideas to form a theory of instruction which could be applied in the learning context. Bruner and his colleagues suggested the notion of categories as a basic unit of cognitive organisation (Bruner et al, 1956). According to Bruner, we assign new information to already existing categories or, if the information does not readily fit into a category, we form new ones. Categories serve five major purposes in our cognitive processes:

1. they reduce the complexity of the environment and allow us to simplify situations, contexts and experiences;
2. they allow us to 'identify' new objects by assigning them to a category;
3. they reduce the need for constant learning by allowing us to assign new objects to existing categories;
4. they allow us to make decisions about appropriate actions, for example, not to tamper with unsafe machines;
5. we can create interrelated categories in order to specify the relationship between objects and events.

The creation of categories is the principal activity involved in the learning process according to Bruner. However, this activity is not taught externally; it is intrinsic to the learner, who must create his or her own categories to make sense of the world. The major implication of Bruner's thinking was made clear in his later work on instructional theory (Bruner, 1966). Learners have to discover the rules and laws which govern the world for themselves. Learners only learn by discovering knowledge for themselves and creating their own categories to store this knowledge. Bruner became the main advocate of 'discovery learning', which swept through schools in the 1960s. He criticised the educational system for being too rigid and pre-determined in its approach to learning. In particular, Bruner felt strongly that there was no topic too complex to be introduced to a learner in the earliest stages, so long as the instructional design allowed the topic to be represented in concrete terms understandable to the learner and revisited the topic at higher levels of complexity later in the curriculum (spiral learning).

Bruner's advocacy of discovery learning techniques was criticised by David Ausubel, who placed more emphasis on the positive role of instruction (Ausubel, 1963). His 'subsumption' theory of learning re-emphasised the role of the instructor in providing reception learning rather than pure discovery learning. The concept of subsumption is similar to the categorisation process of Bruner. The learner absorbs new information by subsuming it under existing categories, creating a hierarchical cognitive structure within which all information can be subsumed.

There is a number of conditions necessary for subsumption to occur (Shuell, 1986). The learner uses 'advance organisers', models of the information to be absorbed, which help to fit the new material into the existing structure. In order to achieve this fit, the material must be discriminable from the existing cognitive structure; this can be facilitated by the trainer, who will point out how the new material is different and repeat this until the learner has successfully subsumed the information. Repetition is often the key to effective learning in this way.

Thus, in Ausubel's scheme, the trainer has a very positive role to play in facilitating learning. Ausubel was quite critical of the excesses to which he felt the idea of discovery learning had been taken by the followers of Bruner. He listed

12 beliefs which he thought characterised the discovery learning philosophy, including (Langford, 1989):

- all real learning is self-discovered;
- problem-solving ability is the primary goal of education;
- expository teaching is authoritarian; and
- discovery is a prime source of intrinsic motivation.

Ausubel proceeded to show how these beliefs were, in reality, myths, and that discovery learning was often extremely inefficient in its use of time, particularly for the teaching of complex concepts which do not lend themselves readily to discovery techniques.

Robert Gagne also emphasised the importance of the trainer. Gagne was concerned with the organisation of knowledge, and used the concept of an hierarchy to distinguish between eight different types of learning which take place when trainees are attempting to learn a new body of knowledge or skill. The most basic form of learning according to Gagne is signal learning, which is, in effect, classical conditioning. Although signal learning is the most elementary form of learning, it does not occupy the lowest position on Gagne's ladder. This is because signal learning can occur at any time and does not need to be preceded by any other form of learning to be effective; it conditions our predisposition to learn in the first place. The remaining forms of learning are placed in the hierarchy thus:

- **Stimulus response learning.** This is Skinnerian operant conditioning.
- **Motor/verbal chain learning.** These are placed at the same position in the hierarchy. They represent the ability to perform a sequence of motor or verbal activities smoothly and automatically.
- **Multiple discrimination learning.** Trainees have learned to discriminate between different objects, ideas, events or stimuli and can tailor their actions accordingly.
- **Concept learning.** This is very similar to Bruner's categorisation process. Information is grouped into concepts which allow the learner to classify other information and to respond to numbers of slightly different things as a class.
- **Rule learning.** Rules enable the learner to respond to a wide variety of situations in a consistent manner. Learners may not always be able to articulate the rules which they use, but they are, nevertheless, learned.
- **Problem-solving.** The highest level in Gagne's hierarchy. In this situation, the learner is able to use the rules and concepts previously formulated to deal with entirely new situations, and so learn anew.

Gagne's model is not developmental, that is, it does not describe the learning abilities of different types of learners. Rather, the hierarchy applies to any learning situation. As the learners progress through the discipline, they travel up the learning hierarchy. An example might be the progress of the craft apprentice. Initial learning would use SR methods to gain some fluency with the basic operations and terminology of the trade (motor/verbal chaining). More advanced training, especially classroom-based education, would enable the apprentice to develop concepts and rules about the trade. Ultimately, the apprentice becomes a fully fledged craftsperson able to use the training to solve entirely novel problems, thus reaching the top of Gagne's hierarchy.

Gagne's theory of learning therefore places great emphasis on the role of the trainer in devising programs and materials which will allow the trainee to move smoothly through the hierarchy. It also draws upon the behaviourist tradition in its use of operant conditioning methods, especially at the lower levels of learning.

Information processing

In the last 20 years, cognitive explanations of learning have increasingly used the concept of information processing as a means of modelling what occurs during learning. As the name implies, information processing theorists use the analogy of the computer to explain learning. Figure 3.4 below illustrates the basic information processing model.

Figure 3.4 — The sequence of information processing

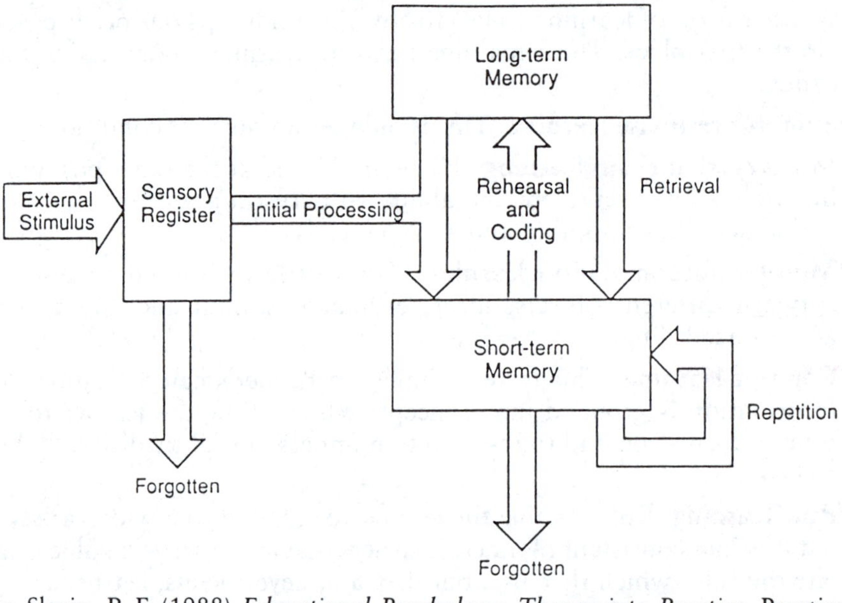

Source: Slavin, R E (1988) *Educational Psychology: Theory into Practice*, Prentice-Hall, Englewood Cliffs, New Jersey, p 145

As the diagram demonstrates, the model focuses on the role of memory. The types of memory identified draw heavily on the metaphor of the computer with both long-term and short-term storage. Memory can be 'accessed' and data 'retrieved' from these stores with varying degrees of success, depending on the efficiency with which the data was stored in the first place. Information processing theorists such as Ellen Gagne (1985) and Schiffrin and Schneider (1977) generally distinguish three types of memory.

The sensory register accepts incoming information and holds it for a very short span of time before it is processed into memory or discarded (forgotten). The sensory register seems to hold large amounts of information in the form in which it was received, that is, visual, auditory etc. As a result, we may have a number of different sensory registers, each of which holds information from a particular sense.

Information from the sensory register is processed and transferred to the short-term store. The short-term store acts as a buffer to the long-term store, holding the information until it can be processed further to be retained longer. It also acts as a working memory into which information from the long-term store is retrieved when it is needed. It appears that information in the short-term store is coded during processing to aid storage, although it is not clear what form the coding takes.

The long-term store is that part of memory where information is permanently recorded. Information entering long-term storage is coded, probably in semantic form to aid recall and organisation. Although information from the sensory register and short-term store is routinely lost (forgotten), it is not known whether information can be lost at all from long-term store, and whether problems of remembering later on are not associated with interference rather than forgetting. Figure 3.5 presents a comparison of these three types of memory.

Figure 3.5 — Commonly accepted differences between the three stages of verbal memory

Feature	Sensory registers	Short-term store	Long-term store
Entry of information	Preattentive	Requires attention	Rehearsal
Maintenance of information	Not possible	Continued attention Rehearsal	Repetition Organisation
Format of information	Literal copy of input	Phonemic Probably visual Possibly semantic	Largely semantic Some auditory and visual
Capacity	Large	Small	No known limit
Information loss	Decay	Displacement Possibly decay	Possibly no loss Loss of accessibility or discriminability by interference
Trace duration	1/4–2 seconds	Up to 30 seconds	Minutes to years
Retrieval	Readout	Probably automatic Items in consciousness	Retrieval cues Possibly search process

Source: Craik, F I H & Lockhart, R (1972) 'Levels of Processing: A Framework for Memory Research' in Norman, D A (1979) *Memory and Attention: An Introduction to Human Information Processing* (2nd ed), Wiley, New York, pp 121–6

Other cognitive theorists have emphasised the importance of organising information for learning. In the 1930s, Bartlett introduced the notion of a schema to explain how individuals related new to existing knowledge (Bartlett, 1932). A schema is a body of existing knowledge or experiences which is stored in memory. New information can be transferred to an existing schema in order to aid comprehension. Schema theory has become an important part of cognitive explanations of human learning. Rumelhart and Norman (1978) elaborated the notion of a schema to produce a cognitive theory of learning. They suggest that the process of learning involves three activities: accretion, in which new information is simply added to the existing schemata (plural of schema), restructuring, in which new schemata are created to accommodate entirely new information, and tuning, where existing schemata are modified as a result of experiencing new situations with which existing schemata cannot cope.

Cognitive theorists also distinguish between different types of knowledge. A basic distinction made by most theorists is between procedural and declarative knowledge. Declarative knowledge is factual knowledge about things in the world; procedural knowledge refers to our ability to perform various tasks using declarative knowledge. John Anderson has used the computer analogy explicitly to create a program (or theory) which links the two forms of knowledge together, called ACT (Anderson, 1983). Anderson suggests that new knowledge is grasped as declarative at first. After processing, it is transformed into procedural knowledge through inference. Thus, the learning process is a search for rules by which operations can be carried out. ACT seems to be the most elaborate and ambitious modern cognitive theory of learning, and demonstrates the power of the computer analogy (Shuell, 1986).

Finally, information processing theory attempts to explain higher order processes in learning. Using the computer analogy once more, information processing theorists use the concept of executive control to describe the way in which the mind exerts control over the learning process itself, that is, selecting what to learn and how to learn it. The notion of executive control is clearly based on the central processing unit (CPU) found in computers which controls the running of programs within the machine. In cognitive terms, executive control emphasises the conscious participation of the learner in the process of learning and the ability to think about one's own learning. The process of thinking about one's own thinking (metacognition) or about one's own memory (metamemory) can bring about improvements in thinking and learning through the development of more effective learning techniques.

Some of the modern debates within cognitive learning theory centre on the possibility of teaching learners to improve their metacognitive abilities. There is a growing body of literature that suggests it is quite possible to improve learners' metacognition by imparting simple techniques that enable them to focus on their learning performance and improve the effectiveness of their memorisation processes (Flavell, 1979; Derry and Murphy, 1986).

Illustration 3.1 — Learning to learn in the Tax Office

The Australian Taxation Office (ATO) is now using work-based learning to deliver its competency-based training to its middle and senior managers. The ATO's research into the learning needs of its management ranks revealed that staff at the higher levels were primarily motivated by their work needs. They were looking for training that was immediately useful to them in terms of their current workload and would enable them to perform better at work. Together with Sydney-based consulting group, Telechy, the ATO developed a new approach to their management training.

Key features of the approach are modules which meet core competencies for the ATO and modules to meet the competency requirements for specific job functions. Sessions introduce the program, provide skills in learning at work, choose work-based activities and provide information on learning outcomes, support mechanisms and timeframes. Learning sets are important because groups of participants encourage and support each other. Learning sets are not tutorials, lectures or training sessions unless the learning set negotiates for that to happen. Rather than creating a project which may be somewhat artificial in order to satisfy their learning requirements, participants select an aspect of their current job and make this the focus of their learning.

Participants are largely self-directed in their learning but have guidance and support to help them. Learning facilitators are being appointed in the work areas to provide additional support. The Honey and Mumford learning cycle has been a key feature in the design of the program. Initial training for the participants includes having them identify their personal learning preferences and some discussion about how their learning preference may help or hinder them. Various features of the program are used to reinforce stages on the learning cycle.

Learning facilitators' primary task is to ensure that participants progress both with their learning activity and through the stages of the learning cycle. Typically participants begin with an initial burst of enthusiasm and high expectations. When they get into it and discover the process requires work and self-discipline, with no firm guidelines to help them through, energy levels tend to drop right down. The ATO has addressed this by spending more time in the initial training on 'learning to learn' and some strategies to get them through the low points. To help the learning facilitators in this task, the program has a module called 'Learning Strategies' for which the work-based learning activity is being a learning facilitator. A major advantage of this approach is the organisation can be seen to practise what it preaches at every level.

Source: Holloway (1997)

Conclusions

Cognitive theories of learning emphasise the importance of the active participation of the learner in the learning process. The nature of the activity may differ according to the theory under consideration, but the central principle remains: learning is active, not passive. There are a number of implications for instructional design in the cognitive approach.

1. **Learner activity should be a central feature of any design.** Learners are active and will learn more effectively if they have some control over the

learning process. This is not to advocate Bruner-style discovery learning programs for everything; however, a moderate amount of discovery can be effective.

2. **Information should be organised to facilitate learning.** Information can be presented in such a way that the links between its various parts can be highlighted to aid schema accretion and tuning. It can also be organised on a hierarchical basis, so that learners progress from the simple to the complex using the notions embodied in Gagne's writings.

3. **Learners need to learn how to learn.** Metacognitive ability improves learning performance and the evidence seems to suggest that this ability can be taught and improved.

Cognitive principles now inform most training design, even programs with a behaviourist foundation. This is not surprising given the focus of the cognitive theorists on the process of learning rather than its observable outcomes. In many ways, behaviour can be viewed as the result of learning, which is best explained using cognitive theory.

The Adult Learner

Adult learning is still a discipline in search of a theory (Hartree, 1986). It has long been thought by adult educators that the differences between children and adults mean that adults must learn in a qualitatively different way from children and that, as a result, a distinctly adult theory of learning is possible. Unfortunately, as the criticisms of the work of Knowles in this area reveal, the differences between adults and children in terms of their learning may be more apparent than real. Adult learning theory, therefore, is a misnomer. Much of what is described by the term are, in fact, theories of adult teaching based largely on cognitive theories of learning and humanistic theories of psychology. The expansion of post-compulsory education in the twentieth century has given rise to a body of literature on the teaching of adults. Perhaps the earliest and best known of the adult learning theorists is John Dewey.

Progressive education

Dewey was a central figure in the progressive education movement in America in the early part of the century and was, for a number of years, principal of a progressive school. His writings, however, were not confined to the teaching of children. Dewey was a fervent believer in the notion of lifelong learning. Learning for Dewey was a process of growth, with all of life's experiences playing a part in our learning and in forming the kind of people we are. Adults learn from their experiences and, as they develop and grow, they can become better learners. Thus, the role of the trainer in Dewey's view would not be that of the didactic instructor, but rather that of the facilitator, establishing the conditions under which people learn for themselves (Dewey, 1938). Therefore, the trainer comes to develop a unique relationship with the trainee: one of guiding and helping rather than directing and imposing.

Dewey also believed that the process of learning was self-directed and that we learn by solving problems using scientific method. Thus, the individual is presented with a problem. Consideration of the problem leads to the formation of tentative hypotheses about possible solutions. The learner then tries out these hypotheses in a trial and error way to arrive at the solution. Again, the role of the trainer would be to facilitate rather than direct the problem-solving process (Jarvis, 1983). Dewey's view of the role of the trainer could be summarised as:

- being intelligently aware of the capacity, needs and past experiences of learners;
- making suggestions for learning, but being prepared for the learners to make further suggestions so that learning is seen to be a cooperative, rather than a dictatorial, enterprise;
- using the environment and experiences, and extracting from them all the lessons that may be learned;
- selecting activities that encourage the learners to organise the knowledge they gain from their experiences;
- looking ahead to see the direction in which the learning experiences lead to ensure they are conducive to continued growth.

Dewey's thinking has been very influential in adult education; his ideas were operationalised by Eduard Lindeman in America. One can also detect intimations of later cognitive approaches to learning: particularly the ideas of Bruner, in the role of experience in learning, and of Gagne, in the importance of problem-solving method.

The humanistic approach

The humanistic approach to psychology was first developed in the 1940s by the psychotherapist Carl Rogers as a reaction to what he saw as the extremes of behaviourism then gripping the discipline. Rogers objected to the reductionism of Skinner and his colleagues who, as we have seen, regarded any phenomena incapable of being accurately scientifically measured as not worth researching. Rogers could not accept that people were simply a product of their conditioning. They had free will, and the differences between people were so great that they could not be explained by exposure to the same environment. Rogers applied his notions of the freedom of the individual to education and learning. Like Dewey, Rogers does not offer a theory of human learning in any comprehensive sense. He is concerned with improving the way in which people are instructed and allowing their natural propensity for learning to flourish.

People prefer to manage their own affairs and, according to Rogers, they prefer to manage their own learning. The role of the trainer is therefore that of a facilitator; a term Rogers did much to popularise during the 1970s and 1980s. The facilitator creates the conditions under which people will learn (Rogers, 1983). Rogers compares his facilitator with the conventional teacher:

> The traditional teacher — the good traditional teacher — asks her or himself questions of this sort: 'What do I think would be good for a student to learn at this particular age and level of competence? How can I plan a proper curriculum

for this student? How can I inculcate motivation to learn this particular curriculum? How can I instruct in such a way that he or she will gain the knowledge that should be gained? How can I best set an examination to see whether this knowledge has actually been taken in?'

On the other hand, the facilitator of learning asks questions such as these, not of self, but of the students: 'What do you want to learn? What things puzzle you? What are you curious about? What issues concern you? What problems do you wish you could solve?' When he or she has the answers to these questions, further questions follow. 'Now how can I help him or her find the resources — the people, the experiences, the learning facilities, the books, the knowledge in myself — which will help them learn in ways that will provide answers to the things that concern them, the things they are eager to learn?' And, then later, 'How can I help them evaluate their own progress and set future learning goals based on this self-evaluation?'

Rogers defines the conditions which the facilitator creates as maximising the freedom of the individual to learn. This involves removing threats to the learner's self-esteem, involving the learner in decisions about the program, learning by doing, using self-evaluation techniques and, finally, enabling students to learn how to learn. Again, echoes of cognitive theory, especially information processing, can be discerned in Rogers' writings, although he is not propounding any new theory of learning per se. Rogers' humanistic approach has had a profound influence on the conduct of adult learning since the 1960s.

Andragogy

Perhaps the most influential thinker on adult learning in the latter part of the twentieth century has been Malcolm Knowles (1913–88). Knowles was for many years the chief executive of the Adult Education Association in the United States, putting him in a direct line of descent from John Dewey, via Lindeman. However, the two differ substantially in their approach to adult learning (Fisher and Podeschi, 1989). For Knowles, adult learning was a socially transforming experience which would lead to the creation of a better society. Learning took place in the organisations in which the vast majority of adults lived and worked. Individuals learn through their experiences in organisations, and organisations will become better places by providing their employees with significant opportunities to learn and develop.

Although he did not invent the term, Knowles can be credited with the popularisation of the concept of andragogy (Knowles, 1970). Knowles differentiated the way in which children learn (pedagogy) from the way in which adults learn (andragogy). Although at first stressing that these differences were absolute, Knowles later acknowledged that, in fact, the differences between adults and children in his writings were rather differences of degree (Knowles, 1984). He describes six assumptions that differentiate andragogy from pedagogy:

1. **The need to know.** 'Adults need to know why they need to learn something before they undertake to learn it.'
2. **The learner's self-concept.** 'Once they have arrived at that self-concept they (adults) develop a deep psychological need to be seen by others and treated by others as being capable of self direction.'

3. **The role of the learner's experience.** '...for many kinds of learning the richest resources for learning reside in the adult learners themselves.'
4. **Readiness to learn.** 'Adults become ready to learn those things they need to know and are able to do to cope effectively with their real-life situations.'
5. **Orientation to learning.** 'In contrast to children's and youth's subject-centred orientation to learning (at least in school), adults are life-centred (or task-centred or problem-centred) in their orientation to learning.'
6. **Motivation.** 'While all adults are responsive to some external motivators (better jobs, promotions, higher salaries and the like), the most potent motivators are internal pressures (the desire for increased job satisfaction, self esteem, the quality of life and the like).'

Knowles continues to show how his concept of adult learning translates into conditions for effective learning which the trainer needs to ensure are present in any adult learning situation (Knowles, 1984):

- the learners feel a need to learn;
- the learning environment is characterised by physical comfort, mutual trust and respect, mutual helpfulness, freedom of expression and acceptance of the differences;
- the learners perceive the goals of the learning experience to be their own goals;
- the learners accept a share of the responsibility for planning and operating a learning experience, and therefore have a feeling of commitment to it;
- the learners participate actively in the learning process;
- the learning process is related to, and makes use of, the experience of the learners;
- the learners have a sense of progress towards their goals.

Knowles clearly draws on the humanistic theorists in his approach to adult learning. He acknowledges his debt to Maslow's idea of self-actualising man, and the learner-centred approaches of Rogers. Knowles does not dismiss the claims of the other learning theorists; far from it. For Knowles, each theory of learning, from classical conditioning to information processing theory, has its place and is appropriate in certain situations. The task of the training and development practitioner is to pick the theory most appropriate to the learning task in hand and to the organisation concerned. Figure 3.6 on p 60 illustrates Knowles' views on this point.

The ideal vehicle for andragogic learning according to Knowles is the learning contract. This is a joint agreement between student and teacher about the goals, methods and evaluation of the learning to be undertaken. Knowles describes the main features of the learning contract:

> ... in traditional education the learning activity is structured by the teacher and the institution ... This imposed structure conflicts with the adult's deep psychological need to be self directing and may induce resistance, apathy or withdrawal. Learning contracts provide a vehicle for making the planning of learning

experiences a mutual undertaking between a learner and his helper, mentor, teacher and, often, peers. By participating in the process of diagnosing his needs, formulating his objectives, identifying resources, choosing strategies and evaluating his accomplishments, the learner develops a sense of ownership of (and commitment to) the plan.

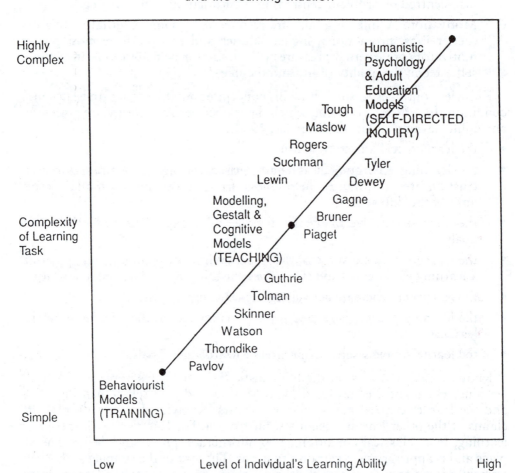

Figure 3.6 — Relationship between teacher models and the learning situation

Source: Knowles, M (1984) *The Adult Learner: A Neglected Species* (3rd ed), Gulf Publishing Company, Houston, Texas (Used with permission. All rights reserved.)

Knowles' ideas have been the subject of much criticism (Jarvis, 1983). The principal target of this criticism has been the concept of andragogy itself. Tennant (1986) summarises Knowles' description of andragogy under five headings and shows that each one of the supposedly unique qualities of the adult learner can be discerned in children also, and that there is no real difference between learners of any age in terms of the processes they undergo during learning. This line of attack on Knowles' theory leads to the charge that andragogy is not a theory of learning at all, but rather an ideological position characterised by an adherence to the principles of humanistic psychology and a belief in the basic individualism of the human learner (Hartree, 1986).

Nevertheless, it is an ideological position which many trainers have found particularly appealing in their approach to their work, and Knowles remains one of the most widely read and popular of the adult learning theorists.

Experiential learning

Implicit in the various approaches to adult learning is the notion of experience. Dewey, Rogers and Knowles all acknowledge the importance of experience to the adult learner. Their prescriptions for effective instruction all embody the concept of learning through experience; they all embrace the concept of experiential learning. Kolb has used the concept of experiential learning to build what he considers to be a theory of learning (Kolb, 1984). He defines learning as:

> ... the process whereby knowledge is created through the transformation of experience.

This definition has four major implications for Kolb. First, the content and outcomes of learning are not so important as the process of adaptation involved in undergoing new experiences. Secondly, knowledge is not a static thing which is acquired once, but a process of transformation in a state of continuous change. Thirdly, learning changes our experience of the world so that we see and experience things differently as a result of it. Finally, the process of learning cannot be understood without also understanding the nature of knowledge. Thus, learning occurs as a result of undergoing an experience which is then transformed into new knowledge which enables the learner to cope more effectively with the world.

Kolb described experiential learning in two dimensions. These are summarised in Figure 3.7 on p 62. The first dimension relates to the way in which we grasp experience. Concrete experience is the state of understanding reality by becoming involved with experience in an immediate way. Abstract conceptualisation emphasises the role of thinking and deriving general rules from the experience. The second dimension refers to the way in which that experience is transformed within the learner so that learning actually occurs. Reflective observation is based on the process of understanding the experience and digesting the implications of what has happened. Active experimentation is the state of changing reality as a result of the experience; particularly influencing people and situations.

The four states which Kolb describes can be thought of as a cycle: the experiential learning cycle. Experiential learning consists of a process of concrete experience, followed by a period of reflective observation in which those experiences are digested. This leads to a phase of abstract conceptualisation, in which understanding crystallises into a theory which explains the experiences, followed by an active experimentation phase, in which the new theory is put into practice in order to change the situation.

Figure 3.7 — Structural dimensions underlying the process of experiential learning and the resulting basic knowledge forms

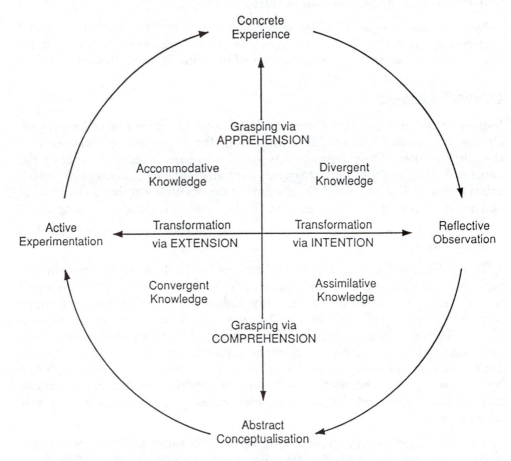

Source: Kolb, D (1984) *Experiential Learning*, Prentice-Hall, Englewoods Cliffs, New Jersey

Kolb takes the concept of the learning cycle further, however, with his notion of learning styles. Although it is generally true, according to Kolb, that we all go through this sort of process when we learn, individuals also have preferences which lead them to emphasise one or other of the four states in their learning. These states or learning styles correspond to the four quadrants bound by the dimensions of the learning process we have just reviewed. Kolb describes the four learning styles thus (Kolb, 1984):

- **The convergent learning style** relies primarily on the dominant learning abilities of abstract conceptualisation and active experimentation. The greatest strength of this approach lies in problem-solving, decision-making, and the practical application of ideas.
- **The divergent learning style** has the opposite learning strengths from convergence, emphasising concrete experience and reflective observation. The greatest strength of this orientation lies in imaginative ability and

awareness of meaning and values to organise many relations into a meaningful Gestalt.

- **In assimilation,** the dominant learning abilities are abstract conceptualisation and reflective observation. The greatest strength of this orientation lies in inductive reasoning and the ability to create theoretical models: in assimilating disparate observations into an integrated explanation.

- **The accommodative learning style** has the opposite strengths from assimilation, emphasising concrete experience and active experimentation. The greatest strength of this orientation is in doing things, in carrying out plans and tasks, and getting involved in new experiences. The adaptive emphasis of this orientation is on opportunity seeking, risk taking and action.

There is a number of forces Kolb identifies which predispose individuals to adopt one or other of the learning styles. These include the basic personality of the individual, his or her educational history, professional career, current job role and the specific, immediate task that the individual is working on. Thus, the balance of these forces may act to shift individuals between learning styles, but the importance of previous choices in terms of education, career, etc, will tend to lock individuals into one of the four learning styles most of the time, with a consequent distortion in their ability to function throughout the full range of the learning cycle.

Kolb's work has been criticised, particularly the questionnaire which he developed to test the learning styles of individual learners which has been the focus of much of his later work. However, his writing remains the clearest exposition of the concept of experiential learning which forms one of the major themes in the body of adult learning literature.

Illustration 3.2 — Honey and Mumford's learning styles inventory

Kolb's learning styles have been adapted by two management development specialists, Peter Honey and Alan Mumford. They use a four-way classification that closely resembles that of Kolb but is simplified for use in a practical training situation.

You can find out your own learning style by completing and scoring the following questionnaire. A description of the Honey and Mumford classification follows for use after the questionnaire has been scored.

Learning Styles — General Descriptions

Activists

Activists involve themselves fully and without bias in new experiences. They enjoy the here and now and are happy to be dominated by immediate experiences. They are open-minded, not sceptical, and this tends to make them enthusiastic about anything new. Their philosophy is: 'I'll try anything once'. They tend to act first and consider the consequences afterwards. Their days are filled with activity. They tackle problems by brainstorming. As soon as the excitement from one activity has died down they are busy looking for the next. They tend to thrive on the challenge of new experiences but are bored with implementation and longer term consolidation. They are gregarious people constantly involving themselves with others but, in doing so, they seek to centre all activities around themselves.

Reflectors

Reflectors like to stand back and ponder experiences and observe them from many different perspectives. They collect data, both first hand and from others, and prefer to think about it thoroughly before coming to any conclusion. The thorough collection and analysis of data about experiences and events is what counts so they tend to postpone reaching definitive conclusions for as long as possible. Their philosophy is to be cautious. They are thoughtful people who like to consider all possible angles and implications before making a move. They prefer to take a back seat in meetings and discussions. They enjoy observing other people in action. They listen to others and get the drift of the discussion before making their own points. They tend to adopt a low profile and have a slightly distant, tolerant unruffled air about them. When they act it is part of a wide picture which includes the past as well as the present and others' observations as well as their own.

Theorists

Theorists adapt and integrate observations into complex but logically sound theories. They think problems through in a vertical, step by step, logical way. They assimilate disparate facts into coherent theories. They tend to be perfectionists who won't rest easy until things are tidy and fit into a rational scheme. They like to analyse and synthesise. They are keen on basic assumptions, principles, theories, models and systems thinking. Their philosophy prizes rationality and logic. 'If it's logical it's good'. Questions they frequently ask are: 'Does it make sense?' 'How does this fit with that?' 'What are the basic assumptions?' They tend to be detached, analytical and dedicated to rational objectivity rather than anything subjective or ambiguous. Their approach to problems is consistently logical. This is their 'mental set' and they rigidly reject anything that doesn't fit with it. They prefer to maximise certainty and feel uncomfortable with subjective judgements, lateral thinking and anything flippant.*Pragmatists*

Pragmatists are keen on trying out ideas, theories and techniques to see if they work in practice. They positively search out new ideas and take the first opportunity to experiment with applications. They are the sort of people who return from management courses brimming with new ideas that they want to try out in practice. They like to get on with things and act quickly and confidently on ideas that attract them. They tend to be impatient with ruminating and open-ended discussions. They are essentially practical, down to earth people who like making practical decisions and solving problems. They respond to problems and opportunities 'as a challenge'. Their philosophy is: 'There is always a better way' and 'If it *works* it's good'.

Learning Styles Questionnaire

This questionnaire is designed to find out your preferred learning style(s). Over the years you have probably developed learning 'habits' that help you benefit more from some experiences than from others. Since you are probably unaware of this, this questionnaire will help you pinpoint your learning preferences so that you are in a better position to select learning experiences that suit your style.

There is no time limit to this questionnaire. It will probably take you 10–15 minutes. The accuracy of the results depends on how honest you can be. There are no right or wrong answers. If you agree more than you disagree with a statement put a tick by it (✓). If you disagree more than you agree put a cross by it (X). Be sure to mark each item with either a tick or cross.

❑ 1. I have strong beliefs about what is right and wrong, good and bad.
❑ 2. I often act without considering the possible consequences.
❑ 3. I tend to solve problems using a step-by-step approach.

☐ 4. I believe that formal procedures and policies restrict people.
☐ 5. I have a reputation for saying what I think, simply and directly.
☐ 6. I often find that actions based on feelings are as sound as those based on careful thought and analysis.
☐ 7. I like the sort of work where I have time for thorough preparation and implementation.
☐ 8. I regularly question people about their basic assumptions.
☐ 9. What matters most is whether something works in practice.
☐ 10. I actively seek out new experiences.
☐ 11. When I hear about a new idea or approach I immediately start working out how to apply it in practice.
☐ 12. I am keen on self-discipline such as watching my diet, taking regular exercise, sticking to a fixed routine, etc.
☐ 13. I take pride in doing a thorough job.
☐ 14. I get on best with logical, analytical people and less well with spontaneous, 'irrational' people.
☐ 15. I take care over the interpretation of data available to me and avoid jumping to conclusions.
☐ 16. I like to reach a decision carefully after weighing up many alternatives.
☐ 17. I'm attracted more to novel, unusual ideas than to practical ones.
☐ 18. I don't like disorganised things and prefer to fit things into a coherent pattern.
☐ 19. I accept and stick to laid down procedures and policies so long as I regard them as an efficient way of getting the job done.
☐ 20. I like to relate my actions to a general principle.
☐ 21. In discussions, I like to get straight to the point.
☐ 22. I tend to have distant, rather formal relationships with people at work.
☐ 23. I thrive on the challenge of tackling something new and different.
☐ 24. I enjoy fun-loving, spontaneous people.
☐ 25. I pay meticulous attention to detail before coming to a conclusion.
☐ 26. I find it difficult to produce ideas on impulse.
☐ 27. I believe in coming to the point immediately.
☐ 28. I am careful not to jump to conclusions too quickly.
☐ 29. I prefer to have as many sources of information as possible — the more data to think over the better.
☐ 30. Flippant people who don't take things seriously enough usually irritate me.
☐ 31. I listen to other people's points of view before putting my own forward.
☐ 32. I tend to be open about how I'm feeling.
☐ 33. In discussions I enjoy watching the manoeuvrings of the other participants.
☐ 34. I prefer to respond to events on a spontaneous, flexible basis rather than plan things out in advance.
☐ 35. I tend to be attracted to techniques such as network analysis, flow charts, branching programmes, contingency planning, etc.
☐ 36. It worries me if I have to rush out a piece of work to meet a tight deadline.

❑ 37. I tend to judge people's ideas on their practical merits.
❑ 38. Quiet, thoughtful people tend to make me feel uneasy.
❑ 39. I often get irritated by people who want to rush things.
❑ 40. It is more important to enjoy the present moment than to think about the past or future.
❑ 41. I think that decisions based on a thorough analysis of all the information are sounder than those based on intuition.
❑ 42. I tend to be a perfectionist.
❑ 43. In discussions I usually produce lots of spontaneous ideas.
❑ 44. In meetings I put forward practical, realistic ideas.
❑ 45. More often than not, rules are there to be broken.
❑ 46. I prefer to stand back from a situation and consider all the perspectives.
❑ 47. I can often see inconsistencies and weaknesses in other people's arguments.
❑ 48. On balance I talk more than I listen.
❑ 49. I can often see better, more practical ways to get things done.
❑ 50. I think written reports should be short and to the point.
❑ 51. I believe that rational, logical thinking should win the day.
❑ 52. I tend to discuss specific things with people rather than engaging in social discussion.
❑ 53. I like people who approach things realistically rather than theoretically.
❑ 54. In discussions I get impatient with irrelevancies and digressions.
❑ 55. If I have a report to write I tend to produce lots of drafts before settling on the final version.
❑ 56. I am keen to try things out to see if they work in practice.
❑ 57. I am keen to reach answers via a logical approach.
❑ 58. I enjoy being the one that talks a lot.
❑ 59. In discussions I often find I am the realist, keeping people to the point and avoiding wild speculations.
❑ 60. I like to ponder many alternatives before making up my mind.
❑ 61. In discussion with people I often find I am the most dispassionate and objective.
❑ 62. In discussions I'm more likely to adopt a 'low profile' than to take the lead and do most of the talking.
❑ 63. I like to be able to relate current actions to a longer term bigger picture.
❑ 64. When things go wrong I am happy to shrug if off and 'put it down to experience'.
❑ 65. I tend to reject wild, spontaneous ideas as being impractical.
❑ 66. It's best to think carefully before taking action.
❑ 67. On balance I do the listening rather than the talking.
❑ 68. I tend to be tough on people who find it difficult to adopt a logical approach.
❑ 69. Most times I believe the end justifies the means.
❑ 70. I don't mind hurting people's feelings so long as the job gets done.
❑ 71. I find the formality of having specific objectives and plans stifling.

- ☐ 72. I'm usually one of the people who puts life into a party.
- ☐ 73. I do whatever is expedient to get the job done.
- ☐ 74. I quickly get bored with methodical, detailed work.
- ☐ 75. I am keen on exploring the basic assumptions, principles and theories underpinning things and events.
- ☐ 76. I'm always interested to find out what people think.
- ☐ 77 I like meetings to be run on methodical lines, sticking to a laid down agenda, etc.
- ☐ 78. I steer clear of subjective or ambiguous topics.
- ☐ 79. I enjoy the drama and excitement of a crisis situation.
- ☐ 80. People often find me insensitive to their feelings.

Learning Styles Questionnaire — Scoring

You score one point for each item you ticked (✓). There are no points for items you crossed (X).

Simply indicate on the lists below which items were ticked.

2	7	1	5
4	13	3	9
6	15	8	11
10	16	12	19
17	25	14	21
23	28	18	27
24	29	20	35
32	31	22	37
34	33	26	44
38	36	30	49
40	39	42	50
43	41	47	53
45	46	51	54
48	52	57	56
58	55	61	59
64	60	63	65
71	62	68	69
72	66	75	70
74	67	77	73
79	76	78	80
Totals ___	___	___	___
Activist	Reflector	Theorist	Pragmatist

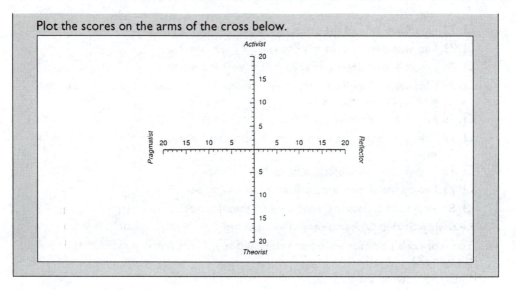

Conclusions

The adult learning literature is not propounding new theories of learning. Dewey, Rogers, Knowles and Kolb are not concerned with the scientific exploration of the cognitive processes involved in learning or the modification of behaviour. Their concern is instructional; improving the way in which people learn by improving training practice. Their writings give the impression of being interlocking. They build on each other's ideas and readily acknowledge their debt to the pioneering work of Dewey. As a result, it is not surprising that a number of common themes emerge.

1. **The role of the self.** The focus of attention is on the individual learner. The effectiveness with which the individual learns is a function of the development of the self. The individual learner is self-directing and the process of learning is the growth of the self. Individuals, following Kolb, can determine their own preferred learning style. The ultimate goal of the learning process is fulfilment of the potential of the self: what Maslow referred to as 'self-actualisation'.

2. **Experience.** Learners draw on their fund of experience and learn through experience. Thus, the best training design must incorporate experiences which the learner undergoes in a self-directed manner, rather than relying on traditional didactic techniques.

3. **Facilitation.** The role of the trainer needs to change to accommodate the emphasis on self and experience for adult learners. The trainer becomes a facilitator, helping the students by clarifying their personal goals in the learning process and creating the conditions for those goals to be achieved, rather than directing the content and process of learning.

These central ideas of adult learning have had a decisive influence on training and development, especially in the areas of management development and organisation development. Most management training programs embody the concepts of self, experience and facilitation to some degree in their instructional methods. Managers have come to expect that the trainer will not give them all the answers but will, rather, provide the setting in which they will discover the important principles for themselves. The methodological consequences of this are explored in later chapters.

The Workplace Learner

The work of the adult learning theorists has been used extensively in recent years to explain how people learn in their workplaces (Burns, 1995; Rylatt, 1994). The workplace has become the central focus for the debate about improving the way we learn as a result of the changes outlined in Chapter 2 and Chapter 4. Training and development has become viewed as a key strategy for improving the economic performance of Australian organisations, and organisations themselves have introduced significant changes into their workplaces which demand considerable investments in training and development with an increasing emphasis on the development of behavioural skills.

In considering learning in the workplace, a critical distinction is often made between training and learning. As discussed in Chapter 1, training refers to the deliberate activities mounted by an organisation to encourage the development of skill, attitudes and behaviours in employees. Thus, training activities tend to occur at particular times and in particular places in organisations. Learning, on the other hand, occurs all the time and in no particular place. People learn, consciously or unconsciously, from many of the things they do and many of the things that happen to them in the workplace. Forrester, Payne and Ward (1995) attempted to clarify the distinction between training and learning in the workplace by contrasting them with education and processes of socialisation. In their view, training and education can be concerned either with the socialisation or the development and emancipation of the individual. Socialisation is concerned with the individual learning the rules by which the society of the organisation works, and adapting his or her behaviour to fit. Thus, managers are keen to socialise their employees so their behaviour fits the requirements of the organisation. Emancipation refers to the development of individuals in their own right so that they eventually fulfil their potential. Forrester, Payne and Ward put these terms into a matrix which is reproduced in Figure 3.8.

In the matrix, training in organisations may be concerned either with the socialisation of employees or with their development and emancipation. Forrester and others argue that much traditional training is concerned with socialisation — getting employees to behave in certain ways — whereas the new organisational forms are increasingly concerned with the development of the total individual, which involves a shift towards work-based learning. This involves the training and development practitioner designing opportunities for employees to learn and develop rather than mounting traditional training programs which employees 'attend'.

Cheren (1990) has emphasised the importance of learning to learn at work. He quotes studies by the American Society for Training and Development in the United States which show that learning to learn is a key basic skill that employers wish to foster in their employees. This involves the development of learning management skills so that employees take responsibility for their own learning rather than relying on training specialists to set up learning opportunities. The development of learning management skills can be built into existing training programs in the organisation so that employees are encouraged to take responsibility for their own learning. In effect, this involves a change in the trainer's role to one of facilitator in the way envisaged by Rogers.

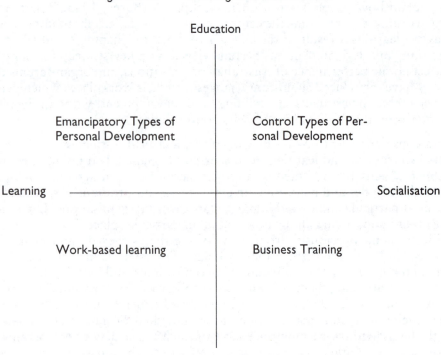

Figure 3.8 — Training and socialisation

Source: Forrester, Payne and Ward (1995)

Informal and incidental learning

Much of the learning that takes place in the workplace is informal or incidental — it takes place outside formal learning situations such as training programs. However, informal and incidental learning are not the same. Incidental learning occurs as a by-product of experiences at work and is usually unintended. Thus, the machine operator who is told to concentrate on turning out parts and not worrying about the quality will learn that the organisation does not really value quality despite what its managers may say in other quarters. Or a young graduate trainee may learn about the important relationships at work through everyday conversations with employees who have been in the organisation for some time. These are important learning experiences, but they are unstructured and fortuitous.

Informal learning, on the other hand, still takes place outside the formal training program but is structured and more intentional. Thus, a newly appointed manager may decide that he or she needs to learn about how to run successful meetings. The manager could read about running meetings, could systematically observe other managers running meetings and learn what was successful and what was not, and could deliberately talk to others who run meetings regularly about what they had learned. This learning is all informal in the sense that it takes place outside a formal meeting skills training program, but it is intentional on the part of the new manager and it is structured.

Marsick and Watkins (1990) distinguish two factors that affect the way learning occurs in the workplace — action and reflection. All learning in the workplace involves a combination of action and reflecting on what has happened. Incidental learning tends to be more action-based. People experience situations at work from which they learn. Some reflection on the importance of what has happened occurs but the focus of the learning is on action. If these actions are random and unplanned, the learning is incidental. People may deliberately seek out situations at work from which they can learn. This will involve action, but a higher degree of reflection on the part of the learner on what they are learning. This is informal learning. Finally, formal learning in a training program typically involves far less action than either incidental or informal learning. However, the emphasis in a formal training program will be reflection on, and understanding, what has been learned in the program. These differences between incidental, informal and formal learning are illustrated in Figure 3.9 on p 72.

According to Marsick and Watkins, three conditions are necessary to enhance the effectiveness of workplace learning:

- **Proactivity** Learners need to be able to take the initiative and understand when and what they need to learn. Thus, proactive learners are 'empowered' to take control of their own learning, and set up situations in the workplace from which they will learn what they need to develop.

- **Critical reflectivity** It is not always enough for the learner simply to reflect on what he or she has learned from a particular experience. Learners need to reflect in a critical way, that is, questioning the basic assumptions on which they operate. Popularised by Jack Mezirow (1990), the radical education theorist, critical reflection encourages questioning of the most fundamental assumptions. This form of reflection is not usually encouraged in organisational training programs, which are more inclined to stress the importance of uncritical acceptance of the organisation's norms and rules. Critical reflection may lead to an almost subversive questioning of the organisation's values and culture.

- **Creativity** Learners need to be able to see beyond the learning situation and imagine what the implications of their learning might be. This might involve reframing situations so that they are seen in a different light and allow the learner to understand their full implications. Alternatively, creativity might involve the ability to play with ideas through activities such as brainstorming, which allow associations between ideas to be made without the censorship of others or the self.

The workplace as a setting for learning

If informal and incidental learning are such an important part of the learning experience for people, it is important to understand how the workplace can be improved to encourage learning to take place. Billett (1993) used the example of the apprenticeship as a model for structuring workplace learning. He identified four phases of workplace learning:

- **Modelling** An expert will perform the task to be learned so the learners can observe the important aspects of the work, and can build a model for themselves which they can subsequently follow in their performance of the task.
- **Coaching** The expert allows the learners to perform the task and monitors their performance, providing feedback and shaping their behaviour until it is correct. This phase is very similar to the role of the sports coach who uses the behaviourist notion of shaping gradually to improve learners' performance.
- **Scaffolding** This is the support which the expert gives to the learner. This support may be at a distance, but will often involve providing further opportunities for learning or additional suggestions and help.
- **Fading** The gradual removal of support until the learners are performing the task for themselves.

Under this 'guided apprenticeship' system, the expert acts as a mentor to the learner, providing the learner with opportunities rather than direct instruction. Learners regulate their own learning and use the expert as a resource, thus remaining independent of the trainer.

Figure 3.9 — Action and Reflection in Learning

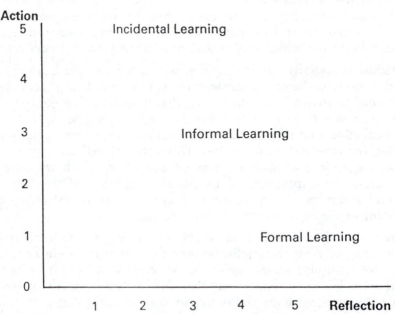

Source: Marsick and Watkins (1990:9)

Illustration 3.3 — Work-centred learning at Alcan

Work-centred learning (WCL) is a radical approach to corporate training which has been described as a 'strategy for sharing and growing the wisdom of the workforce'. By developing a culture of continuous learning, WCL unifies the workforce and reinforces a team-based work culture. Learning becomes part of the industrial process. The WCL program at Alcan's Kurri Kurri plant is a successful example of this new form of on-the-job learning.

The program began with an analysis of the company's existing training. Then a pilot program was designed, consisting of a series of learning modules. A group of experienced workers assumed responsibility for the analysis, development and improvement of each module. For Alcan, the beauty of the system is that the modules are tailored to its specific needs and remain with the company, ensuring ownership of the learning program. According to Daniel Wilkinson, engineering manager at the plant, WCL bridges the gap between off-the-shelf training packages and material available from institutional or private providers.

'This Workplace Centred Learning program provides the means by which ownership of the learning system can be taken up by the line organisation. Learning becomes part of the job and individuals actually seek the learning they need,' Wilkinson explains. WCL was developed to overcome the failure of traditional training methods. 'The classroom method was drowning us' he says. 'It was ineffective and uneconomic. We found it difficult to take groups of workers off the job for classroom training and, quite frankly, most adults didn't like going back to the classroom.' The problem with the traditional approach to training, according to Wilkinson, is that companies are trying to achieve sustained changes in employee behaviours and attitude using methods that are better suited to short-term results. WCL addresses these problems by adopting a process orientation to learning. Under WCL, learning and maintaining the skills and knowledge required for the job is seen as part of the job, rather than as a separate activity.

This means that programs can be tailored for employees by varying the pace, style and content of the program or material: some with interactive computer systems, some with mentor based training and so on. Moreover each individual is able to develop his or her own pace of learning, a factor which encourages those individuals who want to learn or succeed. Part of the reason for the success of the Alcan project is that management has been fully behind the plan and realises that everyone gains from a workforce where the attitude has changed from 'I'm just doing my job' to 'I'm responsible for what we produce'.

Source: Savellis (1996)

Conclusions

Modern approaches to adult learning are concerned with the application of the principles of adult learning in a workplace setting. It has been argued that traditional training does not provide the skills employers and employees need to cope with the rate of change in workplaces. Thus, training needs to become a process for creating opportunities to learn rather than giving direct instruction. The implications of this approach to workplace learning are:

- **Trainer as facilitator** Following the advice of Rogers and the humanistic school of learning, trainers should no longer focus on formal, off-the-job training programs as the principal vehicle for learning, but should change their role to one of creating opportunities in the workplace and within the normal work tasks of individuals, which give them structured learning experiences.

- **Worker as learner** Employees are not simply a resource to be manipulated but individuals who are constantly learning at work. If the organisation wants employees to gain certain skills and avoid habits that are detrimental to the organisation, then it has to structure the workplace in such a way that employees learn and develop as a natural consequence of doing their jobs.

Although the practice of workplace learning does not involve the application of new theories of learning, it means that theory has to be applied in a new setting. That is, within the jobs of employees themselves rather than being confined to the classroom, as the traditional model of training implies.

Summary

This chapter explored some of the theoretical background to learning in organisations. The earliest explorations of learning focused on behaviour, especially on the phenomenon of conditioning. Pavlov showed how animals can be conditioned to respond to certain stimuli in the environment so long as the stimuli are associated with a predictable outcome. Thorndike used the notion of classical conditioning to formulate the law of effect, which holds that individuals will respond in predictable ways to certain stimuli if the stimuli are associated with a desirable outcome.

The most influential of the behaviourists in the twentieth century has been Skinner, who built on the work of Thorndike to establish the theory of operant conditioning. Operant conditioning differs from its classical counterpart in its emphasis on eliciting desired responses (behaviour) from the subject, rather than simply creating the conditions under which they may occur. Thus, Skinner used various forms of reinforcement and punishment to shape behaviour in a desired direction and to eliminate undesired behaviour. Behaviourism is clearly a very powerful explanation of learned behaviour.

Cognitive psychologists, however, have criticised the behaviourist approach for its determinism and its refusal to credit the individual with a role in the learning process. Cognitivists believe that the learner must play an active part in the learning process, and are concerned with investigating those mental activities that take place, better to explain what happens when learning occurs. The Gestalt psychologists of the early twentieth century hypothesised that humans attribute meaning to their perceptions so that they see things as interrelated 'wholes' rather than as a collection of separate items.

The Gestalt notion of 'insightful' learning led to cognitive theorists such as Bruner and Ausubel emphasising the importance of organising information so that it could be learned and retained by the mind, creating the conditions under which learners could become active in the learning process and 'discover' knowledge for themselves. The information processing theorists used the analogy of the computer to explain the activities of the human memory during learning. In this model, information enters a transient sensory register from which it is passed in coded form to a short-term or working memory. At this level, the learner decides whether or not the information is worth storing and processes that which is judged worthwhile into long-term memory. This line of explanation has led to research into the improvement of human learning abilities through processes of metacognition and metamemory.

Other writers have focused on the improvement of the training process. Rogers emphasised the importance of self-direction in the learning process, and suggested that the role of the traditional trainer needed to change from director of learning to a facilitator, helping the learner to learn. Knowles attempted to draw a distinction between adult learning (andragogy) and child learning (pedagogy). He stressed the importance of the self and of the previous experience of the adult learner, advocating learning contracts as the most compatible form of learning for adults. Kolb and others have emphasised the role of experience not only in relation to the previous learning, but also on its centrality to the entire learning process, which can be viewed as a transformation of experience into knowledge.

More recently, the focus of study in adult learning has shifted to workplace learning. Studies of workplace learning emphasise the role of the learner rather than the trainer, and are based on the notion that people learn all the time at work. Marsick has distinguished informal and incidental learning, and shown that improvements in learning can be made through the structuring of opportunities for workplace learning. Under this approach, the role of the trainer becomes one of designing learning opportunities, rather than direct instruction.

None of these competing explanations offers a comprehensive account of the learning process. However, they all have implications for successful program design and implementation.

Discussion Questions

1. How much of human learning is explicable using behaviourist theory?
2. How could the assumptions of the information processing theorists be applied to an industrial training program?
3. What techniques might be useful in a metacognitive training program?
4. Is there such a thing as an adult learner?
5. Does experience help or hinder learning?
6. What are the disadvantages of learning carried out in a workplace setting?

Chapter 4

Training and Organisations

In recent years, the governments of developed countries have increasingly looked to improvements in work force skills as a major part of their response to the increase in global competition. In Europe, North America and Australia, governments have attempted to reform the training systems of their countries to ensure that the work force has the skills to enable organisations to become internationally competitive. However, as Cappelli has remarked, improvements at the national level can only occur in the context of improving training provision at the organisational level (Cappelli, 1994). There has been little systematic research on the operation of training and development at the organisational level. Much of the research undertaken into training and development has focused on the supply-side of the training market — the institutions such as TAFE that provide training services to industry (McDonald et al, 1992). It is only comparatively recently that researchers have begun to inquire into the causes and consequences of training in organisations. As a result, there is no comprehensive theory of training in the organisation.

However, the role of training and development in the organisation is covered by a variety of theories, particularly in the disciplines of management and economics, that deal with the question of the importance of skills in organisations. This chapter reviews the important research and theories that have emerged, to help explain the role of training and development in the modern organisation. Broadly, the chapter may be divided in two. The first half deals with the major economic explanations of the role of training and development, including human capital theory, internal labour market theory and the empirical work carried out by the Organisation for Economic Co-operation and Development and the London-based National Institute for Economic and Social Research. The second half examines the issues raised by research into the management of organisations, including the role of the manager, and the role of training in industrial relations, human resource management and corporate strategy.

Human Capital Theory

Human capital theory is the orthodox approach to the economics of training. Human capital theory was originally proposed in the 1950s as an explanation of the role of education in the growth of developed economies during the long boom after World War II (Schultz, 1959). According to economists such as Schultz, the growth of the United States economy in that period could not be explained by the growth in physical capital alone. He proposed that education had played an important role in economic growth by raising both the productivity and expectations of the population for a better material life. In this sense, education was treated by the human capital theorists as a form of investment. Schultz explained his basic assumption in these words (Schultz, 1960: 571):

> I propose to treat education as an investment in man ... I shall refer to it as human capital .... it is a form of capital if it renders a productive service of value to the economy. The principal hypothesis underlying this treatment of education is that some important increases in national income are a consequence of additions to the stock of this form of capital.

A colleague of Schultz, Edward Denison, calculated that education had contributed 42 per cent of the growth in labour productivity during the period 1929–57 (Denison, 1962). Becker extended Schultz's and Denison's work to examine the private returns to individuals of investment in education (Becker, 1964). It is these rates of return calculations which have become the basis of the debate around human capital theory since that time. Becker's work showed that a higher level of education results in higher earnings for individuals over their lifetimes. Thus, a university graduate who has invested many more years in education will earn many times more in his or her lifetime than the high school dropout who has made only a minimum investment in education.

Becker also applied this theory to the impact of training in organisations. Becker and his colleague, Joseph Mincer, argued that industry-based training was also a form of investment in human capital made by organisations to increase the productivity of their employees. These industry-based investments produce positive rates of returns for individuals who reap the reward of undergoing training through better jobs and higher earnings. Thus, training leads to higher wages for individuals as a result of their higher productivity. Training increases the skill levels of individuals. This will result in higher productivity for the enterprise as individuals use the new skills, and, in the long run, higher earnings for individuals as their higher productivity is reflected in their earnings. Figure 4.1 on p 78 shows a typical age-earnings profile, with university graduates earning far more than those with high school or trades qualifications and unskilled workers having little chance of earning high wages.

However, the human capital theorists also argued that training does not always produce the same benefits for the organisation and the individual. They distinguished two forms of training given to employees by organisations. The first form of training is general training. General training raises the productivity of individuals generally, without regard to the organisational context in which the training takes place. The most frequently cited example of this form of training is the apprenticeship, in which the trainees learn a generally applicable skill which can easily be transferred to another organisation. Because general training improves the job mobility of individuals, the enterprise takes a considerable risk in providing this form of training, as employees may easily move soon after the training is completed and the organisation not realise any real return on its investment. As a result, human capital theory posits that individuals will contribute to the costs of providing general training by accepting lower earnings during the training period, offsetting the organisation's risk. Thus, apprentices do not earn full adult rates of pay until they have completed their apprenticeship. This lower rate of pay is their contribution to the costs of their general training.

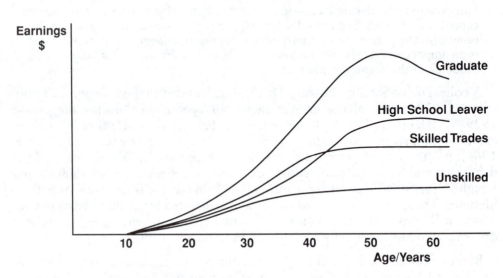

Figure 4.1 — Typical Age-Earnings Profile

The second form of training is specific training, which raises the productivity of employees only within the context of the organisation which provides the training. Specific training does not improve the mobility of individuals, as the skills learned are only applicable within the organisation. In this situation, the organisation is taking less of a risk, in training individuals who will not be able to use the skills acquired during their training in any other organisation and so will not be able to move. As a result, human capital theory posits that organisations will bear the cost of providing specific training. The employees who receive this training will not be required to forgo income in the same way as those undergoing general training.

The evidence for human capital theory

Although human capital theory has become accepted by economists, and many policy-makers, as the best explanation of how training operates in organisations, there has been much debate about whether the basic assumptions of the theory are borne out in practice. In particular, the link between training and higher earnings for employees has been attacked by researchers, as has the distinction human capital theorists draw between general and specific training.

Training and earnings

The basic assumption of human capital theory is that training will lead to higher productivity by the employee, who will recoup the benefit of his or her higher productivity through higher earnings. Although the links between higher earnings and higher levels of training is quite well established, the link between higher earnings and higher productivity is not so clear (Strober, 1990). If this is the case, training may not lead to higher earnings for employees as predicted by human capital theory.

In a classic study of the productivity-earnings link, Medoff and Abraham (1980) compared data on education, experience (on-the-job training), productivity and earnings from 7600 employees in two large United States manufacturing plants. Using supervisors' ratings as the measure of productivity of individual employees, they found there was no relationship between either experience and earnings or experience and productivity. A second study (Medoff and Abraham, 1981) of 8000 managerial and professional employees in a single large company yielded the same results. These two studies suggest that the close links between training (as represented by experience), earnings and productivity do not exist in the way forecast by human capital theory, and that the factors which lead to productivity increases may be quite different from the factors which lead to earnings growth. Although Medoff and Abraham have been criticised on methodological grounds, particularly for their calculations of the returns to experience (Beggs and Chapman, 1988) and for their lack of an occupational dimension in their work (Maranto and Rogers, 1984), the large sample sizes used in both studies have given their work considerable credibility.

In a study of the impact of differences in earnings on workplace attitudes and behaviours, Levine surveyed the earnings, job characteristics and attitudes of 8000 employees in 100 manufacturing plants in the United States and Japan (Levine, 1993). Levine found that higher earnings were positively related to a variety of human resource outcomes including labour turnover, job satisfaction and commitment. The survey measured the extent of both general and specific training received by the employees. Contrary to the predictions of human capital theory, Levine found that plants with high levels of training did not display lower turnover rates or higher earnings for employees. Nor was training (either general or specific) associated with higher levels of job satisfaction or commitment. To the extent that these attitudes reflect higher levels of productivity, Levine's data suggests that training is not correlated with either higher earnings or higher productivity.

Thus, there is no clear evidence that training is related to higher levels of earnings for employees. Nor are higher earnings necessarily correlated with higher levels of productivity. A number of other explanations have been made as to why employers will pay their trained employees higher wages if their productivity is no greater. Most of these explanations have centred around the notions of 'screening' and 'signaling' (Arrow, 1973; Spence, 1974). Under screening theory, organisations use the level of education or training received by employees as a means of filtering better educated or more highly trained employees into higher paid jobs. This notion is developed by signaling theory, under which it is assumed that organisations know little about the potential productivity of employees when they are hired. However, a higher level of education or training signals to the employer that the potential employee has the ability to learn more and, presumably, to work more productively. If employees continue to invest in their own education and training after joining the enterprise, they will be paid more, as the enterprise interprets the employees' efforts to improve themselves as a sign of higher ability or motivation. In either case, neither screening nor signaling theory make a direct causal link between training and productivity. It is the innate ability of the employee that generates higher productivity for the enterprise. Undertaking training simply signals to the enterprise that the employee is capable of working more productively.

General and specific training

The notion that organisations will distinguish between general and specific training, and allocate costs accordingly, has not been the subject of much empirical analysis. In general, commentators on human capital theory have admitted that the distinction between general and specific training is difficult to sustain in practice (Maglen, 1990; Bosworth, Wilson and Assefa, 1993). Very few enterprise training programs can be categorised as purely general or specific. Most training programs contain elements of both forms of training. The major reason for the distinction between the two forms of training in human capital theory from the enterprise's perspective is to reduce the risk of losing the investment in training through employee turnover. Thus, the enterprise will invest in specific training because the employee is unlikely to be able to use enterprise specific skills elsewhere. Also, investing in specific training will bind the employee to the enterprise, as the employee is unlikely to receive recognition for their skills in the form of higher earnings from other enterprises.

However, the evidence from studies in the United States and Australia suggests that employers are moving away from highly specific technical training and are leaning towards giving their employees more general training, in behavioural skills such as problem-solving, communication and teamwork. These are skills which are readily transferable to other organisations. In the United States, Osterman (1994) has shown that organisations in the process of implementing 'high-performance' work practices such as total quality management and teamwork, are more likely to require general, behavioural skills from their employees rather than specific technical skills. The training they provide is also more likely to be focused on general, rather than specific, skills. In Australia, Smith (1995) and Hayton (1996) have confirmed that organisations appear to be placing greater emphasis on the importance of behavioural skills rather than the traditional technical skills that human capital theory would predict they would favour.

These studies contradict the human capital theory prediction that organisations will be more interested in giving employees specific training for technical skills than giving them general behavioural skills enhancement. These studies suggest that, as organisations move towards the implementation of new working practices, the demand for enterprise training becomes more general and behavioural in nature. The prediction of human capital theory that enterprises will favour non-transferable specific training is not borne out by the empirical evidence.

Illustration 4.1 — Training and productivity at Motorola

> A case study often cited in relation to the productivity potential of training is that of US-based electronics giant, Motorola. Between 1987 and 1992, Motorola, through Motorola University, achieved a doubling of employee productivity, a 1,700 per cent improvement in quality (measured in terms of reduced rejects and faster production times) and a $31 billion saving in the total cost of its operations. Motorola requested two US universities to evaluate its return on investment in training. They identified three groups of Motorola plants:
>
> 1. In those few plants where the workforce absorbed the whole curriculum of quality tools and process skills and where senior managers reinforced the training by introducing appropriate new work methods, Motorola achieved a $33 return for every dollar spent on training, including the cost of wages paid while people sat in classrooms.
> 2. Plants which made use of either new quality or process skills and then reinforced what they taught, broke even.
> 3. Plants which taught all or part of the curriculum but failed to reinforce with follow up meetings and a new, genuine emphasis on quality had a negative return on training.
>
> Motorola considers that it has learned some important lessons in ensuring the successful training and education of employees, namely:
> - top-down commitment and involvement in training is essential;
> - training programs must be linked to corporate initiatives;
> - training policies need to set expectations and be tracked;
> - it is essential to have solid pre-requisite skills across the organisation's workforce;
> - the training curricula need to form an integrated system to deliver consistent messages;
> - the most significant current trend is towards quality, with all employees receiving 28 days full-time quality training covering quality tools, strategies, techniques and feedback mechanisms.
>
> Motorola's experience thus very much supports the notion that investments in training can yield substantial improvements in productivity — but that such investments need to be integrated into an overall strategic system.

Source: NSW Department of Training and Education Co-ordination, 1997

Internal Labour Market Theory

Human capital theory, despite its attractive central notion of treating training as a form of long-term investment akin to investment in physical capital, does not seem to explain the mechanisms by which skills are formed, either at an individual or a social level. An alternative approach is to examine the market for labour. Economic studies of the labour market normally focus on the external labour market; that is, the mechanisms by which workers are matched to jobs in the economy. The assumption behind this conventional approach is that all exchanges of labour take place in an open external market situation in the same way as exchanges of other goods and services in the economy. However, many job vacancies within an organisation often are not open to applicants from the external labour market; they are filled from within, that is, from the internal labour market of the organisation concerned. In fact, many larger, multinational organisations have human resource policies which actively encourage the practice of filling vacancies from within the organisation wherever possible. These organisations may only recruit from the external labour market at specifically defined entry points, often at the lowest levels in the organisation. From these entry points, the organisation prefers to develop its own staff to fill promotional vacancies as they arise. The concept of the internal labour market has come to be closely linked with the existence of effective training within the organisation.

Internal labour market theory finds its intellectual roots in the attempts by labour market economists soon after World War II to explain the apparent disparity in earnings between similar jobs in different enterprises (Cappelli and Cascio, 1991). Early work showed that earnings varied according to a variety of factors, some external to the enterprise, such as product markets, and some internal, such as enterprise size and plant characteristics. The modern delineation of internal labour market theory springs from Doeringer and Piore's (1971) seminal book from the late 1960s. In this work, Doeringer and Piore define the internal labour market as:

> ... an administrative unit, such as a manufacturing plant, within which the pricing and allocation of labour is governed by a set of administrative rules and procedures. (Doeringer and Piore 1971: 1–2)

They contrast the regulated internal labour market with the competitive external labour market, in which the price of labour and decisions about training are determined by economic variables. Creedy and Whitfield (1992) describe four characteristics of internal labour markets:

- **Employment stability** A major reason for the creation of internal labour markets is the need employers have to protect their investments in human capital by establishing conditions of employment that encourage employees to remain with the enterprise rather than move to better improve their prospects. A notional labour turnover rate of less than 10 per cent per annum is usually taken as indicative of the presence of an internal labour market.

- **Ports of entry** Entry to the internal labour market is restricted to lower level jobs in the enterprise. Recruitment to higher level jobs is carried out from the ranks of existing employees at lower levels. This process creates career paths for employees, and the expectation of promotion binds them to the enterprise.

- **Constrained wage adjustment** Unlike the external labour market, earnings in the internal labour market are protected from the operation of market forces and do not adjust to changes in the supply and demand for different forms of labour. Employers will use other means of responding to labour shortages, such as restricting output and reducing recruitment, rather than increase earnings.

- **Attachment of wages to jobs** A key feature of the internal labour market is the fact that wages are paid according to the classification of the job rather than the productivity of the employee. Wage structures within internal labour markets are rigid.

The internalisation of the employment relationship depicted in internal labour market theory seems to have come about for two reasons (Cappelli, 1995). First, the organisation attempts to reduce turnover in order to capitalise on the benefits of the skills of employees and their investments in training. Secondly, the internal labour market is an attempt to reduce the transaction costs associated with recruitment of skilled labour and the constant renegotiation and policing of the effort-reward contract. Thus, under internal labour market arrangements, organisations will create job ladders along which satisfactory employees can expect to progress. Earnings will be a function of an employee's position on the job ladder rather than his or her inherent productivity. Internal labour market theory breaks the essential human capital theory bond between earnings and productivity (Osterman, 1984).

Internal labour market theory questions the role of training in increasing earnings and productivity which is advanced by human capital theory. Earnings may reflect the desire of organisations to retain certain employees or the placing of employees on an internal job ladder. While organisations may train their employees to improve their productivity, the operation of an internal labour market may provide other reasons for training. Progression along job ladders may be subject to the acquisition of certain skills — whether or not employees actually use those skills in practice. The existence of internal labour market arrangements also gives managers greater decision-making power (Strober, 1990). Rather than simply making decisions about who receives on-the-job training, managers also make decisions about where specific jobs are placed on job ladders. Access to training under these conditions becomes a political decision, as it affects the future earnings prospects of employees.

The OECD/CERI Studies

The criticisms leveled at human capital theory in the 1970s tended to make the theory go out of fashion as an explanation for the operation of training in organisations. However, in the 1980s, human capital theory re-emerged as governments of developed countries sought to address the economic problems caused by the rise in global competition (Marginson, 1993). These governments began to look to education and training as means of increasing the capacities of the work force to adapt to change.

Studies of the adoption of technological innovation in the agricultural sector suggested that farmers who were better trained and educated tended to use technological changes more effectively than those who were not so well educated. It appeared that education and training were vital in enabling workers to adapt to the pace of technological change. Bartel and Lichtenberg (1987) found that more educated employees were able to adapt more efficiently to new technology than were less educated employees. They theorised that the adoption of new technology created uncertainty in the workplace, and that it was the ability to cope with greater levels of uncertainty that characterised more educated employees. It was, thus, during the implementation phase of adopting new technology that educated employees were most in demand. Industries that had high rates of innovation tended to create the highest demand for educated employees.

This new twist on human capital theory meant that training increased the productivity of employees by increasing their capacity to adapt to change and innovation, especially technological innovation. Neo-human capital theory therefore places innovation, particularly technological innovation, as a mediating variable between education and training, and productivity. It is the ability to adapt to innovation that yields the productivity dividend to the enterprises. The implication for training is that organisations will not capture the benefits of new technology unless they hire educated employees and/or train their existing work forces. Under this new approach to human capital theory, technological innovation should be a major driving force for enterprises to train their employees. It was the implications of this theory that the Organisation for Economic Co-operation and Development's (OECD) Centre for Education Research and Innovation (CERI) investigated in a series of studies in the mid-1980s (OECD, 1988; OECD/CERI, 1986, 1988).

In a project titled 'The development and utilisation of human resources in the context of technological change and industrial restructuring', CERI researchers examined developments in both the manufacturing and service sectors in France, Germany, Japan, Sweden and the United States. The first phase of the project examined developments in the automotive industry and focused on five car manufacturers (Ford, Renault, Toyota, Volkswagen and Volvo). The researchers summarised the developments in the automotive industry in technology, work organisation and human resource development:

- **Technology** All manufacturers had introduced new technologies in both products and processes within their plants. This included the use of robotics, flexible manufacturing, just-in-time inventory systems and computer-aided design.

- **Work organisation** There was a move away from the classic work organisation of the car assembly line. Innovations in this area included the elimination of repetitive tasks, use of group work, and the simplification of job classification systems.

- **Human resource development** Enterprises had tended to lag in the area of training, compared to the rate of change in the other two areas examined. Thus, training tended to be provided retrospectively to suit changes in technology and work organisation. The major training effort was focused on the creation of polyvalence amongst employees, the use of competency-based standards and a changing mix of training provision with greater use of external training providers.

The second phase of the project examined developments in the financial services industry, and found similar, though less pronounced, changes in the three areas of technology, work organisation and human resource development. In this case, the new technologies, such as automatic teller machines in banks, had forced changes to jobs at the teller level, but more extensive changes to work organisation were less evident and training within the enterprises lagged behind these developments. Many enterprises relied on the educational system to provide them with the skills they required in their work forces. The case study evidence accumulated by the CERI research team demonstrated that technology, training and work organisation were inextricably linked, and that the performance of enterprises depended on training to support changes to technology and work organisation. Ford (1989) has represented the CERI model of training in the enterprise in a diagram showing the mutual interactions of all the elements that surfaced during the research — training, work organisation, technology and employee relations. This diagram is reproduced in Figure 4.2 on p 86.

The CERI research highlighted two important findings. First, it recognised that the enterprise could not reap the benefits of technological innovation unless other factors in the enterprise were addressed to allow individuals to use the skills they acquired through training. Thus, training was not sufficient to guarantee a productivity return for the enterprise. In particular, work organisation had to change to allow employees to work productively with new technology. In general, this meant the adoption of some form of teamwork, giving greater autonomy to employees. These changes rested on the enterprise being able to develop a level of trust through its employee relations system. Secondly, enterprises were slow to train. Despite the need to obtain quick returns on investment in new technology, employees were often trained late and poorly. This was especially true in European and United States enterprises that participated in the study. CERI linked this training lag to the uncertainty surrounding the introduction of new technology, and highlighted the cost of the lags to enterprises in terms of the under-utilisation of new production capacities (OECD/CERI, 1986). However, CERI also linked the training lag to differences in work organisation between the enterprises studied. It was clear that in enterprises with a greater teamwork orientation, employees adapted to the new technology much more quickly. Training was built into team-based organisations through 'collective learning' not present in more Taylorist work organisations.

The NIESR Studies

The adaptability and flexibility of the work force, particularly in relation to technological innovation, was also a central conclusion of a long series of studies undertaken by Wagner and her colleagues at the National Institute for Economic and Social Research (NIESR) in London (Daly, Hitchens and Wagner, 1985; Steedman and Wagner, 1987; Steedman and Wagner, 1989; Prais, Jarvis and Wagner, 1991). During the 1980s, the institute had begun to investigate the impact of national vocational education and training (VET) systems on the economic performance of selected countries in the European Union (EU) in particular. At a general level, these studies had shown how vocational training in Britain lagged far behind that of its competitor countries, and had drawn conclusions that seemed to link economic success with the existence of well-funded VET systems such as those in Germany and Sweden, or a greater emphasis on vocational preparation at secondary level, such as occurred in Japan and France.

Figure 4.2 — Ford's model of the OECD/CERI studies

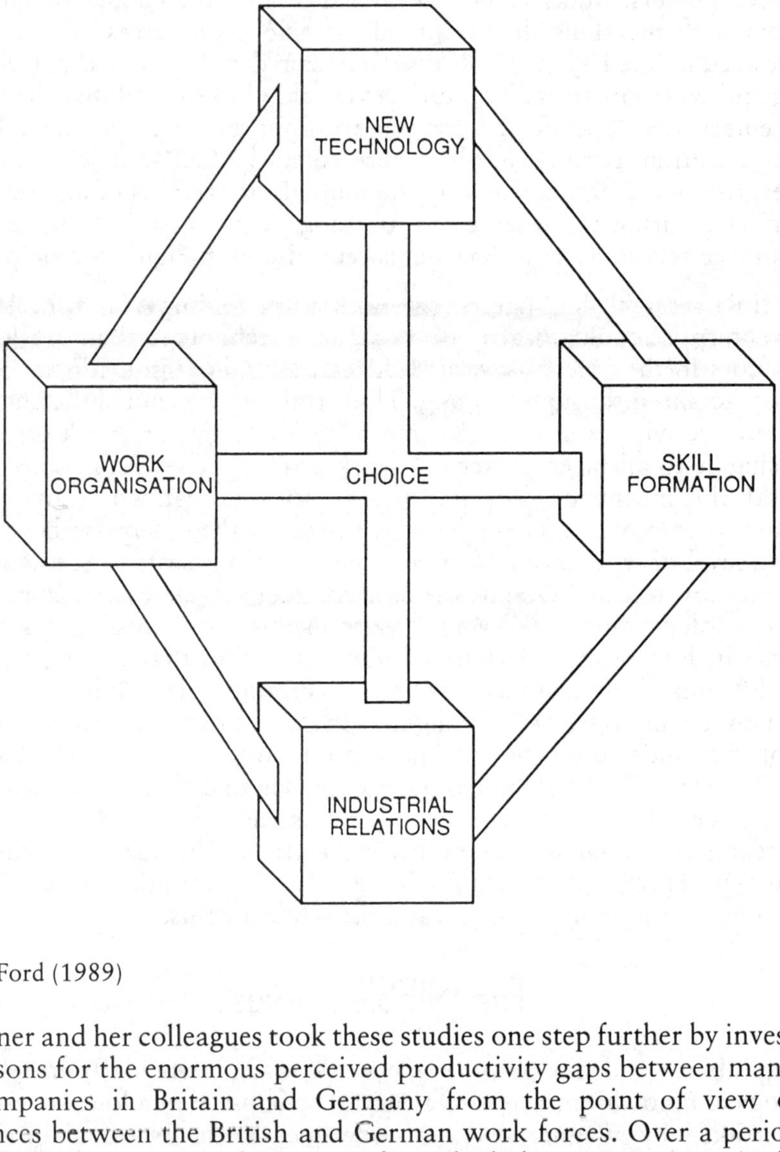

```
                    NEW
                  TECHNOLOGY

      WORK                        SKILL
   ORGANISATION — CHOICE —    FORMATION

                  INDUSTRIAL
                  RELATIONS
```

Source: Ford (1989)

Wagner and her colleagues took these studies one step further by investigating the reasons for the enormous perceived productivity gaps between manufacturing companies in Britain and Germany from the point of view of skills differences between the British and German work forces. Over a period of six years, the NIESR team made a series of matched plant comparisons in the metal working, furniture making and clothing industries in the two countries, followed later by a similar study of the hotel industry. The matching process was scrupulously arranged by the NIESR team to ensure that as little bias as possible crept into the research at the sampling stage; where possible, not only factories but products within factories were matched to give a true reading.

Generally, the conclusions of the studies showed a similar picture emerging in each of the sectors examined:

- German enterprises enjoyed productivity advantages of between 100 and 230 per cent over their matched rivals in Britain.
- German enterprises made more extensive use of computer-aided systems in manufacture, materials handling and design (and in hotel reservation systems) than did the British enterprises.
- There were fewer maintenance and breakdown problems in the German factories.
- Managers with intermediate level skills (supervisors in Britain, meister in Germany) enjoyed far more autonomy in planning and decision-making in Germany than did their British counterparts.
- German enterprises had a much clearer strategic direction than their British rivals. In some industries, such as clothing, this meant that the German companies had abandoned some markets altogether to pursue high margin, niche markets, leaving British enterprises to compete at the low cost end of the market.
- At all levels, from shop floor operator to general manager, German employees were more highly qualified than British employees. German shop floor operators usually possessed 2–3 years of formal qualifications in the industry; German craftspersons had been given more specialised training than British tradespersons; German *meister* had undergone significantly more technical and managerial training than British supervisors; and, at middle/senior manager level, undergraduate and higher degrees were common amongst German managers, rare in British managerial ranks.

The NIESR researchers concluded that higher levels of skill and training, as represented by the qualifications of the German work force, was the determining factor in the success of the German sample enterprises in all cases. Skills, according to the NIESR, produced an adaptable and flexible work force at all levels in German enterprises, able to cope with new technologies, new products and new markets. The training of the shop floor employees made German employees more adaptable to change, particularly to the introduction of new technology. The smooth running of the production systems in the German factories was a result of the superior technical and managerial training of the supervisors, who had the ability to carry out many management functions on the shop floor. Finally, the education and training of German managers enabled them to take a broader, strategic approach to business, in contrast to their British counterparts, and direct their businesses into profitable markets. The superior training of the German workers created a virtuous circle which increased their adaptability and enabled the firms to compete in profitable niche markets. This virtuous German circle contrasted with the vicious circle in which British firms were often trapped.

The superior skills of the German work force were the product of the German VET system. This system is based on apprenticeship. Many jobs carry the requirement for an apprenticeship to be served. The system is jointly funded by employers through their Chambers of Commerce and the Federal Government (hence, the term 'dual system' often used to describe German VET). Thus, large numbers of German employees have three-year qualifications, unlike their counterparts in the English-speaking world. Training for intermediate skills is particularly well developed in Germany. Supervisors (*Meister*) undergo a four-year college-based training program before they are certified as *Meister*. This program covers both technical and managerial skills. Finally, many more Germans attend university than in Britain or Australia with larger numbers studying technical degrees such as engineering. It is these technically qualified graduates German enterprises hire in large numbers to fill their managerial ranks.

Later studies by the NIESR researchers highlighted the role of 'intermediate' skills in the performance of the organisation. By the late 1980s, British manufacturers were closing the productivity gap with their German rivals through restructuring and investment in physical capital. European enterprises still enjoyed a skills advantage, but it was clear that the critical area was the intermediate level. It was here that supervisory skills and technical/professional skills were located. These skills, the NIESR researchers argued, enabled the European enterprises to innovate more effectively through the skills of their professionals and to run their plants more smoothly through the skills of their shop floor supervisors (Steedman, 1993). Rather than giving the European enterprises a straight productivity advantage, intermediate skills enabled them to innovate and pursue a quality strategy more effectively than their British competitors.

The Skills Equilibrium Model

The importance of the interaction between the nation, system of VET and the training delivered in organisations has been highlighted by the work of David Finegold, who has argued that there are two basic paths which countries and enterprises can follow in relation to VET systems (Finegold and Soskice, 1988; Finegold, 1991; Finegold, 1992). The first path he labels a 'low skills equilibrium model'. This low skills equilibrium is characterised by a poorly coordinated VET system which provides few training pathways outside the formal education system. At the same time, and, perhaps, as a result (Glynn and Gospel, 1993), enterprises offer their employees little training, preferring instead to organise work in such a way that it can be carried out by relatively unskilled employees, thus reducing labour input costs. In such a situation, individuals have little incentive to invest in their own training. The state does not provide the access to training that they might seek and employers do not put much value on the qualifications that they may gain. Finegold sees the Anglo-Saxon economies as examples of such low skills equilibria. Thus, in Australia, apart from traditional apprenticeships, the VET system does not offer qualifications for lower-level employees. As a result, there are no training-related career pathways employees can take to improve their skills and employability. At the same time, Australian employers have traditionally offered little enterprise-based training for their employees.

Figure 4.3 — The NIESR circles

VIRTUOUS CIRCLE

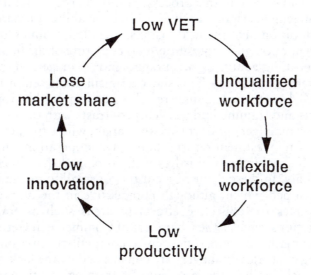

VICIOUS CIRCLE

In contrast, economies such as those of Japan or Germany have encouraged the formation of a high skills equilibrium. In this model, the government frames policies that encourage the development of training programs for all classes of employees. In the European examples of high skills equilibria, governments have actively created VET systems that enable all groups of employees to participate in post-school training. This is supported by significant employer investment in training, providing the individual with a high level of incentive to undertake it.

Finegold models both these systems on the basis of game theory, with three principal actors — the individual, the enterprise manager and the government policy-maker. All three are faced with choices about investments in training. Whether they make the high skills choice depends on a number of factors. The first factor is whether the players take a long-term perspective in their decision-making. VET systems do not produce results in the short term. If the players take a short-term perspective, then they will not be willing to make the investments required to produce a high skills equilibrium. The second factor is the possibility for cooperation between the players in a competitive environment. Enterprises, individuals and countries exist in competition with each other. But excessive competition between, for instance, capital and labour results in a climate in which the massive investments needed to create a high skills equilibrium are not forthcoming, because they are beyond the capability of the players in isolation from each other. Players need to cooperate in an almost corporatist manner to secure the investments required. Finally, an export orientation amongst enterprises is needed to encourage the players to see that investment in training is necessary for survival. In sectors that are relatively cosseted from international competition, there is little incentive to improve the skills of the work force. If all three of these factors are in place, then the conditions are favourable for the creation of a high skills equilibrium. The Finegold model is illustrated in Figure 4.4 on p 91.

Managers play a key role in this process. Finegold argues that national financial market arrangements significantly influence the ability of managers to take a long-term outlook on investment decisions, including training decisions. The annual profit orientation and acquisition/merger culture of the financial markets in the English-speaking countries encourage senior managers in these countries to take a short-term perspective. This short-termism at the senior manager level is transmitted to lower level managers who are responsible for operational training decisions and training budgets. This contrasts with the longer-term perspectives taken by managers in Germany and Japan, where financial markets are geared to long-term investment returns. Similarly, cooperation amongst managers in the English-speaking world is less well developed than in countries such as Sweden and Italy. In these countries, clusters of small to medium-sized enterprises have developed which, although competitive in the marketplace, often pool their resources for collective efforts in areas such as training. Strong employer associations, such as the Chambers of Commerce in Germany, encourage a similar climate of cooperation in a competitive environment. In the English-speaking countries, managers are constrained by the lack of cooperative mechanisms, which inhibits the provision of training, particularly in general transferable skills.

Training, Technology and New Working Practices

Both the CERI research and the NIESR studies emphasised the impact of technology on training provision in enterprises. The relationship between technology and training has been heavily influenced by debate over the impact of technology on skills. This debate had heavily influenced the work of Harry

Braverman. Braverman published his seminal book, *Labor and Monopoly Capitalism*, in 1974. In this work, Braverman described the impact of technology on the experience of workers since the industrial revolution in the early nineteenth century. Braverman's thesis was that managers are driven to cut labour costs in their organisations by competitive pressures. As a result, they will use technology to replace highly paid skilled workers with lower skilled workers by systematically seeking to 'de-skill' work in their organisations. Technology helps them do this by replacing workers with machines.

Figure 4.4 — The skills equilibrium model

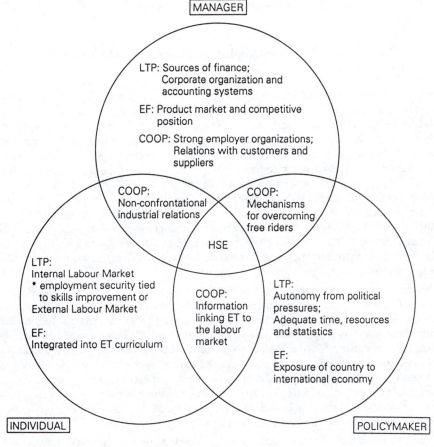

Legend:
Long Term Perspective (LTP)
Export Focus (EF)
Cooperation within a Competitive Environment (COOP)

Source: Finegold (1991)

Adherents of Braverman's labour process theory have argued that the general impact of new technology is negative for skills in most industries (Edwards, 1979; Wilkinson, 1983). From this perspective, enterprises invest in new technology primarily to reduce the costs of production. As a result, managers use new technology to reduce the size of the work force and de-skill the remaining employees. Jobs become more repetitive and routinised, and the higher level tasks, such as programming, are restricted solely to professional and technical employees. More recently, theorists in the labour process tradition have also argued that enterprises use the new technology to increase the degree of managerial control on the shop floor and intensify the work effort rather than enhance the skill of employees (Sewell and Wilkinson, 1992; Delbridge, 1995). In either case, the effect on skills is the same, as it is unlikely that the introduction of new technology would lead to an increased training effort in the enterprises.

Illustration 4.2 — Training for technology at NZI Insurance

In 1993, senior management at NZI Insurance knew there was a shake-up in store for the 120 employees in the group's Sydney-based business services division which was facing major technological change. The division's assistant General Manager, Mark Webb (also responsible for HR), saw the writing on the wall well in advance: he knew that when it came to implementing the new technology in 1995, the business services group was going to have to work in a highly cooperative fashion. 'We were a group of people working together in some cases for 12 or 13 years on the old technology platform, and that had associated with it a lot of cultural and people issues which built up over the years. People were set in their ways' said Webb. In August 1993, 12 months before the technology changeover, Webb employed a psychologist to work out a plan for the division's 35 senior managers with the aim of developing the management group to be team leaders, with a particular focus on running more effective teams.

The psychologist conducted a 3-day workshop with the senior managers and for the next 12 months came in every three months to conduct individual interviews with everyone in the senior management team. According to Webb, the success of the interviews in giving an accurate picture of the workplace culture and in turn identifying the work that needed to be done was in no small part due to the confidentiality of the interview process. At no stage did the psychologist relate specific employee complaints back to any individual employee. He would listen to employee concerns and then take the accumulated information back to Webb in the form of recommendations. Webb said that the confidential interview process proved far more effective than other employee survey methods such as questionnaires.

Webb said that the 12 month training program was a success. 'Everything didn't run smoothly, but we were so much better prepared when problems came up. It didn't stop the fact that we had problems, but it put everyone on their right foot forward, ready to go.' Webb said that the program's success was partly due to NZI's foresight in instigating training well in advance of the new technology actually being installed.

Source: Human Resources Report No 109

More recently, the labour process theorists have been challenged by the post-Fordist school of thought. The post-Fordists, such as John Mathews in Australia, take a much more optimistic view of the impact of technology on skill. They have argued that the global economy is moving away from mass production for mass markets (typified by the Henry Ford dictum that his customers could have any colour of car they wanted so long as it was black) towards niche production for highly specialised and discerning markets (Mathews, 1990, 1994). Thus, they argue, enterprises invest in new technology primarily to increase the flexibility of the enterprise and compete in niche markets. This requires employees to become more skilled as work organisation changes to accommodate the new technology. The net effect is that skill levels rise for employees in all the major occupational groups. Enterprises thus require more training to enhance the skills of their employees and take full advantage of the new technologies.

The debate between advocates of the Bravermanian de-skilling hypothesis and the post-Fordist up-skilling position have been usually conducted at a theoretical, even rhetorical, level. The debate has been marred by a lack of firm empirical data on skills trends in the advanced industrial economies. However, in the 1990s, studies of the actual trajectory of skills have appeared. These studies have, however, not provided clear support for one side of the debate or the other. The results of the studies have revealed a far more complex picture than the protagonists in the skills debate have suggested (Adler, 1992). Evidence from Britain and the United States has generally indicated that both de-skilling and up-skilling are taking place simultaneously but in different sectors. This is resulting in an increasing polarisation of skills with certain groups reporting an increase in skills while others become less skilled.

In a study of production and clerical jobs using data from Hay and Associates, Cappelli (1993) found that the skills of production employees in manufacturing had been rising during the period 1978–86. Rising skill levels had also been accompanied by rising earnings. Clerical jobs, on the other hand, showed both up-skilling and de-skilling effects. However, up-skilling effects did not seem to reflect the impact of technological change. Amongst the production jobs, up-skilling effects appeared to be the result of the disappearance of complete families of low skilled jobs (such as housekeeping on the factory floor) and from the reorganisation of work within other jobs to encompass more high-level activities such as quality control and production planning. On the clerical side, the impact of technological change had been felt with the de-skilling and/or disappearance of jobs under the impact of new office technology such as word processing and user-friendly photocopying. Those clerical jobs that had increased in skill level, however, were those associated with customer service, which again reflected the increased responsibility in jobs as a result of work reorganisation rather than the impact of new technology. Thus, although Cappelli's evidence points to a significant up-skilling of work, the new skills required are not the traditional technical skills but behavioural skills associated with greater decision-making powers and the need to deal with customers more effectively.

Survey evidence from Britain confirms the differential skill patterns that Cappelli found. Researchers from the Social Change and Economic Life Initiative interviewed 6000 individuals from all occupational categories and regions in Britain in 1986 and gathered information on changes to jobs since 1981 (Gallie, 1991). The results showed that 52 per cent of respondents reported an increase in skill levels while only 9 per cent reported a decrease. The commonest experience had been an increase in skills. However, although this was true across all occupational categories, those in the most skilled occupations were more likely to report an increase in skill than those in the less skilled occupations. The Employment in Britain survey in 1992 confirmed the findings from five years earlier (Gallie and White, 1993). This survey revealed that the proportion of respondents who had experienced an increase in skill levels since 1986 had grown to 62 per cent, whereas those reporting a decrease had stayed at 9 per cent. Again, professional groups reported the highest incidence of up-skilling with semi/non-skilled employees reporting the lowest incidence. This polarisation of skills in the British work force is hard to explain through the impact of technology. The British evidence reinforces Cappelli's finding that the impact of technology is greatest amongst the less skilled occupations, serving to reduce skill levels still further or eliminate certain categories of jobs altogether. The up-skilling associated with more highly skilled jobs appears to be the result of changes to work organisation and management techniques, rather than the introduction of technology.

The impact of new working practices

The association of increasing skill levels with the adoption of new management and working practices has been linked to the emergence of new forms of working, particularly with 'lean production' and the high-performance work organisation. The term 'lean production' was coined by the MIT research team that explored the state of the worldwide car industry in the late 1980s (Womack, Jones and Roos, 1990). The project examined various aspects of the performance and management practices of 90 car assembly plants worldwide, and is widely regarded as the most comprehensive international comparison of automobile producers ever undertaken. The MIT team argued that the Toyota Motor Company had been so successful in the car industry because it pioneered highly efficient systems of working in its plants that combined teamwork with high intensity work practices that enabled the organisation to produce cars at very high quality and productivity levels.

MacDuffie and Kochan (1995) analysed the data from the MIT project to explore the impact of lean production organisation on training practices. MacDuffie and Kochan used data relating to training from the study, and compared this to the implementation of lean production and the use of technology in the manufacturing process. Lean production was defined as the use of certain production practices based on reduced buffering in the plant and a set of related human resources practices, including:

- the use of teamwork;
- job rotation;
- involvement of production employees with quality tasks;
- emphasis on interpersonal skills in hiring decisions;

- performance-related pay systems;
- the reduction of status barriers between managers and employees.

They found that technology appeared to have no impact on the level of training in car plants across the world. However, training was closely related to the implementation of lean production systems. More training was provided for employees in lean production plants than in traditional mass production plants. This finding was not related to the location of the plant. However, it appeared from the data that mass production plants in Europe provided more training than mass production plants in other parts of the world. MacDuffie and Kochan explained this through the impact of national VET systems on the overall level of training in enterprises within those countries. MacDuffie and Kochan also speculated on the content of training in flexible production plants:

> Flexible production plants appear to require some mix of general skills for effective problem-solving (reading, math and reasoning skills) and firm specific skills related to the firm's technology and production system ... Furthermore, because of their reliance on work teams, these plants are likely to emphasise interpersonal and communication skills as well.

Thus, the importance of behavioural skills in supporting the implementation of high performance or lean production work practices is borne out by the MIT project.

High performance work organisations combine some of the elements of lean production, but are more oriented towards the use of teamwork and total quality management systems. High performance workplaces have adopted a set of employment practices which are designed to gain the commitment of employees, including:

- employee empowerment and participation in decision-making;
- teamwork: quality circles, QWL programs, semi-autonomous teams, etc;
- job rotation and cross training;
- supportive personnel policies, including profit sharing, job security, payment for skills training in communication and interpersonal skills (Capelli, 1994: 208–9).

These practices are designed to foster employee commitment, so that enterprises can develop a highly skilled work force which is trained to innovate and retain America's competitive edge in the international economy through new product development rather than low cost production. The full extent of the adoption of these practices by United States enterprises is the subject of much debate (Capelli, 1994; Osterman, 1995); however, training plays a central role in the design of these workplaces.

This high performance work organisation has been described by the acronym 'SET', standing for 'security of employment, employee involvement and training'. SET workplaces can be contrasted with the traditional 'JAM' workplace, which is based on 'job classifications, adversarial employee relations and minimal training' (Brown, Reich and Stern, 1993). The three elements of the SET system are interlinked so that one cannot be fully implemented without the others. Thus, employees will only become involved with the company's decision-making if they are assured of job security. Similarly, job security, or rather its obverse, employment stability, plays a significant role in the company's decision to train, as it will not train workers likely to leave the company for higher wages elsewhere. These three elements exist in an interlocking relationship shown in Figure 4.5.

The empirical evidence for high performance work practices tends to highlight the importance of training. In a survey of 694 United States manufacturing enterprises, Osterman (1994) assessed the extent of adoption of four high performance work practices: total quality management (TQM), teamwork, job rotation and quality control circles.

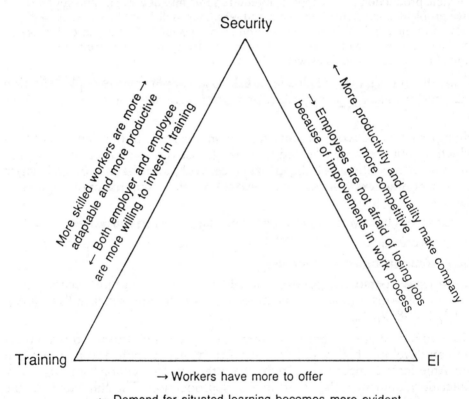

Figure 4.5 — SET theory

Source: Brown, Reich and Stern (1993)

Osterman found that the implementation of high performance work practices was accompanied most frequently by innovative pay schemes such as pay for skill, a high valuation of work force commitment and extensive training. The implementation of high performance work practices also tended to require more skills, but only for technical/professional employees and skilled blue-collar employees, reinforcing the skills polarisation thesis advanced by Gallie (1991) and Cappelli (1993). There was also a distinct difference in the type of skills required. While technical/professional employees were selected on the basis of their professional competence, blue-collar employees tended to be selected on the basis of behavioural skills such as interpersonal skills and the ability to take responsibility (Osterman, 1995). In terms of training, Osterman found that enterprises faced a clear 'make or buy' decision. The implementation of high performance work practices encouraged more extensive training, but this training tended to die away over time as employees became skilled in the new practices. The most important work practices associated with ongoing training were the quality-related practices of TQM and quality circles, that required higher levels of responsibility and problem-solving behaviour from employees. Training was also highly correlated with more humanistic managerial values which accepted the need for enterprises to take some responsibility for the personal and family well-being of employees.

Training and Industrial Relations

Central to the introduction of new working practices in Australian organisations have been the reforms to the centralised Australian system of industrial relations undertaken since 1988. Since 1904 Australian industrial relations has been governed by a quasi-judicial system of arbitration exercised at the federal level through the Industrial Relations Commission and at the state level through industrial relations tribunals (Hancock and Rawson, 1993). Originally established to deal with the recurrent industrial unrest of the late nineteenth century, the arbitration system enabled employers or unions to apply to the industrial relations tribunals to arbitrate in the case of disputes. The result of the arbitration was the system of industrial awards which governed the terms and conditions of large numbers of Australian employees. By the mid-1980s, however, it was widely acknowledged that the award system had become unnecessarily complex and outdated and was restricting the ability of managers to introduce greater flexibility into workplaces and of employees to gain recognition for their skills. Since then two major processes of industrial relations reform — award restructuring and enterprise bargaining — have encouraged the development of workplace reform and the devolution of bargaining to the enterprise. Both of these processes have had significant implications for training in Australian organisations.

Training and award restructuring

In 1988 the Industrial Relations Commission began the process of award restructuring with the introduction of the structural efficiency principle (SEP) as the basis for wage negotiations. Under the SEP, wage rises would not be granted by the commission unless employers and unions could demonstrate that they had made significant progress towards the simplification of awards and had implemented measures to improve the efficient operation of Australian industry. The commission also specified the measures for which it would be looking in the new awards, including the need to:

- **establish skill-related career paths** which provide an incentive for workers to continue to participate in skill formation;
- **eliminate impediments to multiskilling and broadening** the range of tasks which a worker may be required to perform. (Australian Arbitration and Conciliation Commission, 1988:6)

Both of these measures refer specifically to the improvement of training opportunities in enterprises covered by the new awards. Over the following three years, employer groups and individual enterprises overhauled their awards to enable greater workplace flexibility and to create career paths for employees so that they could obtain progression and higher rates of pay as they acquired more skills (Curtain, Gough and Rimmer, 1992). Thus, the award restructuring process was centrally concerned with the improvement of training arrangements within Australian enterprises. In many cases, Australian enterprises followed the traditional route of industry level negotiations with unions to review their awards. In some industries, this resulted in the development of industry level training programs that followed the principles of the National Training Reform Agenda — based on nationally recognised competency standards and leading to a formal qualification — and were aimed at improving the overall skill level of the work force in a particular industry. Examples of this approach to award restructuring include the automotive industry, where employers and unions devised the six-step Vehicle Industry Certificate for production workers in the industry, and the metals industry (the largest industry award in Australia), which produced the Engineering Production Certificate. In other cases, enterprises negotiated training arrangements at the enterprise level and often established joint union-management committees to oversee the process. These enterprise level consultative committees would take the general principles agreed at the industry level and develop procedures for the implementation of improved training within the enterprise (Curtain, Gough and Rimmer, 1992; Hayton et al, 1996).

The process of award restructuring not only encouraged the development of enterprise training directly through agreements reached between the parties but also indirectly through the acceleration of workplace change. The newly restructured awards contained many provisions for workplace change, including the multiskilling of employees, the removal of demarcation barriers, the establishment of career paths and changes to working time. Many of these changes also entailed significant increases in training at the enterprise level (Teicher and Grauze, 1996). However, it was increasingly recognised by all the parties in the industrial relations system (employers, unions and governments) that increasing the pace of workplace reform would require a greater devolution of bargaining to individual enterprises. All three parties argued vociferously in the early 1990s for the Industrial Relations Commission to begin the process of dismantling Australia's centralised industrial relations system and shift the focus of bargaining from the national/industry level to the workplace.

Illustration 4.3 — Giving a XXXX for employee empowerment

> Brisbane's Castlemaine Perkins has used its latest enterprise agreement to set up tailor-made training programs for each employee. This individualised training will help the company establish self-managing work teams and restructure the workplace from the shopfloor up. The program involves designing personal development and training plans looking at technical, team and customer relations skills. The importance of employee skills is emphasised by a commitment from the company to three levels of training. Technical and core business skills training will occur during normal working hours or will be paid at overtime rates. Castlemaine Perkins will pay at single time for 'useful' training involving broader business skills such as supplier seminars and quarterly review sessions. It may pay for books for approved courses for training the employee wants to do and will reimburse reasonable expenses incurred on approved training.
>
> The courses are based on new skills classifications agreed with the unions. Any questions are to be settled between the employee, team leader and training co-ordinator. Queensland LMHU Assistant General Secretary, Chris Barrett, says that the union is happy with the changes as they make jobs more efficient. CP is the latest brewery to go down the path of workplace teams in the search for a competitive edge, following on from the success of Sydney's Kent Brewery. Barrett believes that this enterprise agreement has better chances of success than the last in 1993 which he alleges the company promptly broke by proposing huge redundancies leading to an 'enormous blue' between CP and the unions.
>
> The enterprise agreement codifies a series of agreements on pay and conditions worked on since 1993 and focuses on developing mixed-skill work teams as the basic workplace unit with the power to make decisions within their operational area.

Source: Human Resources Report No 114

Training and enterprise bargaining

Bowing to pressure from the parties, in 1991 the Industrial Relations Commission began the process of gradually devolving greater responsibility for wage bargaining to employers and unions through the establishment of the enterprise bargaining principle. Under enterprise bargaining, the commission still played a role in vetting enterprise agreements for productivity-related offsets and the maintenance of the basic terms and conditions of employees described in the relevant awards, but under the enterprise bargaining principle, local enterprise level agreements gradually replaced the old industry-based awards. Training was a key element in the agreements arrived at under the enterprise bargaining principle. A survey by the federal Department of Industrial Relations in 1992 revealed that 59 per cent of workplaces had introduced multiskilling in their enterprise agreements and a further 38 per cent had initiated major training programs (Short, Preston and Peetz, 1993).

A study of the first 1000 enterprise agreements (DIR, 1993) revealed that four types of training measures were often included in enterprise agreements. First, training needs analyses, and skills audits were a common feature in agreements that contained training clauses. However, references to skills audits appear to have declined in more recent agreements, with only 9 per cent of agreements mentioning training needs analyses (Australian Centre for Industrial Relations Research and Teaching, 1995). Secondly, many agreements contained references to the implementation of training based on national competency standards. Curtain (1994b) found that 28 per cent of all enterprise agreements contained references to training based on competency standards. Thirdly, some agreements linked training directly to pay, and, finally, many of the agreements that mentioned training made provision for the establishment of training committees. Training committees are joint management–union bodies, often established in highly unionised enterprises under award restructuring and enterprise bargaining. They are usually subcommittees of larger plant bargaining committees, and are concerned specifically with the planning and implementation of the training arrangements arising from award restructuring and enterprise bargaining. The powers of such committees vary from a consultative role to a direct role in the implementation of training programs.

A survey of enterprise agreements made before the end of 1994 found that 44 per cent contained references to the development and management of training committees which include both management and union representatives, sometimes with the assistance of staff from the relevant industry training advisory committee (ITAB). The Department of Industrial Relations summary of the references to training in enterprise agreements is reproduced in Figure 4.6 below.

Figure 4.6 — Training provision in enterprise agreements, 1994 (n=1360)

Training Provisions	Proportion of Agreements (%)
Entry level training	6
Skill/competency-based classification structure	26
Training leave	29
Training for broader tasks	27
Any indicator	67

Source: Teicher and Grauze (1996)

As Guthrie and Barnett (1996) have pointed out, these issues reflect many of the concerns of the National Training Reform Agenda. However, they also demonstrate that in subsequent enterprise agreements struck since 1994, the incidence of training-related clauses has declined, so that only 34 per cent of enterprise agreements contain specific clauses relating to training issues.

The diminishing incidence of training clauses in enterprise agreements raises the question of whether training represents a new province for bargaining between the industrial parties, or whether it is simply another issue over which management and unions confront each other in the traditional adversarial relationship. The former point of view has been championed in Australia by post-Fordist theorist, John Mathews (Curtain and Mathews, 1990; Mathews, 1993). Mathews has argued that the advent of post-Fordist production has brought issues of training and skill formation onto the industrial relations agenda at the enterprise level. The adoption of new, flexible technologies and new working practices such as teamworking have raised the requirement for higher levels of skill and, as a result, training has become an industrial relations issue. He develops this theme by arguing that the implementation of post-Fordist work organisation requires the commitment of employees and the abandonment of traditional adversarial patterns of industrial relations. Training is thus an issue on which consensus can be found between management and employees. Skills are necessary to the managers of the new, post-Fordist organisation, and training is important to individuals to guarantee their employability. From Mathews' point of view, it is natural that training should become an important part of enterprise level industrial agreements.

However, the consensus approach taken by Mathews has been criticised by Stuart (1996), who has argued that there is no evidence to show that bargaining over skill formation and training issues has led to the emergence of a more consensual industrial relations climate. On the contrary, he believes that British managers, at least, have to be coerced into improving their training arrangements. He also goes on to demonstrate, however, that the incidence of training may not be a direct result of industrial relations pressures and is affected by a variety of factors. The text of enterprise or collective agreements may not account for the reality of training within individual enterprises, and the training that does take place may not be the subject of formal negotiation. Thus, the declining incidence of training clauses within enterprise agreements, noted by Guthrie and Barnett (1996), may not signal the declining importance of training in Australian organisations but rather a divorce between training matters and other, more traditional, industrial relations issues, engendered by the decentralisation of bargaining brought about through the operation of the enterprise bargaining principle.

One explanation for this separation of industrial relations and training issues under the enterprise bargaining principle may be found in one of the key criticisms made of the training reforms by employers, who have suggested that the reforms were supported by the unions as a means of achieving higher pay rises for their members at a time of national wage restraint imposed through the Industrial Relations Commission (Butterworth, 1995). In conditions of relatively low pay settlements for employees, progression through the new job classification structures by acquiring new skills represents a practical alternative for improving employee incomes. In these circumstances, it is not surprising enterprises should resist the inclusion of training matters in the new enterprise agreements.

Training and Human Resource Management

Since the late 1970s, the old paradigm of personnel management has given way to new approaches to the management of people in organisations, known as human resource management (HRM). There has been a number of factors that have led to emergence of human resource management. These include, first, the globalisation of competition which led to the development of a more strategic approach to the management of human resources; secondly, the example of Japanese enterprises held up in the early 1980s as exemplars for Western enterprises, particularly in their management of human resources (Ouchi, 1981); and, finally, the growth of the 'enterprise culture' under the impact of neo-classical macro-economic policies that provided a benign environment for the growth of a new approach to employee relations (Legge, 1995).

From its earliest formulation, training has always occupied an important role in models of HRM. Often the discussion of training-related issues has been in the broader context of employee development (Beer et al, 1984), but training, as a strategy to ensure the development of employees, has been viewed as central to the implementation of human resource management. Training has been referred to as the 'litmus test' of whether an enterprise is serious about the implementation of HRM (Keep, 1989).

In their groundbreaking work on human resource management, 'Managing Human Assets', Beer and his colleagues at Harvard University attributed employee development with a critical role in gaining the commitment of employees and increasing their competence (Beer et al, 1984). Beer regarded employee development as an investment that would result in flexibility and adaptability, reflecting strongly the neo-human capital views of the CERI and NIESR researchers. However, Beer's interpretation of employee development is far wider than the skills training of human capital theory. For Beer, training is one amongst a number of methods that can be used by the enterprise to develop the careers of employees.

Beer's emphasis is on the development of the employee's career rather than simply training to meet the objectives of the enterprise. Thus, the process of employee development is as much about meeting the needs of the individuals as about achieving the objectives of the enterprise.

Walton, one of Beer's co-authors, made the goal of commitment explicit in his later typology of control and commitment models of HRM (Walton, 1985). Walton described how many United States enterprises were moving from an old work force strategy based on control. This involved tightly specified job descriptions, measured work standards, hierarchical structures and adversarial labour management policies. The emerging work force strategy was based on commitment, and involved greater employee autonomy, flat structures, job security and mutuality in labour relations. Although Walton did not address the issue of training specifically, priority for training and retaining the existing work force was a key element in employment assurances that helped to build the commitment strategy.

Guest, in his theory of HRM (1987), elaborated on the Harvard model for Britain. His theory is illustrated in Figure 4.7 on p 103. In this theory, Guest proposes that groups of HRM policies will lead to human resource outcomes that improve the performance of the enterprise. Training is quite clearly linked to adaptability/flexibility and commitment, following Beer's description of the aims of employee development. In a later article (1990), Guest linked HRM to a set of values that emphasised the importance of the individual (the 'American Dream'). In particular, HRM was based on the human growth theories of writers such as Herzberg (1966) and McGregor (1960) who emphasised the importance of challenge and recognition at work for individual motivation. Thus, HRM provides managers with a chance to allow individuals to develop at work through opportunities for growth and development (Guest, 1990).

Building on the work of Walton, Kochan and Dyer (1993) have described the notion of the 'mutual commitment' enterprise, in which human resources are treated as a source of competitive advantage by engaging employee commitment. The principles of the mutual commitment enterprise are organised at three levels — strategic, functional and workplace. At the functional or human resource policy level, Kochan and Dyer identify three principles:

- staffing based on employment stabilisation to reinforce employment security and promote commitment and flexibility;
- investment in training and development so that employees adopt the principles of lifelong learning;
- contingent compensation that can attract and retain a committed, cooperative and involved work force.

Figure 4.7 — Guest's model of HRM

	A theory of HRM	
HRM policies	*Human resource outcomes*	*Organisational outcomes*
Organisation/job design		**High** Job performance
Management of change	Strategic integration	**High** Problem-solving Change
Recruitment/selection socialisation	Commitment	Innovation
Appraisal, training, development	Flexibility/adaptability	**High** Cost-effectiveness
Reward systems		
Communication	Quality	**Low** Turnover Absence Grievances
	Leadership/culture/strategy	

Source: Guest (1987)

Again, the emphasis in the mutual commitment model of HRM is firmly on employee development — through job security, training and compensation for commitment — in order to create a committed, loyal and involved work force that enables the enterprise to meet its objectives.

Many other models of HRM have been developed but, as Dyer and Kochan (1995) have observed, these models share a number of common characteristics:

> ... high levels of employee participation, involvement or empowerment at the workplace level, primarily through enriched jobs and/or self-managed work teams; high selection standards; extensive investments in training and development; opportunities for high levels of earnings through skills-based and/or performance-based schemes; free flow of information up as well as down the organisation, and stability of employment. All also emphasis the need for mutual trust and co-operation through the organisation. (Dyer and Kochan, 1995:143)

Although these models may differ in terms of emphases placed on particular aspects, they all highlight the importance of employee development and, within that overall umbrella, the importance of training to the process of development. From the perspective of HRM, training assumes a far broader function than the CERI and NIESR studies suggested. Although central to the adaptability and flexibility of the work force, training is also important for engaging the commitment of employees. This involves not simply training for the skills to be used on the job, but a broader notion of employee development in which the enterprise is committed to the career development of employees. Training thus becomes part of the psychological contract which enterprises strike with their employees in return for high levels of commitment, loyalty and adaptability. It is not surprising therefore that training has been described as the litmus test for the implementation of HRM (Storey, 1992).

Training and Corporate Strategy

In their research into the role of HRM in the process of strategy formulation, a team from the Warlock University's Centre for Corporate Strategy and Change, led by Andrew Pettigrew, focused on the role of training. In the mid-1980s, Pettigrew and his team undertook a series of longitudinal case studies of strategic change in 40 British enterprises, focusing on the part that HRM played in the strategy process. Pettigrew found that HRM and strategy are inextricably interwoven, and emerge from the broader process of managing change (Hendry and Pettigrew, 1992). The research team focused on the role of training in the HRM process within these enterprises as a result of further work commissioned by the Training Agency in Britain.

Building on the perception that the lack of training in British enterprises was contributing to their declining international competitiveness (Sparrow and Pettigrew, 1985), the Warwick researchers identified two sets of factors that affected the provision of training in their sample (Pettigrew, Sparrow and Hendry, 1989):

- factors that set training in progress (triggers); and
- factors that establish training within the enterprise (stabilisers).

These factors are represented in Figure 4.8 on p 105. The forces that 'trigger' training provision are clearly linked to the strategy-making process. Enterprises come under competitive pressure and make changes to their products and services. These changes highlight a skills gap in the work force, and training becomes part of the corporate strategy. However, this process is not enough to secure the long-term commitment of the enterprise to training. A skills gap can be remedied in a number of ways, including by recruitment from the labour market (a non-training solution). Training is only stabilised by a combination of factors inside and outside the enterprise. External factors include:

- the availability of skills on the labour market;
- external support for training (grants, etc); and
- legislative requirements (government levies, etc).

Figure 4.8 — Corporate strategy and training

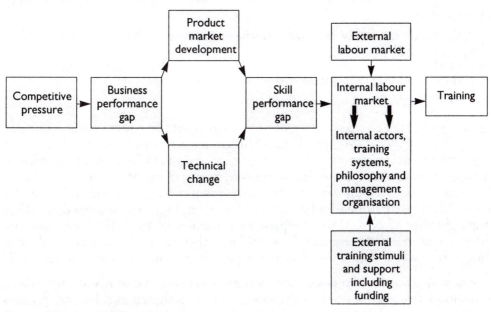

Source: Hendry (1991)

Factors operating within the enterprise include:
- the existence of a training 'champion';
- senior management commitment;
- training infrastructure within the enterprise;
- budgetary constraints; and
- trade unions acting as a watchdog on training provision.

The Warwick researchers argued that most of these factors need to be present for the enterprise to display a long-term commitment to training. They suggested that the conditions for greater enterprise training provision were created by the decentralisation that characterised the restructuring of British enterprises in the 1980s.

More recently, the resource-based view of the enterprise has shed a different light on the role of training and its relationship to strategy. The resource-based view of the enterprise has been popularised in recent years by the work of Hamel and Prahalad, who have developed the notion of 'core competencies'. Core competencies are learned attributes in the enterprise that give it long-run competitive advantage over its rivals. As Hamel and Prahalad (1990) argue, core competencies are not always visible to observers who focus on the end products or the capabilities of the enterprise. Core competencies are buried deep in the enterprise and are only developed over a long period of time.

Organisations may enjoy an immediate competitive advantage, such as a new technology, but this will not last for long, as competitors can copy such advantages. Sustained competitive advantage, on the other hand, is based on resources or competencies that cannot be easily copied. Such resources would have to meet four criteria:

- they should add positive value to the enterprise;
- they should be scarce;
- they should be inimitable; and
- they should be non-substitutable.

The human resources of an organisation can meet these four criteria convincingly (Wright and McMahon, 1992). Human resources can add significantly to the performance advantage of the enterprise, and the skills which they possess may be rare in the population. Moreover, the investment of an enterprise in building a stock of skills will not be easily imitable by rivals, and skills may be such that they cannot easily be replaced by technology. The intermediate skills highlighted as so critical to enterprise performance by the NIESR fall into this latter category. If these conditions are met, then human resources will be a source of resource-based, long-term competitive advantage to the enterprise.

The competencies of individual employees can bring two forms of competitive advantage to organisations — human capital advantage and human process advantage (Boxall, 1996). Human capital advantage accrues when the enterprise recruits and retains people with high potential. Human process advantage refers to processes such as learning, cooperation and innovation, that release and build on the potential of people. Both are required to achieve sustained competitive advantage through human resources. Human process cannot work without human resources which possess skill and potential. Likewise, talented individuals will leave enterprises that do not develop their potential. The combination of human capital with human processes for developing that capital has been labelled human resource competence (Kamoche, 1996).

In the resource-based view of the enterprise, the process of training and development becomes crucial. Human resources are a major core competency for the enterprise. They yield a potentially inimitable source of competitive advantage for the enterprise. However, the potential of human resources may remain unrealised if the enterprise does not have the processes that will enable it to release that potential. In the resource-based view of the enterprise, training is a means of both creating and realising the competitive advantage that human resources can give the enterprise.

What Drives Training?

Research in Australia by Charles Sturt University's Group for Research in Employment and Training (GREAT) and the University of Technology, Sydney has explored how training operates in Australian enterprises, and why organisations adopt different forms of training arrangements (Smith et al, 1995; Hayton et al, 1996). Over a two-year period from 1994–96, the research team studied 42 organisations in depth, and carried out a survey of 1760 studies of Australian private sector organisations. Organisations in five industry sectors were studied:

- building and construction;
- food processing;
- electronics manufacturing;
- retailing; and
- finance and banking.

The research team developed a model of how training operates at the organisational level. The model is illustrated in Figure 4.9 below. The basic logic of the model is focused on the distinction between those factors that give rise directly to training — training drivers — and those factors that shape the type of training which the organisation eventually adopts — training moderators.

Figure 4.9 — Model of enterprise training

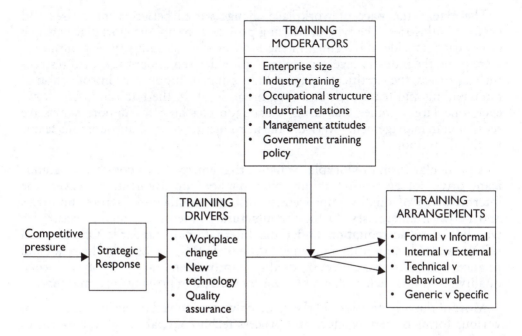

Training drivers are those factors that immediately give rise to a demand for training within the organisation. The operation of one or more of these drivers will produce an impetus to train. This is a similar concept to Hendry and Pettigrew's description of the 'triggers' which cause training (Pettigrew, Sparrow and Hendry, 1989). However, the creation of a training impetus within an organisation does not explain the vast variety of training arrangements that emerge from organisations which appear to be operating under the influence of the same training drivers. The diversity of the training arrangements that eventually emerge from the impetus is explained by another set of factors — the training moderators. These factors moderate the training impetus and determine the type of training which is carried out in each organisation. Because the combination of training moderators tends to be unique to the circumstances of each individual organisation, the operation of only a relatively small number of training drivers can produce an almost infinite variation in the training arrangements that finally emerge.

The operation of the model starts outside the enterprise, with the competitive pressure exerted by the business environment. Competition in itself does not directly give rise to training. However, it is the force that ultimately compels the organisation to take actions which result in the creation of a demand for training.

Drivers of training

It was the changes introduced as part of the strategic response to the new competition that were the real drivers of the training effort. These training drivers were remarkably simple, and recurred consistently throughout the research. The first of these drivers was workplace change.

The extent and pace of workplace change varied between enterprises and between industries. The type of training provided to support workplace change also varied considerably. Thus, in the food processing industry, organisations were using the industry level training program devised under the award restructuring process, the Certificate in Food Processing, to support the introduction of multiskilling and teamwork at a very broad level. In the retail industry, however, one large retailer was using on-the-job coaching to support a massive reduction in management levels and the introduction of semi-autonomous teams on the shop floor.

A particular form of workplace change that emerged as a consistently significant driver of enterprise training was quality improvement. However, the interpretation of quality improvement differed significantly across industries and between enterprises. In the manufacturing enterprises, quality assurance was linked to accreditation under the International Standards Organisation (ISO) standards and/or the implementation of TQM processes. In the retail and finance organisations, however, quality improvement rarely involved formal quality programs such as these, but was focused on improving customer service.

Most of the organisations in the research were involved in the introduction of various forms of new product and process technology, although the extent of technological innovation was greater in the manufacturing and finance sectors than in construction or retail. Generally, the training implications of investing in new technologies in the case enterprises were relatively straightforward. New product technologies often involved on-the-job training for employees who would be producing the new product. Training for new process technology was more extensive. In most cases, training for new process technology was supplied by the vendor of the equipment. Firms would look to the vendor for the training of key personnel, often a mix of engineers and shop floor employees, who would then, in turn, be responsible for the training of other staff involved in the new process.

Moderators of training

The training moderators were the factors which emerged in the research that were strongly associated with enterprise training but did not automatically produce a demand for training. Instead, the training moderators influenced the type of training arrangements that the organisation eventually put in place. The model of enterprise training identified six training moderators:

- enterprise size;
- industry traditions of training;
- occupational structure;
- industrial relations;
- management attitudes; and
- government training policy.

Enterprise size

The effect of the size of the enterprise on training provision was as marked in this study as other Australian research has shown (ABS, 1994a,b; Fraser 1996). Enterprise size was very strongly associated with training. The case studies provided a useful commentary on the reasons for the importance of size. Size is a proxy for a variety of other factors that impact on the ability of the organisation to provide training:

- **Resources** The larger the organisation, the greater the economies of scale that can be achieved in training and the greater the ability of the enterprise to provide internal, formal training, and to support this training with high investments in training infrastructure.
- **The nature of the work force** Larger enterprises have more skilled and professional employees who require higher levels of training. In Australia, the percentage of jobs requiring post-school qualifications in enterprises of fewer than 20 employees is 18 per cent. For enterprises with more than 100 employees, this figure rises to 32 per cent (ABS, 1994b). Thus, the demand for training is greater in proportional terms in larger enterprises.
- **Networking** Small organisations have particular problems in accessing training providers, whereas larger organisations, particularly those employing training specialists, often have well-developed relationships with a network of training providers and with the training authorities.

Industry traditions of training

The industry sector in which the organisation operates was strongly correlated with training in the research, and was revealed very clearly in the case studies as a major influence on the type of training that was to be found in any individual organisation. Industries clearly have their own traditions of training that have developed over long periods of time. Training in the construction industry, for example, is focused tightly on the apprenticeship system, and apprentice training is to be found in all the enterprises in this sector. Similarly, the finance industry has a tradition of expecting employees to undertake finance and banking qualifications in their own time if they wish to progress, and the industry has developed close links with the providers of this form of external accredited training. More recently, as a result of award restructuring, certain industries have established industry level training arrangements, partly in response to developments in the industrial relations system. A good example of this is the Certificate in Food Processing developed by the food processing industry training bodies. However, there were similar developments taking place in the electronics, construction and finance industries.

Occupational structure

Occupational structure refers to the mix of occupational groups found in the organisation's work force. Occupational structure is closely linked to initial vocational training. Different occupations clearly require different qualifications in terms of duration, content and level of post-school qualifications. There is much evidence in Australia to show that workers with initial post-school qualifications are more likely to receive subsequent formal training than those without (ABS, 1994c; McKenzie and Long, 1995). Seventy-eight per cent of managers and professionals in Australia have a post-school qualification — higher than any other occupational group (Karpin, 1995). Those enterprises with higher numbers of managers and professionals in their work forces will tend to provide more training, and often this training will be formal and off-the-job in nature.

Industrial relations

Industrial relations — defined in the research as the number of employees covered by an industrial award and the presence of training provisions in awards or agreements — was correlated with training, but the correlation was not very strong. This finding reflects the results from the case studies, that industrial relations has a strong influence on the climate for training, although it is not, in itself, a driver of training. Thus, industrial relations processes, particularly award restructuring and enterprise bargaining, have emphasised the importance of training for the operation of the new restructured awards, without specifying the form that the training should take. In some industries, as we saw above, these processes have led to the implementation of new, wide-ranging, industry-based training programs. The findings of the research confirmed the importance of industrial relations in creating an organisational climate which is conducive to the improvement of enterprise training.

Management attitudes

As Finegold and others have noted, management attitudes are very important in decision-making on training (Finegold and Soskice, 1988; Finegold, 1991; Karpin, 1995). However, management attitudes may be fragmented within the enterprise. There were many examples in the case enterprises of senior managers who pledged their commitment to the training of their employees. However, attitudes were often quite different at the middle and junior management levels. Managers at the operational level often preferred training that was short, sharp and tightly focused and, since many of the decisions regarding the implementation of training were taken at this level, operational managers had a significant influence on the form that the training would take.

Government training policy

Few of the organisations studied were engaged with the National Training Reform Agenda, and the impact of the Training Guarantee appeared to be very limited. However, other elements of government training policy could be discerned having an effect on enterprise training decision-making. Thus, the availability of grants for innovative training programs had persuaded some enterprises to make substantial investments in training infrastructure. The work of the government sponsored industry training advisory bodies had been particularly effective in persuading some industries to move to more industry-wide training arrangements. The development of national competency standards had also had an effect in some enterprises, guiding the development of training programs designed to meet these standards. Thus, like industrial relations developments, government training policy seems to create a framework within which certain forms and approaches to training are more likely to occur.

Training arrangements

The outcomes of the processes of interaction between drivers and moderators are the training arrangements finally put in place. The diversity of the arrangements in terms of the dimensions of training activity — formal versus informal, external versus internal, technical versus behavioural, generic versus specific — as well as the overall levels of expenditure on training and the distribution of that training between occupational groups in the work force, is the product of the unique interactions between training drivers and training moderators that take place within each enterprise.

Summary

This chapter has explored the principal theoretical approaches to the role and function of training and development at the organisational level. Economic explanations for training and development focus primarily on the role of the individual and the returns to both individuals and organisations from their investments in training.

Human capital theory is the most well known of the economic explanations for training and development in organisations. Human capital theory assumes that training will increase the skills of the individual. This will lead to higher levels of productivity for the organisation and higher wages for the individual. However, empirical evidence on wages and productivity in organisations does not support the assumptions of human capital theory.

Internal labour market theory explains the role of training and development as a means of developing and retaining skills in an organisation. Productivity in individual jobs is determined by a variety of factors, not simply the skills of the employee, and wages are determined in many ways rather than simply as a reward for higher productivity. Thus, training is an essential part of the internal labour market which determines the terms and conditions of work within the organisation.

Research by the OECD/CERI in the mid-1980s investigated the role of training in helping organisations respond to technological innovation. The CERI research demonstrated training does not take place in isolation from many other factors operating in the organisation at the same time. Training is part of an organisational nexus involving work organisation, employee relations and technology. Changes in any of these need to be supported by training. The work of the NIESR also highlighted the importance of training and skills in enabling German organisations to remain more adaptable, innovative and competitive than their British counterparts.

The relationship of training and skills to technological change has been the subject of fierce theoretical debate. Labour process theorists have argued that technology is used by managers to de-skill work, while post-Fordists have argued the opposite case. Empirical research in recent years has revealed a more complex picture, with some occupations experiencing an upgrading of skill as a result of technological innovation, while other jobs are de-skilled or disappear. It is clear that it is the introduction of new working practices and management techniques that has the most impact on training and development in organisations.

In Australia, training has become a central issue in industrial relations since the advent of award restructuring in 1988. Under award restructuring, new training opportunities were created, especially for blue-collar workers. This has been continued under enterprise bargaining, with many enterprise agreements containing clauses on training and development issues. However, the incidence of training clauses in enterprise agreements appears to be diminishing as enterprise bargaining focuses on more traditional industrial issues.

Training is closely related to the rise of human resource management in modern organisations. In most models of HRM, training is a key element increasing the competence and commitment of the work force. For this reason, training has been referred to as the litmus test of an organisation's commitment to HRM. Training also has a key role to play in the formulation of corporate strategy. New strategies require new sets of skills, and training is critical in ensuring the organisation retains and develops the core competencies on which it competes.

Discussion Questions

1. What is human capital theory, and how well does it explain the training behaviour of individuals and enterprises?
2. How did the OECD/CERI studies of the 1980s rework traditional human capital theory, and with what success?
3. How is skill related to productivity?
4. What is the high performance work organisation, and to what extent is it dependent on training?
5. How does industrial relations affect the provision of training in enterprises?
6. What is the relationship between business strategy and training?

Chapter 5

Analysing Training Needs

The conventional starting point in the training process is the training needs analysis (TNA). The training effort in many organisations is often wasted as a result of a poor TNA, or no TNA at all (Goldstein, 1986). Using a medical analogy, the TNA can be likened to the diagnosis of a patient; no self-respecting doctor would dream of embarking on a course of treatment until the illness had been satisfactorily diagnosed. So, training needs analysis is the process by which the instructional needs of the organisation are identified and interpreted prior to the preparation of a training plan. McClelland (1993) has defined the goals of a TNA as follows:

> ... to identify training needs as they currently exist or have the potential to exist at a future time, and to design and develop the ways and means of addressing and satisfying those needs in the most cost-effective and efficient manner possible.

Yet many of the human resource needs of an organisation may not be training or instructional needs at all. There is a variety of needs that must be met in an organisation for individuals to perform. These might include, inter alia, the need for effective supervision, the need for a well-designed job, the need to be given clear performance targets, etc. None of these are training needs for the individual (although they might imply training needs for others). The training needs analysis is therefore an analysis of a particular set of needs; those which can be met, at least partially, by a training solution. The analysis of performance problems may only occasionally lead to the implementation of a strictly training-based solution (Smith and Delahaye, 1987). This point is discussed in greater depth later in the chapter.

This chapter is concerned with the analysis of training needs at the broadest level, and the variety of approaches that can be taken to the problem. The conventional three-level approach in which training needs are analysed successively at organisational, operational and individual levels is examined, together with the notion of a 'performance problem' and the extent to which it can be said to be a 'training problem'. A central notion to the debate in Australia in recent years has been that of 'competency'. This concept is analysed and discussed with reference to occupational analysis. The second half of the chapter examines the different methods of analysis most commonly used in the TNA process: direct observation, information search, group methods and inventory methods.

Three Level Analysis

The most frequently cited approach to needs analysis is that of McGehee and Thayer, who modelled the process on a three-level view of the organisation, involving: organisation analysis, operations analysis and individual analysis (McGehee and Thayer, 1961).

Organisation analysis

At this level, the analyst is concerned with identifying where in the organisation training is needed. It is concerned with macro-training needs that emerge from a study of the organisation's performance as a whole (Laird, 1986). This is essentially a statistical study of the information which is produced within the organisation on an everyday basis. A wide variety of sources exist for this data, such as:

- organisational goals and objectives;
- work force measurements, including analysis of labour turnover, age profiles and expected retirements, etc;
- skills inventories;
- measurements of organisational climate, including industrial disputes, labour turnover, absenteeism, productivity, accident rates, etc;
- measurements of efficiency, such as labour costs, material costs, product quality, downtime, waste and so on.

Organisation analysis does not, of itself, throw up actual training needs, but provides clear indications of where performance problems exist and which areas of the organisation would repay closer analysis.

Examination of the organisation's goals and climate is particularly important in this respect (Goldstein, 1986). Unless the training is in line with the organisation's goals, it is unlikely to be perceived as effective by managers; similarly, an organisational climate antithetical to training will make it difficult for the trainee to apply new knowledge and skills on the job.

Operations analysis

The focus of this level of analysis is on a job or group of jobs. The literature on job analysis is voluminous and, of course, organisations routinely undertake this sort of activity for reasons other than training: for example, job evaluation and organisation design. Sources for this data include:

- job descriptions;
- job specifications, which differ from job descriptions in that they will list the skills required from the incumbent as well as job duties;
- performance standards;
- direct observation of jobs;
- literature review;

- asking questions about the job.

The measurement of the knowledge, skills and abilities (KSA) required to perform the job is important at this level of analysis (Prien, Goldstein and Macey, 1985). The concept of KSAs has become a central focus of much of the literature concerned with training analysis and program design. Prien (1985) popularised the notion of KSA and defines them as follows:

> Knowledge (K) is the foundation upon which abilities and skills are built. Knowledge refers to an organized body of knowledge usually of a factual or procedural nature, which, if applied, makes adequate job performance possible ...
>
> Skill (S) refers to the capacity to perform job operations with ease and precision ...
>
> Ability (A) usually refers to cognitive capabilities necessary to perform a job function. Most often abilities require the application of some knowledge base.

KSAs can exist at a number of different levels. McGehee and Thayer's methodology is concerned with the identification of KSAs at the surface level; that is, the KSAs needed to perform the operations being measured. At this level, KSAs are fairly narrowly focused on the task in hand: knowledge of the actual job, skills in performing the job and the cognitive abilities to operationalise the knowledge. However, a closer analysis may reveal that there are many other KSAs required to perform the job in addition to those which are immediately obvious or measurable. These 'under the surface' KSAs may include a broad knowledge of the processes that take place before and after the job is performed, skills in anticipating problems or in working in team situations with other members of the workgroup, and the ability to differentiate information relevant to the job from the massive amounts of information presented by the job environment (Field, 1990).

Individual analysis

This level of analysis is focused on measuring how well the incumbent is performing the job under review. McGehee and Thayer (1961) produced a long list of techniques that could be used for analysis at this level, which has also been considerably expanded since. These include:
- performance appraisal data;
- job observation;
- interviews;
- questionnaires;
- job tests;
- critical incidents;
- attitude surveys.

For McGehee and Thayer, 'man' analysis was the focus of the TNA process. Training was concerned with improving the performance of the employee at the job, and hence the employee was the key unit of analysis. The number of techniques they list for this level of analysis indicates the centrality of the employee in the TNA process.

The three levels approach has dominated the literature on needs analysis since McGehee and Thayer first articulated it in 1961 (Moore and Dutton, 1978). Subsequent writings in the area have done little more than develop the number of techniques which can be used within the overall framework; no new model of needs analysis has been developed. Attention has been concentrated, in particular, on the person level of analysis. As a result, there is considerable overlapping of techniques and ideas in the analysis process as envisaged by McGehee and Thayer, especially at the operations and person analysis levels, leading to some conceptual confusion. More importantly, however, the McGehee and Thayer prescriptions seem to ignore important contextual factors which can impinge significantly on individual jobs. An example might be the influence of the workgroup on job design and individual performance, which is well documented in the industrial/organisational psychology literature.

Ostroff and Ford (1989) have highlighted the one-dimensional character of the three-levels model. They argue that the three levels correspond to content areas which can classify the data captured in a needs analysis. However, these content areas should themselves be analysed at three different levels in the organisation. Organisational, task and person issues have different implications at the organisational, sub-unit or individual level. As an example, consider the notion of goals. The organisation may well have a clearly articulated set of goals expressed in terms of expected rates of return on investment, profits or market share. However, departments or sub-units within the organisation may pursue entirely different goals concerned with growth or political influence, which may subvert the expressed goals of the organisation. At an individual level, it is obvious that people bring to their work a variety of personal objectives which may or may not be consistent with goals of either the sub-unit or the organisation. Hence, an analysis based on the presumption that employees will identify with the stated goals of the organisation will be inherently unsound. Figure 5.1 on p 118 illustrates this two-dimensional approach to needs analysis.

Analysing Performance Problems

The focus in the needs analysis literature on the individual highlights the notion of performance and performance deficiencies. It is tempting to draw the conclusion that a performance deficiency is the result of a training need and is therefore capable of a training solution. Even a cursory examination of the reasons for performance deficiency, however, will reveal that there are many other factors that impinge upon the performance of an individual besides the absence of training.

Consider, for example, a machine operator whose quality of work declines. Is this a case of poor training? Will training the operator improve his or her performance? Perhaps, if the reason for the decline in performance is related to a deficiency of knowledge, skills or ability. But, quite obviously, there may be many other reasons for the decline: the machine may be faulty, the raw material out of specification, the supervisor's instructions unclear, the workgroup in dispute with management, the operator unwell or suffering from the impact of domestic problems and so on.

Figure 5.1 — A two-dimensional approach to needs analysis

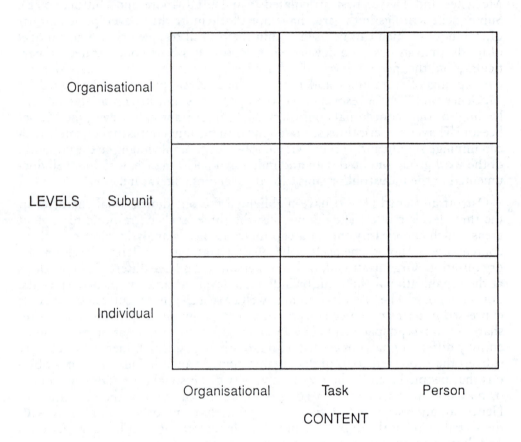

Source: Ostroff and Ford (1989)

And yet, managers will often jump to the conclusion that the performance problem can be rectified by the application of training, regardless of the true causes of the problem. Mager and Pipe (1984) developed a model of performance problem analysis which revolves around the key question of whether or not a skill deficiency exists. The model is reproduced in Figure 5.2 on p 120.

If the problem is the result of a skill deficiency, training or an opportunity to practise the skill may be required. However, the model highlights a number of alternative reasons for the problem which are not susceptible to a training solution:
- performing to the required standard may hurt or punish the individual; for example, working in a cramped or confined space;
- performance may not be adequately rewarded;
- performing to standard may not matter to the individual;
- there may be obstacles which prevent performance;
- there may be a simpler way to do the job;

- the individual may simply not possess the potential to do the job, regardless of training.

None of these reasons is related to training, so training undertaken in these circumstances will be useless. For Mager and Pipe, the analysis process needs to go beyond a simple focus on training needs, and take in the contextual factors that influence the individual at work.

Occupational and Competency-based Analysis

In recent years, the focus of analysis in the training area has shifted away from the more traditional TNA approaches discussed above, to the notions of skill and competency. Changes in the workplace involving new forms of work organisation, multiskilling and new technology, have highlighted the need for skills audits and training programs based on measurable competencies. In Australia, these changes have assumed greater significance with the development of industry competency standards and industry-based training programs such as the Vehicle Industry Certificate or the Food Processing Certificate: see Chapter 2. Together with these industry level developments, Australian organisations have been undergoing an unprecedented period of change in working practices across all sectors of Australian industry; changes which, because of the centralised nature of the award system, are often negotiated and implemented at the industry level rather than at the enterprise level: see Chapter 4 for a full discussion of these and related issues. This process involves training analysis at a level above that of the individual workplace at the enterprise or industry level. Thus, techniques of occupational analysis have become important to the trainer.

Definition of competency

The terms 'competency', 'task' and 'skill' are often used in an interchangeable way which confuses the real differences that exist between the concepts.

A task is a fundamental building block of a job. A job, at the simplest level of analysis, consists of a series of tasks which the incumbent may be required to carry out. It is a routine, sequential and predictable activity which can be clearly observed and measured. Thus, the job of a machine operator could be broken down into tasks that might include loading a component onto the clamp, closing the safety guard, inspecting the finished component for certain defined defects, etc.

In order to perform those tasks, the operator will require certain skills. These would include the obvious psychomotor skills to place components into the machine and take them out correctly and safely. They would also include, from our previous discussion of KSAs, cognitive skills such as the capacity to identify faulty components and reject them or to recognise malfunctions in the machine and correct them.

Figure 5.2 — Analysing performance problems

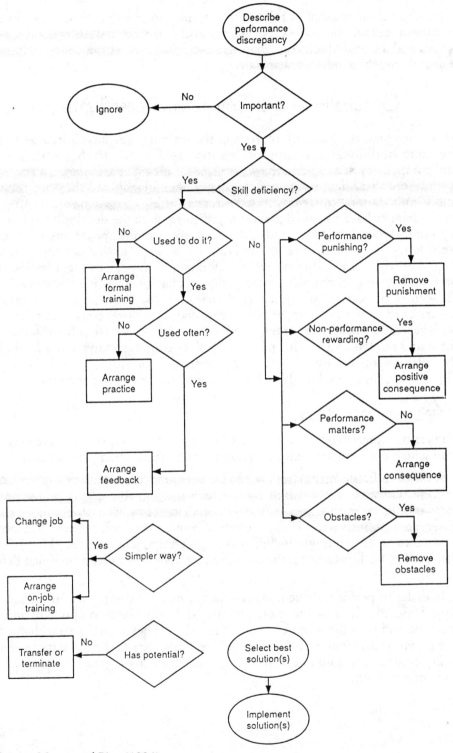

Source: Mager and Pipe (1984)

Illustration 5.1— Multiskilling for nuts and chips

> Smiths' Snackfoods are Australia's largest manufacturer and marketer of snackfoods with famous brands such as Smiths' Crisps, Twisties, Cheezels and so on. The snackfood market in Australia is worth $850 million and Smiths' have 56 per cent of the market. The company has four manufacturing plants across Australia and employs more than 2000 people. At the company's Adelaide plant the company employs 550 people over three shifts. Smiths' at Adelaide identified the need for the development of enterprise specific competencies and assessment criteria for engineering staff in the plant. An attempt to develop competency standards for engineering personnel in 1993 proved to be more difficult than first thought. To accelerate the project, a consultant's brief was developed which called for the development of competency standards and training modules for processes and related equipment.
>
> The process used by Smiths' to select the most suitable consultant was to guide short-listed candidates through all sections of the plant, then have them make a presentation to a project committee comprising an equal number of tradespersons and management. Trengrove Consulting Services, a South Australian based human resource development consulting firm was chosen. A project timeline was set in place and employees' briefing sessions followed with the associated methodology explained. A modified DACUM-storyboard approach was used to gather sufficient engineering/maintenance data from expert groups (4 to 8 members) about each topic to enable the consultants to develop the competency standards.
>
> The skills matrix that was developed for each module from the competency standards, provided an opportunity for self-assessment by each of the engineering personnel. This analysis identified the extent of training required and also ensured that Smiths' would not be trapped into over or undertraining. A comprehensive needs analysis led Smiths' to develop a highly successful, competency-based training program.

Source: Trengrove (1997)

Competencies include both skills and tasks. Thus, a key competency for the machine operator might be 'to place a component in the machine ready for a drilling operation'. This involves both the task of placing the component in the machine as well as the skill of placing it correctly for the machining operation. Another competency for the machine operator would be 'to remove the component after machining and place in the appropriate bin'. Again, this involves both the physical operation of removing the component as well as the skill of judging its quality to determine in which bin to place it. However, a statement of competency will usually go further than describing task and skill requirements. A competency also includes a level of expected performance and any other factors which may influence the outcome of its performance.

The National Training Board (1992) defined the notion of competency as:

> ... the specification of knowledge and skill and the application of that knowledge and skill within an occupation or industry level to the standard of performance required in employment.

Competencies are normally expressed in terms of a unit of competency, its constituent elements and linked performance criteria.

A unit of competency refers to the general area of competency. Thus, in a hotel kitchen, a unit of competency might include: 'clean and maintain equipment and premises' or 'prepare pastry, cakes and yeast goods'. Within the overall unit of competency, each distinct task will appear as an element. Elements of competency describe the lowest, logical and discrete subgrouping of actions and knowledge which form part of the unit of competency. Finally, attached to each element will be a standard of performance, the criteria by which the person can be assessed as competent or not. Figure 5.3 on p 123 shows the unit of competency, 'prepare pastry, cakes and yeast goods', broken down into its constituent elements and performance criteria.

Thus, competency embraces the whole notion of KSA as discussed previously, but goes beyond it in including the conditions under which the task is to be performed and the standard or level of performance required. It is this latter emphasis on standards that has led to the notion of competency becoming so important in the modern practice of training and development, because standards imply the ability to assess performance in training. Thus, competency-based training programs are distinguishable, amongst other things, by the importance attached to regular assessment through the program.

Occupational analysis

The process of identifying the competencies within an occupational area is known as occupational analysis. An occupational area may refer to a number of related occupations across particular industries or it may involve only a small part of one occupation, that is, a single job (Hermann, 1987). The information generated from an occupational analysis, of course, is often used for a wide variety of purposes, not simply for training. However, the technique has come to be associated with the design of competency-based training programs. Three phases may be identified in an occupational analysis: determining the nature and scope of the occupational area, developing a competencies list and collecting data on each competency (Hermann, 1987).

General parameters of the occupational area

The first step in an occupational analysis involves generating a written description of the area. This description will specify the scope of the occupation; that is, what the occupation covers and what it does not cover. Consider the example of a debtors clerk position (Hermann, 1987):

> The person whose primary function is to perform clerical and monitoring activities to ensure the amount of money owed to the enterprise is kept to a minimum. This includes 'chasing' debtors by phone and by letter.
>
> It does not include:
> - approaching debtors in person
> - setting up the system
> - determining policies.

This step may also include the definition of different branches or subsets of the main occupation and the identification of new or emerging occupations.

Figure 5.3 — Units of competency

Industry: Tourism (Kitchen Stream)	
Unit: Prepare pastry, cakes and yeast goods	
Element	Performance criteria
Prepare, decorate and present pastries	• Sweet and short pastry produced to basic standard recipe • Puff, filo and strudel dough pastry-based products correctly identified • A variety of choux-based products prepared and presented to standard recipe • A variety of pastry products produced to restaurant dessert-trolley standard
Prepare and produce cakes and yeast goods	• A selection of sponges and cakes prepared and decorated to standard recipe • A variety of yeast-based products produced and served to industry standard
Prepare and decorate petits fours	• Petits fours selected to complement given situation • Petits fours prepared and decorated to industry standard
Apply portion control and storage procedures	• Portion control applied to minimise wastage • Storage procedures identified and applied correctly for cakes and pastry products
Apply basic hygiene principles and occupational health and safety standards	• Basic hygiene principles and occupational health and safety standards applied according to industry regulations

Source: National Training Board (1991)

Competencies list

Phase two of the occupational analysis process specifies the actual competencies required for the occupation. As we discovered when examining KSAs, there are two types of competencies. Surface or conventional competencies are those skills required to carry out the activities of the occupation, and would normally include psychomotor and cognitive skills most easily identified in the analysis process. Under the surface, or refractory competencies, are those skills which underpin the ability of the person to carry out the activities. Refractory competencies would typically include interpersonal, problem-solving or communication skills. The competencies list includes both types of competency.

It is likely that the analysis process will identify up to 100 or more elements of competency for any occupational area. Using the NTB guidelines, these elements can be grouped into units of competency; around eight units of competency is the usual outcome for an occupational analysis (Curtain, 1989). Figure 5.4 on p 126 shows part of a competency analysis for an engineering draftsperson developed in the United States.

The general format of the competency analysis, with the specific elements of competency placed horizontally next to the general unit of competency, emerges from the group techniques often used to generate this sort of data.

Data on each competency

Unless the resources of the organisation are infinite, some priority order will have to be established for training in each of the competencies identified. This involves collecting data on the relative importance of each competency, which can be used in the training design process. Three types of data can be collected as part of the analysis process. The extent to which each competency is performed may be gauged by examining the percentage of time spent on each competency by typical jobholders. Participants in the occupational analysis exercise may rank the competencies in order of their importance to performing the job. Finally, competencies can be judged on the basis of their difficulty to learn. All of these measures will indicate the competencies which require most attention in terms of the training program.

Methods of Analysis

There is a wide variety of methods which can be used in the needs analysis process. Many of these methods find their origin in the scientific management concepts of management control over the work process that emerged in the early twentieth century. In order to exert control over work and ensure higher levels of productivity, managers began to use techniques of analysis that enabled them to measure jobs in fine detail and develop standard times for most of the operations that occurred in their workplaces.

The information generated by these studies can, of course, be used for many purposes other than simply controlling the work process. They provide a rich source of data for the generation of training material. As a result, trainers make use of these and other methods in their analysis of training needs in the organisation. This section will examine five types of analytical methods used in this process: direct observation, interviewing, information searching, group methods and inventory methods.

Direct observation

Techniques most closely associated with scientific management are those based on direct observation. Since the Gilbreths first introduced the notion of time and motion studies onto the factory floor, the industrial engineer (with or without stopwatch) has become the symbol of management control of the work process. The information generated by a time study is very similar to the information that the trainer needs in order to design training programs for new jobs or the improvement of performance. In order to improve efficiency, the industrial engineer investigates how the jobs in question are being performed. The basic method of analysis employed is one of breaking the job down into its specific duties or competencies. More detailed analysis breaks the competencies down further into specific tasks. Needless to say, this is the starting point for competency-based programs. There are three levels at which methods of direct observation can be used: the simple job breakdown, the medium depth analysis and the detailed analysis (Turrell, 1980).

The simple job breakdown was the technique adopted by the Training Within Industry (TWI) movement in the 1940s in response to the wartime demand for better and quicker training for new workers in the arms factories of the United States. Sometimes referred to as a 'stages and key points' analysis, the basis of the technique is the observation of a job over a number of cycles. The analyst records the activities of the worker, and later breaks the job into what seems to be its 'natural' elements or stages. Each stage is separated from the others by a recognisable 'breakpoint'. For each stage, the analyst generates instructions to guide the new worker and makes notes of any 'key points' that the trainee needs to remember, such as safety precautions, complementary activities, etc. The final form of a stages and key points analysis is shown in Figure 5.5 on p 127, which lays out an analysis of the task of performing a job breakdown.

The medium depth analysis goes much further in its analysis of the job. In this case, the analyst will break each stage down into its constituent parts, that is, each competency into its component tasks. This level of analysis will involve the identification of the most detailed activities such as movements of limbs, hand/eye coordination requirements and so on. The result will be a set of detailed instructions on the performance of the job, with an inventory of attention or care points for the trainee. The usual format of a medium depth breakdown would be similar to that of the stages and key points analysis, with instructions and attention points laid out against competencies.

A detailed analysis would be unusual in the training context. Based on the international industrial engineering standards derived to establish agreed times for all human movement, a detailed analysis breaks the competencies and tasks into discrete actions, with full information on the sensory and mental inputs into the job processes. The advantage of such a breakdown is that it can be done for jobs that do not currently exist, by using the international standards (synthetic data). It is, however, a level of analysis that would be considered too detailed for normal training projects.

The level of analysis required depends on the complexity of the job, the rapidity of its execution (defying clear observation) and the numbers of employees involved in the job (Turrell, 1980). The more complex, rapid or wide ranging the job, the more detailed the level of analysis which is appropriate.

Figure 5.4 — Part of competency profile for a draftsperson

COMPETENCY AREA	COMPETENCIES						
A — Conduct Field Work	A-1 Take measurements	A-2 Determine site orientation	A-3 Make site inspections	A-4 Use surveying techniques	A-5 Develop working sketches		
B — Develop Preliminary Studies and Presentations	B-1 Prepare rough sketches	B-2 Prepare preliminary drawings	B-3 Make models	B-4 Prepare presentation drawings			
C — Prepare Final Drawings	C-1 Determine type and size of medium	C-2 Attach medium to board	C-3 Prepare surface for drawing	C-4 Determine details to be shown (isometric)	C-5 Lay drawings	C-6 Select and use appropriate line weights	C-7 Draw detail views
D — Prepare Written Documents	D-1 Develop written instructions	D-2 Generate job orders	D-3 Write change orders	D-4 Submit requisitions for drafting supplies	D-5 Submit requisitions for services	D-6 Develop inputs for contracts	D-7 Prepare memos and letters
E — Check Drawings	E-1 Check accuracy of dimensions and scale	E-2 Check coordination of prints	E-3 Check revisions	E-4 Check for completeness	E-5 Check line quality	E-6 Verify compliance with building codes	E-7 Check clarity of notes
F — Maintain Document Storage	F-1 File masters	F-2 File media materials	F-3 Retrieve media and masters	F-4 Maintain file of persons	F-5 Maintain drawing log		

Source: Field (1990)

Figure 5.5 — A 'stages' and 'key points' breakdown sheet

JOB TITLE: How to make a job breakdown		
Stage (what to do in stages to advance the job)	Instructions (how to perform each stage)	Key points (items to be emphasised)
1. Draw up table	Rule three columns. Allow space for column headings and job title	Use this sheet as an example
2. Head the columns	On top line insert the title of job Insert: Column 1 (Stage) Column 2 (Instructions) Column 3 (Key Points)	Headings — summarise what the worker needs to know to perform each job Watch out for steps which are performed from habit
3. Follow through the job to be analysed	After each step, ask yourself — 'What did I just do?' Note places where the worker could go astray. Note items to be emphasised. Note hazards. Stress safety points.	Write notes clearly and concisely Keep stages in order Ensure directions are complete — never assume they are
4. Fill in Columns 1, 2 and 3 as stage 3 above is performed	Make brief and to-the-point notes	Review and emphasise these 'Key Points' decisively
5. Number the stages	Follow the sequence a worker must follow when learning the job	
6. Follow the job through using directions in Columns 1 and 2	Follow the instructions exactly	
7. Check that all 'Key Points' are included	Record in Column 3 all points where the worker may be confused	

Behaviour frequency counts analyse specific behaviours in a job which may be causing poor performance or excellent performance. The analyst pinpoints the particular behaviours in question and observes the job, counting the number of times that behaviour is manifested. The analyst may also make notes on the quality of the behaviour or others that may be involved with it (in the case of an interpersonal behaviour). The final statistical analysis of the behavioural observations will highlight behaviours causing poor performance and those leading to excellent performance. It will also reveal whether poor performance can be rectified with training (see Mager and Pipe) or whether other contextual factors require attention. Zemke and Kramlinger (1982) quote the rather unusual example of a behavioural frequency analysis carried out in a Nevada casino. The results showed that contrary to the conventional wisdom of the hospitality and entertainment industry, dealer effectiveness (measured in the number of dollars produced at each table during the night) was not related so much to good customer relations as to the simple number of hands of cards dealt by the dealer. The more hands dealt, the higher the takings. Thus, effective training would concentrate on the dealing competencies of the dealers rather than their customer skills.

Direct observation is also the basis for more subjective methods of analysis, such as personal diaries kept by incumbents or management reports about the job in question. Although the validity of such subjective data may be open to question, they, nevertheless, often form the basis for the initial TNA.

Interviewing

Interviews are a well-established method for collecting information in a TNA. The interview allows the opportunity for direct interaction between the analyst and the subject of the TNA. McClelland (1994a) distinguishes between two forms of the interview — the face-to-face interview and the telephone interview.

Bloom (1988) has shown that face-to-face interviews can be the most effective method for gathering information in a TNA. The face-to-face interview can use structured and unstructured methods. Structured interviews are best used when the problem is fairly clear, and it has been established that a training solution is the most appropriate answer to the problem. In this case, closed 'yes/no' questions can be used by the analyst. An unstructured approach is best used when the problem is not clear, and requires discussion and exploration with the subject. In this case, open-ended questions are used to collect the information. Individual interviews can be very effective, but they have a number of drawbacks:

- they are an expensive method of gathering data;
- they are very time consuming, particularly unstructured interviews;
- they usually require the use of an experienced interviewer.

A variation on the individual interview is the telephone interview. This approach has the advantage of cost-effectiveness, and is particularly useful when collecting straightforward data of the 'yes/no' variety. It is also less intrusive than the face-to-face interview, and respondents are often more relaxed and truthful over the telephone (Peterson and Wilson, 1992). However, McClelland (1994a) points out a number of disadvantages with the telephone interview:

- little opportunity to 'break the ice' with respondents;
- lack of visual clues to the respondent's reactions to questions;
- respondents quickly become tired of telephone interviews; and
- telephone interviews produce less qualitative data than face-to-face interviews.

Information search

The work may have been done already. In this case, it is a matter of finding out where information on the jobs or occupations exists, and determining whether or not it is relevant to those under consideration. There is a wide variety of published sources which can be consulted for analysis purposes including:

- dictionaries of occupational titles. The principal Australian dictionary is the Australian Standard Classification of Occupations (ASCO);
- databases such as ERIC, the education database which is available on CD-ROM and on-line;
- national TAFE Clearinghouse, based in Adelaide;
- industry and occupation specific data;
- documents from equipment suppliers;
- labour force data (Australian Bureau of Statistics);
- data from employment authorities such as the Australian National Training Authority or the various state training authorities;
- government training authorities.

It is likely that the information revealed by such a search will be of a fairly general nature, although lists of competencies for most industries are now available through ANTA.

Group methods

Group methods of analysis allow the knowledge and experience of both employees and supervisors to be tapped, as well as building consensus around the results of the exercise. It seems that the process of award restructuring encourages the use of group methods so that the work force is fully involved in the analysis, generating commitment to the aim of the analysis (Curtain, 1990). This section will examine four group methods: focus groups, DACUM, critical incident analysis and the Delphi technique.

The focus group is an informal meeting of peers to discuss a problem situation, usually moderated by a convenor or facilitator. The purpose of the group meeting is to focus very specifically on an identified and agreed problem. This may be a performance problem or an analysis of competencies pertaining to a job. The job of the convenor is to keep the group discussion focused on the issue and to help the group express its opinions and arrive at some form of conclusion.

Although the meeting of the focus group may proceed in a fairly informal manner, the convenor needs to prepare the ground well in advance by clarifying the purpose of the meeting with both group participants and other stakeholders (management, union officials, etc). Focus groups are generally small, requiring between eight and 12 members to function well. The group must have a clear idea of the issue for discussion before arriving at the meeting. The focus group, in contrast to other group activities such as team development groups, is a group of peers (McClelland, 1994b). It is unlikely that employees will be willing to divulge their knowledge and opinions on sensitive issues in the presence of their superiors, and vice versa (McClelland, Harbaugh and Hammett, 1993). A particularly important issue in the use of focus groups is the role of the moderator. In many cases, the use of an outside moderator can help to bring objectivity to the discussion. However, this has to be balanced against the cost of using an outside moderator, and the lack of understanding such an individual may have of the key issues in the organisation. The analysis procedure may require the formation of a number of different focus groups representing different constituencies concerned with issues. Although discussion in the focus group is structured around a carefully prescribed issue, the methods used by the convenor will often be more unstructured, aimed at encouraging the members of the group to open up and give information which can be transcribed later by the convenor.

DACUM, by contrast, is a much more structured approach to analysis. DACUM (Developing a Curriculum) was developed in Canada in the 1960s and has since been extensively used in occupational analysis throughout North America. It has been used in New Zealand as part of the reform of the apprenticeship system (Burleigh, 1989). The DACUM technique involves the analysis of occupational competencies by an expert group of jobholders led by a facilitator. The process normally takes four to six hours to complete, but can take up to three days. It is generally regarded as a timesaving method of occupational analysis, particularly where large numbers of jobholders may be involved. Three premises on which DACUM depends include (Railton and Milhall, 1990):

1. Expert workers are better able to describe/define their work than anyone else.

2. Any job can be effectively and efficiently described in terms of the skills required by workers to perform successfully the tasks within the job.

3. All tasks have direct implications for the knowledge, skills and attitudes which workers must have in order to perform the tasks correctly.

The outcome of the DACUM process, therefore, is a listing of the competencies required of a job in terms of KSAs, drawn up by the people most expert in that job, that is, the employees themselves. The process of DACUM involves seven steps (Hermann, 1987):

Step 1. *Orientation to the DACUM procedure.* The DACUM panel is briefed by the facilitator on the reason for the meeting and the general procedure to be followed. Examples of competency statements may be given to familiarise the participants with the language of analysis.

Step 2. *Review of the occupational area.* The facilitator gives the group an overview of the occupation/job under consideration.

Step 3. *Identification of the general areas of competence.* The facilitator leads the group to identify the major competency areas. These are normally refined to between eight and 12 key statements of competence.

Step 4. *Identification of the first band of competencies.* Against each competency area, the group lists the specific competencies required. Up to 10 competencies may be identified for each general area.

Step 5. *Identification of the remaining bands.* Completion of the work started in Step 4.

Step 6. *Review and refinement of the competency definitions.* Insert any competencies that may have been overlooked in the previous two steps. A statement is acceptable when the group feels that it would be understandable to most people with a background in the occupation.

Step 7. *Possible subsequent steps.* The examination of additional data, such as sequencing, prioritising, etc.

The final documented outcome of the DACUM will be a list of general competency areas followed by specific competencies, not unlike the example in Figure 5.4. The participative nature of the DACUM process has led to its increasing popularity in recent years as a method of competency analysis prior to programs of multiskilling or award restructuring.

Critical incident technique was developed in the United States during World War II to find out why trainee pilots were crashing their training planes at such an abnormal rate. Military psychologist John Flanagan adopted a very simple technique to find out the answer: he asked questions of the pilots. In fact, Flanagan asked the pilots who crashed their planes to describe exactly what it was that they had done incorrectly, that is, to report incidents of ineffective behaviour. Critical incident technique is a means of establishing the competencies required in a job by asking incumbents to describe incidents of both effective and ineffective behaviour (critical incidents).

The technique can be employed on an individual basis, but it is most often used in a group setting where the participants can use the synergy of the group to gain a clearer picture of the job competencies. Group members are asked to relate, usually in writing, incidents that have occurred in their jobs in the last six months or so that have resulted in either successful or unsuccessful outcomes. Each incident is described in some detail, including information about what training was of assistance, what KSAs led to effective performance, what could have been done to avoid failure, etc. Up to 200 critical incidents may thus be generated by the group (which may include supervisors and other interested parties as well as job incumbents). The task of the facilitator is to help the group refine the incidents into eight to 12 general areas of competence, as in a

DACUM session. Individual incidents can then be classified under each of the competency areas to produce a competency analysis.

The critical incident technique can also be used to arrive at scales for measuring performance. Each of the incidents classified under the general areas of competence can be arranged in order of their indication of an effective performance of the job. Thus, each competency area could be scaled from one to eight; one denoting very poor performance, eight denoting outstanding performance. Each number on the scale can be illustrated by an appropriate critical incident. Such behaviourally anchored rating scales (BARS) are becoming widely adopted as the basis of performance appraisal systems.

Illustration 5.2 — Using DACUM in the textile, clothing and footwear industries

An integral part of the Award Restructuring process in Australian industry was the implementation of improved training programs based on comprehensive skills audits in the enterprises concerned. In the Textile, Footwear and Clothing (TCF) Industries this process was conducted at an industry level as many of the smaller companies that make up the industry did not possess the resources to carry out such an intensive exercise alone.

The first phase of the audit produced a profile of the TCF industries by examining issues of products, processes and work organisation. The result was a grouping of eight clusters in footwear and six in clothing based on similar configurations of product, process and work organisation. Consultants working with the TCF Council on this project advised that the next stage in the process, the identification of competencies, would be best approached using a DACUM method.

Experienced DACUM facilitators convened panels of employees and supervisors representing each of the industry groupings to examine the jobs that were common throughout the industry. The DACUM panel initially focused on the task of identifying the general areas of competence that constituted each job. For instance, the expert panel on outworkers (a very common form of work in TCF) identified six major areas of competence: servicing machines, preparing work, planning work, operating the machine, removing work and maintaining records.

Each of these competency areas was then examined in greater detail in order to specify the actual tasks performed and the knowledge, skills and attitudes required by the worker. The result was a comprehensive report outlining the skills requirement of an entire industrial sector for the future.

Source: Curtain (1989)

Delphi is a less tightly structured technique, developed to deal with future scenarios or situations of great uncertainty. Named after the classical Greek oracle, Delphi involves using recognised subject matter experts to make 'best guess' forecasts about the situation or problem under consideration. In this sense, the group of experts may not be formally constituted as a group at all. Group members may be contacted individually to give their responses which are then processed by the facilitator who produces an overall report. The procedure may be highly repetitive, with group members asked to present their opinions a number of times on the same question after feedback on the previous round. As a result, consensus will begin to emerge within the group on the solution to the problem without a physical meeting having taken place.

Inventory methods

Occupational analysis, particularly at the industry level, often involves the analysis of a very wide range of jobs performed by very large numbers of people. In these situations, inventory methods based on questionnaires and surveys are frequently a popular choice by analysts. They are also methods most often criticised for their lack of completeness, or bias. The public scepticism about opinion polling, or the typically low response rate to mailed questionnaires, is symptomatic of the lack of faith observers tend to have in the results of such methods. On the other hand, a well designed survey or questionnaire can yield a great deal of information in a relatively short space of time, and often in a format that is readily able to be processed. The effective design and administration of questionnaires is beyond the scope of this book, and is the subject of many publications (McClelland, 1994c), however, a number of do's and don'ts can be summarised. These include, inter alia:

- begin with non-threatening items;
- make items as brief as possible;
- group items into coherent categories;
- include clear, concise instructions;
- use professional production methods;
- have a plan for analysis;
- pilot questionnaires;
- don't use jargon;
- don't use negatively worded questions;
- don't hint at desired responses;
- don't put important items at the end; and
- don't allow respondents to fall into 'response sets'.

There is a number of different questionnaire types commonly found in occupational analysis.

Competency inventories can be designed specifically for the occupation in question. Alternatively, there is an increasing number of 'off-the-shelf' inventories available, designed to cover a variety of occupations (Hermann, 1987). The position analysis questionnaire (PAQ) is a structured inventory consisting of 187 job elements. These elements are grouped into six divisions:

1. information input;
2. mental processes;
3. work output;
4. relationships with other persons;

5. job content;
6. other job characteristics.

Each element is scored on one of six different rating scales and analysed to produce a job profile. The PAQ has been the subject of extensive research which has validated the dimensions which the questionnaire uses to measure job competencies (McCormick, 1979).

Comprehensive occupational data analysis programs (CODAP) are a suite of 50 computer programs that analyse occupational data. The term CODAP, however, is now generally used to refer to the data gathering methods used before the computer analysis as much as the programs themselves. CODAP was developed in the United States to analyse military occupations and is used extensively in the Australian Defence Force. It is a questionnaire-based technique that lends itself to the analysis of large numbers of jobs and large population sizes. A CODAP study will (Hayton, 1988):

- find what job groups exist, each job group consisting of workers having similar job profiles;
- provide a job profile on each job group;
- provide a general profile on each job group on variables such as age, sex, job experience, education and location.

The CODAP procedure involves the selection of a relatively large sample of the population who receive the questionnaire normally through the mail. The large sample size helps to offset the bias caused by low return rates. The questionnaire is constructed from a comprehensive task inventory which details all the tasks performed by the population and classifies them into a smaller number of duty statements. This part of the process may be carried out using a DACUM type method, as the outcome is very similar to competency inventory. The resulting task inventory may contain up to 500 specified tasks.

The CODAP questionnaire asks participants to indicate whether or not they perform each of the tasks and if they do, how much time they spend on the task and how important the task is to their job. Other information such as age, sex, education, work experience, etc, is often also included in the questionnaire. Completed questionnaires are then analysed using the CODAP programs which, typically, group the respondents into clusters based on the similarity in tasks performed and provide a job profile for each cluster. The clusters identify the occupations, and the job profiles the competencies (tasks) and general competency areas (duties).

The drawbacks of the CODAP method centre on the expense of the process and its narrow focus on tasks as opposed to the underlying knowledge and skills which form the basis of competency. The resource intensity of the CODAP method has meant that only a few such studies have been implemented outside the military. A survey of 13 CODAP studies reported that each study cost on average $12,000 to perform and took 10 months to complete (Williams and Hayton, 1987). Nevertheless, the CODAP method has enjoyed some popularity in Australia within industries where training arrangements are organised at the industry level, such as tourism, and building and construction (Curtain, 1990).

Illustration 5.3 — Skills audit produces concrete results

> Concrete Constructions decided to take a new approach to industrial relations in 1987 when the construction industry was riding high and projects took an average of 40 per cent longer to complete than they should. A log of claims filed by the 'lofty crane crew committee' in 1988 was the catalyst for Concrete Constructions to begin to talk directly to workers and establish a relationship with them rather than through a union. It turned out that the crane drivers were just as frustrated as the company with work practices that meant they could not repair defects in their own cranes, but had to climb down and wait for a fitter to arrive on site to do the job.
>
> The company now employs only building workers rather than a multitude of classifications such as crane drivers, with people progressing up the pay scale according to the skills they acquire. A bonus was the findings of a skills audit which uncovered a wide range of skills among employees that the company did not know about and can now use. To underpin the changes, Concrete Constructions is spending 4 per cent of its total payroll on training and completed an enterprise agreement with its staff. Today, crane drivers perform maintenance, hydraulics, and even welding work, and have moved out of their cabins to perform general building work as the need for high-rise cranes has disappeared. The bottom line for the company has been improving competitiveness which has allowed it to win new jobs large and small. While major projects in the past typically ran 40 per cent overtime, the company is now experiencing delays of less than 10 per cent.

Source: *Australian Financial Review*, 2 June 1993

Which Method When?

All of the methods discussed are used in analysing training needs, competencies and occupations. Often they are used in combination with one another. Thus, a CODAP survey may involve a DACUM session to establish the task inventory; direct observation of jobs may be supplemented by a questionnaire or focus group and so on. However, each method has its own strengths and limitations.

Direct observation methods have the obvious advantage that they produce first-hand information about the tasks observed. However, they can also be a highly threatening method for those being observed, and the presence of the observer may often lead to distortion in the responses of the participants. Nevertheless, many organisations use these methods for other purposes such as standard setting, and the information so generated may be of invaluable assistance in a training situation.

Interviewing has the advantage of producing very detailed, qualitative information. However, it is a time-consuming and expensive process, and can be very intrusive.

Information searches save time. If the information already exists in the public domain (government reports, etc), then why not use it? Very frequently, of course, that sort of information will not be specific to the organisation or occupations under scrutiny, and will have to be supplemented by more varied methods. Information searches are a place to begin an analysis rather than complete it.

Group methods have the major advantage in that they involve the participants and can engender a sense of commitment to the analysis project. This is one of the main reasons that DACUM and related techniques have become so popular in recent years. DACUM, in particular, is a relatively quick and low cost method of analysis, which seems to yield reliable data. However, facilitators often experience great difficulty in forming DACUM groups, as employers are unwilling to give employees the time out necessary to participate in the sessions. Group techniques also tend to rely heavily on the skills of the facilitator in the group situation for their success. An inexperienced facilitator may easily be led astray.

Inventory methods are most useful when there are large populations and a wide diversity of jobs to be analysed. If run successfully, questionnaires can yield massive amounts of data in a very short space of time. CODAP, in particular, is a tried and trusted method which generates information in a form specifically suited to the occupational analyst. It is, however, expensive and time consuming to run, and the expertise needed to handle the computer analysis is lacking outside the United States.

A comparative study of the value of each of the major occupational analysis methods for phases two and three (competency listing and collecting data on each competency) of the process concluded that an extended information search yielded the most reliable and comprehensive data for the competency lists, and that a competencies inventory was the most effective means of collecting data on the competencies (Rayner and Hermann, 1988). However, the authors also report that they experienced some difficulty in organising a DACUM session and CODAP was not included in the methods trialled.

More recently, the value of the TNA process itself has been questioned. Critics have claimed that the TNA yields only a static picture of the organisation at one point in time, and that it is impossible to determine what the training needs of an organisation may be in the future through such a process. Berger (1993) has suggested that TNAs, particularly for management staff, need to focus on the changing environment and how the organisation is adapting to those changes, in order to get a complete picture of the present and future training needs of managers.

Summary

This chapter has explored the first phase of the training process: analysis. Analysis is a much wider activity than the conventional notion of the training needs analysis (TNA) might at first suggest. This chapter has argued that the process of analysis explores all the aspects of a particular job in its entire context rather than limiting itself to the determination of specific training requirements. In this sense, the analysis phase is a process of problem analysis.

The conventional approach to analysis was pioneered in the early 1960s by McGehee and Thayer, who characterised the TNA process as a three-level mechanism. Training needs were analysed at the organisational, operational and person level. This approach has dominated the literature on training needs analysis since, despite a number of criticisms. A possible alternative involves adding a further dimension onto the McGehee and Thayer model so that the organisation, the operational sub-unit and the individual's training needs are all analysed at each of the three levels.

The concept of competency is important in the design of modern training programs. Competencies are the basic duties and skill requirements of a particular job. In order to make a training program effective, the competencies of the jobs in question must be analysed. Competencies differ from other job-related concepts such as tasks and skills. They can be grouped together into general areas of competency which become the basic skills requirements for a job.

Competencies are often analysed by means of occupational analysis. Occupational analysis can examine jobs at the plant level or at the broader industry level, and is therefore becoming much more widely used as a result of award restructuring and multiskilling. The process involves three phases: an initial description of the occupational context of the job, a listing of the competencies of the job and, finally, the collection of data on the competencies.

There is a variety of methods used in analysis. Broadly, they can be grouped into four. Methods of direct observation based on the principles of industrial engineering; information searches, where the analyst makes use of information that is already published and available; group methods, which involve employees in analysing the competencies associated with their own jobs; and inventory methods, relying on questionnaire and survey-based approaches. Different methods are applicable in different situations.

Discussion Questions

1. Why is the concept of the training needs analysis so narrow?
2. What is a competency?
3. What are the implications of performance analysis for the training practitioner?
4. What are DACUM and CODAP? How do they differ?
5. What are the shortcomings of direct observation as a means of analysis?
6. How do different methods of analysis reflect different assumptions about human learning?

Chapter 6

Designing Training Programs

This chapter will examine the next stage in the training process: the design of training programs. Since the 1960s, the concept of systems approaches human resource development has become increasingly popular. The chapter begins with a short examination of systems theory and its application to the training process. The first step in the process is the specification of objectives, and the chapter discusses a number of different approaches to the formulation of objectives. The process of design is examined at two levels. Instructional theory is the application of learning theory as discussed in Chapter 3 to the design of training programs. Instructional strategy examines the basic division between learner-centred techniques (discovery learning) and trainer-centred techniques (exposition). Finally, the chapter concludes with a discussion of the issue of how training is transferred to the workplace.

The Training System

The use of systems theory in training and development reflects the pervasive use of the systems approach throughout the social sciences in the post-war period. Based on general systems theory (Von Bertalanffy, 1968), the systems approach attempts to integrate the contributions of the different disciplines into a single model which will better explain the workings of the phenomena under scrutiny. Thus, a typical systems approach to understanding a phenomenon would involve the construction of a model representing a process which is fed by inputs and which, in turn, produces certain outputs. The system may also incorporate a control mechanism known as feedback, by which the output of the system is monitored and changes can be made to the inputs to ensure that the system continues to function smoothly. The basic model of the system is shown in Figure 6.1 on p 139.

Figure 6.1 — A 'systems' approach to training

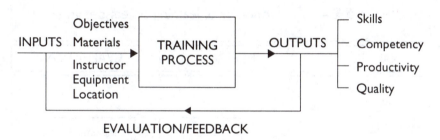

Training can be described in systems terms also. Certain inputs are made into the training system; these might include training objectives, training materials, and other training resources such as an instructor, training equipment and the physical location of the training. Inputs are then processed by the learner, resulting in outputs from the process. Outputs from training might include improved skills and competencies for the learner and improved productivity and quality for the organisation. The performance of the training system is monitored by the process of evaluation. This systems-based approach emphasises the importance of certain elements in the system; in particular, the use of objectives specifying what the trainees will be capable of doing when they have completed the learning, that is, what output to expect. Other aspects of the systems approach highlight the importance of systematic needs analysis before the design phase (so-called front-end analysis), systematic design of programs and materials, and measures to ensure the transfer of training to the work environment.

Advocates of the systems approach to the design of training maintain there is a number of problems which face the designer in any training situation. These problems include trainees not understanding the goals which they should be achieving as a result of participating in the program; how to structure the content of the program so that trainees will achieve those goals; and the resources that will be required in order to run the program effectively. To overcome these and similar problems, the designer needs to adopt a systematic approach. The systems approach to training design has been characterised in five steps (Davis, Alexander and Yellon, 1974):

1. Describing the current status of the learning system. Anticipating the problems that might be encountered in designing the program, such as the background of the trainees or the availability of resources.

2. Deriving and writing learning objectives. Providing guidance to trainees in terms of what they will be expected to achieve.

3. Planning and implementing evaluation. Defining how the trainer will know whether the objectives have been met.

4. Performing a task description and task analysis. Defining the tasks to be learned and the competencies that make them up.

5. Applying principles of human learning. Deciding how best trainees will learn the tasks in the program.

Figure 6.2 puts the steps into a chronological sequence.

Figure 6.2 — A chronology of learning system design

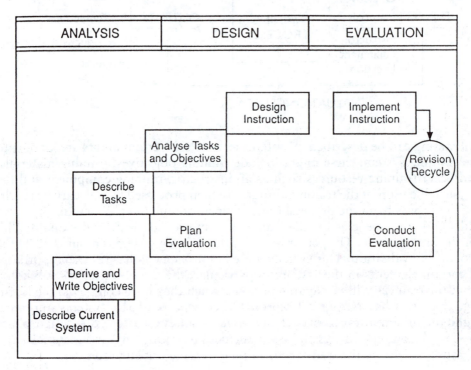

Source: Davis, Alexander and Yelon (1974)

Thus, the systems approach defines an overall method which is structured and sequenced so that no potential problem escapes the attention of the designer. The inputs to the system are specified in terms of the background of the trainees and the objectives they must achieve as a result of undergoing the program, the training material is constructed in accordance with the objectives, and relevant learning theory and the outputs of the system are measured through carefully tailored evaluation.

Romiszowski in his exhaustive three volume study of the instructional design process (1984) uses an explicitly systems-based framework. Preferring the term 'instruction' to training or learning, Romiszowski defines it as:

> ... a goal directed teaching process, which has been pre-planned and tested.

Thus, instruction is a process characterised by clear objectives, planned in advance. Program content is then developed on the basis of the objectives which are, finally, tested out through an evaluation system. Romiszowski identifies four levels of instructional design:

Level 1. The overall objectives for the program and how the program will solve the problems identified in the analysis.

Level 2. The learning objectives for the program, that is, what the trainees will be able to do as a result of going through the program.

Level 3. Detailed planning of the individual components of the program: lesson plans, session plans, etc.

Level 4. Development of instructional media to support the program: the resources needed to administer the program in terms of exercises, audio-visuals and so on.

Romiszowski therefore describes a top-down approach to the design of instructional systems. The designer starts with the large-scale problems uncovered in the analysis phase and works down to the detailed design of the program and the resources required to administer it. Although differentiating between skills and knowledge, this is done at the level of curriculum planning (Levels 3 and 4) rather than higher in the system. Thus, the system Romiszowski advocates can be used in any learning situation.

The prescriptive common sense approach of the systems theorists has made systematic design models very popular among trainers. It seems to lay out an easy, step-by-step guide to the development of programs that will achieve their objectives. There are a number of criticisms of this approach that can be made. First, it places great emphasis on the importance of objectives, but many activities cannot be measured or specified very well using objectives. This point is discussed later in this chapter. Secondly, the systems approach is a highly prescriptive model of the learning process; that is, it states how learning systems should be designed rather than examining the reality of design as it occurs in the workplace. In practice, the designer may work under a number of constraints which prevent him or her from the realisation of an ideal design as recommended by the systems theorists. These constraints can take many forms:

- **Resources are scarce** Typically, training departments do not enjoy great power within the organisation and are not in a position to bid for resources as they are made available. Nadler (1989) has shown how in times of economic restraint it is the budgets of training departments that are cut first to achieve immediate cost savings.

- **The lack of political power of training practitioners** This may impact on the design process itself. Thus, managers may be unwilling to release participants to an off-job training course for long periods of time, compelling the designer to devise a program which will accommodate the needs of others in the organisation apart from the trainees.

- **The systems approach is specifically top-down** This is so, starting with objectives and working through to detailed session design. However, this linear approach to program design may not reflect the reality of the design process, which may be highly iterative in character. Thus, the design and implementation of one program may lead to the discovery of new problems or training needs that are related to the present program. As a result, another program may be designed. A program to train machine operators in programming computer numerical control (CNC) machines may highlight the fact that many of the operators do not understand the total manufacturing process in their plant, resulting in some resistance to the implementation of new technology such as CNC. The trainer may then design a program to introduce operators to plant processes as a prerequisite to the CNC program. New needs emerge from the implementation of training, resulting in a bottom-up design philosophy in contrast to the top-down approach of the systems theorists.

Training Objectives

The design of training systems emphasises the importance of the direction of the curriculum. Trainees need to understand what they will be expected to achieve as a result of the program. The learning needs to have some goal. Those goals are expressed in the form of objectives. Mager identified three reasons why training programs require objectives:

> Objectives, then, are useful in providing a sound basis (1) for the selection or designing of instructional content and procedures, (2) for evaluation or assessing the success of the instruction, and (3) for organizing the students' own efforts and activities for the accomplishment of the important instructional intents.

Objectives serve a variety of functions for the instructional designer, and are the important first step in linking the analysis of training needs with the content of a training program. This section will examine three possible approaches to the specification of learning outcomes: Bloom's taxonomy of educational objectives, behavioural learning objectives and Gagne's taxonomy of instructional outcomes.

Bloom's taxonomy

Benjamin Bloom and his colleagues at the American Psychological Association (APA) first became interested in specifying outcomes for the educational system through a concern with the processes of assessment and testing in the early 1950s. Bloom chaired a subcommittee of the APA, which was charged with the task of devising ways in which college examiners could compare and contrast their methods of assessment for American students. It quickly became clear, in Bloom's words, that:

> ... a theoretical framework might best be obtained through a system of classifying the goals of the educational process, since educational objectives provide the basis for building curricula and tests and represent the starting point for much of our educational research.

Bloom eventually came up with a threefold taxonomy of educational objectives that could classify all learning. He divided learning objectives into domains:

1. The cognitive domain deals with the learning of knowledge and the acquisition of intellectual skills.
2. The affective domain includes the development of attitudes, values, interests and appreciations.
3. The motor skill domain includes physical skills and abilities.

Each domain is ordered into levels of competence. Within the cognitive domain, the student progresses through six levels of mastery: knowledge, comprehension, application, analysis, synthesis and, finally, evaluation. Five levels are specified for the affective domain: attending to specific phenomena, responding to them, learning to value them, organising one's own values and, finally, creating a system of personal values to guide one through life. Educational objectives are developed on the basis of the domains and levels of competence within them.

The taxonomy also represented a hierarchy to Bloom. The cognitive domain was of prime importance in the education of young people, followed by the affective domain, which dealt with the wider development of students as human beings and citizens in society. The physical domain was not considered by Bloom to be an issue of concern for the educational system in the 1950s.

Although the Bloom taxonomy may seem to be all-embracing, there are two major shortfalls in the context of the training and development of adults (Romiszowski, 1984). First, it dismisses the importance of the motor skill domain. Much of the training effort in industry and commerce is concerned explicitly with the development of physical skills. That many of these skills also include elements of the cognitive and affective domains leads on to the second major problem with the taxonomy: the rather exclusive nature of the categories. Thus, the CNC machine operator from the example above may need to acquire not only the physical skills of operating and adjusting the machine, but also the attitude and motivation to do so (affective) and the knowledge to diagnose and rectify simple problems (cognitive). Thus, the content of many industrial training programs will be concerned with achieving objectives that are a mixture of all three domains.

Behavioural (competency-based) objectives

Perhaps the most popular way of constructing objectives for learning is the use of statements of expected behaviour for trainees. As the name implies, behavioural objectives are rooted in the behaviourist tradition of the observation and measurement of recognisable behaviours: see Chapter 3. These are based on Skinner's belief that only measurable behaviour is important in the learning context to the formulation of objectives for training programs. Behavioural objectives clearly specify the outcomes of the learning process in terms of the observable and measurable behaviour of trainees. Robert Mager, perhaps the greatest advocate of behavioural objectives, describes the typical behavioural objective as encompassing three parts (Mager, 1975):

1. **Performance** What the learner is expected to be able to do as a result of undergoing the program. The performance part of the objective has to be written in unambiguous language, using words that express an action rather than a state of mind or intention. Activities such as turning, switching, removing, holding and so on, can be seen and measured. On the other hand, states of mind such as understanding, appreciating or realising cannot be observed and are therefore not useful in constructing behavioural objectives.

2. **Conditions** The important conditions under which the performance is to take place. Thus, a performance may be specified as having to take place without the aid of reference manuals, with a standard set of tools, without interference from the instructor and so on.

3. **Criterion** The standard of performance expected of the trainee. This might be expressed in terms of speed (words per minute for a word processor operator), accuracy (tolerance for a machine operator), quantity (numbers of insurance policies sold in the next three months) or quality (number of customer complaints for a retail assistant), etc.

Mager gives examples of well-specified behavioural objectives. These are illustrated in Figure 6.3 below.

Not surprisingly, the form of behavioural objectives bears a strong resemblance to that of competencies discussed in the previous chapter. Just as behavioural objectives specify the performance, conditions and criteria of an expected behaviour, so competencies detail the task, conditions and criteria associated with a given level of competency. Competencies are expressed as behavioural objectives because they are concerned with the measurement of the same thing: an observable, behavioural outcome.

Figure 6.3 — Mager's behavioural objectives

> *Given any centrifugal pump containing one malfunction, and being told of one symptom of that malfunction (condition), be able to describe and point to the malfunction (performance). Any tools, instruments and references may be used (condition). Four of five malfunctions must be located within ten minutes each (criterion).*
>
> or
>
> *Be able to run the hundred-yard dash (performance) on a dry track (condition) within fourteen seconds (criterion).*

Source: Mager (1975)

The widespread use of behavioural objectives has come under criticism for the same reasons that the behaviourist tradition of learning theory has been criticised within psychology. The major limitation of the behavioural objective is its narrowness. Not everything learned can be reduced to a statement of performance in behavioural terms. It is not always clear what constitutes behaviour, and it may be wrong to equate behaving with learning or knowing (Collins, 1993a). Certainly a glance back at Bloom's taxonomy would reveal that although objectives in the motor skill domain may be simply expressed in behavioural terms, this may not be so simple for objectives in the cognitive or affective domain. Educating machine operators about the importance of maintaining quality standards, or teaching supervisors to use a more flexible style of management may be valuable training activities in some cases, but may be very difficult to reduce to behavioural outcomes measurable in the workplace.

Nevertheless, the definition of competency in behavioural terms for non-motor skills has been attempted with some success, particularly in the area of management development. The expected competencies of a manager, while primarily cognitive and affective, may be observable indirectly through some specified behaviour which indicates the presence of competency (Saul, 1989). For instance, Westpac Bank used a behavioural approach to define competency for their managers in areas as intangible as 'people orientation', 'personal commitment' and 'entrepreneurship'. Thus, the degree of a manager's people orientation was assessed by defining behaviours such as:

- clearly communicating performance standards to staff;
- following through to improve poor performance.

Thus, the scope for behavioural measurement may be greater than critics of this approach admit.

Learning outcomes

Gagne and Briggs (1988) recognised the multiplicity of outcomes that can be expected from a learning situation. The education system is vested with a variety of expectations from different groups in society. Similarly, training programs are often expected to achieve a wide variety of objectives: cognitive, affective and motor skill. To draw up a list of objectives for a training program which may extend over many months may be extremely time consuming and wasteful. Gagne focused on human capabilities rather than domains of learning or behaviour. Program objectives could be classified into categories which described the capabilities the program was intended to enhance. He produced five categories of learning outcomes, which are shown in Figure 6.4.

Figure 6.4 — Gagne's learning outcomes

1. **Intellectual skills** are those which enable a person to do something of an intellectual sort. How to read and write are basic forms of intellectual skill. More advanced skills might include how to diagnose a machine fault or how to construct a road bridge. Intellectual skills are very similar to the notion of procedural knowledge (see Chapter 3).
2. **Cognitive strategies** govern the cognitive processes of the person. Similar to the notion of executive control used by the information processing theorists and of metacognition, cognitive strategies enable the person to decide how to approach a task or solve a problem.
3. **Verbal information** is the knowledge which the person can state, that is, declarative knowledge in the terms of the information processing theorists.
4. **Motor skills** are the physical skills necessary to complete a task. Similar to Bloom's notion of the motor-skill domain.
5. **Attitudes** are those capabilities that determine how a person will make choices between alternatives: values, beliefs, feelings, interests, etc. Attitudes are consistent with Bloom's affective domain.

Source: Gagne, Briggs and Wager (1988)

Learning objectives can therefore be classified according to the types of capabilities to be developed. Gagne does not stipulate the way in which the objectives have to be written, but stresses that performance is the criterion by which the effectiveness of any program ought to be measured. Thus, objectives need to be written on the basis of performance. The taxonomy of learning outcomes assists the designer to decide on the sequence of learning and the types of instruction appropriate to the different skills. Each outcome requires a different approach to instruction. Thus, verbal information may best be taught using an expositive method, whereas motor skills require practice in order to be learned.

It will be clear, of course, that Gagne and Bloom share a cognitive orientation regarding the question of learning objectives. They are more concerned with the processes of learning than the behaviours associated with its outcomes. Nevertheless, the notion of performance as the criterion by which the effectiveness of the training should be evaluated, indicates that objectives need to be written in fairly unambiguous terms, although not necessarily with the same focus on behaviour that Mager would advocate.

Designing Training Programs

The design of training programs can be examined at four levels. First, instructional theory informs the overall structure of the program. Behaviourists, information processing theorists and adult learning theorists make different assumptions about the nature of human learning and instructional design. In practice, these assumptions will have a considerable impact on the way in which trainees will be expected to learn in the program. Secondly, instructional strategy, or the way in which learning occurs in the program, will be shaped by the content of the program. Thirdly, the context of the program, whether delivered away from the workplace in an off-the-job situation or at the workplace in an on-the-job situation, will impact on design. Finally, questions of instructional theory, strategy and context will determine the options available to the designer in terms of the techniques which can be used in the program. Issues of context and technique are the subject of a later chapter on methods and media. This chapter will address the questions of instructional theory and strategy.

Chapter 3 examined the basic theories of human learning that underpin training design. While concerned with explaining the phenomenon of learning, that is, how behaviour is changed, learning theories have obvious implications for the design of the instructional events that produce learning. Adult learning theory, of course, in so far as it may be characterised as a philosophy of teaching rather than a theory of learning, is much more instructional in its orientation than is behaviourism or information processing theory. The latter theories can be developed in terms of instructional prescriptions for program design; the former generally consist of a series of guidelines already developed for design purposes (Hartree, 1986).

Behaviourist approach

Behaviourist learning theory is based on the principles of conditioning first described by Pavlov and later modified by Skinner in his theory of operant conditioning. Operant conditioning states that learning is the production of a specified response to a given stimulus. Instructional design therefore focuses on the provision of an environment in which the stimuli to which the trainee has to learn to respond are present. This environment or context must resemble as closely as possible the context in which the responses will have to be elicited in the real world, usually the workplace. However, the context will be bristling with stimuli, to only some of which the trainee will be expected to respond. These are discriminative stimuli.

The first task of the designer, therefore, is to design instructional events that will enable the trainee to distinguish discriminative stimuli in the context. This is achieved by the use of cues. Cues are stimuli other than the discriminative stimuli which are capable of eliciting the correct response on the part of the trainee. Such cues may be instructions given by the trainer or, perhaps, a physical list of steps to be performed which the trainee can follow until the correct response is learned. True learning in the behavioural sense, however, will not take place until the trainee has been 'weaned' from the cues and emits the desired responses to the discriminative stimuli themselves.

The second major task of the designer, therefore, is to 'fade' the cues to the point where the trainee is responding to the discriminative stimuli. Thus, the trainer may give gradually fewer instructions to the trainee or withdraw the list of steps to follow.

If difficulties arise in the learning process, the trainer may use a number of non-routine treatments to help the trainee. One of the most common of these non-routine treatments is the process of shaping discussed in Chapter 3. Most training programs involve the learning of a number of responses to a series of stimuli; any work task can be broken down into a series of steps or responses. A trainer, using the shaping treatment, will concentrate on each response in turn, not moving onto the next response until the cues for the previous response have been successfully withdrawn. The task will only be performed in full once each individual response has been correctly learned. Sports coaching is a good example of shaping in practice.

From a behaviourist point of view, there appear to be only four underlying skills that are ever learned (Gropper, 1987). These are:

1. **Discriminations**: the ability to distinguish discriminative stimuli from others.
2. **Generalisations**: the ability to recognise stimuli in situations outside the usual context.
3. **Associations**: the ability to identify the response appropriate to a given stimulus.
4. **Chains**: the ability to string together a number of stimuli and responses (often associated with learning a procedure).

A behaviourist approach to the training of a machine operator to operate a new machine might typically begin with the trainer asking the operator to 'have a go' at operating the new machine without any instruction. This serves two purposes: first, it demonstrates the level of prior learning the trainee is bringing to the new situation so that the trainer can focus the training activities on those responses the trainee is unaware of; secondly, it produces greater efficiency by reducing the necessary training time if the trainee has some prior knowledge. The trainer might continue with a routine treatment of providing cues for the operator in the form of a verbal description of the operation of the new machine and/or a written step-by-step operating guide which the operator can follow.

The trainer might then have the operator work the machine using a step-by-step guide, noting any difficulties the operator experiences. These difficulties may then become the focus for non-routine treatments such as shaping, until the trainer is satisfied that the operator is capable of operating the new machine using the guide. At this point, the trainer will begin the process of fading the cues by withdrawing the guide altogether (sudden fading) or replacing it with a briefer or partial guide (gradual fading). When fading is complete and the operator can use the new machine competently without any cues, the training is finished.

Information processing approach

Cognitive approaches to the process of learning stress the importance of the active involvement of the learner. Learning occurs within the mind of the trainee, and the task of the trainer is to set up the conditions to enable trainees to undergo this process for themselves. The trainee is a processor of information. There has been a number of writers who have developed theories of instruction using an information processing approach (Ausubel, 1963; Bruner, 1966; Anderson, 1983). Gagne (1988) based his approach on the five categories of learning outcomes examined in the previous section.

Having established the outcomes of the learning process, Gagne goes on to describe the critical events of instruction that must take place to result in learning. He views these events as setting the external conditions so that the essentially internal process of learning can occur. Gagne (1988) identifies nine events of learning shown in Figure 6.5 on p 149.

For Gagne, these events must take place in any instructional situation. Although the events tend to follow logically one from the other, they are not necessarily in a rigid sequence. For instance, Event One (gaining attention) is something that the trainer is likely to have to do a number of times in any training session as the attention of trainees naturally wanders from the task. The material to be learned may be broken down into discrete units so that Event Six (eliciting performance) may take place a number of times as the trainee undertakes different aspects of the tasks to be learned.

This description of Gagne's learning events presupposes, however, a linear program design. That is, each unit of material can be treated as separate for the purposes of instruction, and the trainee progresses from one to the next as though on a straight line. For more complex or extended bodies of material, this linear approach may not be practicable. It may be necessary for the trainee to grasp all of the material at a fairly simple level of understanding before being equipped to deal with the complexities of the material at a more advanced level. Thus, the trainee may revisit each of the topic areas a number of times during the program, extending and deepening his or her knowledge each time. This 'spiral' approach to learning is illustrated in Figure 6.6 on p 150.

Figure 6.5 — Gagne's nine learning events

1. **Gaining attention** Some rapid stimulus to engage the interest of the trainee and focus attention on the learning to take place.
2. **Informing the learner of the program objectives** The trainee needs to know what they are aiming for and why they should give the trainer their attention.
3. **Stimulating recall of prior learning** Establish the connections of the current learning material to things that have already been learned. Also establishes the deficiencies in the trainee's knowledge which needs to be addressed by the trainer.
4. **Presenting material with distinctive features** The trainer highlights what is new or different about the material, drawing the trainee's attention to where the learning effort needs to be focused.
5. **Providing learning guidance** Making the material as accessible as possible to the trainee. This would involve the use of concrete examples and relating ideas to those with which the trainee is already familiar.
6. **Eliciting performance** The trainee is required to demonstrate his or her mastery of the new material. This may involve carrying out a task of explaining new concepts or ideas.
7. **Providing information feedback** The trainee is told how well the performance went. Feedback can be given in various forms, for example, results of a test, comments on performance, machine-based as in computer-based training.
8. **Assessing performance** The trainee undertakes a final performance which is formally assessed by the trainer to ensure that the learning has taken place.
9. **Enhancing retention and transfer** Providing extra practice for the trainee after the period of formal instruction is over. This may involve the use of skills and knowledge in new situations or simply improving performance in the work situation.

Source: Gagne, Briggs and Wager (1988)

Based on Bruner's (1966) instructional theories, the spiral design requires the designer to state the prerequisites for each unit of the program so that the material is sequenced in such a manner that each part of the spiral is firmly founded on the material below it. As Romiszowski (1981) observes, this approach demands very close attention to detail on the part of the designer; particularly if there is more than one trainer involved in instruction.

Figure 6.6 — The spiral curriculum: schematic representation of the concept of the spiral curriculum with 6 topics — A to F

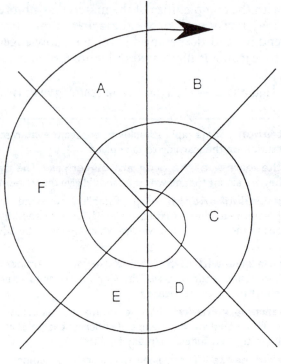

Source: Romiszowski (1981)

The information processing approach therefore sets the conditions for the internal processes of learning which are to take place within the learner. The design focuses on ways and means of guiding the thought processes of the trainee rather than eliciting a required behaviour attached to a particular stimulus. Thus, certain techniques are relatively common in the information processing approach. These include the use of advance organisers which give the trainee a 'preview' of the material which is coming next in the program and serve as 'maps' through the material. The importance of using all the senses to gain attention and help with retention is stressed by the information processing approach; thus, any means of displaying information through the use of visual and audio aids is common practice in this approach to design. Generally, the importance of sequencing material is highlighted by information processing theorists as critical to the understanding of the trainee; this is particularly true, of course, in the spiral design.

A program to teach staff about a new company procedure based on information processing principles might run as follows. The trainer gains the attention of the trainees by handing out a copy of the new procedure to each trainee (event one). This also serves to help trainees to recall prior learning (event three). The trainer then proceeds to outline the structure of the training session and review the sort of material the trainees will be learning during the program (event two).

The trainer might point out how the new procedure is based on similar procedures already used in the company (events three and five) and proceed to give a description of its operation highlighting the important points as the session unfolds (event four). To help the trainees understand the material, the trainer uses a series of visual aids and a number of exercises in which the trainees are required to apply the procedure in a variety of possible situations (event six). Finally, the program ends with a paper and pencil test (event eight) and some feedback on individual performance (event seven).

Adult learning approach

Writers on adult learning, such as Rogers, Knowles, Kolb and others, are not propounding new theories of learning: see Chapter 3. Their concerns are centred on how to satisfy adult needs for responsibility and autonomy within the context of an educational or training program. Thus, the adult learning literature tends to prescribe instructional practices for the trainer which will fulfil the needs of the trainees without investigating how the learning takes place.

Figure 6.7 — Conditions of adult learning and implications for trainers

Conditions of Adult Learning	Implications for Trainers
Learning is a basic human activity and need	Training is not essential to learning but may facilitate it
Adult learners need to feel that they are treated as adults	Trainers and trainees need to structure the learning together so that it is relevant to the needs of the trainees
Adults bring their needs to the learning situation	Training should be individualised where possible
Adults bring their own experiences to the learning situation	Trainers must build on trainee experiences so that new knowledge can be integrated into old
Adults learn best when the self is not threatened	Trainers must create an ethos in which no trainee feels threatened or inhibited
Adults learn at different speeds	Trainers should use self-paced methods where possible
Adults have a variety of learning styles	Trainers must recognise these styles and be flexible in their approach
Adults bring declining physiological features to the learning situation	Trainers must ensure that material is not presented too quickly for processing

Source: Burns (1995: 256–7)

Typical of this literature are the writings of Malcolm Knowles (1970; 1984) who, as we have already seen, makes a number of key assumptions about adult learners which, he feels, differentiate them from children learning in a school environment. Generally, Knowles believes that adults will be more motivated to learn those things of practical relevance to them and will tend to draw on their experience of life to explain the new material they encounter. As a result, the trainer (facilitator) needs to involve the adult trainees as much as possible in the design of the program and play a guiding, rather than an instructional, role. This approach remains very popular within the training community, particularly in the sphere of management and organisational development, where many management development activities emphasise the importance of managers taking responsibility for their own development.

In designing a program based on adult learning principles, the designer might begin with an unstructured group discussion amongst potential trainees about the nature of the training need and the variety of learning activities that might best suit their circumstances and dispositions. Thus, the trainees are closely involved in the design process from the very beginning. The designer adopts the role of a facilitator in much the same way as the analyst facilitates the activities of the group-based methods of training analysis discussed in Chapter 5. The resulting program design will have the commitment of the trainees who will participate in it. The program itself would also have a significant element of trainee control. The emphasis would typically be on the group of participants drawing up rules governing their own behaviour on the program and ensuring that their own actions and attitudes were directed towards the achievement of the objectives of the program.

The content of the program could vary a great deal depending on the nature of the group. There may well be, in fact, no hard and fast design; activities may vary from one group of trainees to the next. However, activities may well be based on an experiential approach, in which simulation, role plays, case studies and open group discussion play a significant part: see Chapter 8 for a full discussion of these methods. Generally, the role of the trainer will be that of guiding the group through the exercises, and ensuring that the group meets its own objectives, sticks to its own rules and receives feedback on the performance of each member.

Training Strategies

Within all three theoretical approaches to design, a basic division can be discerned in the methods and techniques employed. Trainees can be informed by the trainer using an expositive strategy, or trainees can discover things for themselves through a discovery strategy. This section is concerned with the application of these basic strategies, and their relationship to the content of the program.

Exposition versus discovery

Although the concept of expositive strategy is often associated with the behaviourists, and discovery strategies with the cognitive school, the discussion above clearly shows that both these strategies cut across the traditional theoretical boundaries. The behaviourist approach to the training of machine operators employs elements of both exposition (the trainer explains the operation of the machine or produces a step-by-step guide) and discovery (the trainee practises on the machine itself and learns about its operation). Similarly, Gagne's events include a considerable degree of exposition (events 4 and 5) with some discovery (events 3 and 6). Needless to say, the adult learning model tends to lean heavily in the direction of discovery while retaining room for elements of exposition if the trainees decide it is appropriate.

The basic steps involved in each of these strategies are almost mirror image reversals of one another. Romiszowski (1981) describes the features of each strategy in four steps, starting with the *expositive strategy*:

1. Presenting information through either explanation or demonstration.
2. Testing for reception, recall and understanding. Repeating the information if necessary.
3. Presenting opportunities for practice.
4. Presenting opportunities for applying the information in the real world.

For the *discovery strategy*:

1. Presenting opportunities to act and observe the consequences of action.
2. Testing for understanding of the cause and effect relationship.
3. Testing for the formation of general principles in the minds of the trainees.
4. Presenting opportunities for testing the applicability of the principles to real situations.

The expositive strategy is therefore working *from* an explanation of the principle *to* action in the real world. The discovery strategy is working in reverse, generalising *from* experience in the world *to* the general principle. The choice of which strategy to use depends not on the theoretical framework within which the design is cast, but upon the content of the program itself.

Knowledge versus skill

In the previous chapter, a distinction was drawn between the different elements of a job in terms of knowledge, skills and abilities. For practical purposes, a basic division can be drawn between knowledge on the one hand and skills and abilities on the other. In so far as an ability may be defined as a higher level cognitive capability to perform a job, then the distinction between skills and abilities becomes somewhat artificial. Knowledge, however, can be viewed as that foundation upon which skills/abilities rest, consisting of facts, concepts and procedures, etc. The content of any training program will include elements of either knowledge or skill, and usually both. Which instructional strategy is suited to which form of content? The answer to this question depends on the type of knowledge or skill under consideration.

Romiszowski (1981) analyses knowledge into facts, concepts, procedures and principles. The sheer volume of facts it is necessary to learn makes it impractical for discovery techniques. Facts can be learned this way, but exposition is a much more efficient method. The same can be said for procedures in which the trainee has to learn to follow a given series of steps; since learning procedures do not require the deep understanding of the reasoning behind them, exposition is often a more effective method for learning. Concepts and principles, however, require a deeper level of understanding, as they form the basis for the accumulation of factual and procedural knowledge. Again, although exposition of concepts and principles is possible (and frequent), discovery enables the knowledge to be more deeply absorbed and retained.

Skills stand on a foundation of knowledge. Thus, any attempt to learn skills will also involve the learning of the necessary knowledge. Skills training involves three basic steps:

1. Imparting necessary knowledge. This may be in any of the forms discussed above.
2. Demonstrating the skill and providing the opportunity to practise.
3. Providing more opportunities to develop the skill further.

The knowledge content of the first step will determine the type of strategy which is appropriate. Demonstration of a skill is basically expository, although the practice may involve the use of discovery techniques as the trainees work out for themselves the best way to accomplish the task. The final step of ongoing practice, possibly without the presence of the trainer, will be more discovery-based.

Both strategies are therefore required in the learning of either knowledge or skills. The type of knowledge and the level at which the skill is being practised will determine the type of strategy which is appropriate.

Competency-based design

Using the data from the type of competency analysis discussed in the previous chapter, many modern skills training programs are based on the notion of competency profiling (Foyster, 1990). The competency profile takes the process of analysis a stage further, and builds up a picture of the competencies required by a competent worker. The profile is constructed from the units of competency, and their constituent elements identified at the analysis stage. This information is then transformed into performance objectives which are the basis of the training program design.

Often, groups of workers will not be required to be competent in every area identified. Thus, the competency profile will also include the specification of which groups of workers will require which competencies and to what level they have to be mastered. The program can then be structured around the actual needs of the workers, rather than giving all workers 'blanket' coverage of all the competencies identified in the analysis process.

The process of training reform in recent years (see Chapter 2) has embedded competency-based design as the major design principle governing the development of training programs in Australia. This is because, in order to gain national recognition for their training programs, training providers must design their programs around the relevant industry competency standards. Smith and Keating (1997) identify six main stages in the design of competency-based training programs.

Illustration 6.1 — Competency-based training at Pirelli Cables

> CBT is an integral component of the enterprise agreement at Pirelli Cables. Pirelli employs approximately 560 staff at two factories in Sydney. The primary focus of the company's training strategy has been the development of CBT programs for the company's operational staff. Since 1977 when the company commenced operations in Australia, either semi-skilled people with no experience in the industry were recruited as operators, or sometimes experienced employees were poached from other firms. Training was unstructured. The lack of structured training meant there was no career path for employees in the company.
>
> Pirelli's CBT program is based on the skill units identified for each of the factories. The skill units were identified as part of the workplace restructuring process which led to the enterprise agreement. Rather than engaging a consultant to undertake the skills audits the company decided to go it alone. The company believes that by doing their own analysis employees acquired a sense of ownership over the process and the enterprise agreement.
>
> Once the skill units were established and agreed, each unit was divided into five levels and definitions appropriate to the skill unit applied. The five levels were:
>
> - trainee
> - basic skilled
> - skilled
> - multi-skilled
> - advanced multi-skilled.
>
> Pirelli then embarked on the development of the CBT program for each of the skill units. The aim was to have a system whereby an operator could complete all or part of the CBT program depending on their need and their skill level. Training was to be self-paced and self-directed, allowing employees to complete activities within a module and move on to the next activity when they felt confident about having mastered a certain skill.
>
> In 1993 Pirelli changed their approach to the development of CBT to avoid the perception amongst employees that CBT was a Human Resource Department project. Supervisors felt excluded from the process. Under the new approach, the Technical Training Manager co-ordinates CBT development and the supervisors conduct the brainstorming sessions with employees and write the modules.

Source: New South Wales Board of Vocational Education and Training (1994) Vol 2 21–23

1. **Use of competency standards** As discussed in Chapter 2, most industries are covered by competency standards. These have been developed by the competency setting bodies, usually the relevant industry training advisory bodies (ITABs), and cover all the occupations found in those industries. Some larger organisations, such as McDonald's and the National Australia Bank, have set their own enterprise competency standards to cover their own unique operations.

2. **Curriculum development** 'Curriculum' is an educational term that refers to the planned learning experiences trainees undergo during the training program (Print, 1993). In order to gain accreditation and recognition for

the training program, the curriculum for the program has to be produced in a standardised format. This is to ensure that the accreditation body can be sure that the proposed training program meets all the requirements of the competency standards for the occupation. In some cases, specialist training providers have established themselves as curriculum developers. These curriculum developers then sell their curriculum 'products' to other training providers who wish to develop particular training courses.

3. **Modularisation** A key feature of competency-based training programs is that they consist of freestanding modules. Usually between 20 and 60 hours in length, training modules allow a variety of training programs to be constructed from already existing training materials. They also allow training programs to be customised to the needs of different groups of trainees, and allow trainees to enter and exit training programs at a variety of points in the program.

4. **Learning outcomes** Learning outcomes state what trainees are able to do as a result of undergoing the training program. As we noted earlier, learning outcomes are closely related to behavioural training objectives, and should state what trainees will be capable of doing in a clear and measurable way. The correct statement of learning outcomes enables assessment of trainee progress to be more effectively carried out.

5. **Mode and place of learning** Under the principles of competency-based training, training can take place in a variety of settings. In particular, developers of competency-based training have tried to break down the traditional reliance of trainers on formal off-the-job classroom-based training and, instead, turned to the workplace as the most important venue for training activities. In practice, competency-based training can include elements of both on-the-job and off-the-job training, as well as learning materials which trainees can study in their own time in a setting of their choosing.

6. **Accreditation** When the training program has finally been developed, the program needs to be accredited in order to gain national recognition. National recognition means that trainees will be able to gain recognition for having undergone accredited training in any state in Australia. Each state and territory has its own accreditation body which accredits training programs. The accreditation process involves the use of a number of national criteria. If the program meets the accreditation criteria, it automatically gains national recognition. Accreditation for training programs is normally given for up to five years.

This is now the standard process for the development of competency-based training programs in Australia. However, the process has not been without its critics. In particular, critics have highlighted the complexity and time-consuming nature of the accreditation process (Smith and Keating, 1997). Many enterprises have been compelled to accredit their training programs so that their employees possess recognised qualifications at the end of their training. However, the process of accreditation is very bureaucratic, can often take many months and may be very expensive for the enterprise. Many private training providers feel that the public training providers such as TAFE are often given precedence in the accreditation process by government bodies anxious to protect their training systems.

The Training Environment

The effective implementation of training programs, however, does not simply depend on how well the program has been designed. The environment in which the training takes place must encourage the trainee to learn. Thus, the trainer needs to ensure that the training environment is correct for the training program. There is a number of aspects of the training environment highlighted as particularly critical for the implementation of training programs (Wexley and Latham, 1991).

Trainees need to be able to practise what they are being taught. The level of practice required may decline as the trainee becomes more competent, but the opportunity for practice is very important. It is the improvement of practice opportunities that is one of the key reasons for the favouring of a workplace setting for training in many modern training programs. The workplace provides the trainee with the actual setting in which the new skills will have to be used. This also enhances the transfer of training: see below pp 158–162. A particular issue in practice is how it should be distributed. Should practice be given in one session (massed training), or should practice opportunities be made available for shorter periods but more frequently (distributed training)? Industrial psychologists have shown that rest between practice sessions is important in improving the performance of trainees (McGehee and Thayer, 1961). However, distributed training is often difficult to arrange in workplace settings where equipment cannot be made available or where managers are reluctant to release trainees more than once from their jobs for training sessions.

In some cases, trainees need to be able to practise their new skills beyond the point at which they might be expected to have reasonably acquired the new skills. However, in some occupations, an automatic response is required for changing conditions in the job. An example of this might be an aeroplane pilot, who needs to be able to carry out procedures correctly and quickly. In this case, training will emphasise overlearning so that the skills of the pilot will become reflex actions. Overlearning involves the opportunity to practise a skill beyond the point of mastery so that the performance of actions becomes drilled into the subconscious of the trainee.

The size of the unit to be learned also impacts on the design of the training environment. The parts of a training unit may be broken up to facilitate learning. Figure 6.8 on p 158 illustrates the three main ways in which training can be broken up.

Figure 6.8 — Breaking up a training program

	Phase 1	Phase 2	Phase 3
Whole Training	A+B+C	A+B+C	A+B+C
Pure-Part Training	A	B	C
Progressive-Part Training	A	A+B	A+B+C

Source: Wexley and Latham (1991)

Whole training consists of practising all the components of the training program in each phase. Pure-part training involves practising each component of the training program separately. Progressive-part training allows the trainee to build up a picture of the whole of the training as the program progresses. In effect, the choice of strategy depends on the nature of the task. For tasks that involve a high interdependency of sub-tasks, whole or progressive-part training may be appropriate. For tasks in which the sub-tasks are relatively independent of each other, pure-part training is possible.

The final element in the training environment is feedback. Locke and Latham (1984) have shown that feedback is essential for trainees to learn and retain their learning. Feedback shows trainees when they have completed a task correctly, increases interest in the training and enables trainees to set themselves goals that aid learning.

The most powerful form of feedback is positive. This echoes the behaviourist approach to shaping behaviour, in which negative feedback is viewed as a punishment for a trainee exhibiting the wrong behaviour, and which encourages the use of positive feedback to ensure the development of the positive aspects of trainee behaviour. However, feedback does not have to be exclusively external. A well-designed training program will allow trainees to generate internal feedback by setting goals which they can achieve. The achievement of the goal provides the internal feedback which may be supported by the external feedback from the trainer.

Transferring Training to the Workplace

The key question in any design is how to ensure the transfer of training to the working environment. Annett and Sparrow (1985) define the concept of the transfer of training thus:

> Transfer of training is the term used to describe the benefit obtained from having had previous training or experience in acquiring a new skill or in adapting an old skill to a new situation.

Three possible types of transfer are generally recognised. Positive transfer occurs when the skills acquired in the one situation produce a significantly better performance in another situation. Negative transfer occurs when the skills acquired produce a lower level of performance in the second situation. Zero transfer occurs when the skills acquired in one situation have no impact on performance in the second situation. A common example of transfer is driving a car. A person trained to drive an automatic car will have little difficulty in adjusting to drive another automatic. This is a case of high positive transfer of the original training. However, the same driver may encounter considerable problems in dealing with a manual change car, which requires a set of different responses such as depressing the clutch, changing gear, etc. This would be an example of negative transfer, where the original training on an automatic car intrudes on the driver's ability to learn how to drive a manual vehicle. Learning to drive a car would, of course, have virtually no impact on the driver's ability to ride a bicycle (zero transfer).

Illustration 6.2 — Accrediting training at BHP Steel

BHP Steel is one of the key divisions of Australia's largest company. The division employs 27,000 people at a range of locations from the large steelworks at Port Kembla to small service centres with less than 20 employees. In 1994, BHP Steel became a self-accrediting body with the power to grant an externally recognised qualification for training programs developed in the company. Margrit Stocker, Training Consultant at BHP Steel, described the benefits of accreditation to the company:

> This accreditation process is a benefit to us as it provides standards and guidelines for good practice in the writing and delivery of training for our employees. Hence it provides a logical and structured competency-based approach to divisional training: so we know what competencies employees have or acquire. A major benefit of this accreditation is that our training will have clearly defined learning outcomes in the form of required competencies related to qualifications, so becomes widely recognised and thus portable across workplaces.

BHP Steel established a three tier process for accreditation of their training.

- **Tier 1.** Training material is submitted to the Divisional Accreditation Panel which includes external specialists who review the material. Once the committee is satisfied that the material meets the accreditation standards it recommends it to the second tier.
- **Tier 2.** The Steel Group Accreditation Council comprises both BHP and non-BHP members. The non-BHP members include the chair of the NSW accreditation authority (VETAB), a union representative and independent training experts.
- **Tier 3**. The decision of the Steel Group Accreditation Council is forwarded to VETAB which registers the decision and returns the appropriate certification which is then forwarded to the relevant department via the Divisional Accreditation Committee.

BHP Steel believes that accreditation not only benefits the company but also its employees. Accreditation means that employees will be able to get recognition for the competencies they already possess. They will also know exactly what skills and knowledge they require to progress within the company.

Source: New South Wales Board of Vocational Education and Training (1994) Vol 1 13–20

In behavioural terms, positive transfer will occur when the stimuli in the work situation and the responses required are as close as possible to the stimuli experienced and the responses learned in the training situation. As the stimuli experienced and the responses learned begin to differ, the transfer will become increasingly negative (Holding, 1965). Misko (1995) identifies two forms of positive transfer of training: near transfer and far transfer. Near transfer occurs when skills learned in a slightly different situation are applied successfully to the new situation. Thus, to continue the driving analogy, drivers of a manual car should be able to use their knowledge to learn how to change gears on trucks. These are different, but near, situations. Far transfer involves using skills learned in one context to help develop skills in a very different situation. Thus, the driver of a car might be able to use the general principles of reading and using the instruments on the dashboard to help in learning to use the instruments in an aeroplane. These are very different situations, but the general principles of instrument reading can be transferred. The difficulty for trainers therefore lies in designing programs which maximise positive transfer, that is, designing training situations which replicate the work environment and teach the actual skills required.

Theories of transfer

There are two major theoretical explanations of the transfer process. The theory of identical elements is a behaviourist explanation first put forward by Thorndike in the early twentieth century (Thorndike and Woodworth, 1901). Identical elements theory argues that transfer will only occur if there are considerable similarities between the two situations or tasks. These similarities may lead to either positive or negative transfer. Highest positive transfer will occur if both stimuli and responses are identical, as in the example of driving the two automatic cars above. Highest negative transfer will occur in situations where the stimuli are the same but the responses required are different, as in the case of changing from driving an automatic to driving a manual car. Where both stimuli and responses required are different, no transfer will take place.

The second theory emphasises the importance of general transferable principles. Some writers have argued that if trainees are given an understanding of general principles that apply across a range of tasks, trainees will become adaptable enough to deal with a wide variety of situations (Fleishman, 1972). This approach has obvious cognitive orientations, as distinct from Thorndike's behaviourist account of training transfer. Transfer through principles highlights the ability of trainees to be able to apply general principles in a wide variety of situations and so dramatically reduce the amount of time they require to become proficient at new tasks. Research sponsored by the American Society for Training and Development seems to indicate that it is general transferable skills, rather than specific task skills, that employers require of their employees, so reinforcing the transfer through principles concept (Carnevale, Meltzer and Gainer, 1990).

Both explanations of training transfer, however, have been criticised as being founded on outmoded and discredited psychological theories. Annett and

Sparrow (1985) argue that human skills can be viewed as 'plans'; that is, a series of actions which are learned to deal with specific situations. These plans are formed from more detailed sub-plans and, in turn, are often parts of higher-level superordinate plans (that is, abilities). Learning involves acquiring a new sub-plan. However, in situations which call up an existing superordinate plan, we may revert to the old sub-plan which has not been completely erased from memory. Also, as situations change, so the plans we have learned become out of date and inhibit our ability to respond in an appropriate manner: this is negative transfer.

This point is highlighted when considering the skills required by operators working in complex industries such as the nuclear power or chemical industries (Hirschorn, 1984). In these industries, operators are required to monitor processes using instruments on a control panel. They are trained to react in certain ways to particular combinations of instrument indications; plans are created. However, as the nuclear accident at Three Mile Island in the United States showed, there may be a variety of possible interpretations of instrument readings. In this situation, the readings the power station operators saw on the control panel did not reflect the situation they had been trained to expect; their plans were defective.

The resulting response of the operators was fatally flawed. Operators trained to react in a particular way can make disastrous mistakes (negative transfer). Training may need to focus on the vagaries of the control system rather than on understanding the processes which it represents; continuous training may also be required to minimise the possibility of negative transfer in critical situations.

Latham and Crandall (1991) have shown, however, that it is not simply the design of the training program that affects transfer. Organisational and social factors in the workplace may have a profound impact on the ability of trainees successfully to use their new skills. The key factors that affect transfer of training in the workplace appear to be:

Pay and promotion

As behaviourist psychologists have long noted, pay is a major determinant of work behaviour. If trainees are not paid to use their new skills, or are rewarded for not using them, then transfer of training will be inhibited. At a managerial level, executives who feel they have not been rewarded with promotion for learning new skills through MBA programs and the like may be more inclined to leave the organisation.

Environmental constraints

Work has to be organised and the technology made available for trainees to use their new skills. Smith (1997) reports the case of one organisation that trained its production workers in the skills of collecting statistical quality data as part of a quality improvement campaign. However, on the job, workers were not allowed to collect or record the data, which was viewed by local managers as a technician level activity. Thus, the quality improvement skills of the trainees quickly faded.

Peer group

The power of the peer group at work has been recognised since the Hawthorne experiments of the 1920s and 1930s first investigated the impact of social relations at the workplace. The support of the peer group is needed if trainees are to be able to use new skills.

Supervisory support

Similarly, the behaviour of the supervisor is critical to the ability of trainees to use their new skills. The supervisor controls key aspects of the trainees' work environment and can make a substantial difference to their ability to perform.

Figure 6.9 shows eight points which need to be considered in the design of programs to enhance transfer.

Figure 6.9— Enhancing the transfer of training

1. **Rote learning discourages transfer**. Rote learning cannot teach the comprehension needed to apply skills across a range of situations.
2. **Meaningful learning promotes transfer**. In the information processing sense, material is placed within a context to facilitate understanding.
3. **Integrate theory and practice**. The knowledge base underlying skills should be used to highlight the common principles underlying different skills and their application.
4. **Use varied examples and experiences**. Examples which point out relationships and distinctions are useful in promoting transfer.
5. **Use discovery learning**. Plans created by the trainee rather than imposed by the trainer are likely to be more durable and flexible.
6. **Making use of abilities**. If abilities are viewed as higher level skills, then trainees who can be selected on the basis of their ability in a particular area may be more capable of transferring skills between tasks than others without that ability.
7. **Learning to learn**. A metacognitive strategy to enhance learning skill and transfer.
8. **Motivate learners**. Convincing learners of the benefits to them of learning a skill and structuring the program so that trainees work to short-term, realistic goals and achieve them.

Summary

This chapter has examined aspects of designing and implementing training programs. Training and learning have often been characterised as systems. In this view, training is a process which has certain inputs and outputs. Inputs can be in the form of trainees or training materials; outputs can be in the form of skilled workers. The systems approach describes a methodical design process which starts with training analysis, moving on to the writing of objectives and, finally, to designing the program. At a systems level, Romiszowski proposes four levels of instructional design: the course system, the lesson level, the instructional event level and the learning step level. However, the 'top-down' systems model has been criticised as rather prescriptive in its orientation and not adequately dealing with the realities of training and development in organisations.

Training design is most heavily influenced by the objectives for the training program. Early attempts to classify learning objectives resulted in Bloom's taxonomy of educational objectives, which divided the objects of learning into three domains: cognitive, affective and motor skill. Gagne developed Bloom's taxonomy into a classification of learning outcomes. Gagne identified five categories, including intellectual skills, cognitive skills, verbal information, motor skills and attitudes. Of these, intellectual skills are the most important, as they are fundamental to the development of the other four outcomes. Mager took a behavioural approach and emphasised the importance of clear performance objectives for the development of effective training material.

The process of design is influenced by both theory and strategy. Behaviourism, information processing and adult learning theory all have major implications for instruction. A behaviourist approach will stress the importance of eliciting the correct response to the stimulus, using the techniques of cues and fading to achieve this. Information processing theorists such as Gagne emphasise the setting of external conditions so that the internal process of learning is facilitated. Adult learning writers focus on the needs of the adult for autonomy and responsibility in the learning process. There are two basic instructional strategies. Expositive strategies involve the trainer giving information to trainees; discovery strategies involve the trainees finding out the information for themselves. The use of each of these strategies depends on the content of the program in terms of knowledge and skill. Competency-based programs focus on training in specific job competencies with clear assessment of achievement, often using self-paced material.

A crucial design problem is how to ensure the positive transfer of training to the workplace. The behaviourist approach stresses the matching of the training and the working environments so that the trainee experiences the same stimuli and responses in both. A more cognitive approach asserts that trainees should be taught transferable general principles that can be used in a variety of situations.

Discussion Questions

1. How useful is systems theory in the design of training programs?
2. What activities might not be reducible to behavioural performance objectives?
3. Give some examples of positive and negative transfer of training.
4. In what situations would a behavioural approach to training design be preferable to an information processing approach?
5. Is the distinction between knowledge and skill a helpful depiction of reality?
6. What are the drawbacks to the competency-based approach to training design?

Chapter 7

Delivering Training

In previous chapters we discussed the process of designing training, from needs analysis through to design. This discussion has largely been conducted at the level of strategy, that is, the overall design that will satisfy the training needs. The process of design, however, does not finish with a plan for instruction. Beyond this, the trainer has to address the question of operationalising the instructional design. Romiszowski (1981) termed this activity the fourth level of instructional design: it is the selection of instructional media; how the training is to be carried out; and the techniques and technologies that will have to be deployed to realise the design.

This chapter is concerned with decisions involved in the delivery of training. The chapter opens with an examination of the role of the trainer in the delivery of training. It then goes on to examine the methods and media which can be deployed in modern training programs. There is a bewildering array of methods and media which trainers can employ in the delivery of training programs. A full discussion of even the most common would itself require a book. The confines of a single chapter therefore means that the topics covered will be highly selective, and cannot be said to be fully representative of the range of methods and media at the disposal of the modern trainer. Methods vary from the techniques that trainers use such as lectures, syndicate work, role playing and so on, to the general types of training in common use in industry and commerce. A wide range of media is similarly available to the trainer, particularly since the advent of computers into training. In the interests of selectivity, this chapter will focus on three of the more significant media coming into common use by the training profession.

The Role of the Trainer

The delivery of training is one of the critical activities for trainers. In Chapter 1, we explored the roles of the training practitioner. In both the ASTD studies in the United States and the research conducted for the development of the workplace trainer competencies in Australia, the role of the trainer as an instructor or facilitator of learning is featured as central to the practice of training. Tovey (1997) identifies three roles for the trainer in the delivery of training: those of instructor, facilitator, and resource.

The **instructor** is the traditional role of the trainer in delivery of training. In this role, the trainer is a subject matter expert and delivers the material directly to trainees. This may be in the form of the traditional 'stand and deliver' model of off-the-job training, or through instruction in the workplace through on-the-job training.

The facilitator role is derived from the application of the adult learning principles developed by Knowles and Rogers, which we examined in Chapter 3. The basic premise of adult learning is that trainees manage their own learning; the trainer acts as a guide through the process. This is the role of the facilitator. The focus of the facilitator is on the trainees rather than on the content of the training, and the trainer may not be a subject matter expert, able to answer all the questions of the trainees. The trainer will arrange for learning resources to be available for trainees when they are needed, and will ensure that the learning is taking place and that no trainees are left behind in the process.

Figure 7.1 — Critical success factors in the delivery of training

Critical Success Factor	Definition
Focusing on Outputs	Creating a shared view of the outcomes of the training rather than focusing on the inputs to the process.
Gaining Managerial Support	Management endorsement of training raises the priority that the training will receive in the workplace.
Knowing Clear Business Outcomes	All training should lead to improvements in individual and business performance.
Creating Systems that 'Sing the Praises' of Learning	Getting the organisation to align its systems with the objectives of training.
Securing Accountability	Learning is the responsibility of everyone in the organisation not simply the training specialists.
Aligning with the Best	Identifying the most suitable application or accessing expertise that can enlighten and stimulate the training effort.
Celebrating Champions	Maintaining energy and enthusiasm by celebrating those in the organisation who get results.
Aiming for 'Just-in-Time' Learning	All training should be delivered to the job at the time it is needed.

Source: Rylatt and Lohan, 1995: 21–43

The **resource** role treats the trainer as simply one amongst a number of resources trainees can use. In this role, the trainer does not need to be present when the trainees are going through the learning process but should be available when needed. The focus of the trainer in this role is on the learning process and ensuring that learning is taking place. The trainer may use learning contracts that set goals for the trainees but leave the achievement of the goals largely in the hands of the trainees.

Rylatt and Lohan (1995) go further than the role of the trainer in the instructional delivery of training, and identify the critical success factors that underpin the effective delivery of training. These are summarised in Figure 7.1 on p 165.

Training Methods

This section will examine four methods of training: induction (sometimes referred to as orientation or socialisation), on-the-job training, behaviour modelling and distance, or open, learning. The inclusion of induction in a discussion of training methods may appear a little surprising. However, induction is a form of training which cuts across the usual categories. Although the induction process is most commonly thought of as the initial training which new entrants to an organisation would receive, initial training may not be confined to these organisation at entry ports. As employees progress through the organisation or simply move between workplaces, they undergo a broad process of socialisation to the new job they have acquired. Thus, induction, whether formal or informal, continues to recur throughout the organisational life of an individual. It is this 'recurring' nature of induction which explains its presence in this chapter.

All four methods discussed in this chapter are becoming increasingly important as organisations strive to improve productivity and efficiency, through induction to enable new employees to contribute as quickly as possible, on-the-job training to improve performance at the operational level, behaviour modelling as a way of improving the 'people skills' of staff and managers, and open learning to deliver off-the-job training outside the conventional classroom format.

Induction training

Three terms are commonly used in referring to the training of new entrants to the organisation: induction, orientation and socialisation. These terms are not interchangeable.

Orientation takes its meaning from the literal meaning of the term, that is, the process of pointing new employees in the right direction, enabling them to find their way about the organisation. It may be argued, however, that orientation is about much more than this; orientation may be viewed as 'the process through which a new hire acquires a commitment to the organization' (Warren, 1979). The process of orientation is located not only in the training which the organisation provides to new entrants, but in the entire recruitment and selection process. Thus, the potential new entrant begins the orientation process by applying to the organisation; the job advertisements or the employment agencies used by the organisation inevitably tell the applicant something about the organisation. The process of building commitment continues through the screening, interviews, induction, training and final review of the new entrant after he or she has spent some time with the organisation.

Socialisation is a still broader process. Originating in sociology, the concept of socialisation refers to the way in which members of society acquire the beliefs and values of the other members of the society. Thus, socialisation takes place through a variety of institutions such as the family, schools and media, as well as organisations over a long period of time. Upon entering any new organisation, the newcomer learns the values, norms and behaviour patterns unique to that organisation. Schein (1988) explains what these values, norms and behaviour patterns are about:

> ... the basic goals of the organisation. The preferred means by which these goals should be achieved. The basic responsibilities of the member in the role which is being granted to him by the organization. The behaviour patterns which are required for effective performance in the role. A set of rules or principles which pertain to the maintenance of the identity and integrity of the organization.

Thus, socialisation can occur through a wide range of activities, formal and informal in the organisation: the selection process, training, interactions with superiors or other workers, critical events at work, etc. In fact, as in society at large, socialisation within the organisation can be a long-term activity, with employees undergoing periodic 'resocialisation' as they change location or workgroup.

Induction is a much more specific term, usually referring to the formal training content of orientation or socialisation. Many of the stages in the process of socialisation are accompanied by some form of training. Most commonly, however, induction training will take place at the time of the new entrant's arrival in the organisation.

There is a number of reasons why induction takes place in organisations. There is evidence to show that labour turnover is highest amongst those who have most recently joined an organisation (Kenney and Reid, 1995). Induction training, by helping to socialise the new entrant, may help to reduce that level of turnover. A study of labour turnover and absenteeism in the Australian car industry demonstrated that both phenomena were strongly correlated with the degree of commitment of employees to the company (Automotive Industry Council, 1990). If induction generates greater commitment on the part of the trainee, then it may be a powerful tool in reducing turnover. Legislative concerns are also of increasing importance. The employer has a duty to inform employees of occupational health and safety rules in the organisation, equal employment opportunity policies and general work rules that govern conduct in the organisation. The formal induction is a convenient forum for this activity, and provides a record of employees having received that information in the case of litigation.

Schein (1988), however, highlights the reason for the current popularity of induction/socialisation in the workplace. He describes how in the 1950s heavy socialisation was standard in the larger American corporations. Conformity was the order of the day in companies such as IBM. In the 1960s, there was a strong reaction to this sort of corporate brainwashing; induction and socialisation became unfashionable until the 'shocking confrontation' with Asian companies in the 1970s and 1980s. In order to emulate their success, consultants such as Peters and Waterman (1982) advocated the creation of strong company cultures with an emphasis on the central role of formal induction for both new and existing employees. The role of induction and socialisation in improving employee performance and commitment became more fashionable.

What part does training play in this process of socialisation? Two ways have been suggested in which formal induction training increases employee commitment to the organisation (Feldman, 1989). First, trainees receive many cues about appropriate behaviour from induction training. These cues might include: the level of bureaucracy (the importance of rules and regulations), the difficulty of training material (the expected performance standards), the choice of trainers (supervisory and interpersonal style) and so on. All of these cues in the training program tell the new entrants how they will be expected to behave and the things which the organisation values. Secondly, induction training helps to develop norms of behaviour in the trainees. Induction programs are a fertile ground for the development of norms for a number of reasons:

1. The training group develops its own group norms which can be influenced by explicit statements from trainers or supervisors.
2. The trainer's reaction to behaviour in the program gives clues about the expected standards of behaviour.
3. The formality or informality of the program tells the trainees about the style of interpersonal relations in the organisation.
4. Organisations often hire people from similar backgrounds (local schools, etc). The induction program serves to show how the new environment is similar to the old, and reinforces group values.
5. Deviant behaviour can be identified and punished, demonstrating the limits of what is acceptable in the organisation.
6. Induction programs help to create and maintain diversity in the group roles, which is then transferred to the work setting.

Thus, the induction program is a powerful vehicle for socialisation. The content of most induction programs is, of course, at the level of the mundane (location of toilets, employment conditions, etc). While these elements of content are necessary and help employees perform more effectively after they are released into the workplace, it may well be that the primary effect of the training is at the level of the process of the program rather than the objective material delivered.

On-the-job training

On-the-job training (OJT) is training which occurs in the workplace. Of course, OJT is occurring all the time, whether it is planned or not (Laird, 1986). Individuals learn about their work constantly, refining methods of working, making the job easier for themselves, learning from others and so on. Very few employers would admit that no OJT takes place in their enterprises, and most would agree that it plays an important part in building the effectiveness of the organisation (Rothwell and Kazanas, 1990). What is not clear, however, is the extent to which OJT is intended and planned in the workplace and, conversely, to what extent it merely 'happens'. OJT is often differentiated from the more structured method of job instruction technique (JIT), in which the training is planned carefully by a trainer/supervisor skilled in instructional techniques (McCord, 1987).

JIT evolved in the United States from the Training Within Industry movement of World War II. Faced with the prospect of retraining an entirely new work force to work in the country's recently converted arms factories, the United States Government formed the Training Within Industry (TWI) service in 1940. TWI developed a series of programs underpinned by the philosophy that the best place to learn was on the job itself, and that the best instructor was the supervisor, who should be trained in the techniques of training and instruction (train the trainer). TWI persuaded industrialists that the jobs which they considered to be too skilled to learn in anything less than years could be broken down, using Tayloristic methods of job and task analysis, and passed on to trainees in a very short period of time, using a structured approach to instruction. This structured method of instruction boiled down to seven simple steps to be followed by the supervisor/instructor:

1. Show workers how to do it.
2. Explain the key points.
3. Let them watch you do it again.
4. Let them do the simple parts of the job.
5. Help them do the whole job.
6. Let them do the whole job, but watch them.
7. Put them on their own.

After the war, the TWI principles became the standard for OJT in American industry, and quickly spread with the adoption of Taylorism in other parts of the English-speaking world, including Australia. Refined into two parts, the TWI system included eight steps covering 'how to get ready to instruct' and 'how to instruct'. Modern JIT has collapsed the eight steps into five (Camp, Blanchard and Huszczo, 1986):

1. Prepare to teach. Decide what should be taught; gather tools and supplies; arrange the workplace.
2. Prepare the trainee. Put the trainee at ease; determine trainee knowledge and motivation.
3. Train the trainee. Describe and demonstrate; question trainee to assure learning; repeat demonstration if needed.
4. Trainee performs the job. Observe trainee; correct errors.
5. Trainee becomes a regular worker. Check to ensure performance is acceptable.

Figure 7.2 — Job instruction card

HOW TO GET READY TO INSTRUCT

Have a Time Table—
how much skill you expect him to have, and how soon.

Break Down the Job—
list principal steps.
pick out the key points.

Have Everything Ready—
the right equipment, materials, and supplies.

Have the Work Place Properly Arranged—
just as the worker will be expected to keep it.

Job Instructor Training

WAR MANPOWER COMMISSION
BUREAU OF TRAINING
TRAINING WITHIN INDUSTRY

KEEP THIS CARD HANDY
16—26793—2   GPO

HOW TO INSTRUCT

Step 1—Prepare the Worker
Put him at ease.
Find out what he already knows about the job.
Get him interested in learning job.
Place in correct position.

Step 2—Present the Operation
Tell, Show, Illustrate, and Question carefully and patiently.
Stress key points.
Instruct clearly and completely, taking up one point at a time—but no more than he can master.

Step 3—Try Out Performance
Test him by having him perform job.
Have him *tell* and *show* you; have him explain key points.
Ask questions and correct errors.
Continue until you know HE knows.

Step 4—Follow Up
Put him on his own. Designate to whom he goes for help.
Check frequently. Encourage questions. Get him to look for key points as he progresses.
Taper off extra coaching and close follow-up.   16—26793—3

If Worker Hasn't Learned,
the Instructor Hasn't Taught

Source: McCord (1987)

This sequence has formed the basis of structured or planned OJT since the 1950s, and is still the fundamental model used in many train the trainer programs in the country. The behaviourist origins of JIT are quite clear in its use of demonstration and feedback/correction, and may be the reason why it is still regarded as so appropriate to the workplace.

The ascendancy of competency-based training in Australia has added impetus to the renaissance of structured OJT. OJT has been described as possessing five characteristics (Connor, 1983):

1. The preparation of a task and skills analysis.
2. The development of performance-based objectives.

3. Training in the work environment.
4. Supplementation by other methods of training.
5. Criterion-referenced certification based on defined competencies.

OJT therefore is clearly based on the identification of skill training needs which are transformed into competencies. Trainees are then 'certified' on criteria which measure the competencies directly. The supervisor who carries the responsibility for OJT cannot certify trainees unless they meet each of the competency standards. OJT is competency-based training outside the classroom.

Illustration 7.1 Structured on-the-job training at IBM Australia

IBM established its manufacturing plant at Wangaratta in Victoria in 1976. The plant employs approximately 160 permanent employees and a further 300 casual staff. The plant was initially commissioned to produce the Selectric electric typewriter. However, it switched to production of personal computers in 1984 when the bottom fell out of the typewriter market. In order to give the plant viable production volumes, IBM decided to use the Wangaratta plant to supply computers to the entire SE Asian region. However, in order to secure this business the Wangaratta plant management had to show that they could meet Asian standards of cost and quality.

In order to achieve this, the plant hired only casual employees to staff the production areas of the plant. This lowered the costs of production significantly but raised the problem of achieving high levels of quality with a casual workforce. The answer for IBM was to put in place a structured on-the-job training program that ensured that production employees were highly skilled in their jobs.

New production employees receive a half day general induction from the training instructor in their area. New employees are given information that is directly relevant to their job covering health and safety, protective clothing and some product knowledge. After induction the new employees proceed to their section where they begin an intensive period of on-the-job instruction. The training is handled by the supervisor and the training instructor for the section. The training that each production employee receives is carefully documented in a manual that is given to the employees to help them master each task in the process of computer assembly. As employees achieve the required standard on the tasks they are 'signed-off' by the Engineering department. The sign-off process involves close observation and questioning of the employees by an engineer who then certifies employees on the basis of their performance.

The aim of the training is to achieve a fully qualified casual workforce. Production worker training at Wangaratta is a lengthy and highly structured activity. The use of casual staff and the quality standards which the plant has to meet have compelled IBM to adopt this structured approach to manage the problems associated with a large, shifting workforce.

Source: Smith et al, 1995

OJT has a number of distinct advantages as a training method. First, it optimises transfer of learning to the job. Since the training takes place on-the-job itself, full transfer should be possible once the trainee has been certified as competent. Secondly, the training process is accelerated as there is no off-the-job learning which has to be applied in the workplace; trainees have learned the job directly. Finally, OJT can appear to cost substantially less, as specialist training resources do not have to be committed to the training, which is carried out by the supervisor or an appropriately trained operator. There is no doubt that it is this latter factor of cost minimisation which attracts employers to the notion of OJT. This assumption is, however, less justified in specialised areas of work where the risk of damage to expensive equipment or the production of large quantities of scrap materials may be higher than the cost of setting up off-job training centres.

The difficulties with OJT centre on the informal nature of much training when placed in the workplace. The exigencies of production may easily relegate OJT to a lower priority in the minds of managers, with a consequent deterioration in the standard of training and lengthening of training time. Supervisors and 'expert' operators, although trained in instructional techniques, may not be as competent as a dedicated training instructor. Generally, OJT may be outside the control of the training practitioners in the organisation, with the result that training programs which involve extensive periods of training in the working environment may not be an efficient means of improving skills.

A compromise between off-the-job and on-the-job training is vestibule training. In this case, training takes place in an off-line production facility often near the actual workplace itself. The trainee learns to use the actual tools of the job but without the pressure of work. Although vestibule training shares with OJT a high level of transferability, the cost involved in dedicating equipment to training often dissuades managers from using this technique.

Behaviour modelling

Based on Albert Bandura's theory of social learning, Behaviour Modelling (BM) has grown in popularity since the mid-1970s. In Chapter 3 we reviewed Bandura's ideas, placing the notions of social learning in the context of the behaviourist tradition. Bandura himself preferred to think of his theory as part of the cognitive school, emphasising the activity of the individual in the learning process. Most writers in the area of learning theory have viewed social learning as a compromise between the two schools, incorporating the participation of the individual but also firmly based on Skinnerian operant conditioning. Bandura did not apply his ideas in the industrial/commercial area but originally used them to treat phobic individuals. Whatever the particular fear or phobia, the trainees observed models performing fear-provoking activities and experiencing no fear themselves. Bandura was able to show that in a short time phobias could be extinguished in individuals by modelling their behaviour on the models (Bandura, 1977). The process of learning new behaviours through modelling has been applied since in a number of situations: training salespersons and job interviewees, and eliminating racial prejudices at work. However, the technique of modelling has been most frequently used in the context of leadership, particularly for front-line supervisors.

The BM technique is based on four major sub-processes that Bandura identified as part of the social learning process:

- **Attentional processes** These engage the individual in the modelling. Particularly important for capturing the attention of the individual is the authenticity of the model and the situations which are being modelled. If the individual feels that the modelling does not accurately reflect his or her own situation, he or she is less likely to imitate the modelled behaviour.
- **Retentional processes** These are primarily the repetition of the desired behaviour in the training situation.
- **Motor reproduction processes** These are the use of simulation situations that allow the trainees to practise the behaviours in the classroom.
- **Motivational processes** These are the use of positive feedback from trainers and other trainees on the individual's performance in the simulations.

The process of behaviour modelling therefore involves the creation of a model which trainees observe and imitate in subsequent simulations. The repetition of the simulations under the control of the trainer and the feedback received from other trainees reinforces the desired behaviour in the mind of the trainee to the point where it becomes an automatic response in similar situations. A typical BM program might focus on handling difficult supervisory situations with employees, such as dealing with grievances or correcting unacceptable behaviour. The session begins with the trainer outlining a simple step-by-step approach to dealing with the situation. This outline is followed by a model of the situation being handled correctly, usually recorded on video. Trainees observe the video model and afterwards practise handling similar situations in one-to-one simulations controlled by the trainer. In most programs, trainees are involved in at least two simulations as both supervisor (handling the situation) and employee (reacting to the behaviour of the supervisor). After the simulation, the trainee receives feedback from both trainer and trainees. The emphasis in the feedback is on providing positive reinforcement, highlighting what the trainee did correctly rather than his or her mistakes.

Thus, BM reverses the traditional cognitive approach to learning, in which an understanding of theory leads to attitudinal change which, in turn, creates changes in behaviour (Bandura, 1969). BM addresses the problem of behaviour first, and relies on the successful application of the desired behaviours to effect changes in attitude and an understanding of theory. The key to the effectiveness of the BM process is the delineation of the critical steps of behaviour the trainees must follow. It is only in the light of the steps that the trainees can create any understanding of the modelling process and what they are expected to imitate (Latham, 1989).

The use of BM in the training of supervisors was pioneered by Melvin Sorcher at General Electric in 1970 (Goldstein and Sorcher, 1974). Sorcher's success precipitated a rash of interest in the technique which was, later, the subject of fairly intensive research and evaluation. Major evaluations of BM carried out by Moses and Ritchie (1976) and Latham and Saari (1979) have shown that BM is one of the most effective methods of producing permanent behavioural changes. Whether it leads to greater understanding on the part of the trainee has not been so clearly established.

Generally, BM has proved to be a successful method for changing behaviour. It is solidly grounded in learning theory and involves the active participation of the learner. However, the technique has been criticised as being too manipulative and oversimplifying the responses required of managers and supervisors in complex interpersonal situations. Although popular amongst trainers, it remains to be seen whether BM can be used in a wider variety of training situations than is currently the case (Ferguson and Smith, 1988).

Open learning and distance learning

Open learning and distance learning (OL/DL) are ways of making training and learning more flexible. The notion of distance (often known in the past as 'external' or 'correspondence') programs is not new to Australia. The size of the country and the remoteness of some of its locations has meant that Australia has pioneered many of the techniques of distance learning. A large number of tertiary students complete degrees and diplomas through universities such as Charles Sturt University in New South Wales which is specifically geared to distance learning. Less familiar is the application of OL/DL techniques to industrial and commercial training.

What is the difference between OL and DL Coffey (1977), one of the pioneers of open learning in the United Kingdom, viewed it as a form of learning without constraints. There were two main forms of constraints on traditional learning: administrative and educational. Administrative constraints forced learners to attend programs in certain places, at certain times, for a defined period. Educational constraints referred to the teacher-centred nature of most training programs, where the learner had little or no input into the content of the program or the way in which the training was delivered. An open learning program is one that removes these constraints. Distance learning is a form of open learning. DL programs can be defined as those where there is:

- separation of teacher and learner;
- use of technical media to unite teacher and learner;
- provision of two-way communication;
- teaching of people as individuals.

DL therefore removes the administrative constraints Coffey referred to in his definition of open learning, although not necessarily the educational constraints. Nevertheless, OL and DL share many common features. The program material is delivered in a way to facilitate individual, rather than group, learning. The learner can decide the pace and the sequence in which the material is studied, and new training technologies such as video, multimedia or the Internet are used to supplement traditional print-based materials. OL and DL are not synonymous, however; distance learning is remote, whereas open learning will often take place in a training centre and involve frequent contact with the trainer, albeit in a one-on-one situation.

OL/DL requires changes to both trainee and trainer behaviour. The trainee has far more control than in the traditional learning situation. Trainees exercise choice over what they learn and the speed and sequence in which they learn it.

The emphasis on individualised instruction means that trainees have less contact with each other and this may pose a problem for some people. In many DL situations where the lack of contact is inherent in the structure of the program, group work may have to be scheduled into the program at certain times to overcome the problems of student isolation.

Illustration 7.2 — Open learning and flexible delivery in the WA Police Force

> The Western Australian Police Force has officers all over the State, some as far from Perth as Sydney is. It is obliged both by common sense and industrial agreements to provide in-service training for its officers. Amongst an officer's duties the highest priorities are the maintenance of the law, apprehension of lawbreakers and appearances in court. That means that for officers in rural and remote communities, it is not really practicable to take days off to go to Perth for training nor even to have set times for training, since these might conflict with an emergency or a court requirement. Yet, the training must be provided.
>
> The police force has met this dilemma with the flexible delivery of training. Training materials are prepared, sent out to officers in printed form, supplemented by televised instruction relayed via satellite and with telephone, computer or videoconference communication between the distant officer and the training base in Perth. Not only has this proved effective as a form of training but it has also saved a great deal of officer time, hotel bills and plane fares.
>
> 'Open Learning' and 'Flexible Delivery' are two phrases in common use and are likely to become even more common. They do not mean quite the same thing but there is a lot of overlap between them. Open Learning focuses on the learner and describes an approach which makes access to education and training and progress through it as suitable as possible for the learner's individual situation. Flexible delivery focuses on the provider of education and training who overcomes restrictions of place and time and provides training in the way and place most suited to the situation of the learner, whether classroom, home or workplace. The two phrases go together but open learning is wider than flexible delivery.

Source: Johnson, 1994

The trainer is similarly isolated from the students. The individualised nature of the program imposes a heavy burden on the trainer to produce materials which are comprehensible to the trainee without the intervention of the trainer. All OL/DL material has to be produced before the program runs, so that it is relatively self-contained and comprehensive. This may often involve the use of a variety of different instructional media with which the trainer needs to become very familiar. Providing feedback outside the formal training situation may also pose problems of communication and student interpretation of feedback. As a result, the production of OL/DL material may be very expensive and resource intensive. The advantage, of course, lies in the fact that the per capita cost will reduce in direct proportion to the number of trainees who undergo the program. One of the advantages of OL/DL is its capacity to process large numbers of trainees in a relatively short space of time.

OL/DL is not a panacea for traditional training problems. OL/DL solutions may be appropriate in the following instances (Wilson, 1987):
- where there are large numbers of trainees or trainees are far-flung;
- when flexibility in offering options is needed to make the training relevant to students;
- where job demands make release for traditional training difficult;
- where consistency and continuity in training is required; or
- where students possess very different degrees of knowledge about the subject area.

OL/DL is not appropriate where:
- trainee motivation is low;
- the number of potential students is low;
- only a short time is available to prepare materials; or
- motor skills training is the main part of the training.

In short, in terms of flexibility OL/DL can offer major advantages over traditional training methods, but its use is circumscribed by what can be taught and the resources needed to operate the system effectively.

Training Media

This section is concerned with the technological aspects of training. Trainers have for many years used audio, visual and audio-visual media in the delivery of programs. Blackboards, whiteboards, overhead projectors and tape-slide productions have become the stock in trade of the training practitioner. However, in recent years, many more powerful technologies, largely developed outside the training field, have been adapted for use in the training setting, with significant implications for the trainer. It is these more recent developments that will be examined in this section.

Video

The conventional audio and visual media used by the training practitioner, such as those alluded to above, are by nature static. That is, they act as illustrations to the text the trainer is using. By contrast, dynamic media present sequences involving movement and are capable of standing alone as a training device (tape-slides may be seen as a transition medium). Sixteen mm and 8 mm film developed as a training medium in World War II, and were used in industrial and commercial training in the 1950s. The use of films in training proved very popular, and a number of training film production houses emerged in the 1960s, specialising in the production of film for this purpose. Many training films were made, and used extensively throughout the training industry. Popular performers such as John Cleese were able to develop alternative careers in the industry because of its size. Since the 1970s, however, film has given way to video as the most popular audio-visual medium. The ubiquity of television as an entertainment and information medium in the household has given video a very high level of credibility in the eyes of most trainees. We tend to suspend disbelief very easily when watching television and relax critical standards, accepting what appears on the television screen as 'true' (Fawbert, 1987). This rather uncritical acceptance of television as a medium, while it may give rise to controversy over the role of political advertising at election times, makes video an invaluable tool for the trainer.

Five major roles may be identified for video in the context of training (Smith, 1987). First, video is being used with increasing frequency in the strictly non-training role of organisational communication. Many organisations produce in-house magazines or newsletters as part of an employee communications policy. Research has shown that these pieces of paper are rarely accorded much attention and vital messages from management may be missed by employees. The use of video magazines, sometimes broadcast within the workplace through permanently stationed monitors (electronic noticeboards), are generally held to be more effective in eliciting an employee response than are conventional bulletins.

Short prerecorded video sequences (triggers) can be used at the beginning of a training session to start discussion or provoke a response from trainees. The value of video in this situation is that it can depict reality and, indeed, it would seem that the credibility of the medium is linked to the extent with which the content accords with the trainees' understanding of reality.

Videos can be used as training sessions in their own right. Many companies are now selling their training packages as a set of prerecorded videos which form the heart of the training material for the session. This is particularly useful in the OL/DL situation.

Video can present a model. The most extensive use of video in this situation is in behaviour modelling programs discussed earlier in the chapter. Again, the credibility of the video depends on the extent to which it is regarded by trainees as depicting reality.

The final common use of video in training is in the non-prerecorded mode: closed circuit television (CCTV). Here the trainer uses video as a form of feedback for the trainees. As the trainees perform a newly acquired skill the camera records what happens, and the trainer later uses edited highlights to show the trainee what went right and what went wrong. Obviously, the use of CCTV is not confined to the classroom. The portability of modern camcorders means that on-the-job training may also benefit from the instant feedback that CCTV can bring.

The rapid diffusion of video in training has come about, of course, for the same reasons as its current diffusion as a substitute for the static camera. In the last 10 years, the size, weight and price of portable camcorders, players and monitors has decreased dramatically, putting reasonably sophisticated video equipment well within the budget of many training organisations. However, video has some major drawbacks as a training medium.

The cost of production of prerecorded material is high. Few organisations can afford to equip and staff a recording studio with the editing suites, mixers, lights and so on, required to produce a professional video. The expectations of trainees, having been exposed to very professional broadcast productions, are high, and the trainer cannot afford to have the credibility of the video damaged by its amateur production. Thus, although the cost of the basic equipment is decreasing, the cost of production is still determined by the studio (principally labour) costs of good production, and are likely to remain high.

Secondly, there are a number of video standards and formats that have emerged in different parts of the world. North America and Japan established the NTSC standard, which is completely incompatible with the European and Australian PAL system, which, in turn, is incompatible with the French and Russian SECAM system. As a result, videos produced in America cannot be shown through normal television equipment in Australia, and vice versa, without first undergoing a costly electronic translation operation. It does not seem likely that a common standard will emerge in the near future.

Finally, there is a range of video formats. Most commercial television is produced on the Sony U-matic, 3/4 inch tape format. This produces high quality recordings that can be used as a master for subsequent copies. However, most domestic (and industrial) video cameras and recorders use the 1/2 inch VHS format. Needless to say, one cannot be played back through equipment designed for the other. In addition, there are other formats, such as the now dying Beta format, the miniature 8 mm VHS format designed for hand-held camcorders, and Super VHS with very high definition produced for the newly emerging technology of high definition television. It appears, however, that unlike the situation with standards, formats are gradually moving towards VHS/Super VHS as a worldwide system.

Nevertheless, despite these drawbacks, video offers the trainer substantial advantages as a support to training programs.

Computer-based training

Computers have been the growth technology of the 1980s and 1990s. In a decade, the power formerly only associated with large mainframe systems working in specially designed, air-conditioned environments has been vested in the desktop personal computer. Moreover, the microchip revolution appears to be far from over, as computer companies compete fiercely to be the first to the market with ever smaller and more powerful laptop and notebook machines. The potential of this technology for training has been one of the most discussed topics in the training literature. It would also be fair to say that while the potential certainly exists for a myriad of training applications the realisation of that potential has been relatively slow. As a result, while most training practitioners in Australia would have had some experience of computer-based training, it is unlikely that many would have explored its full potential.

Computer-based training covers a wide variety of applications of computers in training. Three major applications are usually distinguished (Kearsley, 1983). First, computers can be used to control and manage the training process. Computer managed instruction (CMI), also known as computer managed learning

(CML), generates information about the trainees in the training program. Typically, this information would be concerned with student records, the test results of the students and their progress through the program. By accessing these databases, the CML system can produce a variety of reports which help the trainer to control the training program and pace the students through it. Figure 7.3 shows the components of a typical CML system.

Figure 7.3 — Components of a CML system

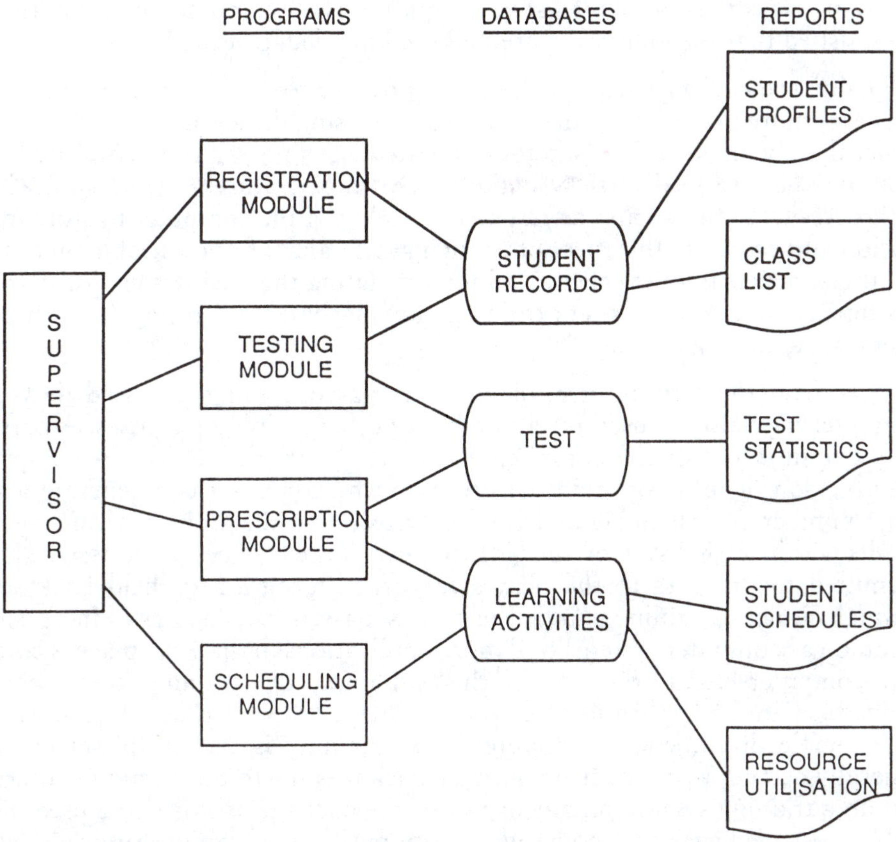

```
PROGRAMS              DATA BASES           REPORTS

                                           STUDENT
                                           PROFILES
           REGISTRATION
           MODULE
                          STUDENT
                          RECORDS          CLASS
S                                          LIST
U
P          TESTING
E          MODULE
R
V                         TEST             TEST
I                                          STATISTICS
S
O          PRESCRIPTION
R          MODULE
                          LEARNING         STUDENT
                          ACTIVITIES       SCHEDULES
           SCHEDULING
           MODULE
                                           RESOURCE
                                           UTILISATION
```

Source: Kearsley (1983)

Secondly, the computer can be used to instruct: a process known as computer assisted instruction (CAI). In CAI, the power of the computer is used to instruct the trainee directly, taking the place of the trainer. CAI systems usually revolve around three strategies. Drill and practice substitutes for the practice sessions so important in many skill training programs. Typical of these drill and practice programs would be the typing tutor sessions now available with most word processing packages. However, the computer can generate a number of different problems on which the trainee can try his or her newly acquired knowledge and skills. In the tutorial mode, the computer gives information to the trainee. In the early days of computer-based training in the 1970s and 1980s, most computer-based training tutorials were little more than 'page turning' programs in which the trainee simply sat in front of the computer screen and read information in the same way as he or she would read a book. With the development of more sophisticated computer graphics and animation, information can be presented in a much more interesting way for the trainee, and involve the trainee in an interactive way. Nevertheless, tutorial programs are basically informational in content. The Socratic method of CAI uses the power of the computer to store a large volume of information on a given range of topics and requires the trainee to learn the information he or she needs by means of inquiry. In this situation, the trainees ask the computer a series of questions about the topic area until they are satisfied that they have acquired all the knowledge needed.

Finally, the computer can be used as a broader tool of learning in which the learner is more in control of the process and is using the computer in a real sense rather than being led by it. Computer assisted learning (CAL) is associated with more open-ended uses of the computer. The most common method associated with CAL is the simulation or game. The ability of the computer to store information and calculate the effect of changing the value of one variable on a series of others, makes it an excellent tool for simulating the business environment of a company for the purposes of training in management or in steps to be used in operating a new machine.

Apart from the various forms of computer-based training discussed above, the computer may also be used for a number of other training purposes. A particularly common use of the computer is to test the trainee. Within a computer-based lesson or in a conventional program, the computer can generate a very large number of test items and randomly examine the trainee. Using the test results within a CMI system, the performance of the trainee can be assessed, and permitted to progress to the next stage of the program or held back to go through remedial training until the test is passed satisfactorily. Increasingly common as computer systems find more applications in the workplace is embedded computer-based training. In this situation, the training component is 'embedded' in the application software (Bentley, 1988). Perhaps the most familiar example of embedded computer-based training is the 'Help' screens that generally accompany modern computer packages. Here the computer user can call up a training session on any aspect of the package as it is being used. Similarly, most packages will come with computer-based training tutorials which may be accessed while the package is used, or in an 'off-line' situation.

Computer-based training first emerged in the early 1960s. The first systems, such as the PLATO system, developed at the University of Illinois, were usually designed for dedicated equipment. That is, the training system could only run on hardware designed specifically for it. Often this involved the purchase of a large mainframe computer with a series of terminals attached to it. As computer technology progressed, however, the need for dedicated equipment disappeared and 'piggyback' computer-based training systems which could run on existing equipment began to appear. Most modern computer-based training programs now do not involve the purchase of anything other than the software which will be compatible with most personal computers. The computer-based training industry is therefore concerned with the development or 'authoring' of software;

the expertise of the computer-based training specialist is in writing programs or, more particularly, in developing systems which enable non-programmers to develop their own computer-based training. These latter systems are known as authoring languages.

Computer-based training offers the trainer a number of advantages over conventional training formats. The most frequently quoted advantage is that of cost reduction. This usually comes about as a result of the individualised nature of computer-based training. Trainees progress at their own speed and start at a point in the program where they are ready to learn. Computer-based training therefore is a very good way of taking prior learning into account. It has been estimated that computer-based training can offer up to 30 per cent cost reduction over conventional training on these grounds alone (Hart, 1987). The other major reduction in cost is a result of the substitution of the trainer by the computer. The initial costs of developing the training can be distributed over all the trainees who go through the program, without incurring the variable expense of the trainer's time. It is doubtful, however, that computer-based training could fully substitute for the trainer. Some topics are better taught in a group or interactive setting, and trainees in a computer-based training program will often require the assistance of a human trainer, if only to switch on the machine!

The principal limitations of computer-based training also relate to cost, this time to the very high cost of developing material. Like open learning, computer-based training programs require enormous commitments of resources to develop. The finished product has to be capable of being used by a trainee alone on machines with which he or she may not be very familiar. But, unlike more conventional OL material, computer-based training has to be programmed. It is not uncommon to find that quality computer-based training may require the investment of 200 hours to produce one hour of training material. The refinement of authoring languages will bring this ratio down, but the production of sophisticated material will always be very costly.

A further criticism that has been made of computer-based training concerns its assumptions about human learning (Galagan, 1987). Until recently, most programs followed a very linear format in which trainees were given some information via a tutorial and were then tested on what they had learned. If the test score was not high enough, the trainees were prevented from going any further in the program until the previous sections had been mastered. This stimulus-response design is, of course, very behaviourist in its orientation. Recent computer-based training has utilised the power of the computer to produce more interactive sequences that invite the participation of the learner in the program, although the behaviourist basis of much computer-based training still inhibits the development of the medium.

Combining the two technologies of computer-based training and video has led to the emergence of multimedia as a separate training medium since the early 1980s. The combination of the two has been made possible by the development of the CD-ROM by Phillips in the late 1970s. Operating on the same principles as an audio compact disc (CD), CD-ROMs have the capacity to store around 54,000 video frames on one disc side. The information stored on the CD-ROM may be video, audio or computer data and thus lends itself to training applications. The major difference between CD-ROM and videotape, and its principal advantage, is the capacity of CD-ROM for random access. Unlike the serial nature of videotape, where particular sequences can only be accessed by winding or rewinding the tape, information stored on CD-ROM can be accessed immediately by the laser reading device incorporated in the CD player. When combined with a computer-based training program, this means that the trainee can switch between the computer and the CD-ROM (displayed on the same monitor) at will, or as the program directs, with no time lost in searching for material.

Two main uses for multimedia have been distinguished (Smith, 1986). As a tool for information retrieval, the random access capability of the CD-ROM lends itself to practical uses in the sales promotion and training field, where product information is important, or in an OJT situation, where the CD-ROM can demonstrate the steps that need to be followed by a technician in diagnosing or rectifying machine faults. For training purposes, the power of the CD-ROM is more fully harnessed when it is combined with a computer-based training program, allowing the trainee to interact with the program. The trainee can chose which sequences on the CD-ROM to access, in what order and over what period of time. Multimedia is therefore something of a natural technology for open learning.

The Internet

The explosive growth in computer applications in the last five years has come from the convergence between computing and telecommunications. The most well-known expression of this new dimension for computing has been the development and spread of the Internet. The Internet began as a distributed computing and communications system designed in the late 1960s to enable military planners to safeguard their communications networks in the case of a nuclear war (Myburgh, 1996). The system developed by the military allowed the communications network to be vested in a large number of small personal computers rather than depend on a small number of larger computers that could be knocked out in the event of a nuclear strike. For many years, the Internet remained a military 'toy' accessed increasingly by computer scientists who were intrigued by the possibilities for electronic communication between themselves. The development of more user-friendly software, particularly the graphical user interfaces of Microsoft's Windows program, in the 1980s allowed more and more people access to the Internet. By 1996 it was estimated that 30 million people worldwide were connected to the Internet (Cher, 1996). The number of connections to the Internet is growing at an exponential rate as more people have access to personal computers and the cost of connection declines.

Illustration 7.3 — Cost saving Internet to replace CD-Rom workplace training

> As corporate job skill requirements keep rising, Internet-based training promises individual, interactive and remote learning opportunities that will increase productivity for firms and boost profits for training consultants.
>
> Training on the Web will save valuable workplace time because courses can be done from a desk, from home or even from a hotel room with a small laptop without the need for heavy CD-ROM drive. With courseware installed at a Web site, all a trainee theoretically needs to do is fire up a Web browser and start reading, watching demonstrations and answering questions. And with advances in Internet multimedia transmission, Java and other downloadable applet technology, courses can be engaging and interactive.
>
> Experts tip that Internet-based training is likely to be less expensive than CD-ROM-based computer-based training and far more flexible. The real savings come in eliminating the costs of tracking and handling CD-ROMs says Chuck Aranda, Vice-President of Sales for the St Louis-based Cornerstone Solutions Group, which is developing systems for Web-based training delivery. The field is so new that no vendor yet has available investment metrics for Web-based training. But Aranda believes profit returns to trainers will be based upon distribution, updates and maintenance savings, plus a reduction in travel costs when compared to classroom-based training.
>
> At the same time five of the world's leading technology vendors are to start a global Internet training and certification consortium. The consortium will seek to set a global standard for training on new technologies with the rapid advance of Internets and Intranets. The Big Five are IBM, Lotus Development, Netscape Communications, Novell and Sun Microsystems.

Source: *The Employer*, 112:1–7

The Internet is a worldwide computer-to-computer communications system that allows large amounts of information to be relayed so long as it is encoded into digital form. The information can be text, graphics, sound, video or still pictures. Graphics and sound tend to travel slowly over the Internet as this information is often in the form of very large computer files. Its advantages as a training tool are gradually becoming obvious as the World Wide Web (that part of the Internet that enables documents to be transferred) becomes more sophisticated. Currently, the most important users of the Internet for education and training purposes are tertiary institutions, particularly universities that have specialised in distance and open learning. Universities are major users of the Internet, as academics have long since realised its power for research and other purposes. However, it is now relatively cheap and simple for universities to put much of their teaching material on the Internet. This means that students can access teaching materials from their own computer and print what they find most useful on their own printers. However, the Internet also allows much more than the simple transfer of information. Using e-mail (electronic mail), students can 'talk' to their lecturers electronically. A refinement of simple e-mail is the use of listservs, which allow members to post information onto an electronic bulletin board which may be accessed by all members of the listserv. Thus, lecturers can put new information onto a listserv for all students, or even deliver lectures via the Internet. A further refinement is the Moo, or electronic tutorial, which is a 'realtime' tutorial in the form of group discussion over the Internet.

Business organisations are also beginning to realise the power of the Internet to improve their business performance. Many companies have now established in-house Internets, or 'Intranets'. These Intranets work in the same way as the Internet (to which they are connected) but access is limited to members of the relevant company. A key use for Intranets is for on-line training of staff (Cher, 1996). Using an Intranet, training materials and information can be delivered to all staff with access to a computer instantly. Although on-line training may not supplant conventional methods completely, it is a powerful supplement to the training toolkit. Figure 7.3 explains some of the important concepts of the Internet.

Figure 7.4 — Important Internet terms

Terms	Definitions
WWW	World Wide Web. A Web of hypertext documents located at different sites around the world. To view the Web, you need a browser program such as Netscape
Hypertext	Text with digital links to other (usually related) texts. It is a way of moving from item to item on the Web
HTTP	Hypertext Transfer Protocol is the system which lets you view the Web from the WWW
FTP	File transfer protocol is a way of requesting a file or program from one remote location on the Internet be sent to your computer, or sending it
E-mail	E-mail is a means of sending messages from computer to computer. E-mail addresses are often available on the WWW
Listserv	A program which maintains a mailing list — a sort of group e-mail. You can subscribe to various special mailing lists via e-mail
Telnet	The command and program used to log in from one Internet site to another
Home page	A shop front on the WWW. Home pages usually contain links to other related sites

Summary

In this chapter, a number of contemporary training methods and technologies have been examined. There is a variety of methods available to the trainer. Induction training has often been practised in a very ad hoc manner. However, as organisations become more concerned with developing commitment amongst the work force, the process of induction appears to be an attractive way of introducing new employees to the values and beliefs of the organisation, rather than being merely a simple process of initiating the employment contract. Induction thus becomes an important part of organisational socialisation.

On-the-job training (OJT) has traditionally occurred throughout industry and commerce. Often, however, like induction training, it occurs in a very informal way and without structure. The emergence of competency-based training has highlighted the importance of structured OJT. The most frequently used model for structured OJT is the American Job Instruction Technique (JIT) based on the principles of the Training within Industry movement. Structured OJT has a number of advantages over off-the-job training, particularly in relation to cost and improving the transfer of training to the workplace.

Behaviour modelling (BM) applies the principles of Albert Bandura's social learning theory to the training situation. Through a process of observing a model and defining the important behaviours that occurred during a successful performance, trainees can learn new behaviours and retain them by repeated practice under the guidance of a facilitator. This technique has been widely and successfully used in the context of sales and supervisory training since the mid-1970s.

The search for more flexible methods of training delivery that do not tie the process of off-the-job training to the formation of large groups of trainees has led to the development of open learning; it is 'open' because the learning process is individualised and released from the normal constraints of the classroom. Training packages are designed for self-teaching using a variety of media. A form of open learning popular in Australia is distance learning, where training by means of printed self-study packages is delivered to trainees at a remote location through the post or using electronic media. The advantage of these more flexible methods is the individualised nature of the design and the fact that trainees can progress at their own pace through the training material, often resulting in faster learning.

The variety of media for the delivery of training has increased dramatically with the impact of new technologies. The miniaturisation of video equipment and the decrease in prices for camcorders, players, etc, has put the use of video techniques within the budgets of many training departments. The uses of video are many: from general employee communications via electronic noticeboards, to the preparation of prerecorded training videos, to the use of CCTV for practice and feedback in skills training sessions.

Computers are increasingly used in training, both to control the training process (computer-managed learning) and to deliver the training itself (computer-assisted instruction). Computer-based training has enabled the development of open learning, by releasing trainees from the classroom environment and allowing them to study at a time and pace to suit themselves. The major drawback with computer-based training is the high cost of development of quality training material, which restricts the use of the medium to situations involving large numbers of trainees.

Finally, the combination of computers and communications technologies has resulted in the development of the Internet, which is likely to become a powerful new training medium.

Discussion Questions

1. What kind of skills could be developed using a behaviour modelling approach?
2. What have organisations to gain from formal induction training for new employees?
3. To what extent will the computer replace the trainer?
4. Why has open learning been so slow to develop in Australia?
5. What are the advantages of OJT?
6. Can people learn via the Internet?

Chapter 8

Assessment and Evaluation in Training

The assessment and evaluation of training are becoming critical elements in the debate on how to improve the provision of training in Australian enterprises. In one sense, assessment and evaluation are concerned with the same thing: the determination of the success of training. Assessment focuses on the success of the trainee at mastering the skills and competencies around which the training is designed. Evaluation focuses on the training program and attempts to determine the success of training at a number of levels in the organisation.

The introduction of competency-based training (CBT) has highlighted the importance of assessment (Hall, 1995). Under a CBT system, trainees are certified as competent to perform tasks through the assessment procedures built into the program. This means that assessment carries much more weight than in a non-CBT system because trainees will be given responsibility based on their certification of competence. If the assessment procedure fails to detect a lack of competence on the part of trainees, this might have serious consequences in the workplace, where incompetent employees could cause accidents, or worse. In this situation, the trainer or assessor (they may be different) could be held liable for the incompetence of trainees. It is thus critical to ensure that reliable and valid assessment procedures are built into CBT programs.

Evaluation of a program most often takes place at the end of the program, as an 'add on' activity, by which time it may be too late to remedy any shortfall that the evaluation has revealed.

Commentators often bemoan this add on approach to evaluation (Smith and Piper, 1990) and argue, instead, that evaluation must be a central part of the design process. Evaluation of training happens whether the trainer designs it into the program or not. Trainees will naturally pass judgment on the worth of any training program, and not only at the end of the program. Evaluation of training will be a continuous process in the minds of the trainees. Thus, any procedure that restricts evaluation until after the program is complete is simply ignoring the reality of the processes of human judgment. Perhaps, therefore, evaluation should be built in at every stage of the training process, from needs analysis to final program implementation and afterwards.

The scant evidence from evaluation research, however, would seem to highlight the gulf between theory and practice in the field of evaluation (Lewis and Thornhill, 1994). Research in Australia has also highlighted the lack of evaluation of training programs as a major concern (Collins and Hackman, 1991). Fourteen per cent of companies surveyed reported no evaluation of training programs at all. Of those that reported evaluation, the bulk (66 per cent) used only end-of-course assessments, with only 12 per cent using any before and after measurements of performance. Smith et al (1995) found in their study of 30 Australian enterprises that formal evaluation of training programs was very rare and did not extend beyond the end-of-course 'happiness sheet'. However, it appeared that, contrary to much of the literature in the evaluation area, managers in the enterprises studied did not wish to engage in lengthy evaluation exercises (Smith et al, 1995:115):

> Managers did not speak in terms of requiring a full evaluation of the training they had sanctioned and did not appear to demand elaborate justification of the dollars they had invested in training in terms of demonstrable returns to the business. In this sense, managers seemed to be prepared to take a leap of faith in keeping with the general belief in the efficacy of upskilling the workforce.

Thus, the reticence to evaluate training may not be the result of the incompetence of the training department but an expression of the lack of demand for evaluation in organisations as a whole.

Assessment

Assessment is simply the process of collecting evidence about the performance of trainees in a training program and making a judgment about whether they have met the standards laid down in the program design (Hager, Athanasou and Gonczi, 1994). Thus, assessment involves both an objective and a subjective component. The objective component is the collection of evidence on the performance of the trainee. However, the judgment about whether the trainee has met a particular standard is essentially subjective.

Within a CBT training environment, the judgment about whether trainees have reached a particular standard is based on the competencies around which the training program was designed. This means that trainees are being judged against fixed standards of performance which are specified by the competency standards. The judgment involved in the assessment process, therefore, is a simple 'yes/no' decision. Either the trainees meet the competency standards or they do not. This form of assessment in which trainees are judged against a fixed standard is known as criterion-referenced assessment. This is in contrast to norm-referenced measures which are often used to assess performance in non-CBT education and training programs. Norm-referencing measures the performance of trainees against the overall performance of the group and usually results in some form of ranking. A typical example of norm-referencing would be the public examinations systems, such as the Higher School Certificate in New South Wales or the Victorian Certificate of Education. In these examinations, the performance of candidates is assessed against the performance of all the candidates and results in a score that measures the position of individual candidates within the group that sat the examinations. Many universities also use norm-referencing for marking items of assessment. Hager et al (1994) cite three reasons why norm-referencing presents problems in a CBT training system:

1. Typically, norm-referencing does not specify what trainees can do against explicit criteria.
2. Norm-referencing is concerned with ranking trainees. This causes some trainees to see themselves as failures.
3. Norm-referencing almost always reports against categories which may be of interest to trainees but bear little relationship to workplace performance.

Thus norm-referencing is not suitable for a CBT system. Under CBT, the competency standards lay down the performance criteria to be achieved. Trainees either meet these standards or they do not, and their performance is assessed without reference to the performance of other trainees in the group. Assessment under CBT therefore is based on criterion referencing. However, criterion-referenced assessment also has problems. In particular, the search for ever clearer and measurable criteria against which trainees can be assessed often leads to the development of extremely narrow and specialised criteria which refer only to certain aspects of performance which are directly measurable. Other aspects of the job, even though they may be specified in the competency standards, may not be assessed, simply because unambiguous measurement criteria cannot be developed. This is particularly true of competencies that refer to behavioural traits such as personal skills, which may be very important in industries such as hospitality or retail. The development of increasingly narrow criteria leads to what Wolf (1993) has referred to as a 'never ending spiral of specification' and the atomisation of the competency standards.

Forms and uses of assessment

Assessment can be oriented towards different aspects of the training that trainees receive. Figure 8.1 shows a continuum of assessment practice, from a general assessment of the whole performance of the trainee at the right-hand end to the narrow assessment of specific workplace performance at the other.

Figure 8.1 — A continuum of assessment

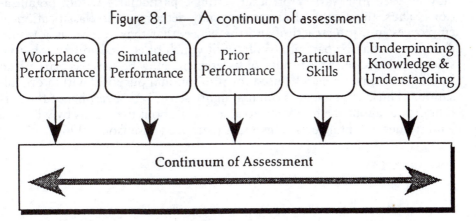

Source: Hager, Athanasou and Gonczi (1994)

There are four principal forms of assessment (Rumsey, 1994): holistic, formative, diagnostic and summative.

- **Holistic assessment** This involves examining the performance of the trainee in all aspects of the training. Holistic assessment is 'integrated' in that it attempts to assess not only the skill, but the underpinning knowledge and understanding of the trainee. Thus, in Figure 8.1, holistic assessment represents the right-hand side of the assessment continuum. Usually holistic assessment will involve assessing the trainee in a variety of contexts to ensure the competency standards have been fully met. This will often involve a mix of workplace and off-the-job assessment on knowledge and theory.

- **Formative assessment** This takes place during the training and is designed to give the trainees feedback on how they are progressing. It is intended to help the trainees learn, rather than to pass judgment on their performance. Thus, formative assessment will often include tasks or assignments which trainees have to complete as part of the learning process. The grade that they receive through the process helps trainees to understand what they need to do to achieve the competencies designed into the program.

- **Diagnostic assessment** This is used to determine the abilities of trainees before entering a training program. Thus, diagnostic assessment would be used by trainers to determine what training ought to take place and how it should be structured to meet the needs of the trainees.

- **Summative assessment** This is the final assessment, that takes place at the end of the training program. It is intended to assess whether or not trainees have met the competency standards for the program. Thus, in summative assessment, trainers collect evidence to make a final judgment of the ability of the trainee. This evidence might include samples of work, observation of performance and written tests. This evidence is then put together, or 'summated', so that the trainee may be assessed as competent or not. The results of assessment are not necessarily confined to the judgments of whether trainees have reached a level of competence or not. They may be used in a variety of other settings, particularly within organisations. Thus, the results of assessment may determine the classification of employees in a job structure and the wages that they receive as a result. Assessment may be part of a skills audit which often feeds into a job classification exercise. The results of assessment may be used as part of an incentive scheme or may be used for promotional purposes within organisations. Thus, assessment is often a highly sensitive matter; hence the current debate about the best ways to assess and about the means by which to gain trainee acceptance of assessment methods (Thomson, 1996).

Illustration 8.1 — Assessment at Hella Australia

> Hella Australia is the Australian subsidiary of the German-owned automotive lighting producer, Hella. In 1995, the company decided to revive its literacy training program for employees on the Mentone site. Hella employs a large number of non-English speaking background workers. The company realised that it had on staff, people without formal qualifications in training but whose knowledge and skill could be used as workplace trainers. Together with local Barton TAFE the company devised a Workplace Trainer Category 1 training program for these potential workplace trainers to be run using an action-learning method. This involved coaching the potential trainers to design and administer a workplace literacy program as the major part of their training program. However, assessment of the trainees was quite complex and had to be done against three sets of standards:
>
> - the workplace trainer competency standards
> - the National Metals and Engineering competency standards and
> - the workplace assessor competency standards.
>
> Hella devised a three tier assessment method. The first tier of assessment tested the trainees against the workplace trainer competencies. This involved an holistic assessment approach which examined the trainees' progress in establishing a workplace literacy training program from needs analysis, through program design and, finally, to observation of the technique in the training room and on-the-job.
>
> The second tier involved a more complex, project-based assessment approach. The purpose of the second tier assessment was to ensure that the trainees had met the learning outcomes of the training program and the Metals and Engineering competencies at the same time. Hella chose to set the trainees a project based on the company's TQM program. The trainees had to research the TQM process, focusing on an internal customer and present their results to a TQM team meeting. The trainees were assessed against a range of criteria involving communication, research and listening skills. This enabled the cross-matching of the learning outcomes of the training program with the Metals and Engineering competencies.
>
> The third tier of assessment involved the trainees being assessed against the workplace assessor competencies. Hella adopted a participatory approach again which involved the trainees using the complex, cross-matching assessment process used in Tier 2 in their own assessment of trainees in the workplace literacy training program. Thus the trainees used their own assessment process in their work.

Source: Newton, S (1996)

The assessment process

The process of assessment is guided by four major principles (Smith and Keating, 1997). First, assessment must be valid. Validity is achieved when the assessment measures what it claims to assess. Thus, in the CBT training system, the assessment process should be able to determine whether or not a trainee is competent as a result of training. Thus, the assessment will gather evidence that the trainee has met the competency standards by testing trainees against the performance criteria.

Secondly, assessment has to be reliable. Reliability involves there being consistency in the assessment process so that all trainees are judged in the same way using the same methods. A reliable assessment process enables the trainee confidently to say that all trainees have been assessed against the same standards and that the results of the assessment are therefore fully generalisable.

Thirdly, assessment has to be flexible. Flexibility is a key element of the training reform agenda and refers to the ability of the training system to meet the needs of a wide variety of trainees who exist in a variety of circumstances. In terms of assessment, flexibility means that there must be variety in the assessment procedures adopted, so that trainees in different situations can be assessed in ways that suit their circumstances. Thus, trainees who do not have a job will require assessment in a college or other environment. Flexible assessment, however, highlights the importance of validity and reliability. If a variety of assessment methods is used, they must be carefully arranged so they are valid and reliable, so that one group of trainees is not disadvantaged by the process.

The final principle of assessment is fairness. No group of trainees should be advantaged or disadvantaged by the assessment process. This means that the assessment process should be equally open to all trainees and should have the confidence of the trainees that it is valid and reliable. In general, fairness in assessment involves making the process transparent so that trainees and trainers know beforehand what the assessment will be and how it will be conducted (Rumsey, 1994).

There are many methods that can be used in the assessment process. Hager et al (1994) identify four major assessment methods:

- **Direct observation** This involves checking and rating the performance of a trainee at a particular task. Observation of trainees has a high level of validity, and a major advantage of observation is that the assessor can focus on the integrated task and assess the trainee against all the relevant performance criteria. However, not all aspects of learning may be assessed through direct observation and observation may be lengthy and costly to administer.

- **Skills tests** This method usually involves taking a sample of work that has been completed or setting the trainee a project which brings together a number of skills or competencies. Skills tests have a moderate level of validity and the more skills tested, the higher the degree of reliability. However, the testing of specific skills may not permit a judgment to be made about the overall level of competency of an individual and it may be costly to set up tests for a long list of skills.

- **Simulation techniques** This involves observation, but of performance outside the real workplace in a simulated environment. Simulations can range from simple case studies to complex computer simulations of real work situations such as aircraft simulators. Simulations can offer a high degree of reliability in that all trainees undergo the same simulation, but they may not be sufficiently realistic to make judgments about behaviour in the real situation, thus impairing their validity.

- **Questioning techniques** Questioning is probably the most common and the simplest form of assessment. Questioning can range from the formative questioning in the training situation to gauge trainee learning (and help in the learning process) to the formal questioning of an examination in which all the trainees have to answer the same questions on their own. Questioning is a very good way of testing cognitive skills, but is very poor for assessing behaviour in the workplace.

Figure 8.2 illustrates each of the major assessment methods and their applicability.

Figure 8.2 — Suitability of forms of assessment

	Knowledge	Skills	Attitudes
Direct observation	3	3	3
Skills tests	3	3	3
Simulations	3	3	3
Questioning techniques • written • oral • computer	3 3 3	3 3	

Source: Hager et al (1994)

A major debate within CBT has been over the question of whether assessment should be graded or ungraded. At the introduction of CBT in the early 1990s, it was envisaged that assessment would be ungraded. This was a logical extension of the use of industry competency standards in training programs. Under the principles of accreditation of courses then established, trainees were trained until they were competent (Smith and Keating, 1997). After they had reached competence, they proceeded to undertake the job. In this situation, it makes sense to reduce assessment to a judgment about whether or not a trainee has reached competence. If a trainee is competent, there seems little point in deciding *how* competent he or she is. The notion of outstanding performance is strictly irrelevant to a CBT training system.

Within the training system, there are vociferous advocates and opponents of graded assessment (Thomson, Mathers and Quirk, 1996). The advocates of graded assessment in the CBT training system argue that:

- grading motivates the trainees to do better and score higher marks, and thus promotes learning;
- grading can provide information for other uses such as selecting highly motivated or high performing trainees for more training or higher-level positions;
- grading provides an insight into the quality of training. If a significant number of trainees score very highly, it is likely that they have received high quality training.

The opponents of grading, on the other hand, argue that:
- the CBT system, and industry competency standards particularly, do not allow for grading and were never established to test for excellence;
- grading creates unnecessary competition between trainees, when the purpose of the training is to achieve competency;
- while grading may be good for high achievers, it stigmatises low achievers as failures, which is an outcome to be avoided in the training system.

The evidence from recent surveys of the use of CBT amongst training providers in Australia suggests that the overwhelming majority of public and private training providers use ungraded assessment (Smith et al, 1996).

A further key feature of assessment in Australia is the move towards assessment in the workplace. Hager et al (1994) argue that workplace assessment can only take place on the job, in the actual workplace of the trainee. Any other form of assessment, even simulation, is not true workplace assessment. Thomson (1996) suggests that competency can only be assessed in the workplace. This is because the workplace is a very different environment from the off-the-job training environment. In the workplace, employees are expected to exhibit high performance not just once, at assessment time, but continuously. The tasks performed have to be carried out under severe constraints such as short deadlines, or with inadequate resources, and interpersonal skills are often required in the workplace in order to get things done. Because the workplace is so different, it is argued that any assessment not done in the workplace will not be a true measure of the ability of the trainee to achieve competence in the 'real world'. Advocates of workplace assessment argue that off-the-job assessment can only judge a trainee to be 'work ready'. Workplace assessment is needed to judge if a trainee is 'work competent'.

Smith and Keating (1997), however, show that although workplace assessment may seem a logical approach in a CBT training system, it is not without its problems. Unless they are qualified trainers already, workplace assessors need to be trained to assess their trainees properly. In many cases, it will be the supervisor who is assigned to the workplace assessor, and the pressures of production may mean that the assessment process is manipulated to fit in with the pressures of the workplace, resulting in a poor or invalid assessment. As a result of these concerns over the role and functions of the workplace assessor, competency standards have been developed for the workplace assessor which form part of the competency standards for workplace trainers discussed in Chapter 1.

Recognition of prior learning

Technically, the Recognition of Prior Learning (RPL) is a fifth form of assessment. However, it is usually treated as a different process in the debates about assessment, because it occurs before the training rather than during it. RPL is one of the key principles on which the CBT training system is built. It is one of the 10 principles used under the National Framework for the Recognition of Training that determines whether a training program may be accredited. Essentially, RPL is the acknowledgment of the skills and knowledge acquired by a trainee through previous training or from life experiences (Wilson and Lilly, 1996). Granting of RPL enables trainees to miss those sections of the training program that relate to their previous skills, and so hasten their progress through training. RPL began in the United States as a means of recognising the skills of returned servicemen from the Vietnam War who had left the forces and wished to acquire civilian qualifications.

RPL is granted by training providers on the basis of documented evidence of previous study or a portfolio of evidence that the trainee has acquired the skill through other means. Thus, RPL is granted against the learning outcomes for the training program. In industry, RPL may be granted against the competency standards for a particular job. Thus, if employees can demonstrate, through a portfolio or a test, that they have achieved competence in certain skill areas, they can be given jobs at particular skill levels in the job classification structure. This process is sometimes distinguished from academic RPL and called the recognition of current competencies (RCC).

RPL is based on five key principles (Smith and Keating, 1997):

1. **Competence** RPL focuses on the competencies a person has acquired, not how or where the learning took place.
2. **Commitment** The training provider must be committed to the value of RPL.
3. **Access** RPL processes must be open to all applicants.
4. **Fairness** All RPL processes must be verifiable, credible and just.
5. **Support** Potential applicants must be given support, as must those administering the RPL process.

Despite the apparent attractions of the RPL process, particularly for trainees who could move through their training more quickly, the adoption of RPL has been low. Research carried out by the Group for Research in Employment and Training at Charles Sturt University has found that the take up of RPL in Australia is remarkably low (Smith et al, 1997). Some reasons for this might include the fact that RPL processes are often cumbersome and bureaucratic and the trainee may have to pay for the privilege. Also, trainees may wish to undertake the full training program as a refresher on the parts that they know, or may prefer to stay with a peer group rather than accelerate their progress.

Evaluation

If evaluation is concerned with the measurement of a program's value or worth, there are four main purposes with which, conventional training wisdom suggests, the process of evaluation will be concerned (Smith, 1987).

First, that the outcomes specified in the objectives of the program are met. Outcomes may be measured at a number of different levels. For instance, trainees can be assessed in terms of what they have learned. This is a relatively simple process, involving some form of testing during the program. The transfer of that learning may be assessed in terms of the extent to which the behaviour of the trainees changes in the working environment after the program is completed. This may involve the participation of the colleagues and managers of the trainees to determine on-the-job changes. Finally, the outcomes for the organisation as a whole may be measured: the 'bottom line' criterion.

Secondly, within the program, the contribution of the various components of the program to the overall effectiveness of the training may be assessed. This is an internal measure which helps to assess the validity of the design of the program in meeting the needs identified at the beginning of the training process. At this level, evaluation is designed to improve the effectiveness of the program by highlighting areas that need attention.

Thirdly, evaluation may be concerned with the costs and benefits training involves for the organisation. The evaluation process in this case is attempting to put a monetary value on the benefits that accrue to the organisation and to compare them with costs involved in setting up the training program.

Finally, evaluation is often used as means of persuading others in the organisation that the program is worth the investment of resources that has been made, and that further training activities can be justified on the basis of the success of the current program.

More pertinent to the debate may be the reasons why evaluation does not occur. Phillips (1991) identified nine myths which are commonly used as reasons not to evaluate training effort:

1. I can't measure the result of my training effort.
2. I don't know what information to collect.
3. If I can't calculate the return on investment, it is useless to evaluate.
4. Measurement is only effective in the production and financial areas.
5. My chief executive officer does not require evaluation, so why should I?
6. There are too many variables affecting the behaviour change for me to evaluate the impact of training.
7. Evaluation will lead to criticism.
8. I don't need to justify my existence, I have a proven track record.
9. The emphasis on evaluation should be the same in all organisations.

None of these reasons denies the possibility of evaluation per se, but they may be considered to be barriers which inhibit organisations from developing evaluation programs. The increased competitiveness of the 1990s has highlighted the need to evaluate, as organisations look for ways to cut costs and training practitioners find it difficult to justify their existence in a quantitative fashion. Certainly, there seems to be evidence that during periods of economic downturn in Australia, training departments have found themselves on the defence against corporate cost cutting programs which resulted in the diminution, and sometimes disappearance, of personnel activities completely (Dunphy, 1987). The answer may lie in the development of a 'results-oriented training function' in which evaluation plays a key role. Such results-oriented evaluation will produce information which can be used for purposes beyond those outlined above (Phillips, 1991). These purposes could include:

- **Identifying strengths and weaknesses in the training function overall** Each input to the program may be assessed individually, particularly the competencies of the internal training staff.
- **Increasing the demand for training** Good communication of the results and style of the program can increase management awareness of the need for training in the organisation as a whole and give training a more strategic position.
- **Evaluation may also include an assessment of who benefited most from the training** Measurement of learning and of learning transfer can be fed back into an appraisal system and form the basis of future development activities.
- **Evaluation can also address the problem of the appropriateness of training solutions to organisational problems** Although the analysis phase of the training process should determine this point, it may only be evaluation which can gauge the extent to which training activities improved a situation.

Types of evaluation

The various purposes of evaluation lead to the development of different types of evaluation. An important distinction is that between formative and summative evaluation (Scriven, 1967). Evaluation undertaken for the purpose of improving and developing the training program is referred to as 'formative'. Formative evaluation is not concerned with the overall impact of the program but rather with its inherent structure and design. Summative evaluation, on the other hand, is concerned with the impact of the program. Summative evaluation addresses the question of whether the program achieved its objectives and is concerned with the measurement of changes in the workplace as a result of the training program.

A related distinction is often made between process and outcome evaluation. Process evaluation focuses on the recording and assessment of what happened during the development and implementation of the program. Obviously, process evaluation data collected for the purpose of improving the program becomes a formative evaluation. Outcome evaluation is concerned with measuring the effects that training programs have on trainees and the organisation. Although related, the process/outcome distinction is distinguishable from the formative/summative dichotomy (Brinkerhof, Brethower, Hluchyj and Nowakowski, 1983). Questions involving the improvement of the program (formative evaluation) may involve both process and outcome evaluations being carried out. Similarly, assessing the impact of a program (summative evaluation) may involve investigating the processes as well as the outcomes of the training.

A further category of evaluative activity sometimes used is that of validation. Whereas evaluation is concerned with the assessment of whether the program achieved its objectives and how effective the program design was in enabling that to happen, validation is concerned with assessing whether the program will have the desired effect in the first place; that is, is the program capable of meeting the needs identified. Thus, validation is a 'predictive' activity (Stanley, 1987).

The distinctions between these different forms of evaluative activity can appear to be academic rather than practical. Nevertheless, there seems to be a consensus in the literature on the distinction between the two forms of evaluation. Evaluation may be focused on activities concerned with the design and development of the program, including the validity of the needs analysis, or alternatively it may be focused on the impact of the program in terms of the individual trainees or the benefits accruing to the organisation as a whole.

Illustration 8.2 — Progressive evaluation at ICI Botany

> ICI Botany is one of Australia's largest chemical production plants located near Botany Bay in Sydney. In 1993 the company introduced a more systematic method for the evaluation of its workplace training at the Botany plant. The new system was agreed with the unions at the plant and was based on the evaluation of the progress of the trainees as a result of their training. The evaluation process was based on six principles:
> 1. The next inline supervisor would be the primary evaluator.
> 2. The work of employees would be evaluated within a competency-based framework.
> 3. Progress of employees would be through an integration of formal and informal training.
> 4. The evaluation process would comply with all regulatory guidelines.
> 5. The evaluation process should be realistic and involve ICI staff only.
> 6. The evaluation process would, itself, be audited.
>
> The process was based on a Training Report card. The report card had 'active' and 'passive' sections. The active sections recognised the nature of the work and carried a training value. The passive sections recognised the trainee and the plant. Both the supervisor and the trainees filled in the report cards which thus documented the training progress of the trainee. The cards were designed to be machine readable which allowed ICI to build up a comprehensive training profile for all employees. Prior learning was also recorded on the report card. The evaluation system built in an auditing process based on both random and prescribed field assessments. Finally the system also incorporated an appeals mechanism. If an employee did not feel that the supervisor's comments on the report card were correct then there was provision for the matter to be referred to an independent, accredited assessor for judgment.

Source: Seary, R (1993)

Models of Evaluation

Research into evaluation has sprung from two sources (Brinkerhof, 1987). Business and industry has been concerned with the development of evaluation techniques which measure the performance of training and its contribution to the 'bottom line'. The focus of these models has therefore been on the outcome type of evaluation. While trainers may have developed methods of assessing the effectiveness of their program designs, the preoccupation of evaluators in the business context is with the results of the programs.

At the same time, from the 1960s, governments have become concerned with the evaluation of the educational and social programs that have increasingly consumed such a large part of government budgets. The models developed for this purpose, although concerned with the ultimate outcomes of the programs, are principally focused on process and on improving and refining the programs over time. Public servants found the models useful in designing, implementing and improving the programs for which they were responsible with the speed often demanded by governments attempting to live up to election promises.

Models of evaluation have also evolved within themselves over time. The historical and theoretical development of evaluation models may be traced through three distinct phases (Smith and Piper, 1990). Early models adopted the rigorous processes of scientific method in the pursuit of objective proof of the impact of training programs on trainees. Control group designs and cost benefit analyses were the preferred methods of the scientific approach in the 1940s and 1950s. Unfortunately, these rigorous proof-oriented models could not take into account any effects that were either unexpected or unquantifiable using the categories of the researchers. In the 1960s, systems models of evaluation began to emerge which, while retaining a focus on outcomes, were also concerned with measuring the processes that occurred within the programs in an attempt to improve evaluation. The systems evaluators provide clear models which are easily operationalised by trainers, and provide clear, if rather impressionistic, data about the program. More recently, 'naturalistic' evaluators have emphasised the importance of capturing the unintended effects of training programs and of not contaminating the evaluation process by eliminating the contact between evaluators and evaluees. While this approach has led to the development of fairly rigorous models for evaluation, the data which the process produces may be too unstructured for use in an organisational setting. This chronology of the development of evaluation is illustrated in Figure 8.3 on p 200.

Since 'scientific' models are clearly oriented towards the evaluation of training outcomes, it would appear that the basic distinction to be drawn is between process-oriented and outcome-oriented models of evaluation.

Outcome-oriented models

Probably the most influential model of evaluation ever developed is that of Donald Kirkpatrick (1959). Kirkpatrick identified four levels, or stages, of evaluation.

1. **Reaction** How much the trainees enjoyed the training program. This is the most immediate level of evaluation, and is generally carried out at the end of the program. The ubiquitous 'happiness sheet' asking participants to rate the program on a series of dimensions is the most frequently quoted method of evaluation at this level. For Kirkpatrick, it is important to evaluate at this level for two reasons: the immediate reaction of the

trainees can often form the basis of managerial judgments on the program as a whole, and it is important that trainees enjoy the program if they are to learn.

2. **Learning** What principles, facts, techniques or skills have been absorbed and understood by the trainees. There is a variety of well-established methods for evaluating at this level, usually involving some form of testing.

3. **Behaviour** At this level, learning transfer is being tested. This measures improvements in job performance as a result of undergoing the training. This may require much more intensive follow-up to the program, where trainees are measured a number of times over the period subsequent to the training to determine real and lasting changes to job performance. At this level, measurement becomes much more difficult, as most methods rely on some form of subjective assessment from others in the workplace, such as subordinates, peers or supervisors.

4. **Results** How has organisational performance changed as a result of the training? This is the most difficult level at which to attempt evaluation. The immediate problem is the separation of variables. Performance at the organisational level is determined by a wide variety of factors; training may only be a very small part of the overall pattern of causality at this level. It is also, of course, the level of evaluation which most interests decision-makers in the organisation.

Figure 8.3 — Evaluating corporate structures: three evaluation traditions

	Scientific	Systems	Naturalistic
Period	1950s	1970s	1980s
Expected outcome	Scientific proof	Improvement	Understanding processes
Typical methods	Measures, controls, statistics	Focus on events, objectives, feedback and control	Qualitative, grounded, progressive, focusing
Features	Rigorous Distanced	Pragmatic Semi-involved	Rigorous Highly evolved
Problems	Results ambiguous Do not explain why	Not practical Limited view of training and development Informal feedback often more useful	Hard to generalise May lose independence Labour intensive Not so convincing?

Source: Smith and Piper (1990)

Kirkpatrick's model is completely outcomes-focused, from immediate outcomes (reaction) to ultimate outcomes at the organisational level. The model also encapsulates the basic paradox associated with outcome models of evaluation: that those results of most value to the organisation are, by definition, the most difficult to achieve.

There is a number of variations on the Kirkpatrick model. The results level, for instance, may be divided into organisational results concerned with operational measures, such as quality, productivity, absenteeism, labour turnover, etc, and ultimate results, which measure the ultimate value of the program to the trainee (career path enhancement, etc) and to the organisation (improved profitability). The CIRO model also builds upon Kirkpatrick's work (Warr, Bird and Rackham, 1970).

Context (C) evaluation gathers information about the workplace background to the needs analysis phase of the design. Input (I) evaluation assesses the relative worth of different training resources used in the program. Reaction (R) and Outcome (O) evaluations correspond to the Kirkpatrick categories.

However, outcome-oriented models of evaluation, particularly Kirkpatrick's, have been criticised because they fail to take into account the whole process of training, and its broader relationship to the organisation (Lewis and Thornhill, 1994; Dyer, 1994). These critics have called for a more integrated model of evaluation, which has led to the development of process-oriented models.

Process-oriented models

In contrast to the outcome-oriented models, which find their methodological provenance in the concerns of business and industry to evaluate training programs, the process-oriented models originate in the attempts of governments to assess the value of their educational and social programs; nevertheless, these models are applicable within the business context, in so far as trainers are concerned with evaluating the training process. All process-oriented models contain some element of outcome evaluation, but they are primarily concerned with collecting information which will help program providers to improve the program design and operation.

A very simple approach is the discrepancy evaluation model, or DEM (Provus, 1971). The DEM method creates a standard for the training program, measures the actual performance and finally reports on the discrepancy. The method uses a systems approach to the creation of standards for the program, specifying inputs to the program such as design, program processes and outcomes. Evaluation questions are carefully constructed to elicit the actual performance of the various elements of the program in relation to the standards, and the discrepancy becomes the focus of the improvement activities.

In the mid-1960s, Daniel Stufflebeam (1983) developed the CIPP model for the evaluation of educational programs in the United States. Concerned with the fact that conventional techniques of evaluation were only assessing the worth of educational programs on the basis of their outcomes, Stufflebeam realised that the reason for the variation in outcomes may well be related to the fact that individual teachers were using entirely different educational processes to achieve the objectives of the programs. Therefore, any evaluation that did not take into account differences in process would be rendered inadequate. The CIPP model attempts to evaluate the whole program design process as well as the outcomes of the program under four headings.

1. **Context (C)** Evaluation of the analysis process, the target population, their needs, underlying problems and whether the objectives for the program address the identified needs.
2. **Input (I)** The ability of the system to deliver the program, and the likelihood that the design will fulfil the objectives.
3. **Process (P)** The assessment of actual or potential defects in the program process. Recording the actual events in the program and the evaluation of their efficacy.
4. **Product (P)** Evaluation of the outcomes of the program and assessment of how well they met the program's objectives.

In contrast to the outcome models based on the Kirkpatrick philosophy of levels of outcome, CIPP is almost entirely based on the evaluation of the pre-outcome processes. Significantly, CIPP introduces the concept of the ability of the training system to deliver the program, under the category of input evaluation. Stufflebeam also viewed evaluation as a predictive process rather than an end-on device. The point about evaluation was to ensure that the program was correct before implementation, rather than trying to change the program in midstream. Evaluation does need to occur at the end of, or during, the program, but CIPP is a model for continuous evaluation from the point of the initial program concept to final implementation and afterwards.

Brinkerhof (1987) elaborated this predictive evaluation process further by linking it to the cycle of training decisions. He identifies six logical steps in the training cycle: establishing worthwhile goals for training; creating a workable design; implementing the design and making it work; trainees exiting with new skills; trainees using the new skills in the work situation; and the organisation finally benefiting from the new skills of the trainees. The training cycle can be evaluated at each of these stages. Thus, Brinkerhof proposes a six-stage evaluation model, summarised in Figure 8.4 on p 203.

- Stage I examines the analysis phase of the training process in much the same way as Stufflebeam's content evaluation. The key question to be addressed at this stage is whether or not training is an appropriate solution to the identified problems.
- Stage II evaluates the production of a training design, that is, whether it is good enough to be put into practice. This stage may also include some evaluation of the inputs to the program, although this is not completely clear in Brinkerhof's analysis.
- Stage III is concerned with implementation, particularly whether the program is being run according to plan or whether departures from the original design are occurring.
- Stages IV to VI, in effect, replicate the Kirkpatrick model. Reactions and learning are the foci of Stage IV, behaviour of Stage V and results of Stage VI.

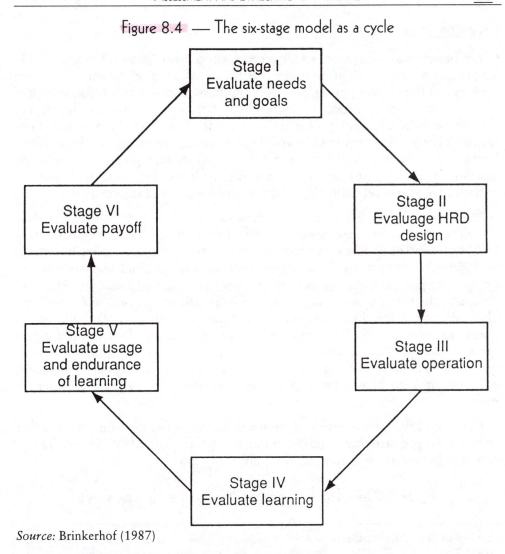

Figure 8.4 — The six-stage model as a cycle

Source: Brinkerhof (1987)

Brinkerhof's model neatly encapsulates both process and outcome, devoting three stages in the evaluation to each. It also brings together the two traditions of evaluation research in both the business and educational communities and produces a model which is of value to each, despite their differing concerns.

Techniques of Evaluation

There is a variety of techniques that can be used in any evaluation situation. While some techniques lend themselves to certain types of evaluation better than others, they are generally value-free to the extent that they can be used within any of the models we have considered in the last section. This section will examine the major types of evaluation techniques and their applications.

Questionnaires

Questionnaires are the most widely used form of evaluation (Dawson, 1993). The most common evaluation exercise is the questionnaire administered at the very end of the training program: the 'happiness sheet'. In this form, the questionnaire is a highly suspect measure of the effectiveness of the training. The term 'happiness' encapsulates the criticism made of this technique: that it is one in which the participants tend to give highly favourable ratings of the program because they have enjoyed the experience, rather than giving any objective assessment of the use of the program in the work context. Nevertheless, Kirkpatrick (1975) still recommends its use as one measure of trainee reaction.

More generally, questionnaires can provide a great deal of valuable information. The advantages of the questionnaire are that it is both simple to administer and relatively cheap. Used in a pre-program setting, questionnaires can gauge the level of trainee knowledge and skills before training, which makes them particularly appropriate in the design of competency-based training. After the program, the usefulness of questionnaires is limited by the response rate. They also suffer from the disadvantage that they can only elicit information on the questions being asked. Thus, information on unanticipated effects and consequences may not be revealed by the questionnaire. The use of open-ended questions to counter this effect may often result in the production of a questionnaire which is extremely time consuming to analyse, thus negating its intended purpose.

Dawson (1995) has devised '10 commandments' of evaluation sheets, which improve the performance of questionnaires as a technique of evaluation. The 10 commandments are summarised in Figure 8.5 below.

Figure 8.5 — The ten commandments of evaluation sheets

1. Use three evaluation sheets — pre-course, immediate post-course and later enquiry sheets.
2. Tailor the evaluation sheets to a particular course. To get information on whether a course has succeeded, it is crucial to ask questions based on the course.
3. Get information on training needs. Questions can be asked which give a useful profile of participants.
4. Make questions logically inclusive and specific. Asking questions about possible additions and deletions will reveal what was found useful.
5. Measure the value to both the organisation and the individual.
6. Ensure that evaluation sheets are returned to the trainers when they are needed.
7. Use later enquiry sheets. Trainers need to carry out interviews regularly with a sample of participants.
8. Get all the information into a database. This permits reporting and analysis.
9. Protect confidentiality and access to records.
10. Settle on a format and then keep to it to allow longitudinal comparison.

Source: Dawson, 1995

Tests

The popularity of criterion-referenced assessment in competency-based training designs has given testing a higher profile in evaluation than hitherto. Regarded in the past as a rather simplistic extension of school grading methods to the complex world of industrial training, the emphasis on skills training in recent years has underlined the importance of testing to ensure competency, particularly in 'payment for skills' wages systems. Testing may be of benefit not only to the instructor but also to the trainees and to management in the evaluation process (Denova, 1979). For the instructor, tests provide the most reliable information on the progress of the trainee during the program, that is, at the level of learning. For the trainee, tests can be a valuable source of impartial feedback, and for management, tests give an indication of the performance of the training program as a whole. There is a variety of possible test types:

- **Essay tests** These are useful in situations where trainees are dealing with abstract concepts that form a whole, and where the conceptual skills of organising information, reasoning and self-expression are important.
- **Oral questioning** This permits the instructor to adapt his or her line of questioning to the responses of the trainee, and can be administered with little formal preparation.
- **Alternate-response tests** These ask questions with two possible answers presented to the trainee, between which he or she must discriminate. They are highly objective, and can be administered and scored quickly and easily.
- **Multiple-choice tests** These present trainees with more than two possible responses. This makes trainees less able to guess their way through the test, but are more time consuming to construct and score.
- **Performance tests** These construct situations in which the trainee has to perform a task. They are different in kind from the previously discussed paper and pencil type tests, as they involve the construction of physical test environments. They have a number of advantages in that they reinforce the learning process and provide explicit proof of the ability of the trainee to perform at a given level.

Testing may be carried out *before* training to assess prior learning, *during* training to determine progress, and *after* training to assess learning and transfer to the job. The flexibility of the testing concept and its apparent objectivity account for its popularity in modern training programs.

Interviews

Interviews, in contrast to tests and questionnaires, provide the evaluator with qualitative data. They are a very popular evaluation technique. Some researchers advocate their use continuously through the program to monitor the progress of the training and enable changes to be made in response to trainee reactions (Parlett and Hamilton, 1977) although most writers advocate their use in the pre-program or post-program situations. The value of the interview is in the opportunity it affords the evaluator to explore issues in depth and search for the unexpected. However, it is a time-consuming process and subject to the subjective biases of the interviewer.

Observation

The use of trained observers is usually confined to the period during the program. The observer, of course, may observe and evaluate a variety of things: the trainees, the trainer or the general conduct of the program. The advantage of observation is that direct, first-hand information is collected. However, as noted in Chapter 5, methods of direct observation have certain difficulties associated with them, particularly the impact of the observer on the behaviour of the group under observation.

Group discussion

The advantages of this form of evaluation are similar to those discussed for group methods of training analysis. The method is flexible in that it may be employed before, during or after the program. Gathering together potential participants in the program beforehand is a method often used to clarify objectives of, and expectations for, the program. During the program, group discussion can yield valuable feedback which can lead to improvements in the way in which the program is running. The use of 'follow-up' days after the program has finished is a useful means of measuring the longer-term impact of the training. Facilitation skills are, however, necessary for the successful conduct of group-based evaluation.

Appraisal

Training evaluation can be very successfully integrated with an appraisal system. Before and after appraisals of the participants can yield useful information about the impact of training at Kirkpatrick's behaviour level. In fact, Kirkpatrick (1983) suggests that appraisal by oneself, superiors, subordinates and peers should form part of the evaluation process. Appraisal is usually viewed as part of a longer-term evaluation strategy.

Impact analysis

Impact analysis provides a means of integrating evaluation into the design phase of the training process (Bramley and Kitson, 1994). It is a group-based process that brings together all the stakeholders in the training — participants, providers and managers — to discuss and agree on the key result areas the training should address. These key result areas can be clustered, and performance measures derived that relate to the various levels of evaluation from reaction to results. The stakeholders can agree on the best way of evaluating the results of the training and implementing the performance measures.

Cost/Benefit analysis

An approach that is becoming increasingly common as the costs of training programs grow, is accounting for the costs and the benefits that result from a training program and making decisions based on economic criteria. The principle that governs this approach is known as the Kaldor–Hicks principle, which states that one situation will be preferred over another when the gainers could compensate the losers and still be better off. In other words, the success of the program is measured by the extent to which the benefits outweigh the costs.

The benefits and the costs are shared between the participants in the program and the other stakeholders in the organisation (for example, managers who send staff through training programs, etc). Typically, there would be six benefits to participants and stakeholders from a successful training program:

1. **Value of work-related education** Benefit of such education to participants other than that usually given a market value, such as promotion.
2. **Attraction for new employees** A benefit for the company in being able to use the existence of training programs as an inducement to high quality recruits to join.
3. **Satisfaction** Increased skills and improved performance may add to the level of satisfaction individuals experience in their work.
4. **Increased knowledge** The extent to which the program was instrumental in the acquisition and retention of knowledge by employees.
5. **Productivity** Whether the program resulted in a measurable improvement in job performance. There are various utility measures that have been developed which enable an accurate assessment of productivity gains to be calculated.
6. **Reduced attrition** One potentially measurable impact of training would be its role in encouraging employees to remain with the organisation because training results in trainees having higher levels of commitment.

These benefits are assigned a market value and weighed against the three major costs that may be linked to training. These are:

- **Participant inconvenience** The costs incurred by the participants as a direct result of undergoing the training program, including lost income, child care, travel, etc.
- **Program costs** The total cost to the company of planning, developing and implementing the program.
- **Opportunity costs** Principally, the loss of worker productivity during training.

Figure 8.6 shows how these benefits and costs may be distributed between participants and other stakeholders in the organisation. For participants, benefits would typically include increased job knowledge and competency leading to higher job satisfaction, together with a general sense of the intrinsic worth of the educational experience. For stakeholders, the presumed benefits of training might include higher levels of productivity, reduced turnover and the ability to attract and retain valued employees; these benefits may be balanced by the cost to the employer of arranging the training.

Figure 8.6 — Benefits and costs

	Participants	Stakeholders
BENEFITS		
(1) value of education	x	
(2) attraction to new employees		x
(3) satisfaction	x	
(4) increased knowledge	x	
(5) productivity		x
(6) reduced attrition		x
COSTS		
(1) participant inconvenience	x	
(2) program costs		x
(3) costs to firm		x

Source: Hawthorne (1987)

The problem, of course, with this approach to evaluation is the difficulty of assigning market values to the rather intangible costs and benefits of training.

Evaluation Designs

If selection of an evaluation model and appropriate techniques constitute an overall evaluation strategy, the question still remains of *when* to evaluate. There is a wealth of research comparing the effectiveness of different evaluation designs. Designs range from the highly scientific control group designs, through statistical methods, to the crude post-test only designs which seem to be the stock in trade of most trainers. This section will present a brief overview of the major designs. Figure 8.7 on p 210 represents the six major designs in schematic form.

Single group, post-test only

This is the simplest and commonest form of evaluation (Clegg, 1987). Only those participants who have undergone the training program are measured. The problems with this design are summarised above in the section on questionnaires.

Single group, pre-test and post-test design

In this situation, a pre-test is administered prior to training and a comparison made with the results of a post-test administered after the program is complete. This design enables some measurement of change to take place. However, valid conclusions about the impact of the training program are difficult to draw, as the measurement is limited only to those who have undergone the training.

Time series design

In this situation, a series of measurements are taken over time, both before and after training. This enables more valid conclusions to be drawn about the pre-training state of the participants and the stability of any changes which occurred. In the diagram, line A shows no performance change, line B shows what appears to be a permanent improvement and line C shows an unstable change taking place.

Simple control group design

In this design, measurements carried out on those undergoing training (experimental group) are compared with measurements made of a similar group, the members of which are not trained (control group). The groups are selected to be as comparable as possible in every respect, other than in the training received. Conclusions may then be drawn about the effectiveness of the training, based on the differences observed between them. The intention of the control group is to eliminate variables from observed performance differences.

Control group, post-test only

A common variant on the control group design is to use a post-test only model. Possible distortions arising from the use of a pre-test, which sensitise participants (see below) are thereby ruled out. However, no pre-test and post-test comparisons are possible.

Experimental design

The most sophisticated of the control group designs involves an extension of the number of the control groups used, in an attempt to isolate scientifically the training variable. A scientifically 'pure' design would incorporate the use of random selection, pre-test and post-test measurement and a number of different 'streams' to ensure the isolation of the training variable. Figure 8.7 illustrates the Soloman 4 Group design.

There are other, more complex variants on these designs, but the basic three-way categorisation of:
- participant only testing;
- correlation designs; and
- control group designs

includes most of the evaluation designs in common use. The choice of design depends on issues such as validity.

Figure 8.7 — Major evaluation designs

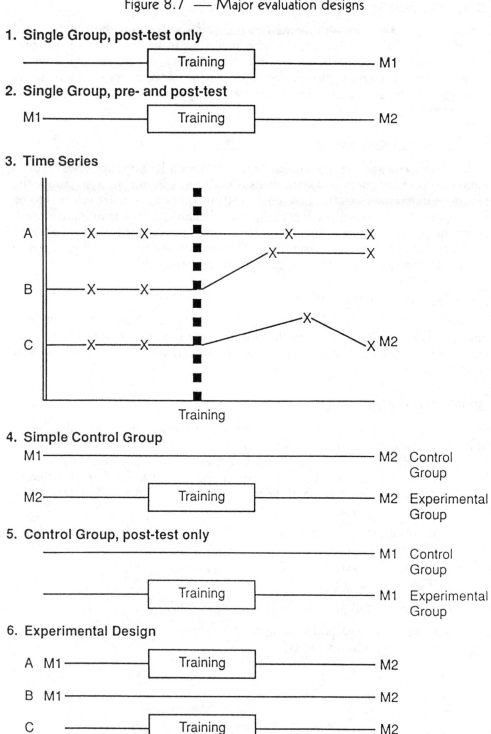

Illustration 8.3 — Cost/Benefit analysis at WMC Resources

> WMC is a major world nickel producer and one of Australia's largest gold producers. It owns the world's largest known multi-metal ore body at Roxby Downs in South Australia. WMC Projects and Engineering is a services group for the nickel and gold divisions. In 1996, the Projects and Engineering Group introduced a Performance Management Scheme for Design Managers. The training program associated with the program contained three components — a residential course, a tutorial and a refresher course after two years.
>
> WMC decided to use cost benefit analysis to evaluate the training program. Program costs were calculated by determining the following costs: consultancy for design and development; travel, accommodation and venue; books and printing; attendee time; training and development specialist time; secretarial support; cost of tutorial and refresher training. The resulting figure was then divided by the number of design managers who attended the program. Other attendees' time was not calculated as their attendance was necessary to achieve the objectives of the program. On this basis, the cost per design manager for the program was $11,254. If the other attendees were apportioned their share of the costs the amount would halve. As the program ran several times it was possible to amortise the establishment costs, resulting in a reduction of the unit costs of each program.
>
> Project benefits were calculated after striking a typical project value of $5 million. Of the 77 projects running in the company at that time, the average project value was $6.126m. Benefits were struck on the cost penalties not incurred as a result of completing the project on time, budget and standard. Savings included in the calculations were based on: labour and materials; on-time start-up with no production loss; on target manufacturing capacity; asset transfer penalty of one month not incurred. The total costs were then discounted by 47 per cent in accordance with the level of competencies covered by the program. The total benefits of a fully competent design manager were calculated at $812,500 for one project and applied to a three year cycle. A further set of calculations showed a substantial return to the company of running the program. At best, there was an internal rate of return on 150 per cent, and at worst 34 per cent. Each of these return figures exceeded the acceptability criteria of WMC for a return of greater than 20 per cent on their training investment.

Source: State Training Board of Victoria, 1997

Design Validity and Criterion Development

As we saw in our discussion of assessment, validity refers to the overall believability of the results of the evaluation. The evaluation process needs to establish that changes in trainee behaviour are the result of training and not some other factor (internal validity), and that the results of the training program will hold true for other groups undergoing the same training (external validity). The key to valid evaluation is developing criteria that will measure the effects the trainer decides are significant to the training. This section will examine the issues of validity and criterion development, and how these impact on competency-based training.

Internal validity

Although the training program is designed to produce changes in trainee behaviour, it may be difficult to establish exactly what changes observed during the evaluation process are the result of the training. Other factors may have intervened to produce, at least in part, the changes that have been observed. These other factors are sometimes referred to as threats to the validity of the evaluation. There are five common threats to validity:

1. **History** Events which occur at or around the same time as the training program and have an effect on the participants or the control group. A typical example might be the introduction of a new bonus scheme for shop floor employees concurrent with new training programs. Is any change in employee performance the result of the training or the new bonus system, or a combination of both?

2. **Individual change** Internal changes may occur within the individual trainees themselves during the period of the training program. Maturation processes may have an impact on the subsequent performance of trainees. This effect may be particularly pronounced with training programs for young people or programs that extend over a long period of time, for example, apprenticeship programs.

3. **Selection** Some groups of trainees will perform better than others. A disproportionate number of over-achievers or under-achievers will tend to distort evaluation measurements and make it difficult to draw general conclusions about the program from measurements of only one group.

4. **Mortality** Groups of trainees may change their composition over the period of the training program as some individuals leave and are replaced by others. This makes comparisons of pre-tests and post-tests particularly difficult.

5. **Hawthorne effect** As Elton Mayo and his associates found in the 1920s, there seems to be a motivational effect in being singled out for special attention. In Mayo's experiments investigating the impact of environmental change on the productivity of factory workers, groups of workers under observation seemed to react positively to the attentions of the researchers, with the result that productivity appeared to improve regardless of the settings of different environmental factors. A similar effect may impact upon the members of experimental or control groups undergoing measurement.

Figure 8.8 summarises the main threats to validity for each of the designs discussed above. In general, single group procedures and correlational methods are prone to most of the threats, in particular those associated with internal changes and selection. Control group designs emerge as the most valid; they are, of course, also the most difficult to put into practice.

Figure 8.8 — Threats to internal validity

	Hsitory	Change	Selection	Mortality	Test Effect	Hawrthorne
Single Group Post Test	*	*	*	*		*
Single Group Pre/Post Test	*	*	*	*	*	*
Time Series	*	*	*	*	*	
Simple Control Group				*	*	*
Control Group Post Test				*		*
Classic Experimental				*		*

* = Threat to validity of test

External validity

External validity refers to the generalisability of the results of one group to another. Internal validity is a prerequisite for external validity, as the results of the evaluation must be valid for the group being studied if they are to be generalised to predict the behaviour of other groups (Goldstein, 1986). There are three main threats associated with external validity:

1. **Effect of pre-testing** The process of undergoing pre-test procedures may sensitise the participants in the experimental group to the training program and lead them to perform differently from a group that has not been pre-tested. For this reason, experimental evaluation designs include groups that have not been subjected to pre-testing.

2. **Characteristics of the group** No matter how carefully the selection process for the training program is carried out, the fact is that groups differ in their composition. As a result, the reaction and behaviour of one group may not be a reliable guide to the behaviour of another group in the same situation.

3. **Effect of the training setting** The 'Hawthorne' effect discussed above. The presence of the evaluator may induce changes in the behaviour of the group which restrict the generalisability of the results to other groups.

Criterion development

The accuracy of the evaluation depends on the measures used to indicate the changes in behaviour or organisational performance. The development of these measures, referred to as criteria, are the subject of much debate in the psychological literature on evaluation. Generally, criteria are expected to meet three requirements if they are to be regarded as valid for the purposes of evaluation.

First, criteria should be relevant to the effects being measured. Criteria are relevant to the extent that the knowledge and skills identified in the analysis phase are represented in the criteria used in the evaluation phase. For example, a machine operator might be trained in the programming of a new computer-controlled (CNC) machine. Part of the evaluation could include a paper and pencil test of the operator's programming knowledge. This criterion (of an adequate performance in the test) may be relevant to the measurement of the operator's knowledge of the programming language and commands, etc, but it may not be relevant at all to the measurement of skill in actually programming the machine. A paper and pencil test is irrelevant to the assessment of the operator's skill in programming the CNC machine.

Secondly, just as criteria should be relevant to the effects they are measuring, the reverse is also true; effects identified in the analysis should not be missing from the criteria. To the extent that effects may be missing, the criteria are said to be deficient. If performance on the CNC machine is identified as the objective for the training program in the analysis, then the criteria will be deficient if they do not measure this effect through some sort of performance test.

Finally, criteria may be contaminated to the extent that they measure effects not identified in the analysis or present in the training program. Thus, the paper and pencil test for the machine operator on the CNC programming course may include general questions about the role of computers in manufacturing. Such knowledge, however, may not have been identified as necessary in the analysis, and so the criteria that are being used to evaluate the performance of the trainee are contaminated. Figure 8.9 on p 215 summarises the notions of criterion relevance, deficiency and contamination.

Criteria are relevant if the KSAs they are attempting to measure are either represented in both criteria *and* needs analysis or represented in neither. Where KSAs are represented in the analysis but not covered by criteria, the criteria are deficient; where KSAs are represented in the criteria but not in the original analysis, the criteria are contaminated.

Strategic Evaluation

A study of evaluation processes in 12 Australian organisations found that, typically, four approaches to evaluation were taken (State Training Board of Victoria, 1997). These approaches represented different stages in the development of the evaluation process.

- **Budget evaluation** This was the simplest and most common form of evaluation, and involved the organisation assessing whether the training budget had been fully spent or not. No attempt was made to evaluate the impact of the training or assess the costs and benefits of training expenditure involved. Budget evaluation was often driven by external requirements such as, in Australia, the Training Guarantee Scheme.
- **Skills evaluation** This involved the assessment of whether training was meeting the skills requirements of the organisation. This form of evaluation did not address the efficacy of any training program in particular, but rather attempted to assess the overall impact of training on the operational requirements of the organisation.

Figure 8.9 — The relationship between criteria and needs assessment

	− Not Represented	+ Represented
− Not Represented (Competency Represented in the Criteria)	Criterion Relevance A	Criterion Deficiency B
+ Represented	Criterion Contamination C	Criterion Relevance D

Source: Goldstein (1986)

- **Project evaluation** This form of evaluation assessed the impact of training within a single project. Thus, as part of project development, training needs would be analysed and targets set. The evaluation process assessed the impact of the training in terms of performance indicators linked to the goals of the project.
- **Strategic evaluation** This was the most sophisticated form of evaluation observed, but also the most unusual. In strategic evaluation, performance indicators are developed for the training function. Thus, performance indicators can be measured and the performance of training in the organisation assessed objectively. The performance indicators for training are then linked to the performance indicators developed for the organisation as a whole, which thus allows assessment to be made of the contribution of training to the achievement of the strategic plan of the organisation.

The implications of each of these forms of evaluation are summarised in Figure 8.10.

Figure 8.10 — Characteristics of different stages of evaluation

Evaluation	Importance of Training	Purpose of Training	Results of Training	Type of Learning
STRATEGIC	high strategic importance for the organisation	to provide long-term competitive advantage	creation of a learning culture	double-loop learning
PROJECT	important for the success of particular initiatives	to provide project benefits that outweigh costs	improved performance in particular areas	goal-based learning
SKILLS	increase in operational skills	to increase workforce skills	increase in skills acquired and used	goal-based learning
BUDGET	to meet external pressures	to meet organisational obligations	increase in skills acquired	haphazard learning

Source: State Training Board of Victoria (1997)

In this typology, strategic evaluation is the form of evaluation process organisations should be aiming to achieve. The other forms of evaluation do not assess the impact of training on the achievement of the organisation's goals. Strategic evaluation depends for its success on the development of performance indicators for training that tie into the performance indicators for the organisation. The use of performance indicators is one way of making training more measurable. Figure 8.11 on p 217 illustrates the link between strategy and evaluation.

Issues in Evaluation

So far, this discussion of evaluation has focused on the philosophy and mechanics of the process. During the discussion, a number of questions were alluded to but not addressed in any depth. These questions include the problem of who does the evaluation. Is it a responsibility of training practitioners or should other interested groups be involved? Does evaluation aim to produce proof positive of change and is this possible? How should evaluation be integrated into the training design process and, finally, how are the results of evaluation best communicated? It is these issues the following section will address.

Who evaluates?

Smith and Piper (1990) identify four stakeholders in the evaluation process: the purchaser of training (patron), the training agency (provider), the trainee (participant) and the independent evaluator (agent). Each has different concerns in evaluation, and each will use different methods for evaluation.

Figure 8.11 — Linking strategy and evaluation

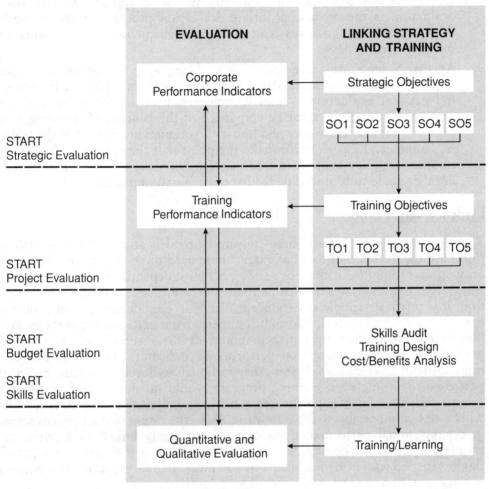

Source: State Training Board of Victoria (1997)

1. **Patrons** Patrons have often invested in training with very little evidence of the potential benefits to the organisation (Smith et al, 1995). Where patrons have become involved in evaluation, their concerns have centred on the feelings and experiences of the participants and the performance of the trainer, particularly if the trainer is a member of the organisation rather than an external provider. Much patron evaluation will be informal.
2. **Participants** Participants, although the prime beneficiaries of training, seem to be involved in evaluation at a peripheral level. Informal evaluation of their own performance and of the effectiveness of the training program through, primarily, post-test only methods is the most common form of participant involvement in evaluation.
3. **Providers** Providers are, by far, the group most commonly involved in the evaluation process. Most of the models and methods discussed in this

chapter are predicated on the involvement of the trainer in the evaluation. Often, the trainer is the only evaluator. It would appear that formative evaluation is the most appropriate evaluation process for the trainer's involvement. This involves issues of improvement rather than issues of training effectiveness.

4. **Agents**   Agents are in the position of being able to provide the most objective evaluation, particularly in summative terms. The occurrence of independent evaluation is limited, however, particularly in the business sector where patrons must be convinced of the benefits of investing in a professional evaluator over and above the original investment in the training. Smith and Piper (1990) make the point that the agent's evaluation is no more 'real' or 'true' than that of the other stakeholders but, rather, is another angle to be added to the overall evaluation picture.

Evidence versus proof

The plethora of complex and time-consuming models and methods of evaluation raise the question of to what extent these need to be used in practice. The answer, according to Kirkpatrick (1977), is that it depends on what the trainer wants. Kirkpatrick draws the distinction between evidence and proof in evaluation. It is relatively simple to produce evidence of the effectiveness of training: that is, at the reaction level, informal comments from participants; at the behaviour level, observation by colleagues; and at the results level, a series of measurements of organisational performance indicators. However, proof is more difficult to evince. Even at a fairly rudimentary level, producing proof of participant learning on a training program would involve the use of control groups and some fairly sophisticated statistical analysis. At the results level, it will be all but impossible to separate variables to the extent that an improvement in organisational performance could be satisfactorily linked to a particular training program. Kirkpatrick's answer to the dilemma is to 'shoot for proof' but be satisfied with evidence, since this will more than satisfy most stakeholders in the evaluation process.

Evaluation and design

Earlier in this chapter, conventional approaches to evaluation were characterised as end-on or add-on activities that appeared almost as an afterthought in the training design process. In discussing process evaluation models, the evaluation activity became linked into the design process at an earlier phase so that data collection for evaluation was taking place constantly over the entire duration of the training program.

This approach highlights the distinction between a 'production' model of evaluation and a 'cooperative' model (Wigley, 1988). The production approach is based on a notion of training as an off-job experience with little or no relevance to the work situation. Evaluation in this model is limited to an end-on assessment of the reaction of participants. The cooperative model, on the other hand, establishes the trainer as an internal consultant who involves other stakeholders in the design process so that training is clearly linked to the job situation.

In this case, evaluation becomes a part of the entire process from needs analysis through to final implementation and results assessment. The relationship of training and management is crucial to the success of the training program, and the collection of evaluation data is an important part of maintaining this relationship. Figure 8.12 on p 220 illustrates the cooperative model.

Communication of results

The impact of the evaluation depends on the way in which the results are communicated to those who make decisions in the organisation. The importance of the communication phase of the evaluation process has been highlighted in the Motorola Corporation, which employed an external evaluator to assess the impact of a total quality control program (Brandenburg, 1987). Five major factors appeared to influence the success of communicating the evaluation results.

1. **The reports told a story** Reports were easy to read and were structured in the form of a story with a beginning, an introduction of key characters, a description of actions taken, an analysis of processes followed and an explanation of results obtained.

2. **There was clear explanation** No jargon was used that was unfamiliar to the target audience.

3. **The reports were an accurate reflection** Managers reading the reports could identify that the results were a true reflection of what had happened.

4. **There was a balance of quantitative and qualitative information** Quantitative information was used sparingly and presented in an easily digestible format. The reports were liberally sprinkled with anecdote to liven the presentation.

5. **The reports were short** The reports were readable in about 20 minutes.

These guidelines may help to ensure the final success of the evaluation exercise.

Summary

Both assessment and evaluation have become important features of the training debate in Australia in recent years. The introduction of CBT has highlighted the critical nature of assessment procedures that can declare a trainee competent to undertake a job. Typically, assessment in CBT is criterion-referenced, which means that trainees are judged against a fixed standard of performance, specified in the competency standards, rather than against the performance of their peer group (norm-referenced assessment).

There are various forms of assessment. Holistic assessment involves judging the trainee against all aspects of the competencies on which the training is based. Summative assessment is the most common form of assessment. This involves judging whether the trainee has met the required standard of performance from having undergone the training. Assessment should be valid — measure what it says it measures; reliable — measure all trainees in the same way; flexible — take into account the differing circumstances of trainees; and fair — equally open to all. An important debate in CBT assessment is whether it should be graded or ungraded. The logic of CBT is that assessment should simply classify trainees as competent or not-competent. However, critics of this ungraded approach think that trainees can be graded within a competence rating.

Figure 8.12 — Training and evaluation process in a cooperative situation

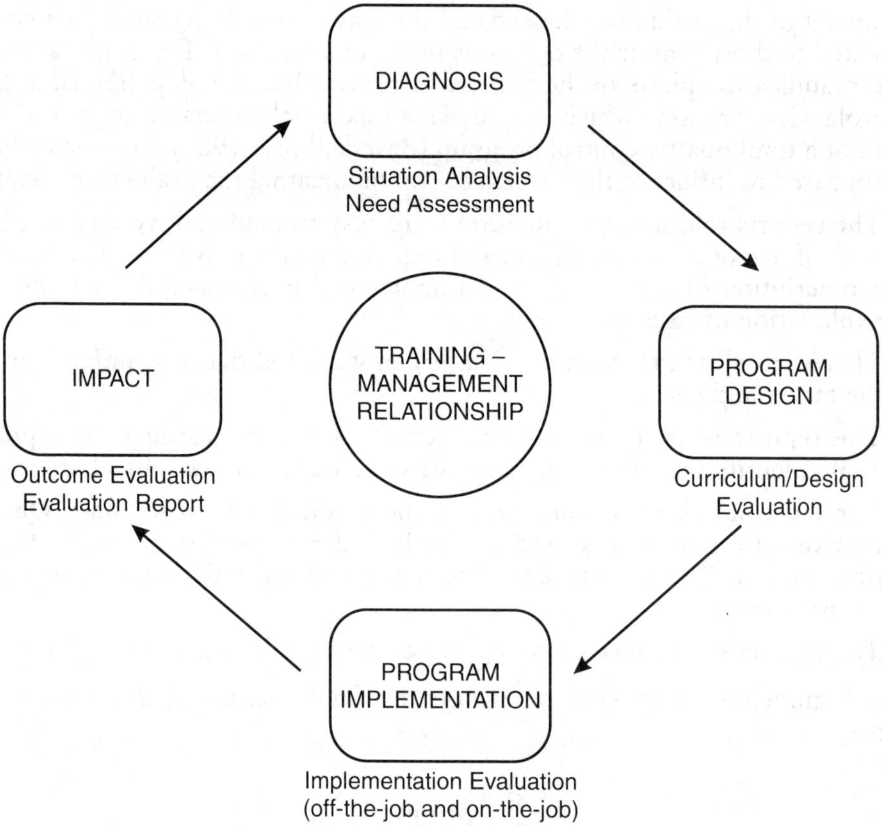

```
                    ┌─────────────┐
                    │  DIAGNOSIS  │
                    └─────────────┘
                  Situation Analysis
                   Need Assessment

    ┌──────────┐   ┌──────────────┐   ┌──────────┐
    │  IMPACT  │   │  TRAINING –  │   │ PROGRAM  │
    │          │   │  MANAGEMENT  │   │  DESIGN  │
    │          │   │ RELATIONSHIP │   │          │
    └──────────┘   └──────────────┘   └──────────┘
  Outcome Evaluation                  Curriculum/Design
  Evaluation Report                       Evaluation

                    ┌─────────────┐
                    │   PROGRAM   │
                    │IMPLEMENTATION│
                    └─────────────┘
              Implementation Evaluation
              (off-the-job and on-the-job)
```

Source: Wigley (1988)

Assessment is increasingly practised in the workplace and on the job. This means that trainees are assessed on their performance in the real work setting as opposed to a classroom setting. Workplace assessment means that trainers have to be trained to assess, and there are competency standards for assessment which workplace trainers need to reach in order to be certified to assess.

Evaluation is an activity that attempts to put a value or worth on any training activity. Apart from the conventional reasons for evaluating training which centre on the formative aspects of improving program performance or persuading others in the organisation to invest in the training process, evaluation is also a way for training practitioners to demonstrate their contribution to the 'bottom line' of the organisation.

There are a number of different models of evaluation. Outcome models stress the importance of measuring the impact of training at the individual and organisational level. These models are epitomised in Kirkpatrick's four-level evaluation model. Process models highlight the importance of examining the whole training process, not only its outcomes (although these are often included in process models). Typically, this involves the evaluation of the context of the training and the inputs as well as the implementation and outcomes.

Within the models, there is a variety of techniques, ranging from individual questionnaires to group methods, that can be used to collect evaluation data. The design of the evaluation (whether pre-tests or post-tests are used or control group methods) is critical to the level of proof that is produced in the evaluation process. In many cases, scientifically rigorous methodologies are beyond the scope of organisations, which may be satisfied with evidence rather than proof.

The reliability of the results of evaluation depends on the validity of the methods, both internal and external, and the accuracy of the criteria in measuring those elements important to the organisation and included in the training program.

Questions of concern to the training practitioner that emerge from this discussion of evaluation include the role of the various stakeholders in the process, the level of proof required, the place of evaluation in training design and, finally, the communication of results.

Discussion Questions

1. Why is assessment such an important issue in a CBT system?
2. Should we grade assessment in training?
3. Should assessment be practised in the workplace? What are the problems with this approach?
4. What is the distinction between process and outcome models of evaluation?
5. Is proof of training evaluation really required?
6. How can problems of validity be avoided in evaluation?
7. Does Brinkerhof provide a bridge between process and outcome models of evaluation?

Chapter 9

Management Development

The success or failure of an organisation is often ascribed to its managers. They are regarded as a separate group within the literature on organisation theory and behaviour, and are often treated as such by the human resource policies of their own workplaces. It seems sensible, then, to regard their training and development as an activity apart from the mainstream training and development practices of the organisation. Indeed, this is certainly the case in the body of training literature, which encompasses a wide variety of books and journals devoted to this aspect of training and development.

Management is not, however, a homogeneous concept. The distinction is usually made between senior managers, who direct the overall strategy of the organisation, middle managers, who implement the strategy, and junior managers, who manage the operational aspects of the organisation. Another critical but much neglected distinction is that between managers and supervisors (sometimes referred to as 'frontline managers'). Traditionally regarded as 'men in the middle', supervisors form a group comprising those who are neither managers nor workers and yet are often viewed as the backbone of management within their own organisations.

This chapter outlines the distinction between management and supervisory development and examines each separately. A review of the state of management in Australia is followed by a discussion of the case for management development. The major methods of management development are examined, with a focus on some of the more recent developments in this area. The section concludes with a discussion of the Karpin report and its implications for management development in Australia. Supervisory development is examined in the context of the historical emergence of the supervisor's role on the shop floor and its gradual transformation in the twentieth century. The current practice of supervisory development in Australia is discussed, followed by an examination of the Frontline Management Initiative.

Managers in Australia

The voluminous literature on management is beset by the perennial difficulty of finding an adequate definition of a manager's job. Four reasons have been advanced for this difficulty (Gamble and Messenger, 1990). First, managers' jobs vary according to their setting. The job of a production manager in the car industry, for instance, is quite different from that of the captain of a large passenger liner; it involves very different behaviours. Secondly, even within the same organisation, managers usually enjoy considerable latitude in determining the content of their own jobs. This is one of the key characteristics that differentiates the manager's job from that of non-managerial occupations, where job content is more carefully circumscribed. Thirdly, managerial behaviour tends to vary with circumstances. It is not always enough to give orders when the support and commitment of a large number of people, many of them not under the direct control of the individual manager, may be required to carry out a particular task. Finally, managers tend to behave differently as they progress up the management hierarchy. They may well not conform to the traditional notions of 'classical' management theory, that is, planning, leading, organising, controlling and directing, but engage in a series of seemingly random, reactive behaviours in their attempt to control the workplace.

Figures prepared for the Industry Taskforce on Leadership and Management Skills, the so-called 'Karpin Committee', revealed that there were approximately 900,000 managers in Australia in 1994 (Midgley, 1995). Of these, 33,000 were general managers, 202,000 were specialist managers, 411,000 were supervisors and 254,000 were farmers and farm managers. This number was expected to rise to 977,200 by 1998 (McCloud and Siniakis, 1995). Two-thirds of these managers were employed in small business (businesses with less than 50 employees) as Figure 9.1 illustrates.

Figure 9.1 — Managers in Australia

	Fewer than 50 Employees	More than 50 Employees
Middle and senior managers	54,000	181,000
Supervisors	213,000	198,000
Farm managers	254,000	n/a
Total	521,000	379,000

Source: Karpin (1995)

Thus, managers in Australia represent about 12 per cent of the work force, which is broadly comparable with the proportions in other countries. However, in terms of education, Australian managers compare very poorly with their international counterparts. About 29 per cent of Australian managers hold a first degree, compared with 63 per cent for Germany, 65 per cent for France and around 85 per cent of managers in the United States and Japan (Handy et al, 1988). The educational position of Australian managers is illustrated in Figure 9.2 on p 224.

Figure 9.2 — Percentage of managers with degrees

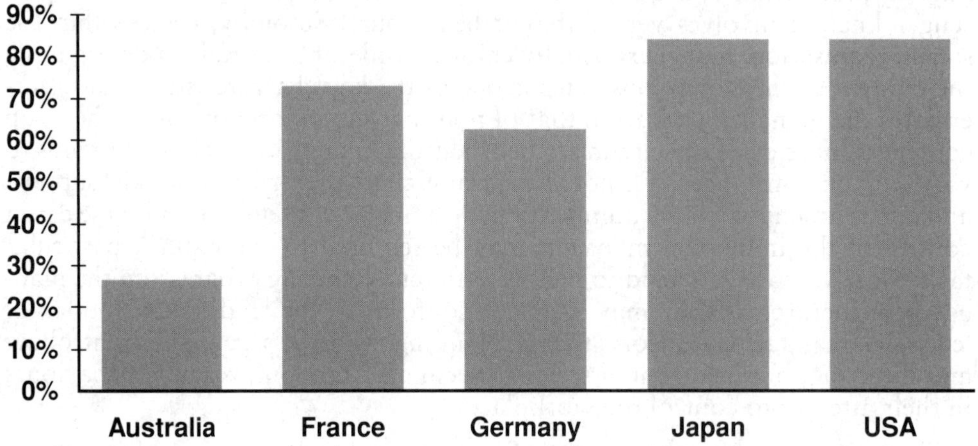

Source: Karpin (1995)

The picture becomes a little brighter when other forms of vocational qualifications are considered, such as trade certificates and associate diplomas. Forty per cent of Australian managers hold some form of post-school qualification. This, of course means, however, that fully 60 per cent of managers in Australia hold no formal educational qualifications beyond secondary school (Dawkins, 1991). Moreover, Australian managers do not spend much of their time in training. Estimates by Midgley (1995) put 'world best practice' in management training at about 15 days per year, or 6 per cent of a manager's time. As Figure 9.3 shows, Australian managers barely achieve half that level, with an average of less than seven days training per year.

Figure 9.3 — Days spent in training by level of manager

Level of Manager	Average Days Spent in Training per Year
Executive	7.8
Senior	7.0
Middle	7.1
Junior	5.3
Supervisor	5.34
Over all Levels	6.9

Source: Midgley (1995)

This lack of formal education and subsequent training may help to explain the poor perceptions of the performance of Australian managers overseas. Savery, Dawkins and Mazzarol (1995) surveyed 502 Asian managers and asked them to compare the performance of Australian managers against the performance of managers from five competitor countries. The results of the survey are summarised in Figure 9.4 on p 225. Asian managers placed most emphasis on long-term perspective, acceptance of responsibility and managerial expertise. Australian managers shared last place with Taiwan's managers on these three criteria — both some way behind managers from the other four countries. They concluded that the weaknesses of Australian managers may be due to their relative lack of international exposure, or to the fact that international best practice is not widely pursued in Australian organisations.

The views of these Asian managers also tally with the conceptions which Australian managers have about themselves (Wawn, Green et al, 1995). A group of 91 Australian management experts and practising managers agreed that while Australian managers were hard working, flexible and innovative, their greatest faults were their short-term view, lack of strategic perspective and poor people skills.

In terms of their social and economic backgrounds, however, Australian managers more closely resemble their overseas counterparts. In the past, managers in Australia tended to come from families in which the father would have had a managerial or professional position. Now there is evidence that managers are being drawn from a much wider social net as merit plays a more significant part in the promotion process. Nevertheless, few Australian managers have direct experience of the shop floor, most coming from a staff or a technical position (Lansbury and Quince, 1987).

Figure 9.4 — Managerial qualities: mean ranking of managers

Quality	Australia	Germany	Japan	Taiwan	UK	USA
Ability to look well into the Future	4.7	3.4	2.1	4.4	3.9	2.5
Acceptance of Responsibility	4.6	3.1	2.0	4.7	3.6	3.0
Management Skills	4.7	3.3	2.3	4.9	3.4	2.2
Entrepreneurial Skills	4.8	3.7	2.3	3.4	4.1	2.6
Leadership Skills	4.6	3.4	2.7	4.8	3.4	2.1
Technical Skills	5.0	2.7	1.8	4.6	4.0	2.8
Cross cultural Skills	3.8	4.0	3.1	3.7	3.7	2.6
Adaptability Skills	4.1	3.9	2.5	3.6	4.1	2.8

Source: Karpin (1995). Means are on a six point scale (1) best to (6) worst

Karpin (1995:65) summarised what we know about the Australian manager as follows:

> It is difficult to speak of a 'typical manager' given the wide diversity of managerial jobs and skill needs, but some broad generalisations can be made:
>
> The typical Australian manager:
> - is male;
> - is of Anglo descent;
> - has the HSC or a qualification from TAFE as their highest educational qualification; and
> - has worked for the same firm for more than six years.

A picture emerges therefore of a large number of underqualified, underexperienced and undertrained managers running Australian enterprises, by comparison with our major trading partners. Any further discussion of management development, however, needs to return to the question of what it is that a manager does and how it can be learned.

Prescriptive theories

The traditional approach to analysing the work of the manager has its origins in the early twentieth century work of the classical management theorists epitomised in the work of Henri Fayol (1949) and Lyndall Urwick (1947). The classical school emphasised the rationality of management activity. Managers were charged with the administration of the organisation, and they 'should' or 'ought' to use a rational, scientific approach in discharging their duties. The emphasis on the words 'should' and 'ought' highlight the prescriptive orientation of much of this literature. The job of the manager entailed the planning, organising, directing and controlling of an organisation established on rational principles. These principles included, inter alia, the notion of unity of command (each individual has only one boss), the division of labour, the distinction between line and staff functions and the centralisation of authority. The work of the classical management theorists was supplemented by the work of Frederick Taylor (1911) who invented the concept of 'scientific management', a concept which became synonymous with the rational approach to management.

Although nearly a century old, classical and scientific management theory still dominate the practice of management. Such modern innovations as management by objectives (MBO) and planning, programming, budgeting systems (PPBS) are clearly based on the rational, prescriptive view of management activity. Research later in the twentieth century has tended to move the focus of management activity from that of the detached classical administrator to that of one who acknowledges, in McGregor's (1960) words, 'the human side of enterprise'. The impact of the behavioural sciences on management theory has emphasised the social nature of work and the individual and intrinsic nature of motivation. Nevertheless, this softer approach still rests on the notion of the manager as a rational planning person who, while understanding the complexities of human behaviour, does not relinquish that rationality in the pursuit of the management task.

A corollary of this prescriptive approach has been the work by occupational psychologists in identifying management traits: those qualities essential to effective managerial performance. However, the variance displayed by different managers in terms of personality profiles has made it almost impossible in practice to identify a set of traits necessary for a manager. In 1940, Bird, at the University of Minnesota, concluded that only 5 per cent of leadership traits were common to any group of four or more studies of leadership (Yau and Sculli, 1990). The outcome of this type of research has usually manifested itself in trait-based personality questionnaires designed to select prospective managers from graduate recruits or other groups within the organisation. Possibly the most successful of these inventories is that designed by Ghiselli (1971), who identified 13 traits which he scaled in order of their importance to management ability. However, the traits that Ghiselli identifies as most significant to managerial ability, such as 'supervisory ability', 'occupational achievement' or 'intelligence', are so generalised that they become meaningless when related to the specific training needs of managers.

Descriptive theories

More successful than the prescriptive approaches in understanding the work managers do has been the more recent research examining the actual behaviours manifested by managers in the workplace. Perhaps the most well known of these research programs was that conducted by Henry Mintzberg of McGill University. Mintzberg (1975) showed that much of the manager's job is taken up with activities which do not fit into the traditional rational model of planning, organising and leading, etc. In fact, the manager seems to perform a number of roles. These roles are present to varying degrees in every managerial position and form an integrated whole. None of the roles can be removed without changing the nature of the others. They are grouped into three major categories:

1. **Interpersonal roles** These comprise the leadership aspects of the manager's job, relating to subordinates and peers, and performing the ceremonial duties of the manager.
2. **Informational roles** Controlling the key resource of information: acquiring it, disseminating it, hiding it and acting as the spokesperson for the group.
3. **Decisional roles** Handling grievances, negotiating, bargaining and allocating resources.

In a separate work, Mintzberg defined eight managerial skills which are related to the roles discussed above. These are illustrated in Figure 9.5 on p 228.

As Yau and Sculli (1990) point out, the notions of management skills and management traits are not unrelated. There is a rough correspondence between Mintzberg's eight skills and the traits identified by Ghiselli. Thus, supervisory ability can be viewed as congruent with the trait of leadership, and occupational achievement may be correlated with entrepreneurial and resource-allocation skills. However, the focus on skills makes the efficacy of management training and development much clearer.

Figure 9.5 — Mintzberg's managerial skills

Peer skills	Deal with the manager's ability to enter into and effectively maintain peer relationships
Leadership skills	Focus on the manager's ability to deal with subordinates — to motivate and train them, provide help, deal with problems of authority and dependence, and so on
Conflict-resolution skills	Include the interpersonal skill of mediating between conflicting individuals and the decisional skill of handling disturbances
Information-processing skills	Managers should know how to build informal information networks, find sources of information and extract what they need, validate information, assimilate it, and build effective mental models
Skills in decision-making under ambiguity	These are important because a characteristic of top management decision-making is the unstructured situation. The manager must first decide when a decision must be made; diagnose the situation and plan an approach to it; search for solutions and evaluate their consequences; and, finally, select an alternative
Resource allocation	Used when managers are required to choose among competing resource demands. They must decide how to allocate their own time, determine what work their subordinates must do and in what formal structure they must work, and pass judgments, sometimes very quickly, on projects that require organisational resources
Entrepreneurial skills	Involve the search for problems and opportunities and the controlled implementation of change in organisations
Skills of introspection	Relate to the manager's understanding of his or her job. A manager should be sensitive to his or her own impact on the organisation; he or she should be able to learn by introspection

Source: Yau and Sculli (1990)

Competency-based management

In the 1990s, the notion of competency has been used with increasing frequency when discussing management training and development. In the management development context, however, the term has been given a far less specific meaning than that generally used in the Australian training system. In that situation, the term 'competency' has been defined in relation to the tasks comprising a particular job and has referred to a basic function carried out by the job incumbent. In the context of management, however, competency has been used interchangeably with the term 'skill'. Thus, the American Assembly of Collegiate Schools of Business conducted an outcomes measurement project (OMP) in the late 1970s in an attempt to make the offerings of the traditional business school programs more relevant to the actual work of a manager (American Assembly of

Collegiate Schools of Business, 1987). The outcomes measurement project identified two types of educational outcomes for management. The first related to content, that is, the essential knowledge a manager requires to perform effectively. The second set of outcomes referred to the 'skills or personal characteristics' which the manager required. It is interesting to note that in this case the traits and skills discussed earlier have been elided into one category. These skills included the familiar leadership, planning, decision-making and communication skills which are the inheritance of the rational approach. Together these outcomes formed a set of management competencies which could be tested as part of a business school program. Thus, the notion of competence referred to the testability of the knowledge and skills the manager should have acquired, rather than defining the basic dimensions of the manager's job.

In a study more closely related to the job tasks of the manager, Boyatzis (1982) defined competency as an underlying characteristic of a manager which can lead to effective performance. Boyatzis identified 19 competencies which he grouped into five clusters as shown in Figure 9.6.

Figure 9.6 — Boyatzis' management competencies

Goal and Action Management Cluster
Efficiency Orientation
Proactivity
Diagnostic Use of Concepts
Concern of Impact

Leadership Cluster
Self-confidence
Use of Oral Presentations
Logical Thought
Conceptualisation

Human Resource Management Cluster
Use of Socialised Power
Positive Regard
Managing Group Process
Accurate Self-assessment

Directing Subordinates Cluster
Developing Others
Use of Unilateral Power
Spontaneity

Focus on Others Cluster
Self-control
Perceptual Objectivity
Stamina and Adaptability
Concern with Close Relationships

Source: Boyatzis (1982)

However, in Boyatzis' work, competencies alone are not a guarantee of effective performance. He places the competency clusters in a complex model which relates them to the demands of the job and the environment of the organisation. Management competency may be only one of several causes of effective performance (Albanese, 1989).

Confusion arises when the tasks that a manager performs are mistaken for the competencies that are required. Thus, to perform a planning task adequately, the manager may require a range of competencies such as being able to diagnose problem situations, evaluate solutions, come forward with ideas and so on. The fact is that, unlike the operational competencies, managerial competencies are wide ranging and enable a manager to perform a number of tasks.

In the United Kingdom, the Management Charter Initiative (MCI), set up in response to the perceived deficiencies of British managers, clearly separated the tasks or 'standards' required of a manager from the competencies needed to perform to the standards. Thus, the MCI identified managerial standards from a conventional 'breakdown' of managerial functions into their constituent tasks. Managerial competencies, on the other hand, are derived from a DACUM-like process of identifying individual managerial behaviours and grouping them into clusters which become competencies. Thus, a typical cluster of behaviours of a manager might be that he or she:

- identifies priorities;
- thinks back from the deadline;
- identifies elements of tasks;
- anticipates resource requirements;
- allocates resources to tasks;
- manages his or her own and others' time.

These could be grouped under the general competency heading of 'organisation' (Woodruffe, 1991). Nevertheless, despite the cloudy definition of the term in the context of management development, the notion of competency provides a much surer framework for creating training programs for managers than the myopic prescriptions of the classical theorists.

In Australia, the use of management competencies is gaining ground in organisations. Recent research has shown that 45 per cent of Australian organisations appear to be using the management competencies (Nesbit and Midgley, 1995). Not surprisingly, larger organisations are using management competencies more frequently than smaller organisations. However, the research also revealed that management competencies are being used for a wide variety of purposes within organisations. Apart from determining training needs, Australian organisations are using management competencies for selection, promotion and appraisal. All these activities link in very well to management development activities. However, management competencies are also being used for other purposes, such as designing training programs, career planning and mentoring: see Chapter 11. Thus, the use of management competencies may benefit organisations beyond the purposes of management development.

Why management development?

There seems to be a number of reasons why Australia needs more effective management development.

1. **The growth of management as an occupation** Even if the stock of managers stayed at present levels, it has been calculated that 30,000 new managers per year would need training to replace those retiring (Dawkins, 1991). However, it is likely that more rather than less people will become involved in management functions in the future. Corporate restructuring and re-engineering programs often focus on thinning the ranks of middle management in larger organisations to create 'leaner', more competitive structures; yet the tasks these managers perform cannot be wished away and, as a result, those at lower levels in the organisation become more involved in aspects of management as staffing becomes tighter. This trend shows no likelihood of abating in the 1990s (Littler et al, 1997).

2. **Work force demographics** The age structure of Western countries is changing as people live longer and fewer children are born. The result is a diminishing number of people entering the productive work force. Australia is no exception to this trend, although the effect of immigration is to produce a slightly younger age structure than that of Europe or the United States (Australian Bureau of Statistics, 1990c). The impact of this demographic downturn in the labour market will be to increase the level of competition between employers to recruit and retain younger workers. Only those organisations offering good development programs will be able to attract the best recruits; this will be particularly true at the premium graduate end of the labour market, containing those traditionally bound for management careers.

3. **The internationalisation of management** The global economy is increasingly dominated by multinational and transnational corporations. Managers are frequently expected to be able to move to other parts of the world during their careers with these organisations (Karpin, 1995). The Australian economy includes a large number of such corporations. However, as discussed earlier in the chapter, Australian managers do not compare favourably with their international counterparts in terms of education and development. As the Australian economy becomes more international, its managers will require a higher level of development.

4. **Management is becoming more strategic** Hamel and Prahalad (1990) argue that the function of top management is to develop the ability of the organisation to think and act strategically by taking a long-term view in decision-making. This contrasts with the short-term results orientation that seems to typify the Australian manager (Dawkins, 1991). Thus, the overall depth and calibre of managers in Australia need to be improved if the organisations they run are to compete in the longer term.

The long-term competitiveness of Australian organisations in a global economy therefore would seem to depend, in part at least, on the quality of Australian managers. Improving this level of quality is the function of management development.

Illustration 9.1 — Woolworths boosts line managers' skills

A Woolworths management training scheme sparked by a surge in unfair dismissal claims against it has evolved into a wide-ranging employee management program that is bearing results. Industrial Relations Manager, Joe Degabriela, says by pointing to the level of disruption and the costs resulting from the claims, he has been able to show the value of training to Woolworths' bottom line.

In the early 1990s the retail environment was increasingly competitive on customer service as well as price. Woolworths' wanted to extend its trading hours to compete with smaller shops and new convenience stores. At the same time the company had launched its 'Fresh Food People' campaign forcing it to abandon its old employment concept of 'a disposable workforce in a vestibule industry.' This threw greater responsibility onto line managers and their ability to motivate and manage their employees, when the company had already weighed them down with increased duties after flattening the management structure.

Degabriela believes the intensive training will turn around managers' employee management skills. The recent company-wide management seminar was developed in-house and used internal trainers at a cost of $300,000. HR was able to convince the company of the training's value because it already had runs on the board in the form of simple training seminars that had been seen to deliver. HR needed to be able to support the company's line managers in delivering in this brave new world.

It started in 1992 by putting line managers through a seminar focused on its most common union disputes which were generated largely from a misunderstanding of the awards, Degabriela said, particularly minor awards that had different conditions to the main Shop Employees (State) Award. Issues included 10-hour breaks between shifts, Sunday rosters and unions' right of entry under the NSW Industrial Relations Act. On each matter the number of store disputes declined at the same time as store managers' employee skills developed. The company followed this up by developing a user-friendly Industrial Relations handbook for managers, plus training on the new supermarket award and a rostering workshop.

Source: HR Report No 140

The objectives and targeting of management development, however, differ between organisations despite the overall reasons for the existence of the activity. Four major objectives for management development can be identified from the literature. First, management development is often viewed as essential for programs of organisational change: see Chapter 10. Managers are a key ingredient in the process of change and need to change their mode of operation in order for the broader organisation to change. Secondly, related to the theme of change, management development is usually one of the first steps in the implementation of quality improvement programs in organisations. Often, new change strategies such as TQM or teamworking involve a heavy dose of management training and development. Thirdly, management development can be used to facilitate the process of merger and acquisition. Where two different organisations are to be welded together, a common approach to management is usually regarded as an essential element for success. Programs of management development can help this common focus emerge. Finally, management development seems often to be associated with the emergence of a broader role for line managers as organisations pare their management ranks in recession (Storey, 1989).

Traditionally, management development in Western organisations has been targeted at two groups of managers: new entrants and non-performers. The latter approach is typified by Odiorne's adaptation of the Boston Consulting Group's portfolio analysis matrix illustrated in Figure 9.7.

Figure 9.7 — Odiorne's management development matrix

	Low Potential	High Potential
High Performance	Workhorses	Stars
Low Performance	Deadwood	Problem employees

Source: Storey (1989)

In this approach, the focus of management development is on those 'problem employees' with high potential but whose actual performance is low. As one advocate of this approach, quoted by Odiorne, put it:

> ... we polish the stars, fix the problems, feed the workhorses plenty of hay and shoot the dogs.

It would appear, however, that this targeting of the management development effort may be a symptom of a lack of integration of management development with the mainstream management of the organisation. Comparative studies of management development in the United Kingdom and Japan have revealed that Japanese managers have difficulty in identifying the concept of management development as a separate activity because it is so embedded in the work of the manager (Storey et al, 1991).

Handy et al (1988) identify three forms of management development. The corporate approach focuses on the organisation as the site of management development activities. The academic approach uses the expertise of external business schools and/or universities to provide development programs for managers. Finally, the professional approach regards the professional institutions (in Australia, particularly those for accountants and engineers) as the basis for developing managers. The predominance of accountants and engineers within the management structures of Australian organisations appears to testify to the power of the professional bodies in this respect. Nevertheless, although the professional bodies may certify managers in certain disciplines, the bulk of general management training and development takes place within the organisation or in the business schools. It is the role of these two approaches that will be examined in the next two sections.

Models of Management Development

Management development within the organisation has increasingly come to occupy a separate position in the overall structure of human resource management. Frequently, this separate nature is institutionalised by the existence of a defined management development function within the organisation. This is in recognition of the fact that management development is not simply a matter of training managers in a formal sense. Management training programs are an important element in management development but they are not the sole means of developing management abilities. Other key elements of the process are career and management succession planning, the establishment of organisation structures which facilitate the development of managers, the periodic rotation of managers between different positions and functions in the organisation and the administration of management remuneration.

Programs of management training in the more effective organisations will be linked into this broader framework of management development. Thus, specific training programs may be planned for individuals as they reach certain predetermined points in their careers. Training programs may encompass project work and on-the-job training activities to supplement the off-the-job parts of the program and so on. Treatment of management development within the broader context of human resource management is the subject of a wide-ranging literature in itself and is beyond the scope of this work. In this section, discussion will centre on corporate management training programs and the techniques most often employed within them.

Finegold et al (1995) have developed a typology of the different models of management development that organisations might pursue. A summary of the seven different models is shown in Figure 9.8 on p 235.

Figure 9.8 — Finegold's models of management development

MODELS	No formal training	Company-based training			Customised training	Advanced apprenticeship	Short courses	Undergraduate courses	MBAs
Who receives training	No one	All	College graduates	Large firms	Cross-functional teams	Skilled workers, supervisors	All	Post-secondary students	Existing managers
Who provides training	Small firms, universities	Japanese large firms			Community colleges, German RKW	Alternating firm and college	Professional organisations, private consultants	College universities	Business schools
What types of skills	Personal qualities	Emphasis on firm specific			General in firm-specific content	General and company-specific	General, wide variety	Emphasis on general	
Who pays	No one	Firm			Firm	Firm, individual, and state	Individual firm, state indirect	State, individual	Individual, firm, state indirect
Role of state	None	Minimal (correspondence course, small firms training)			Small firm subsidies	— Regulate — Fund off-job training	— Direct provision — Funding (institutions, individuals) — Accreditation		

Source: Karpin (1995)

Model 1: No formal management development

This is the most common model, and predominates in small firms around the world. Despite the explosion in management development activities, many firms and managers remain very sceptical about the value of training and developing employees for roles as ill-defined as that of manager.

Model 2: The company-based model

This is an increasingly common form of management development within larger organisations. In this model, the organisation provides its own management development programs which are open to all managers. The programs may be run by specialist training staff employed by the organisation or they may be outsourced to external training providers and consultants. Some very large organisations may run a suite of management development activities which involve a mix of formal off-the-job training with other on-the-job development activities. However, the development is likely to be highly firm-specific and not readily transferable by the individual to other organisations. Large Japanese firms are usually quoted as the prime example of in-company management development.

Model 3: Customised training

This is an amalgamation of the in-company model and Models 6 and 7 which are based in universities and business schools. Universities and non-university business schools (such as the Australian Administrative Staff College at Mount Eliza in Victoria) have, for some time, been offering non-degree executive programs on a fee-paying basis as part of their general programs. These executive programs differ from the usual university business school offerings in a number of ways:

- They are much shorter in duration, typically consisting of a few days or weeks rather than months or years.
- They focus on particular issues, such as strategic planning, general management, personal skills, etc, rather than attempting to cover the range of management activities.
- They employ a wider variety of teaching methods than do traditional programs. In this respect, they resemble in-house corporate training programs. In fact, many of these programs may be run on the organisation's premises using university staff on a subcontract basis.
- They are non-accredited, that is, unrecognised by university accreditation bodies and carrying no value in academic terms.

Most programs of this type are open to all members of the public who are willing to pay the fairly substantial fees charged. This means that these programs tend to be very general in nature, as they cater for a very wide potential audience from a range of different organisations.

In order to increase the relevance of such programs to particular organisations, training practitioners may subcontract the university to develop and run a program for their own specific enterprise. Such programs have the merit of employing independent experts as faculty and being conducted on 'neutral' ground in the university, where managers can be more open about their experiences and opinions. These collaborative designs are becoming increasingly common in the United States and in Australia, as universities seek to make their offerings more relevant to the business world (Verlander, 1989).

Model 4: Advanced apprenticeships

This model is related to the German 'dual system' model of apprenticeship. Under this model, managers undergo both in-company training and attend off-the-job training programs which lead to nationally recognised qualifications. The German model combines both company-specific and general training and is used very effectively for the training of supervisors who eventually attain the status of master or *meister* in the German system. The German *meister* is highly trained, both technically and in management. This combination of management and technical training enables the *meister* to exercise the authority often associated with middle level managers in Australian organisations.

Model 5: Short courses

This is one of the most common models of management development. Organisations send their managers to short courses on particular topic areas run by external training providers and consultants. This model of management development is very flexible in that the organisation can chose where and when to send their managers on training programs. However, often managers go to external training courses and come back into the organisation without the means to implement what they have learned. As a result, short courses are not an effective way of changing behaviour.

Model 6: Undergraduate courses in business

Most of Australia's 39 public universities now offer undergraduate degrees in business. In recent years, there has been an explosion of enrolments in business degrees. From 1979 to 1993 the total number of students enrolled in business programs at universities increased by 140 per cent, from 50,000 to over 120,000, with most of this increase occurring since 1987. This number is expected to rise to over 150,000 by the year 2000 (McCloud and Siniakis, 1995). Thus, undertaking an undergraduate degree in business has increasingly been seen as a necessary element of achieving a career in management. The advantage of this explosion in management education for organisations is that it is almost entirely underwritten by the government, which finances the public universities and subsidises the costs of students studying. However, undergraduate study is only an introduction to management, and rarely contains any element of practical management training that would enable graduates to take up a management position on graduation. In order to make effective managers, undergraduates usually require further training and development by the organisation.

Model 7: Master of Business Administration Programs (MBAs)

As with undergraduate business programs, there has been an enormous expansion of post-graduate business programs, usually MBA programs. Since 1979 the number of MBA programs on offer in Australia has increased from 10 to over 40. Much of this increase has taken place since 1987 (Ashenden and Milligan, 1995). Most of these MBAs are offered by universities but some, such as that run by the Association of Professional Engineers (the largest MBA program in Australia), are offered by private training providers, or by overseas institutions such as the International Management Centre from Buckingham. The growth in student numbers in MBA programs has been even more dramatic, with numbers of higher degree students (most of whom are enrolled in MBA programs) increasing by over 400 per cent, from 2500 in 1979 to 12,500 in 1993. These numbers are likely to reach more than 20,000 by the year 2000 (McCloud and Siniakis, 1995).

Illustration 9.2 — Companies turning from MBAs to in-house training

> Leading Australian companies are increasingly negotiating with business schools and universities to have in-house training contribute towards an MBA. Industry experts query the relevance of stand-alone MBA programs, stating that the quality of MBAs is extremely varied and there aren't enough experienced and able teachers to support the plethora of MBA programs. The national body of MBA graduates, the Graduate Management Association of Australia, says there are at least 38 MBA programs. It has approved only 18 schools from which graduates are eligible for membership of the association, because of quality concerns.
>
> Coopers and Lybrand has negotiated with Monash Mount Eliza Business School to have its in-house management education program incorporated as part of the school's MBA. Coopers and Lybrand's National Education Director, Patrick Blades, said their in-house Certificate of Management supplied knowledge and skills unique to Coopers. Having it count for two-thirds of an MBA gave it the best of both worlds. It was cost-effective as MBA programs often took no account of students' existing competencies and skills and made them repeat courses. And it still gave accreditation to a prestigious MBA program which was important in recruiting and marketing. Blades says new recruits look to continually develop their own skill sets otherwise they will be out of date within five years. Accreditation also impresses clients that qualifications are relevant.

Source: HR Report No 119

Typically, the MBA program is a two-year full-time or four-year part-time course of study covering the essential aspects of management knowledge. This usually includes subject areas such as finance, operations management, marketing and human resource management. Most MBAs, depending on the size and skills of the faculty, include a variety of elective subjects with a work-related project to finish the degree and act as an integrator for the subjects that have been studied. Thus, unlike the more traditional Masters degrees, which stress the development of research skills, the MBA is oriented toward course work and, as a result, has tended to be viewed with some scepticism by the academic community, which has often questioned its 'masters' status. Nevertheless, the number of MBA programs continues to grow, attracting a seemingly unending stream of candidates, with many university faculties of business reporting many applications received for each place in the program.

Yet, despite its popular appeal, the MBA has attracted considerable criticism from the business community it serves, particularly in the United States. The decline of American industry has been attributed by some critics to the flood of overpaid, inexperienced MBA graduates absorbed into business in the last 20 years (Hayes and Abernathy, 1980). There has also been considerable criticism of the content of MBA programs that do not meet the practical day-to-day needs of managers in industry for skills in problem-solving and personal interaction (Porter and McKibbin, 1988). Certainly, it appears that MBA programs tend to be quite stereotyped in their content and teaching methods, and pay little attention to the skills requirements of managers outlined by the outcomes measurement project discussed earlier in the chapter.

Although these criticisms have largely surfaced in the United States, they are still taken seriously by universities in Australia. As a result, spurred by the increasingly deregulated environment of tertiary education, a number of changes are being made to MBA programs in this country (Hubbard, 1990) including:

- A shortening of the duration of the degree to around 18 months full-time and two/three years part-time.
- A mix of part-time and full-time students. Traditionally, MBA students have been reluctant to give up full-time employment for the sake of study and so part-time study has proliferated.
- More variation in both teaching methods and course content to introduce greater variety and more relevance to managerial jobs.
- The growth of the 'corporate MBA', in which a university tailors the MBA to the specific needs of a particular employer in return for a guarantee of student numbers.

Building on the work of Carter and Gribble (1991), who developed a model of work-based learning, Cattegno and Millwood have suggested that management development takes place in a number of different ways, combining elements of all the models presented by Finegold (see Figure 9.9 on p 240).

Thus, the initial education of managers and their subsequent training and development combines with their experiences of their work role and relationships with others at work in their overall development. The key to effective work-based learning for managers is to structure these different forms of experience into an individualised development plan that pulls all their experiences into a coherent whole.

Figure 9.9 — Model of workplace management development

Labels:
- Learning
- Formal management education
- Challenging work role
- Education
- Skills/Competency-based
- Work experience **Work role**
- Training and development
- Work experience **Work relationships**
- Individual management development plan
- Relationships with
  - Immediate managers
  - Peers
  - Team/Group
  - Mentors
  - Role models
  - Networks
  - Experts

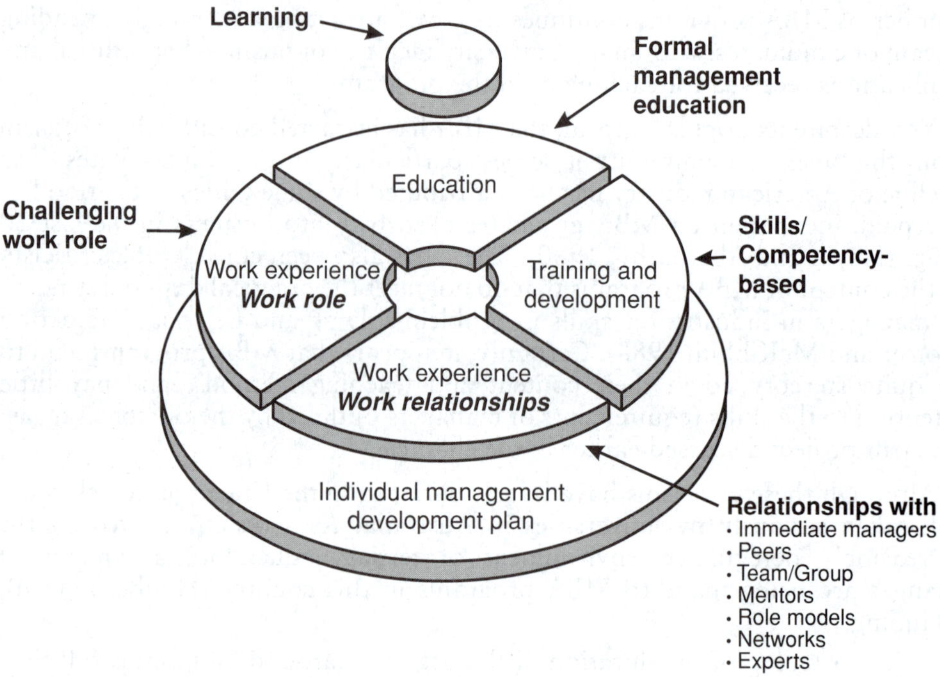

Source: Karpin (1995)

Methods of Management Development

There are many methods used in management development programs. This section will examine some of the more common methods.

Role plays

Role plays involve the enacting of a problem situation in which the trainees are given an opportunity to experiment with and practise the behaviours necessary to solve the problem. The most usual type of role play exercise is the structured role play, in which the participants are given pre-assigned roles to play and some background information as the context for their character's actions. The success of the role play depends on the extent to which the participants can identify with the role. This, in turn, depends on the ability of the trainer to create an environment in which the participants do not feel embarrassed or threatened. Bartz and Calabrese (1991) have identified four goals for role playing in the context of management training:

1. **Active participation** The participants can practise and learn through trial and error.
2. **Behaviour modelling** Role plays are the basis of the BM technique discussed in Chapter 7.

3. **Feedback** Both the trainer and the other participants in the program give the role players constructive comments on their performance.
4. **Practice** The experience is, ideally, repeated so that participants get a chance to learn from mistakes.

In management training, role playing is most suited to training in interpersonal skills, for example, how to handle employee grievances, how to negotiate, how to interview, etc. There is a number of factors critical to the success of the role play technique. First, as stated above, the trainer needs to create an atmosphere of trust and relaxation so that participants can enter their roles as completely as possible. Secondly, the participants require enough information to play the roles realistically, although not so much that their capacity to play the role is overwhelmed. Generally, this means that participants need an adequate framework for the role play so that they can judge which responses are possible in the situation. Thirdly, the handling of feedback is of particular importance to the learning of the participants. Trainers skilled in role play tend to use a form of positive reinforcement by focusing on the strengths of the role players rather than criticising what went wrong. This rewards the desired behaviour, which will tend to be repeated over successive role plays.

Case studies

Case studies present the participants with a documented recreation of a business problem based either on fact or the imagination of the case study writer. Often used in small group work within the context of a training program, cases are capable of setting problems of far greater complexity than the simple role play. Cases vary in length from a few short pages to the massively complex Harvard Business School type of cases, which describe an entire business situation and demand lengthy and careful analysis. The trainer acts as a facilitator in leading group discussion on the case and in highlighting the acceptable possible courses of action participants may recommend.

The complexity that the case method allows enables the trainer to emphasise the fact that there may be no absolutely right or wrong answers to the problems the cases present. The popularity of cases as a means of management training attests to their ability to simulate the reality of management situations with multiple possible solutions and a high degree of uncertainty.

Business games

Perhaps the most frequent expression of the experiential approach in management training is the business simulation or game. The use of the term 'game' to describe these activities implies an element of competition, and games usually involve a number of teams playing against each other in simulated market competition.

Games differ from cases and role plays in that they set up entire business situations and allow the trainees to control a number of different factors. Thus, a business game typically establishes a number of different companies competing in a particular marketplace. The trainees have control over the internal decision-making of the businesses they are running, for example, product innovation, marketing, manufacturing costs, etc. However, the game sets the performance of the businesses in the context of external economic realities such as inflation, interest rates, market conditions and so on. These external factors are controlled by the facilitator and are the same for all players. Thus, the trainees are simultaneously reacting to the market and to the actions of their competitors. Games are normally played for a pre-set number of rounds and are followed by extensive debriefing, critical for learning in this situation.

Business games were first developed in the late 1950s by the American Management Association for use in their executive development program (Camp, Blanchard and Huszczo, 1986). Since that time, they have become a common feature of management training programs all over the world. Early business games were controlled manually, involving the facilitator processing the decisions of the competing teams to determine their impact on business performance according to a set of formulae devised by the game's creators. This manual operation limited the sophistication of the games in terms of their ability to imitate the complexity of the real business world. The development of microcomputers in the 1970s, however, led to the development of a myriad of business games and simulations processed by computer, enabling far more complex games to be devised with almost instantaneous feedback provided to trainees.

Learning takes place in the business game because the participants have control of the situation. Thus, many of the notions of adult learning are incorporated into the business game. The game can be played at a speed to suit the participants, and learning takes place by doing and observing others in similar situations together with feedback provided by the facilitator and other participants. The outputs of business games are both skill building for participants in handling complex business situations, and learning for the facilitators, for whom each run of the game reveals different aspects of the business environment.

Critics of the process, however, have pointed to the fact that the notion of the game stresses competition at the expense of true learning. Participants in business games may become increasingly motivated by the need to win and lose sight of the fundamental purpose of the activity, which is to learn the principles of business management.

Outdoor management programs

Outdoor programs use the challenge of physical tasks and group activities in the natural environment to help managers learn about themselves and their impact on others. The concept of outdoor programs originated with the outward-bound movement in the United Kingdom, which started in the 1940s. The original mission of outward-bound was to assist in the vocational preparation of young people. There are now some 34 outward-bound centres throughout the world, and its activities have extended into adult and management development.

The basic premise of an outdoor management program is the notion of setting managers a problem or individual challenge (for example, abseiling) for which they have no ready answer. The learning takes place through the process of working out a group solution to a problem or overcoming the challenge. After the exercise, the facilitator helps the managers to reflect upon and analyse what happened which leads, via the Kolbian experiential cycle, to the formulation of general principles for handling unknown situations. The process is illustrated in Figure 9.10.

Figure 9.10 — Learning cycle for outdoor challenge program

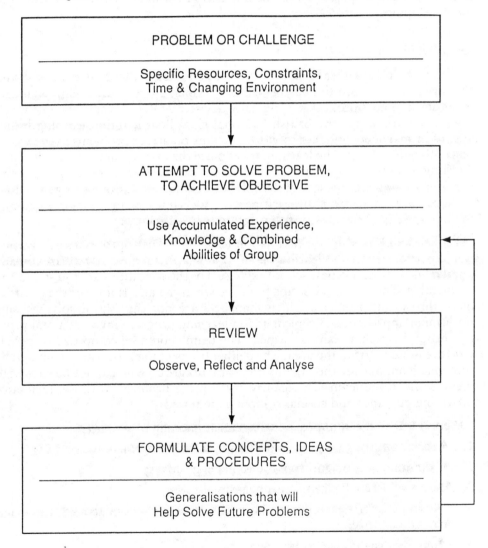

Source: Cacioppe and Adamson (1988)

This type of program is enjoying increasing popularity in Australia and a number of large organisations use some form of outdoor training, often in conjunction with other forms of training, in their management development programs. A survey of training and development practices carried out by the

Australian Graduate School of Management indicated that the number of organisations using outdoor programs increased from 8 per cent in 1986 to 23 per cent in 1991 (Collins and Hackman, 1991).

Critics of management development programs have, as we have seen, focused on the relevance of the content of many of the programs to the practical needs of managers. A number of new approaches have been developed which take management development out of the classroom and ground the activities more clearly in the workplace. These include action learning, self-development and the development centre.

Action learning

The 'action' in action learning refers to the activities of the trainees in problem-solving, in contrast to the passive learning which characterises many management development programs. Originally devised by Reg Revans when he was a physicist working for the British National Coal Board, action learning brings groups of managers together to work in teams on actual problems in the workplace (Revans, 1982). The learning takes place through solving the problem and working in a group, and being exposed to the perspectives of other group members. Groups are composed, preferably, of people from different organisations and occupations, or from different parts of the same organisation, to maximise the multiplicity of perspectives that action teams comprise.

Pedler (1983) has shown that action learning is not appropriate in all situations, particularly if the learning is programmable or the answers are already known (as in most business school exercises) or the conditions are too stable and predictable. The technique seems to thrive when the uncertainty of the environment throws up problems which managers are not capable of solving using traditional approaches. A typical action learning program involves a real problem around which a team is formed. The team should be composed of people who are not experts in the area. The deliberations of the group are facilitated by someone from outside the organisation or workgroup who cannot be subject to pressure from the team. The team works on the problem, with the facilitator providing guidance and specialist input as required.

Action learning can improve management learning in six ways:
1. Working through a process of finding the right problem to solve;
2. Examining a problem from multiple perspectives;
3. Learning to challenge taken-for-granted norms;
4. Learning a process of consultation with those whom the group cannot directly control;
5. Gaining insight into group dynamics;
6. Gaining insight into oneself as a manager.

Action learning is gradually being incorporated into the programs of different institutions, although it has proved to be more popular within institutions than in corporations. The International Management Centre from Buckingham, based in the United Kingdom, has used the technique extensively in its management programs and its MBA course. It has marketed the concept by establishing a network of like-minded institutions across the globe: the International Management Centres (Wils, 1991).

Illustration 9.3 — Outdoor training improves performance

Although outdoor experiential training (OET) is still trying to improve its credibility as a training and development method, when used as part of a controlled traditional training program it can improve organisational performance. A Proctor and Gamble sales team of 2,600 people recently took part in experiential training exercises in the United States. The exercises had team members navigating a raging river, averting a chemical spill, plunging through giant spider webs and doing a trust fall from 1.5 metres up.

Team members learned in a matter of hours how to work together in a creative, problem-solving manner because it pulled them into the learning process emotionally as well as educationally. It broke stereotypes on who was the most valuable, illustrating the diversity of challenges of well designed OET programs that cater to everyone's abilities, physically and mentally. It also cut down work-related barriers and fostered greater appreciation for co-workers.

Outdoor courses do not have to be long and costly. Companies may decide it is more effective, convenient and cheaper to support traditional training with regular OET interventions. Line management is important in this process in terms of cost, ownership, relevance and commitment. The following elements have been identified as common to successful OET programs;

- training activities should be new to all participants;
- participants should be encouraged to take psychological but not physical risks;
- the choice of activities must match the needs of participants and allow for flexibility to extend the experience;
- the program of activities must reflect the workplace environment;
- activities should be multitask not skills-oriented. The emphasis should be on areas such as making decisions and communicating as opposed to developing a skill in a particular area;
- transfer of training is achieved by reviewing the processes used in trying to achieve the desired outcomes in tasks and making links and connections to the workplace

Source: *The Employer* No 118

Self-development

For many managers, the possibility of attending long, off-the-job training programs is becoming increasingly unattractive. Such programs often involve too much time away from the job, resulting in problems during the manager's absence, and frequently their content is not perceived as relevant to the actual job the manager does. Dissatisfaction with traditional methods of instruction in the training community also surfaced during the 1970s, as management educators began to share the misgivings of their students about the value of conventional training programs.

Pedler and Boydell (1981) developed the notion of manager's self-development as an alternative to formal, off-the-job training programs. The central features of self-development are that managers take responsibility for their own learning and that learning can occur anywhere; formal programs are simply one of many possible learning arenas. These notions, of course, display a strong element of the adult learning prescriptions of Knowles and Rogers: see Chapter 3. Pedler and Boydell base their notions on a stage model of human development which describes how adults progress towards an understanding of the interrelatedness of the world and thus develop a capacity to learn from all experiences. The implications for management development are that managers will learn in all situations and that the role of the trainer is to help:

- managers clarify what they want to learn; and
- managers design their own learning situations and follow up with personal counselling.

Thus, a typical self-development program might begin with a workshop during which managers are encouraged to explore their goals in life and think of courses of action that will help them to achieve these goals. The role of the trainer/facilitator is to create a climate in the workshop which helps managers to become receptive to self-development. This may not be possible for all managers, and Pedler and Boydell readily admit that many managers will not be prepared to approach learning in this way. After the workshop, managers embark on their courses of action. This may involve group activities as well as individual actions; self-development does not mean managers working in complete isolation. The facilitator takes on the role of the counsellor, following up with each manager on an individual basis to review his or her progress and help further activities.

Self-development extends the notion of management development into the workplace and recognises what many managers believe. That is, that they learn most from doing a job and working with others rather than attending formal training programs.

Development centres

The development centre is an extension of the use of the assessment centre in the area of training. The assessment centre is a process designed to measure individuals on a number of dimensions, including their personality through profiling, intellectual abilities and behavioural skills. It is used as a more thorough and exacting means of selection for management positions than the simple interview or interview plus paper and pencil tests methods. The origins of the assessment centre lie in the research carried out in Germany during the 1930s to produce a more effective system for selecting army officers. The extensive use of psychological tests, group exercises and in-depth interviews was taken up by the allied powers in World War II, which resulted in the War Officer Selection Boards used in Britain and Australia to select army officers.

It was, however, in the United States that the work of the military psychologists was first used in the commercial context, when AT&T established a series of assessment centres for the selection and promotion of managers. Considerable research into the validity of the assessment centre method in the United States has shown that the technique is a more reliable guide to the potential of individuals than more conventional means of assessment (Moses and Byham, 1977). Since the 1970s, the assessment centre method has spread rapidly through the United States and Europe, although its use in Australia is still limited.

More recently, the assessment centre method has been developed for use in the identification of training and development needs of managers. Recent estimates indicate that up to 50 per cent of major companies now use some form of development centre worldwide. There is evidence that this method is also being used in Australian organisations (McDonald and Heine, 1991). Munchus and MacArthur (1991) show that the typical development centre uses a mix of six techniques for assessment purposes:

1. **In-basket exercise** in which the manager is faced with a simulated work situation in the form of an 'in-basket' of memos, papers, etc, and is required to deal with the issues presented in a defined length of time.
2. **Group exercises** in which managers are given a business-related problem to solve in a group, usually with pre-assigned roles.
3. **Leaderless discussions** in which the managers have to 'sell' their point of view to the rest of the group.
4. **Psychometric tests** designed to capture the personality profile of the individual manager.
5. **Aptitude tests** designed to gauge the intellectual abilities of participants.
6. **Interviews** in which the results of the development centre may be discussed along with the development needs of the individual manager.

Goodge (1991) makes the point that development centres are more than simply assessment centres going under a new alias. However, the differences are concerned more with the way in which the centre is used than with the techniques employed, which remain substantially the same.

The Karpin Report

There have been regular reports into the state of management training and development in Australia. In 1982 the influential Ralph report (Ralph, 1982) championed the university business school model of management development. It recommended that Australia needed to develop a small number of world-class university business schools that would provide high quality MBA programs which would equip Australia's managers with the intellectual skills to cope with the changing world of management. However, as we have seen, the Ralph report's call for a small number of elite management educational institutions did not materialise, and most universities proceeded to establish their own MBA programs.

During the 1980s, concern grew that, despite the proliferation of management education programs in the universities, Australian managers were still rather badly educated in comparison with their international counterparts (Dawkins, 1991). As a result, the then Minister for Employment, Education and Training, Kim Beazley, in 1992 established the Industry Taskforce on Leadership and Management Skills, commonly known as the Karpin Committee after its chairman, David Karpin, CEO of resources giant CRA. As we saw earlier in the chapter, the Karpin Committee's research confirmed the pessimistic picture of Australian management presented above. Karpin argued that a new paradigm was required for Australian managers in order to cope with the internationalisation of business and management. Karpin summarised the old and new paradigms of management in a three-way stylisation of the old and the new Australian manager. This is reproduced in Figure 9.11.

Figure 9.11 — The emerging senior manager profile

1970	Today	2010
The Autocrat	**The Communicator**	**The Leader/Enabler**
• Male	• Male	• Male or female
• Anglo-Celt, British or Australian citizenship	• Anglo–Celt, Australian citizenship	• Wide range of ethnicities, citizenships
• Started as message boy, rose through ranks. All management training on-the-job	• Graduate, possibly postgraduate qualification. Career in corporate centre. Product of internal management development program	• Graduate, probably MBA or AMP as well. Wide-ranging career, many placements. Product of major development program including placements
• Very local focus, possibly one Australian state. Has travelled once, to England.	• Expanding focus, travels regularly to Asia, United States of America, Europe	• Global focus, travels regularly. Has lived in two or more countries
• Established competitors, cartels	• Recently deregulated marketplace, rapidly changing competitors	• Manages in both regulated and deregulated economies
• Paternal view of work force	• Sees work force as stakeholder in business, working hard on communication and information sharing	• Manages work forces in several countries. Shares information and delegates heavily
• Stable environment. Relatively low stress, home to see kids most nights, long term position	• Turbulent environment. High stress, long hours, fears burnout	• Environment typified by rapid change. Limited term appointment, high pressure, results driven

Source: Karpin (1995)

Karpin painted a picture of the evolving Australian senior manager as a globe-trotting, corporate executive, managing work forces in several parts of the world. Whether this will be true of all Australian managers, or simply the corporate executives who formed the samples for much of the research underpinning Karpin's deliberations, is a matter of some debate. However, this is the foundation on which Karpin based his main recommendations. These include:

- the development of an 'enterprising culture', starting at the level of primary and secondary schooling;
- measures to improve the management of small business by using, amongst other things, a system of qualified mentors or advisers to provide advice to small business managers;
- developing a new frontline management development program for the estimated 180,000 frontline managers in Australia who have not received any formal management training;
- the development of a framework of management competency standards for use across all industries so that every manager gains a common core of skills;
- measures to improve the standards of management education offered by university business schools, including accreditation of MBA programs and the establishment of a new national management school;
- the promotion of best practice in management through measures such as international study tours for up to 1500 Australian managers each year;
- the establishment of the Australian Council for Management Development, which will oversee the implementation of many of Karpin's proposals and maintain a national focus on management development.

Karpin argued that if these recommendations were implemented, Australian managers would be able to perform effectively and this would lead to higher growth and improved living standards. The Karpin model for management reform is illustrated in Figure 9.12 on p 250.

However, few of these recommendations have been implemented. In particular, the call for a new world-class business school was regarded as unnecessary proliferation in the context of the increasing numbers of graduate business schools that have emerged since the mid-1980s. Karpin also drew a number of criticisms. Many commentators have disagreed with Karpin's rather stylised presentation of the old and the new Australian manager (Lamond, 1995; Nettle, 1996). The Karpin picture seems to describe the situation in which the managers of tomorrow will work rather than the skills and competencies they will require and, as such, does not provide a clear guide to the form of management development most suited to the 'leader/enabler'. Karpin has also been accused of underestimating the changing nature of managerial work as a result of the introduction of teamwork in many organisations (Emery, 1995). In many cases, teams are taking over the role of the traditional manager and making many decisions for themselves. In this situation, managers may become facilitators rather than leaders. Nevertheless, the Karpin recommendations have set the management development agenda for Australian organisations for the foreseeable future.

Figure 9.12 — Model for management reform

Source: Karpin (1995)

The Frontline Manager

In the first part of this chapter, the distinction was drawn between the manager and the frontline manager or supervisor. Whereas the manager has a definite position within the organisation, the supervisor is often characterised by a more ambiguous status, neither manager nor worker but a 'man in the middle' (Wray, 1949). This has not always been the case. Nineteenth-century supervisors or overseers occupied a very powerful position inside the factories where they were employed. The undeveloped management hierarchies meant that supervisors had the right to hire and fire and often to determine levels of pay for large groups of people. This remained the case until the early twentieth century, when the gradual introduction of the principles of scientific management stripped supervisors of many of their functions, relocating them in the new staff departments such as personnel, finance and industrial engineering (Dawson, 1991).

The position of the modern supervisor

The position of the contemporary supervisor may be analysed into four 'problems' (Smith, 1990). First, there is the problem of role definition. The role of the supervisor is like that of a black box (Thurley and Wirdenius, 1973). Management fills the box with duties and responsibilities appropriate to the particular organisation. Thus, definitions of the supervisory role change from one organisation to another.

Secondly, there is the problem of position. The supervisor is often regarded as the person in the middle, both in terms of the organisational hierarchy and in class terms. This ambiguity can lead to considerable role strain which may result in the ambivalent loyalties that supervisors often display.

Finally, the future of the supervisory role is open to considerable debate. Child and Partridge (1982) identify four possible alternatives:

1. **Abolition** The emergence of autonomous work groups on Scandinavian lines.
2. **Improving the role** Clarifying the role of the supervisor vis-a-vis other managers.
3. **Developing the role** Making the supervisor into a more powerful manager along the lines of the German *meister*.
4. **Changing the role to that of technical supervisor** A specialist coordinator of teams of less qualified employees.

Child and Partridge opt for the second possibility as being the most desirable, and there is evidence that Australian managers share this view (Smith, 1988). Many organisations see the necessity for the supervisory role to change from one of overseer or director to that of a more flexible team-leading facilitator.

Characteristics of the supervisor

Research in Australia has confirmed the picture of a fairly traditional supervisory type inhabiting industrial organisations (Gilmour and Lansbury, 1984). A consistent pattern of characteristics emerges which seems to typify supervisors in Australia. They:

- are generally recruited from the shop floor without any prior training for a supervisory position;
- have a lack of educational qualifications, particularly post-secondary or post-apprenticeship;
- have a tendency to view supervision as a career in itself. Supervisors tend to see themselves as a group distinct from management which has little opportunity for promotion into management;
- have an older age profile;
- have a predominantly working-class position in social terms.

The frontline management initiative

Smith's survey of supervisory training practices in Australia implies that the state of supervisory training is still very conventional (Smith, 1990). In the organisations surveyed, supervisors were primarily recruited from the shop floor with little or no preparation for their role. Selection procedures were based on interviews alone. Training courses were highly standardised, emphasising the knowledge required rather than the skills supervisors might use. Training tended to be of short duration, was given fairly early in the appointment and involved little input from senior managers in the organisations.

The Karpin Committee identified the development of frontline managers as a key priority area for the reform of management development in Australia. Of the approximately 900,000 managers in Australia, over 400,000 are in frontline supervisory positions. Thus, frontline managers are the largest single group of managers in the country. In the light of the lack of training given to supervisors, Karpin recommended that a new frontline management development program should be developed for national implementation through the TAFE system. The Australian National Training Authority (ANTA) took up this recommendation and, in 1995, instituted a National Reference Group to work on the development of what became known as the Frontline Management Initiative (FMI).

The reference group carried out extensive consultations within Australia and overseas and developed a set of competencies for frontline managers. The competencies were developed within a framework of four themes:

- leading by example;
- leading, coaching, facilitating and empowering others;
- creating best practice; and
- creating an innovative culture.

Within these four themes, the Australian Frontline Management Standards comprise 11 units of competence. These are illustrated in Figure 9.13 on p 253.

The FMI can be delivered in a number of ways and by any training provider accredited to deliver it. The FMI comprises a set of four qualifications, from a statement of attainment through to the full Diploma in Frontline Management which is awarded on completion of all 11 competencies. Organisations that use the FMI work from an FMI 'kit' which includes the competency standards user's manual, an assessor's guide, a facilitator's guide, a participant's guide and a database. Organisations can also customise the competency standards to meet the unique requirements of their own situation. Thus, for the first time in Australia the FMI provides a standardised, nationally consistent approach to the training of supervisors.

Figure 9.13 — Frontline manager competencies

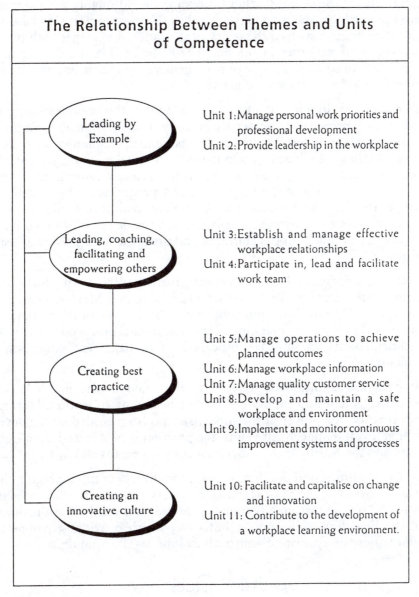

Source: Pickett (1997)

Summary

This chapter has been concerned with the training and development of managers in Australian industry. Managers and supervisors constitute about 12 per cent of the work force in this country, which is comparable to other developed economies. However, by international standards, Australian managers are relatively poorly educated and untrained for their jobs.

The definition of managerial work is fraught with difficulty. The dominant paradigm is that of the classical school, stressing the rationality of management action and prescribing planning and control as the most important tasks of the manager. Mintzberg destroyed this myth of the rational manager with his studies of management activities in the mid-1970s. Since that time, a number of writers have elaborated on the idea of management competencies, which form a more useful guide for development activities.

Management development is pursued both within the organisation (corporate) and outside, primarily in university business schools. Management training within the organisation uses a series of experiential techniques such as role plays, case studies and business simulations to develop management skills. Management education in the universities is increasingly centred on the MBA degree. Despite criticisms of the output of MBA programs in the United States and Europe, the demand for places in Australian institutions still far exceeds supply. Universities and business schools also run a wide range of executive programs which are of much shorter duration and often focus on particular aspects of management.

The lack of education of Australian management was the driving force behind the creation of the Industry Taskforce on Leadership and Management, the so-called 'Karpin Committee'. Karpin concluded that the role of the manager was changing quickly under the pressure of internationalisation, and made a series of recommendations to improve processes of management education and development.

Supervisors are traditionally viewed as the 'men in the middle', caught between management and the shop floor but belonging to neither. During the twentieth century, the power of the supervisor has been eroded by the development of functional management. Thus, the position is problematic in a number of respects and the future of the supervisor is by no means clear.

Supervisory training and development appears to reflect this ambiguity in the supervisor's position. The poor training of supervisors, or frontline managers, was addressed by the Karpin Committee, and this has resulted in the development of the Frontline Management Initiative, which provides a competency-based and nationally consistent approach to supervisory training.

Discussion Questions

1. What is the difference between management training and management education?
2. To what extent are Boyatzis' competencies applicable to all managers?
3. Why has the Karpin Committee's report been so widely criticised?
4. Are supervisors managers?
5. Why has supervisory development been so neglected in Australia?
6. Does management development serve any useful purpose?

Chapter 10

Towards the Learning Organisation

The call for change in organisations has become all pervasive. In the public sector the increasing inability of governments to fund their burgeoning bureaucracies and social programs created, and in the private sector the threat posed by competition from East Asian countries provided, the stimulus for organisations to enter a period of upheaval in pursuit of 'leaner' operations.

Because the processes of change in organisations are consciously created and driven by managers, they often take the form of tangible programs. Organisational change does not simply happen; it is the result of management decisions. Frequently, however, change programs do not achieve the objectives set by the managers who institute them. As a result, organisations may experiment with a number of change programs in the attempt to realise more competitive performance.

Training practitioners often find themselves heavily involved in the implementation of such programs. This is usually because they contain significant elements of training (for example, team building for total quality management programs) and because the human relations orientation of the program is generally considered to be the specialist domain of the training practitioner rather than any other manager. Thus, the field of training and development has come to embrace the area of organisational change, almost by default.

This chapter will examine some of the more common types of change programs found in organisations. The structure of the chapter will follow a roughly chronological order, discussing different schools of thought about organisational change and the resulting forms of change program as they have emerged since World War II. Starting with the human relations-inspired organisation development movement in the 1950s, the chapter will go on to discuss the different forms of employee involvement programs that surfaced in the 1960s and 1970s, through to the quality movement of the 1980s and the emergence of the learning organisation in the 1990s. First, however, the concept of organisational change requires further discussion in order to provide a framework for the exploration of the various forms in which it occurs.

What is Organisational Change?

Organisations in Australia face an increasingly competitive environment. In the private sector, Australian organisations are having to deal with global competition, as the tariff barriers that for so long protected industry are quickly being dismantled. The evidence suggests that Australian organisations do not yet compete at world-class levels of productivity, quality and export performance (Australian Manufacturing Council, 1990). In the public sector, the rolling back of government intervention in the economy and society has created pressure to streamline government bureaucracies and provide more effective services within the context of expenditure cuts. These and similar pressures have led managers to try to implement often radical changes in their organisations in order to ensure their survival.

The pressures for change

Amongst the pressures that managers have to confront in the operation of their businesses are:

- **Privatisation** The sale (or part sale) of government enterprises in the belief that governments are not equipped to run businesses in a market economy. Examples would include the privatisations of Qantas and the Commonwealth Bank.

- **Deregulation** The loosening of governmental and legal controls in the economy to allow more scope for market forces. Thus, the deregulation of the telecommunications industry has allowed the development of private sector competition for Telstra.

- **Quality** The success of Japanese industry in export markets is widely perceived to have occurred as a result of the higher quality of Japan's manufactured goods. This has spurred Western enterprises to make quality a central feature of their operational management. The impact of the quality movement is discussed in more detail below.

- **Globalisation** Multinational corporations, in particular, have re-evaluated their positions in the emerging global market for goods and services, with the result that Australian subsidiaries are compelled to compete in the global market rather than simply the domestic market. Holden's Engine Company, for example, supplies engines not only to General Motors Holden in Australia but to GM subsidiaries all over the world.

- **Downsizing** Levels of unemployment remain high in the 1990s as organisations seek to reduce overheads and improve productivity by drastically reducing the number of employees while maintaining or increasing output (Littler et al, 1997). The pressure to achieve more with less resources has often resulted in the need for major changes within the organisations to accompany the downsizing programs.

- **Takeovers and mergers** The wave of corporate takeovers and mergers in the 1980s and 1990s has produced many larger, more diversified operations than has been the case hitherto. The creation of these diversified groups has often resulted in the need to introduce significant change into the organisations acquired, in order to match the expectations of the new owners.

- **Technology** The exact impact of technological change is the subject of hot debate. The chain of causation is not clear: does technological change cause organisational change or can technology be grafted onto many organisational forms (Appelbaum and Batt, 1994)? Despite the controversy, however, there seems to be little doubt that organisational change is closely linked to the implementation of new forms of technology.

Illustration 10.1 — Downsizing Australia

> Australian businesses and governments have retrenched 3.3 million workers since 1986. In effect, more than one in two full-time workers have been retrenched in just over a decade. Two-thirds of these retrenchments are in the blue-collar or low skill sectors of the economy — manufacturing, wholesale and retail and construction. Men account for three-quarters of the job losses despite holding only two-thirds of the full-time jobs. The job losses represent more than half the number of Australians employed full-time in 1997.
>
> Although there has been substantial job creation over this period, most of the net jobs growth has been in less secure, casual or part-time work, while those in full-time jobs are working harder and longer. The proportion of workers employed part-time now stands at 26 per cent up from 17 per cent in 1986 and 6 per cent in the mid-sixties. The OECD's *Jobs Study* reveals that among major western nations Australia has the highest rate of temporary employment and the fifth-highest rate of part-time employment.
>
> Australian companies have adopted a lean, mean corporate religion that says higher labour productivity is the main path to profits. The downsizing philosophy adopted by the Business Council of Australia in the early 1990s saw major companies adopt a 'core and periphery' labour management strategy. They sacked substantial numbers of full-time workers and replaced them with fewer, casual or outsourced employees whose tenure could be turned on or off like a tap. Research indicates that there is no end in sight to downsizing. A survey of Australian organisations in 1996 revealed that more than half had downsized in the previous 5 years and 42 per cent intended to downsize in the next two years. Telstra, the major banks and BHP all announced major downsizing programs to take place in the next 5 years in 1997.
>
> Companies are shedding about 300,000 full-time jobs a year — or about 500,000 when part-time jobs are included. This is, of course, offset by the creation of new jobs during periods of economic growth, but when this dries up in a recession the in-built dynamism of job shedding will drive unemployment well into double digit figures.

Source: *Sydney Morning Herald*, 20 October 1997

In dealing with these issues, managers have needed to introduce significant programs of change to enable organisations to adjust to the new conditions. The speed and pervasiveness of the change in organisations has been the subject of much debate amongst writers in the field of managerial strategy (Hitt et al,

1995). Should the organisation adjust slowly and continuously to changes in the environment (incrementalism) or does the speed of change in the environment demand radical change (transformation) of those organisations that want to survive?

Dunphy and Stace (1990) identified four types of change strategy observable in Australian organisations, ranging from the slow 'finetuning' approach, to the radical 'corporate transformation' which they suggest is more typical of change strategies in the 1990s. Figure 10.1 on p 259 shows the Dunphy and Stace typology of organisational change.

Many, if not most, of the changes that Dunphy and Stace outline under each of the strategies involve significant change in the management of human resources. It is, in fact, the changes to the management of human resources that characterise the essence of these change strategies. The changes to human resource management are often regarded as an attempt to engage the commitment of people to the organisation in which they work.

Organisational commitment

The notion of organisational commitment may be contrasted with the traditional notions of labour control in Western organisations (Walton, 1985). The traditional 'control' strategy involved the division of work into fragmented, deskilled tasks performed by unskilled operators directly supervised by supervisors whose job it was to exert management control on the shop floor. Organisations were hierarchically based and employees enjoyed little or no input into decision-making. In times of economic downturn, employees could easily be retrenched in order to cut costs. Naturally, the control strategy tended to breed an adversarial industrial relations climate and a consequent lower level of enterprise performance.

In contrast to this traditional strategy, many organisations are attempting to improve their performance by actively engaging the personal commitment of their employees on the assumption that commitment will lead to increased levels of motivation. Such a 'commitment' strategy involves the devolution of responsibility to employees; jobs are redesigned to increase autonomy; management hierarchies are flattened resulting in less direct supervision of employees; and the organisation makes a commitment to job security in return for the commitment of its work force. Figure 10.2 summarises the principal characteristics of control and commitment strategies.

As organisations move from control to commitment, they may exhibit some of the characteristics of both strategies in a 'transitional' form. In some cases, organisations may become stuck at the transitional stage and the resulting hybrid form coalesces into a more or less permanent arrangement.

Figure 10.1 — The scale of change

TYPE 1 Fine Tuning: Organisational change which is an ongoing process characterised by fine tuning of the 'fit' or match between the organisation's strategy, structure, people and processes. Such effort is typically manifested at departmental/divisional levels and deals with one or more of the following:
- Refining policies, methods and procedures
- Creating specialist units and linking mechanisms to permit increased volume and increased attention to unit quality and cost
- Developing personnel especially suited to the present strategy
- Fostering individual and group commitment to the company mission and the excellence of one's own department
- Promoting confidence in the accepted norms, beliefs and myths
- Clarifying established roles (with their associated authorities and powers), and the mechanisms for allocating resources

TYPE 2 Incremental Adjustment: Organisational change which is characterised by incremental adjustments to the changing environment. Such change involves distinct modifications (but not radical change) to corporate business strategies, structures and management processes, for example:
- Expanding sales territory
- Shifting the emphasis among products
- Improved production process technology
- Articulating a modified statement of mission to employees
- Adjustments to organisational structures within or across divisional boundaries to achieve better links in product/service delivery

TYPE 3 Modular Transformation: Organisational change which is characterised by major re-alignment of one or more departments/divisions. The process of radical change is focused on these subparts rather than on the organisation as a whole, for example:
- Major restructuring of particular departments/divisions
- Changes in key executives and managerial appointments in these areas
- Work and productivity studies resulting in significantly reduced or increased workforce numbers
- Reformed departmental/divisional goals
- Introduction of significantly new process technologies affecting key departments or divisions

TYPE 4 Corporate Transformation: Organisational change which is corporation-wide, characterised by radical shifts in business strategy, and revolutionary changes throughout the whole organisation involving many of the following features:
- Reformed organisational mission and core values
- Altered power and status affecting the distribution of power in the organisation
- Reorganisation — major changes in structures, systems and procedures across the organisation
- Revised interaction patterns — new procedures, work flows, communication networks and decision-making patterns across the organisation
- New executives in key managerial positions from outside the organisation

Source: Dunphy and Stace (1990)

Figure 10.2 — Control to commitment strategies

	Control	Transitional	Commitment
Job design principles	Individual attention limited to performing individual job	Scope of individual responsibility extended to upgrading system performance, via participative problem-solving groups in QWL, EI and quality circle programs	Individual responsibility extended to upgrading system performance
	Job design deskills and fragments work and separates doing and thinking	No change in traditional job design or accountability	Job design enhances content of work, emphasises whole tasks, and combines doing and thinking
	Accountability focused on individual		Frequent use of teams as basic accountable unit
	Fixed job definition		Flexible definition of duties, contingent on changing conditions
Performance expectations	Measured standards define minimum performance. Stability seen as desirable		Emphasis placed on higher 'stretch objectives', which tend to be dynamic and oriented to the marketplace
Management organisation: structure, systems and style	Structure tends to be layered, with top-down controls	No basic changes in approaches to structure, control or authority	Flat organisation structure with mutual influence systems
	Coordination and control rely on rules and procedures		Coordination and control based more on shared goals, values and traditions
	More emphasis on prerogatives and positional authority		Management emphasis on problem-solving and relevant information and expertise
	Status symbols distributed to reinforce hierarchy	A few visible symbols change	Minimum status differentials to de-emphasise inherent hierarchy
Compensation policies	Variable pay where feasible to provide individual incentive	Typically no basic changes in compensation concepts	Variable rewards to create equity and to reinforce group achievements: gain sharing, profit sharing
	Individual pay geared to job evaluation		Individual pay linked to skills and mastery
	In downturn, cuts concentrated on hourly payroll	Equality of sacrifice among employee groups	Equality of sacrifice
Employment assurances	Employees regarded as variable costs	Assurances that participation will not result in loss of job	Assurances that participation will not result in loss of job
	Extra effort to avoid layoffs		High commitment to avoid or assist in re-employment
			Priority for training and retaining existing work force
Employee voice policies	Employee input allowed on relatively narrow agenda. Attendant risks emphasised. Methods include open-door policy, attitude surveys, grievance procedures and collective bargaining in some organisations	Addition of limited ad hoc consultation mechanisms. No change in corporate governance	Employee participation encouraged on wide range of issues. Attendant benefits emphasised. New concepts of corporate governance
	Business information distributed on strictly defined 'need to know' basis	Additional sharing of information	Business data shared widely
Labour–management relations	Adversarial labour–management relations: emphasis on interest conflict	Thawing of adversarial attitudes: joint sponsorship of QWL or EI; emphasis on common fate	Mutuality in labour relations; joint planning and problem-solving on expanded agenda
			Unions, management and workers redefine their respective roles

Source: Walton (1985)

Training for commitment

The notion of organisational commitment is not universally accepted. Problems arise when any definition of the term is attempted (Coopey and Hartley, 1991). To what is the employee committed? Organisations tend to have a plethora of goals, many of which are not shared by all members of the organisation; managers may be more committed than shop floor employees to goals of competitive success. Shop floor employees may be more committed to notions of pay equity and fair management.

Nevertheless, despite the definitional difficulties associated with the concept, commitment remains a central feature of most of the programs of organisational change examined in this chapter.

Training is often perceived to play a key role in the development of commitment, particularly amongst new employees (Heyes and Stuart, 1996). The initial socialisation of employees may be the point at which managers can develop the sense of commitment in new employees. The type of commitment that is required by the organisation will determine the form that the socialisation process takes.

Thus, an organisation attempting to follow a business strategy based on high levels of innovation by employees may use an individualised socialisation process which emphasises the professionalism of the employee rather than dull conformance to group norms of behaviour. In contrast, an organisation pursuing a strategy of reducing costs and raising productivity rather than innovation may wish to emphasise the importance of adherence to group norms through a more collective form of socialisation; thus engaging the moral commitment of the individual employee to the sometimes tough decisions that managers in the organisation may make (Schuler and Jackson, 1987).

Organisation Development

The earliest and most systematic approach to organisational change in the post-war period is that of the organisation development movement. Beckhard (1969:9) described organisation development (OD) as:

> ... an effort (1) planned, (2) organization-wide, and (3) managed from the top, to (4) increase organization effectiveness and health through (5) planned interventions in the organization's 'processes', using behavioural-science knowledge.

This definition involves a number of elements. OD is a planned change effort involving a systematic approach to the diagnosis of problems and formulation of plans to overcome them. OD takes a 'total system' approach in that it does not focus on organisational problems in isolation, but rather as part of the overall organisational system. In this respect, OD has been heavily influenced by the systems approach to organisation theory. OD practitioners insist that their projects cannot succeed without support at the highest level in the organisation. The direction of the OD effort is clearly top down. OD is geared toward improving the effectiveness and the health of the organisation, by which OD practitioners mean its ability to achieve its stated goals and the elimination of the unnecessary conflict which acts to inhibit that process. Finally, OD prescribes a set of techniques for intervening in the organisation which are specifically based on behavioural science (particularly applied psychology).

A history of organisation development

The founding father of the OD movement is acknowledged to be Kurt Lewin, the American social psychologist who developed the innovative field theory in his work with family groups in the 1940s and later applied it to large organisations (French and Bell, 1990).

Lewin's first application of his theories came as a result of a workshop run by the Massachusetts Institute of Technology-based Research Centre for Group Dynamics for the Connecticut Interracial Commission in 1946. After the day's workshop activities were over, Lewin and his colleagues developed the practice of meeting informally to discuss the group dynamics observed during the day's proceedings. Gradually, the members of the workshop became involved in these evening sessions, which allowed the members of the workshop to speak freely about what they had felt and observed during the day. These sessions became the most interesting part of the workshop.

From this experience developed the National Training Laboratory in Group Development (NTL) based at Bethel, Maine. Lewin died two years later in early 1947, but his followers developed the concept of the T-(for training) group which became one of the major strands of the OD movement. T-groups used the concepts of clinical psychology to investigate and train participants in the processes of group dynamics and the role of the individual in groups. Led by a facilitator, T-groups were deliberately unstructured training workshops in which the participants explored their own and others' personal styles. The unstructured nature of the sessions led typically to the development of frustration within the group; this frustration often exploded early in the session and provided the catalyst for the group members to embark on intensely introspective examinations of themselves and others. During the 1960s, T-Groups became very popular methods of interpersonal skills training in Europe, America and, to a lesser extent, in Australia. However, their often destructive nature and perceived lack of transferability to the organisational environment of the trainees led to their decline in the 1970s and 1980s.

The second major strand of the OD movement was based on the work of Rensis Likert and his colleagues at the Survey Research Centre (SRC) at the University of Michigan in the 1950s. Likert developed a method of charting personal attitudes (the Likert Scale) which he developed into a tool for implementing attitude surveys in industrial organisations. Working with the Detroit Edison Company in the late 1940s, SRC staff developed the survey and feedback technique in which the results of the attitude survey were communicated back to the work force by means of an interlocking system of discussion groups cascading down the organisation from the top management team. This has proved to be an enduring technique, which is still used extensively in Australian organisations as part of change programs (Saul, 1989).

The third major strand of OD was the development of the action research method. Based on the Lewinian dictum, 'No research without action, no action without research', action research forms the theoretical framework for most modern applications of OD. Action research is discussed in more detail later in this section.

Lewin's model of change

Lewin (1952) pioneered the simplest and most frequently cited model for organisational change in the OD literature. He postulated a three-stage model for the change process: unfreezing, moving and refreezing. Each of these steps has been further elaborated into a number of mechanisms by which the change is effected:

1. **Unfreezing** Present forces compelling individuals to behave in certain ways need to be weakened so that change can occur. This involves disconfirming the current behaviour or attitudes by demonstrating their failure. Disconfirmation sets up a level of anxiety or guilt which needs to be strong enough to motivate a change for the individual. Finally, the creation of psychological safety by reducing the threat posed by change is necessary to induce individuals to make the change.

2. **Moving** Effective change requires gaining enough information to make the change. What is possible may be seen either through the use of a role model (a part often played by OD practitioners themselves) or by looking outside the organisation at what others have achieved. This is a process often referred to as 'benchmarking', and which has become popular with many Australian organisations.

3. **Refreezing** Ensuring the stability of the change process involves individuals receiving confirmation that their new behaviour or attitudes both fit with the person's own self-concept and can be integrated and are acceptable to significant others such as colleagues and superiors. The process of obtaining this confirmation is the final stage of the change program.

An alternative approach to the Lewinian model (although by no means mutually exclusive to it) is that of action research.

Action research

Action research is often compared to the traditional notion of scientific research. Traditional scientific research is problem-centred. A problem is posed and the researcher devises a method for investigating the problem and arriving at an explanation. Action research, on the other hand, is solution, or action, centred. The research is framed in terms of finding and implementing a solution to the problem. Action research also involves others, the clients, in the research and action processes; that is, it is a collaborative process.

Action research is a form of consulting (see Chapter 11) or applied research. It consists of a series of steps, shown in Figure 10.3 on p 264. The researcher develops a client-system infrastructure consisting of ad hoc or permanent face-to-face groups in which the clients are involved in the research. The research procedure passes through a number of steps in which the problem is diagnosed, a plan is formulated and implemented, and evaluation leads to further learning in addition to the stock of behavioural science knowledge.

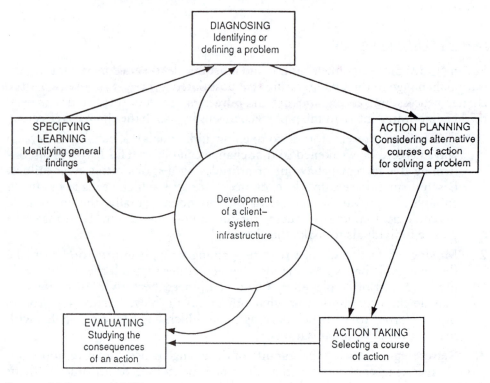

Figure 10.3 — Process of action research

Source: McLennan (1990)

Thus, research leads to action and action leads to learning. This model of diagnosis, research, action and evaluation has become the standard model for OD practitioners since the 1960s.

Values and assumptions of OD

Clearly, the terminology of the OD movement indicates the psychological/psychotherapeutic background of many of the early practitioners such as Lewin, Beckhard and others. Notions of diagnosis, treatment and organisational health conjure up the image of the organisational doctor for whom the organisation is the patient and who possesses a kit-bag of remedies which can be applied to cure organisational ills (Morgan, 1986).

Despite the fact that OD has also been developed in countries outside the United States (most notably at the Tavistock Institute for Human Relations in the United Kingdom), it still retains in its set of assumptions a strong element of American belief in the importance of the individual. In fact, this humanistic orientation can often be a source of conflict for OD practitioners, who find themselves trying to balance the needs of managers for more efficient operation and the needs of individuals for growth and development.

Nevertheless, the OD movement has grown strongly since the 1950s, with many universities offering qualifications in the area (for example, Royal Melbourne Institute of Technology University in Australia) and the existence of a worldwide organisation of practitioners in the OD Network. The relative decline in popularity of some OD methods in the 1970s has been offset by the resurgence of interest in organisational change since the mid-1980s.

Changing the Corporate Culture

The notion of corporate culture became fashionable in the early 1980s, as business leaders sought to find explanations for the success of Japanese commercial and industrial organisations in export markets. Early explanations for Japanese success focused on the differences between Japanese and Western society and on the notion of culture in particular (Pascale and Athos, 1981).

It was observed that Japanese society still retained many of the aspects of feudal nineteenth-century Japan and that these had a positive impact on business performance. For instance, Japanese workers nurtured a strong sense of loyalty to their employers, who in return provided them with guarantees of lifelong employment, subsidised housing and welfare benefits, etc. Thus, Japanese commercial success was explained in terms of the beneficial aspects of Japanese culture which were played out in the factory environment.

The message was clear. In order to compete with the Japanese, Western organisations had to adopt some of the key characteristics of Japanese business culture. In practice, however, this prescription proved very problematic. Part of the problem was, of course, the meaning of 'culture'.

What is culture?

Despite its recent appearance in the literature on organisational change, the term 'culture' has been used in the industrial context for some time. Borrowed from anthropology, culture originated as a description of those norms of behaviour that distinguished one society from another. In the early 1950s, Elliott Jacques (1951:251) used the term to describe life in the factory:

> The culture of the factory is its customary and traditional way of thinking and doing things, which is shared to a greater or lesser degree by all its members, and which new members must learn, and at least partially accept, in order to be accepted into service in the firm. Culture in this sense covers a wide range of behaviour: the methods of production; job skills and technical knowledge; attitudes towards discipline and punishment; the customs and habits of managerial behaviour; the objectives of the concern; its way of doing business; the methods of payment; the values placed on different types of work; beliefs in democratic living and joint consultation; and the less conscious conventions and taboos.

In the more recent literature, culture has come to mean more than simply the outward manifestations of the beliefs of the organisation. Culture is viewed as a deeper level of values and assumptions that bind the members of an organisation together. Moreover, these values are learned by the organisation in a collective manner, in order to help the organisation face a hostile environment

(Schein, 1985). Thus, the implication is that if culture is learned then it can be consciously changed and manipulated by managers to achieve improved organisational performance. Therefore, culture change becomes a key feature of any organisational change program.

Illustration 10.2 — Saturn — a model of corporate change

General Motors' Saturn car plant in Tennessee, USA, was held up as an international icon of best practice in the Karpin Report. The company has adopted a structure of working teams, company–union partnership and consensus decision-making. Role models — 'heroes' and 'legends' in Saturn terminology — who promote the Saturn philosophy that emphasises people, quality and customer enthusiasm, are actively promoted. One such was when Saturn recalled, replaced and scrapped 800 cars which had a minor fault. Saturn's beginnings go back to the 1980s when General Motors decided that it needed a radically new type of manufacturing plant to build a small car that could successfully compete with Japanese imports.

The bold Saturn initiative started when GM selected 99 people — 55 from the union and 44 from management — from all areas of the company to establish a plan. They came up with a plan based around a new relationship between employee and employer contained in five people strategies.

1. **A partnership** with the Union of Automobile Workers sharing management functions within teams at all levels of the company.
2. **The company was organised around teams** with 10–12 members found to be most successful. The teams operate like a small business with responsibility for ordering supplies, resolving conflicts and work planning.
3. **Recruitment** consisted of an 8-page application form, a telephone interview, and a two-day, on-site interview with spouses also brought down and met. GM said they needed people who could work in teams and accept the company philosophy.
4. **Risk and reward remuneration**. Pay rates are set at 10 per cent below the GM rate. That 10 per cent represents a risk: paid quarterly if the conservative training and quality goals are met with a further 10 per cent for meeting more difficult quality and productivity goals.
5. **Training**. The agreement established training as an integral part of the company structure, recognised by its prominence in the remuneration system. After an extensive induction process, 92 hours was established as a minimum training time, with employees having individual training plans. GM said that training by leaders from all levels of the company reflected the twin values of teaching and leaders setting an example for others.

The result has been that Saturn turned a profit within three years of production, has won a swag of awards for its car and its ideas are being followed by companies world-wide.

Source: HR Report No 114

The Elements of Corporate Culture

In just the same way as anthropologists investigate the nature of primitive societies by exploring their myths and rituals, so organisational theorists describe corporate cultures in terms of their outward manifestations. Thus, the corporate culture is composed of a number of distinct elements (Deal and Kennedy, 1982):

- **Ceremonies** Events in the organisation which are designed to reaffirm members' commitment to the organisation and its values. Thus, a training course for new managers may be important for other reasons than the content of the program leads one to believe.
- **Myths and stories** Organisations have their own funds of stories, shared by all members, that serve to highlight the important values and beliefs of the organisation and form a means of communicating them to new members.
- **Rituals** Procedures repeated on a frequent basis in the organisation, for example, the daily production meeting or the weekly report of training activities. These rituals serve to illustrate the sort of behaviour the organisation expects of its members.
- **Symbols** A symbol encapsulates some aspect of the organisation's culture. Often symbols are visual, for example, the location of the chief executive's office at the top of the building, with a view of Sydney Harbour. They may also be written, such as a statement of mission and values that attempts to articulate what is important to the organisation.

Changing the culture

Compared with the Japanese examples discussed earlier, some cultures were viewed as more conducive to organisational success than others. Thus, businesses were often exhorted to develop strong corporate cultures which were regarded as playing an important part in competitive performance. Peters and Waterman (1982) were amongst the first to define what constitutes a strong corporate culture.

Managers and, in particular, the chief executive officer (CEO) are usually seen as crucial in creating a new corporate culture. The CEO and his or her management team need to analyse the existing culture and decide what new values they wish to introduce. These are often published as a 'statement of mission and values.' At this point, managers often turn to training and development specialists to help in the design and delivery of programs to communicate the new values through the organisation.

Training activities that support culture change programs often embody significant elements of off-the-job training. Typically, short two- to three-day courses will be run for all members of the organisation, in which trainers and members of management attempt to explain and attain commitment to the new culture. One automotive manufacturer, for instance, designed a new in-depth induction program for all new employees, the purpose of which was specifically to communicate the values associated with the introduction of the new model (Smith, 1989). Very quickly, however, it was realised that the new program was only influencing new employees, and that the aims of the program would be more effective if the training were extended to all members of the organisation.

The problems of culture change

Despite the popularity of the notion of culture change, however, there is little firm evidence of the success of culture change programs. Those organisations that have changed in this way have often done so not as the result of a conscious management program, but through the shock of some external crisis. Nor is there much convincing evidence of the links between cultural change and organisational effectiveness (Denison, 1990).

A number of problems are faced by organisations that attempt this sort of change program. First, it is exceedingly difficult to measure culture. Definitions of what constitutes corporate culture vary widely and are often very diffuse. Devising scientific instruments that can measure such diffuse phenomena is expensive and often produces unreliable data.

Secondly, organisations, like society as a whole, are not made up of one uniform culture, but a potpourri of subcultures. The culture on the factory floor may be very different from the culture of the offices or that of management. Which culture are managers attempting to change and in what ways? There is evidence to suggest it is the existence of conflicting cultures that produces the most innovative environments (Coopey and Hartley, 1991).

Finally, culture change often means the imposition of management's culture on everybody else. It may be that managers cannot transmit their culture to others in the organisation with any real success. The subcultures already present may simply be too powerful to be supplanted in that way. What managers regard as cultural change may be no more than sullen behavioural compliance on the part of alienated employees who realise they have to go along with management if they wish to retain their jobs (Anthony, 1990).

The Quality Approach

In a parallel response to that of the culture theorists to the emergence of Japan in the 1970s, many Western observers noted the ability of Japanese organisations to produce manufactured goods at lower cost and at much higher levels of quality than did Western organisations. This observation was seemingly at odds with the traditional Western view that high levels of quality involved higher costs, as more workers were employed to inspect products and control the quality system. The Japanese approach, on the other hand, was based on the belief that good quality lowered costs, as fewer workers were needed to inspect goods that were guaranteed to be made 'right first time'.

Western observers were initially confused by the fact that Japanese organisations seemed to employ very few people whose jobs might be described as quality control. It appeared, instead, that the Japanese worker was able to produce goods at a high level of quality without the need for any checking or inspection function at all. Further investigation revealed that Japanese success in combining low costs and high quality was the result of applying some simple managerial techniques which, unlike the cultural differences highlighted in earlier studies, were readily transferable to the Western context.

Perhaps more astounding still for Western analysts was the realisation that many of these techniques were based on lessons learned from American experts hired by Japanese firms in the post-war reconstruction of the country during the 1950s; lessons which the West had apparently forgotten.

Foremost amongst these American experts, and the person considered to be the founder of the modern quality movement, was Dr W Edwards Deming. In the 1950s, Deming showed Japanese industrialists how they could control quality in production through the application of simple statistical process control (SPC) techniques (Deming, 1982). The key to SPC was the concept of variation. The quality of all production systems varies, but SPC techniques allow workers to track the variation and control it, thus ensuring a consistently high level of quality without the need for the large armies of inspectors and checkers typically found in Western enterprises.

Unfortunately, the application of SPC is not so straightforward as the theory suggests. Another expert hired by the Japanese in the 1950s, J M Juran, demonstrated that the successful implementation of the new quality control techniques demanded a different managerial style to the traditional autocratic Western model. Responsibility had to be given back to the worker, and the deep knowledge within the work force of the production system had to be successfully tapped by managers in order to guarantee further improvement (Juran, 1962).

The application of the ideas of Deming, Juran and others in Japan during the 1950s and 1960s led to the development of the characteristic management style which Western observers began to record in the late 1970s. It was the attempts by Western organisations to transfer these notions into their own contexts that became the basis of the quality movement. In particular, Western organisations have experimented with two types of program, quality circles and total quality control.

Quality circles

Quality circles (QCs) are small work-based groups of employees who meet regularly, usually under the leadership of the supervisor, to discuss and resolve quality-related problems in the workplace (Robson, 1982). They are an attempt to tap into the knowledge of the work force on the factory floor in order to solve operational problems which are often left untouched by the management specialists in an organisation. QCs were one of the first Japanese techniques to be imported into the West following the many missions to Japan in the late 1970s.

Quality circles work on the assumption that problems in the operation are most effectively solved nearest to the workplace in which they occur. Thus, QC members are trained in problem-solving techniques which they apply to problems which they, or managers, identify. As they are based on the organisational commitment of their members, QCs are usually voluntary in operation, so that only part of the work force will be involved in the program at any time. Interestingly, this voluntarism distinguishes Western QC programs from those in Japan, where membership of a QC is often compulsory.

As with SPC, however, QC programs do not operate in isolation from what happens in the rest of the organisation. In order to be effective, QCs require the dedication of significant resources from the organisation to make them work, especially in the early stages of a program (Robson, 1982).

Illustration 10.3 — Why culture change and TQM fail

> Culture change and TQM programs are often ephemeral management fads or cycles of control that are abandoned when they fail to deliver measurable productivity improvements. A study by the University of New South Wales into culture change in the NSW Department of Industrial Relations, Employment, Training and Further Education (DIRETFE) revealed that the program was undermined by downsizing and work practice rationalisation and by managers' reluctance to give up their prerogative.
>
> Culture change and TQM's focus on creating a corporate quality culture ignores the potential for conflict to exist both within the management hierarchy and between management and worker. DIRETFE set up process improvement teams consisting of staff at the coalface who were to focus on eliminating waste and improving customer service. However, the autonomy of the teams was limited by middle management guidance teams. These were to provide leadership to the teams by reviewing the issues they realised and selecting those appropriate for investigation.
>
> The study suggests six problems which programs such as this face:
>
> 1. Attempts to alter workforce values through culture change programs may fail in the face of management programs emphasising downsizing and rationalisation.
> 2. Teams members' initial enthusiasm for the chance to research and implement change may dissipate because of increased workloads and the time the process takes.
> 3. Middle management may resist recommendations and tensions may increase both within the management hierarchy and between the different management levels.
> 4. These tensions may cause internal customer service to lose out rather than benefit.
> 5. The union — the NSW Public Service Association — was suspicious the program represented downsizing by stealth. It was kept in the dark about the culture change program.
> 6. The speed with which senior management dropped the program when it was faced by other issues suggested it was little more than a management fad.

Source: HR Report No 131

Foremost amongst these resources is training. QC programs are usually accompanied by large-scale training programs for the different groups involved with them. First, QC members themselves are trained in problem-solving techniques based on simple statistical data collection and analysis methods. It may take several weeks of training, usually administered in modular form, for QC members to become proficient in the use of these methods to solve actual problems in the workplace.

Secondly, QC leaders, who are usually supervisors (although some QC programs make provision for elected leaders), are trained in the problem-solving techniques, and are often involved in the training of the QC members themselves.

Finally, others involved in the administration of the QC program need to be trained. These include coordinators, who oversee the program, and facilitators, who work with the QCs to eliminate organisational barriers to their performance. Their training will often include an appreciation of the problem-solving techniques used by the QCs, as well as training in group dynamics and facilitation skills for their own use.

QC programs enjoyed immense popularity in the early 1980s as the positive results from the first programs launched in the late 1970s became widely known (Ramsay, 1991). In Australia, the Australian Quality Circle Association (AQCA) was founded as an umbrella group for those organisations experimenting with this form of change program. However, many QC programs have since failed. There would seem to be a number of reasons for the failure of QC programs (Drago, 1988):

1. Management commitment, both to providing the resources necessary to establish and maintain the program and to implement the solutions proposed by QCs, may have been lacking.

2. QCs do not appear to work well in highly skilled workplaces, where skilled workers may fear management's intentions and refuse to share their knowledge of the workplace in the way demanded by QC programs.

3. QC programs may be introduced as part of management strategy to weaken the power of unions in the workplace. It appears that QC programs introduced without the participation of unions fail more quickly than those with union support.

Nevertheless, QC programs often bring many benefits to participants, both worker and manager. Circle members receive useful training and some variety in the work routine, and managers obtain practical solutions to operating problems. It may be that QC programs are best understood as a step on the road to organisational change rather than representing an end point in themselves (McGraw and Dunford, 1987). Whatever the reason for their decline, since the late 1980s QC programs have increasingly given way to total quality management.

Total quality management

As the name implies, total quality management (TQM) takes a much broader approach to the problem of quality than do quality circles programs; TQM is a total system approach which stresses the fact that everyone in the organisation has responsibility for ensuring effectiveness. The body established in Australia to coordinate the introduction of TQM, the Total Quality Management Institute (TQMI), defines the process as:

> ... the management philosophy that seeks continuous improvement in the quality of performance of all processes, products and services of an organisation. It emphasises the understanding of variation, the importance of measurement, the role

of the customer and the involvement of employees at all levels in an organisation in pursuit of such improvement.

Based on the principles of Deming, Juran and others, TQM was introduced into organisations under a variety of names. Total quality control (TQC), value adding management (VAM) and common interest programs (CIP), although differing in detail and emphasis, are all expressions of the same TQM philosophy described in the TQMI definition above.

TQM took the work of Deming in particular, and created a management philosophy based on his famous '14 Principles', summarised in Figure 10.4.

Figure 10.4 — Deming's 14 principles

1. Create constancy of purpose for improvement of product and service.
2. Adopt the new philosophy.
3. Cease dependence on inspection to improve quality.
4. End the practice of awarding business on the basis of price tag alone.
5. Improve constantly and forever every process for planning, production and service.
6. Institute training on the job.
7. Adopt and institute leadership.
8. Drive out fear.
9. Break down the barriers between departments.
10. Eliminate slogans, exhortations and targets for the work force.
11. Eliminate work standards and numerical goals — substitute leadership.
12. Remove barriers to pride of workmanship.
13. Institute a vigorous program of education and self-improvement.
14. Put everyone in the company to work to accomplish the transformation.

The TQM approach has a number of distinguishing characteristics:
- It is an organisational system which is designed to become part of the organisation's culture.
- It draws on the efforts of all people in the organisation.
- The aim of TQM programs is continuous improvement; there is no end point in the process.
- It uses the statistical methods of SPC.
- TQM is directed at eliminating all waste in the organisation, whether waste material, time or processes.

The introduction of TQM usually involves three strategies (Oakland, 1989). First, a well-documented quality management system is required. This involves taking an overview of the organisation, its objectives and the various components of the system to decide how they can be made to work more effectively together to produce consistent quality.

Secondly, SPC is introduced. This involves a systematic study of the production process and the construction of dimensions on which its performance (variation) can be monitored. Managers, supervisors and employees then use the

SPC techniques to record the performance of the system and decide when corrective action is necessary.

Finally, the essence of TQM is teamwork (discussed in more detail below). All employees (not only operators) are organised into workplace-based teams. These operate in a problem-solving fashion in the manner of quality circles, but their activities are not restricted to certain meeting times in the week. Teamwork becomes the natural way of organising work at all times.

Training and development has a significant part to play in the introduction of TQM. Typically, a TQM program is introduced from the top of the organisation and cascades through all its levels. At every level, teams are formed to analyse each department's activities. Each team requires training in group processes and the SPC-based methods that are used to collect and analyse performance data. Often, in the case of large organisations, this involves training programs running continuously over periods of years.

The size of such a training task inevitably involves the use of non-training specialists in a training role. As a result, trainer training programs become an immediate priority for organisations introducing TQM. The total training input into the TQM process is heavy and prolonged.

TQM programs became very popular in Australia in the early 1990s. Backed by the Federal Government, the TQMI was established in 1987 as an umbrella body, and now boasts over 100 member organisations, including such large organisations as Telecom Australia, Ford, Kodak, Esso and IBM. By 1995 research by the Group for Research in Employment and Training at Charles Sturt University and the Research Centre for VET at the University of Technology, Sydney showed that most Australian organisations were involved in some form of quality improvement program. Quality improvement, and TQM in particular, had become a major driving force for training in many Australian organisations (see Chapter 4) with large numbers of employees undergoing training in problem-solving and teamwork skills in order to facilitate the introduction of quality improvement programs (Smith et al, 1995; Hayton et al, 1996).

Teamworking

The thrust of the quality approach to organisational change was the emphasis on small group and teamwork. This emphasis is not new. The original pioneers of the OD approach in the 1940s were initially concerned with the impact of informal groups in the workplace. The OD movement grew out of the work of the Research Center for Group Dynamics established by Lewin at MIT in 1945 (French and Bell, 1990). Whereas the work of the OD movement tended to concentrate on the role of the individual in group behaviour, it was left to others to pursue the value of the group or team as a unit of work organisation.

Eric Trist and his colleagues at the London-based Tavistock Institute of Human Relations (including the Australian researcher, Fred Emery) developed the notion of the self-directing workteam as the basis for their successful consultancy with the British National Coal Board in the 1950s (Trist, 1963). From this work, the Tavistock group developed the highly influential socio-technical systems approach to organisational change, which put the development of effective workteams (sometimes known as semi-autonomous workgroups) at the centre of the change process.

Quality of work life

Socio-technical designs became the focus for the attempts in the 1960s and 1970s by large European and American organisations to counter the effects of routine fragmented factory work on the motivation of the work force. Known as quality of work life (QWL), these experiments stressed the importance of redesigning jobs to include higher levels of worker control and group work. The most well-known examples of QWL programs included those at General Motors in the United States, Volvo in Sweden and Phillips in Australia. All of these organisations attempted to change the traditional pattern of work organisation to accommodate semi-autonomous workgroups, with varying degrees of success.

However, most of these QWL programs did not survive for more than a few years, and many of the organisations that had experimented with them returned to more traditional patterns of organising work in the late 1970s and 1980s. It has been suggested that the reason for the failure of QWL was that the rationale for the new work forms was usually grounded in the desire to make the work environment more amenable for the workers in the belief that happy workers are more productive workers. Unfortunately, QWL programs were very rarely linked into the business plans of the enterprises and thus suffered in times of economic downturns (Auer and Riegler, 1990).

Modern teamwork

Despite the mixed success of QWL, the notion of teamwork has proved very durable and has undergone a renaissance in the 1990s. Again, the influence of Japan has played a major role in the renewal of interest in teamworking. Although not associated with QWL, large Japanese corporations have been using a similar, though more restricted, version of teamwork on the shop floor for a number of years. Banker and his colleagues in their research on the impact of teamwork in manufacturing organisations (Banker et al, 1996) identified six variants of modern teamworking:

- **Traditional workgroups** This is the traditional work organisation in which workers have no responsibility and in which the ancillary functions are carried out by staff specialists. This form of work organisation is the outcome of the application of Taylorism.
- **Quality circles** As discussed above, these are voluntary groupings of workers which meet to solve quality-related problems in the workplace. These teams play no part in the regular work organisation, and for this reason are sometimes referred to as 'off-line' teams.

- **High performance workteams** In Chapter 4, we discussed the emergence of the high performance work organisation. The workteams that accompany this form of work organisation are referred to as high performance workteams. They have responsibility for major, but routine, activities, within a strict hierarchical structure. The decision-making authority enjoyed by these teams is more than a quality circle but less than a semi-autonomous team.
- **Semi-autonomous workgroups** These teams are very closely integrated into the production system. Typically, a semi-autonomous team will consist of six to eight members under the direction of a team leader who will also be a production worker. A number of team leaders report to a supervisor. This type of team does not necessarily involve any job redesign, although members will be flexible enough to cover each other's jobs in cases of absence and may carry out simple maintenance tasks: see Figure 10.6 on p 276.
- **Self-managing teams (or autonomous workgroups)** Based on the Scandinavian workgroup concept, this type of team usually involves much more extensive job design, with workers responsible for setting their own work targets and organising themselves to control large sections of the work process. This form of organisation has considerable implications for the role of the supervisor.
- **Self-designing teams** These are a more autonomous variant of the self-managing team. In this situation, the team has control over the design of the team and over who should belong to the team.

The major difference between these six variants is the level of autonomy each possesses to make decisions in the workplace. They are represented in Figure 10.5, which places the variants on a continuum of autonomy.

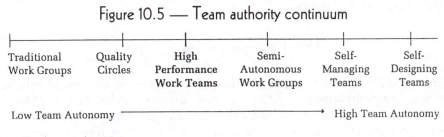

Figure 10.5 — Team authority continuum

Source: Banker et al (1996)

It is not yet clear which type of teamwork will become more widespread. Generally, employers tend to favour the high performance or semi-autonomous types, as they involve little or no delegation of control to the shop floor. Unions are predisposed towards the more worker-centred self-managing type.

Figure 10.6 — Characteristics of effective teams at an Australian car manufacturer

> An effective team:
> - has a high success rate (ie, more often than not it achieves what it sets out to do);
> - agrees on clear, challenging objectives, ie, everyone in the team contributes to, shares an understanding of and is committed to the objectives;
> - has a leader who adjusts the leadership style along a spectrum from participative to autocratic, depending on the circumstances;
> - has a mix of people who contribute in different but complementary ways;
> - operates in such a way that a balance is struck between concern for the task (the 'what') and concern for the process (the 'how');
> - creates a supportive atmosphere where people are happy to say what they really think, develop one another's ideas and commit to an agreed course of action even though there may have been differences of opinion;
> - learns from experience, both successes and failures, by reviewing its processes and constantly improving its performance;
> - works hard and plays hard — ie, its members not only achieve challenging objectives but enjoy themselves as they do so.

Implementation of all variants of teamwork involves considerable training input. Teamworkers need to be extensively trained to cover jobs other than their own and, in the case of the more autonomous teams, to take on more highly skilled tasks. Team leaders and supervisors need to be trained in their new roles as facilitators to the teams. As in all the change programs examined so far in this chapter, of course, the introduction of teamwork has considerable implications for what happens in other parts of the organisation. Banker's (1996) research has shown that training is a key ingredient for the success and longevity of teams. Teams that do not undergo extensive training tend not to work well and to disintegrate in a short period of time.

The Learning Organisation

Many organisations undergo a number of change programs in an attempt to improve competitiveness. Culture change, quality circles and TQM almost become fads or fashions to which organisations subscribe without any lasting impact on their effectiveness (Abrahamson, 1996). Over time, however, some organisations continue to change and improve, while others find it more difficult. A learning process would therefore appear to take place within organisations which enables them to survive in changing environments. Early organisational learning theorists, Fiol and Lyles (1985), described organisational learning as:

> ... the process of improving actions through better knowledge and understanding.

Yet, there is a difference between organisational and individual learning. Organisational learning is not simply the sum of the learning of each of the individuals in the enterprise. Organisational learning implies a capacity to transmit the lessons from one generation of employees to another, and to adapt as a result of the learning process.

Adaptation and learning

The processes of adaptation and learning are not the same. Adaptation is the process of adjustment to changing circumstances. The release of a new product or the adoption of new policies are examples of a gradual incremental adjustment to new conditions. Adaptation may not, however, be enough to secure the long-term survival of an organisation. The fate of the Swiss watch industry confronting the twin threats of new product technology (the electronic watch) and Japanese competition in the early 1970s demonstrates the inadequacy of adaptation in the face of revolutionary change.

Organisational learning is a much deeper process, involving the development of insights and knowledge over a long period of time and the ability to assess critically the assumptions on which the organisation is basing its actions.

Argyris and Schon (1976) first pointed to the distinction between these two processes in organisations. They distinguished between single-loop and double-loop learning. Single-loop learning is essentially equivalent to adaptation. It is short-term behavioural change often associated with previous behavioural responses to similar situations, for example, discounting the price of products when demand slumps.

Double-loop learning involves a process of questioning the assumptions on which the organisation is acting. It occurs throughout the organisation and has implications for everyone. A successful change of corporate culture would be an example of double-loop learning. Organisational learning therefore involves the presence of double-loop processes.

Learning, however, does not imply large-scale change. Figure 10.7 on p 278 shows the possible relationships between learning and organisational change. Position A might represent fairly mature industries in which no new learning or change is taking place as the organisation is in a dominant position. Position B may represent organisations which have undertaken a number of change programs but in which very little real learning has taken place (for example, the Australian car industry). Position C involves relatively few changes but with significant learning taking place. Position D represents the organisation which is involved in both significant change and learning such as the introduction of TQM.

Building the learning organisation

One of the most influential writers on the learning organisation has been Peter Senge, Director of the Centre for Organisational Learning at MIT in the United States. In his book, *The Fifth Discipline: The Art and Practice of the Learning Organization* (1990), Senge identified five conditions necessary for organisational learning to take place:

Figure 10.7 — Learning and change

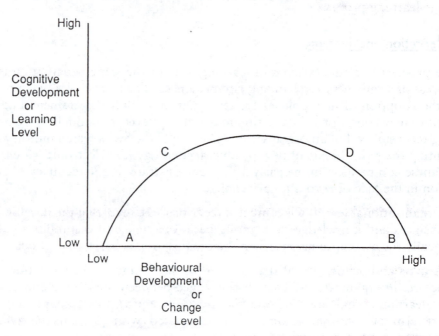

Source: Fiol and Lyles (1985)

- **Systems thinking** This is a reworking of the systems paradigm in organisational theory which was discussed in Chapter 3. Systems thinking involves looking at the organisation as a whole system in which changes to one part of the organisation necessarily produce changes in another. Senge regards systems thinking as difficult for managers in many organisations who are conditioned to think in terms of single causes for events. In systems theory, changes in organisations can be the result of the interaction of a number of concurrent activities and events. Similarly, systems thinking predisposes managers to realise that change may come from many places in the organisation, not only from the top. Thus, change programs may be initiated anywhere within organisations where managers need to recognise and capitalise on changes that take place rather than attempting to fit the organisation to their own view of how change should proceed.
- **Personal mastery** The learning organisation fosters growth and development in all its employees. However, it is the responsibility of the individual to take charge of his or her own destiny and create his or her own opportunities for personal development. Thus, an organisational commitment to learning can only be realised by individuals taking responsibility for their own learning.
- **Shared mental models** The means of overcoming the gap between individual and organisational learning discussed above is through sharing mental models. Kim (1993) has shown that mental models are the routines and frameworks we use every day to make sense of the world and guide

our actions. In the course of individual learning, these mental models change, but this does not benefit the organisation unless these models are shared with others so they can learn also. The learning organisation adopts strategies to enable the sharing of mental models to take place so organisational learning can occur.

- **Shared vision** This is a notion taken from the theory of leadership. A good leader has a personal vision which he or she is able to articulate to other members of the organisation. Thus, in the learning organisation, leadership is a well-distributed capability and all members have their own visions relating to their work and their careers. The learning organisation allows its members to share these visions and to subscribe to a common vision that binds them together.

- **Team learning** At the heart of the learning organisation is teamwork. Effective teamwork allows all the members of the team to learn together, and to set their own direction in line with the shared vision of the organisation.

A particular difficulty with the notion of the learning organisation is to what extent organisational learning is simply the sum of all the individual learning that goes on within the organisation, or whether it is possible for the organisation to learn apart from its individual members. The learning organisation provides opportunities for individuals to learn and develop, but it must also have ways of ensuring that individual learning is retained for the benefit of the organisation. This is the role of memory. Just as individuals learn through committing lessons to memory, so organisations learn by developing procedures that act as an organisational memory. Thus, the learning organisation must be able to develop procedures that ensure the fruits of individual learning are recorded and used by other members of the organisation.

Adler and Cole (1993) illustrated this point in their comparative study of two car plants renowned for their experiments in work design and organisational change — Volvo's Uddevalla plant in Sweden and the joint General Motors/Toyota plant (NUMMI) in California. Both plants had adopted a teamwork approach to work organisation. At Uddevalla, Volvo provided a high level of training for all its employees in areas such as personal skills, presentation skills, training competence and so on. However, the learning at Uddevalla was wholly focused on the development of the skills of the individual employee. There were no mechanisms for linking individuals to organisational learning. At NUMMI, by contrast, the focus of managers had been on developing procedures and standardisation of work methods, so that as one team learned a better way to work, this knowledge was recorded and passed on to other teams in the organisation. Adler and Cole (1993:32) summarised the differences this way:

> At NUMMI, the skill development strategies for individual workers are managed as a component of this process, rather than as a way of maximising personal opportunities (as at Uddevalla). As a result, training focuses on developing deeper knowledge ... of the production system. Understanding a broader range of jobs — the focus of Uddevalla's approach — is recognised as an important stimulus to kaizen (continuous improvement) efforts, but this broadening of skills builds on rather than replaces work process and the deepening of skills.

Field and Ford (1995) examined organisational learning in the Australian situation, and identified a number of barriers to the implementation of the learning organisation. These are illustrated in Figure 10.8, which is an adaptation of earlier diagrams by Bill Ford summarising the OECD/CERI research on training in organisations: see Chapter 4. In this model, organisational learning will only take place when employee relations, work organisation, skill formation and technology and information systems are aligned to the purpose of learning.

Figure 10.8 — Factors affecting organisational learning

- Work organisation
- Technology and information
- Skills training and learning
- Consultation and agreements

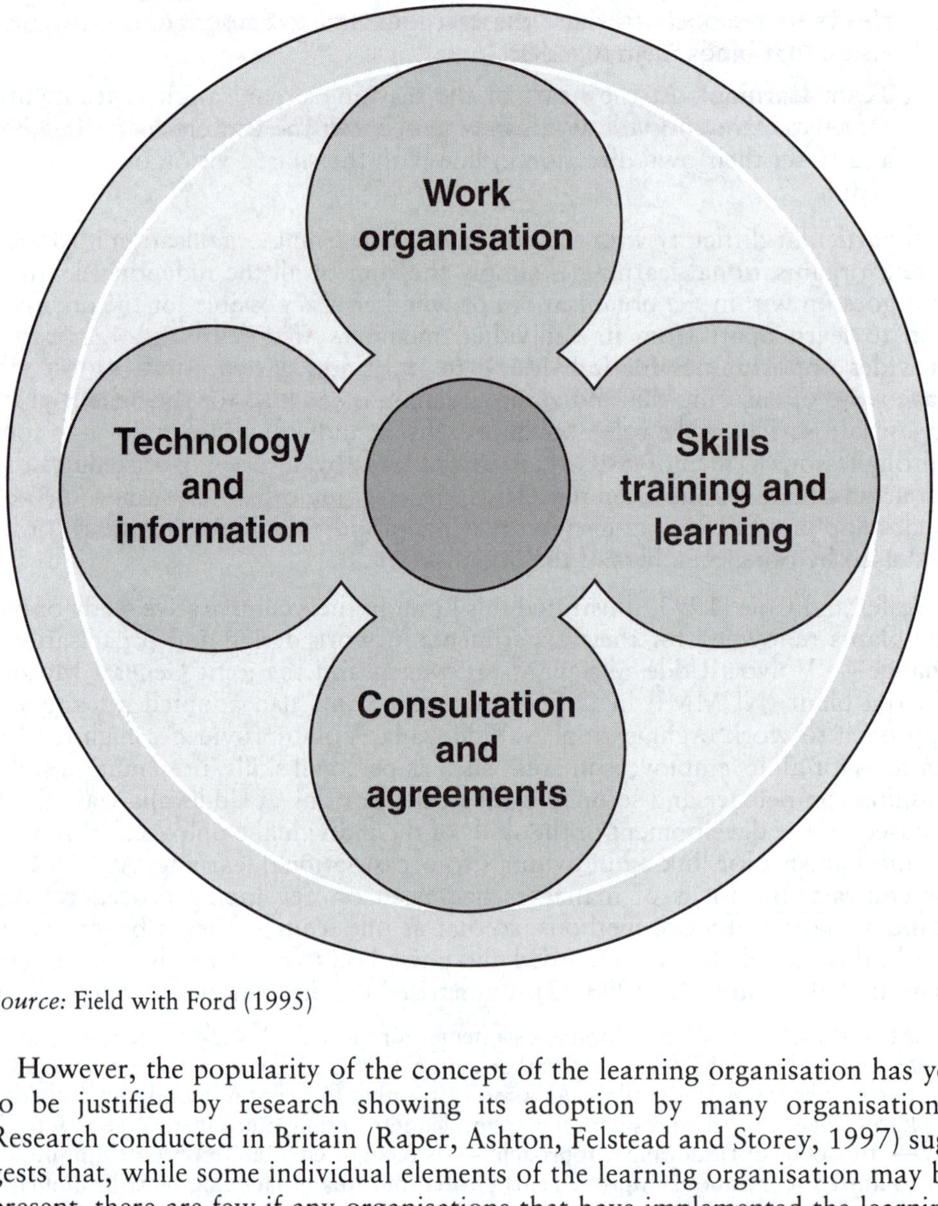

Source: Field with Ford (1995)

However, the popularity of the concept of the learning organisation has yet to be justified by research showing its adoption by many organisations. Research conducted in Britain (Raper, Ashton, Felstead and Storey, 1997) suggests that, while some individual elements of the learning organisation may be present, there are few if any organisations that have implemented the learning organisation as a 'total package', and that Senge's idea may remain an ideal towards which organisations strive rather than an empirical reality.

Summary

This chapter has examined programs of change commonly found in contemporary organisations and their links to training and development.

The economic situation of the West, including Australia, particularly in the face of Far Eastern competition, has produced a dynamic for change in many organisations in both the public and private sectors. Most of these change programs are designed to improve organisational performance by engaging the commitment of employees through some form of devolution of control to the shop floor. This movement has been characterised as one of moving from a control paradigm to one of commitment.

The origin of many of these change programs is to be found in the organisation development movement which began in the United States in the 1950s. OD is based on humanistic notions of reconciling the needs of organisations for improved performance with the needs of individuals for growth and development. The OD movement gave rise to a number of different change programs, including the use of T-groups for sensitivity training for individuals, the use of employee surveys and feedback as a catalyst for change and the action research method for diagnosing and implementing organisational change.

In the 1980s, the notion of corporate culture gained popularity as a result of attempts to explain the success of Japanese firms in export markets. A number of writers and consultants advocated the development of a strong corporate culture to harness the motivation of the work force and achieve significant breakthroughs in organisational performance. However, the reality of culture change has proved to be far more elusive than its advocates would suggest, and there are few examples of successful culture change programs.

In the 1990s, the concept of quality became very important in discussions of organisational change. Again, inspired by the success of Japanese corporations in producing high quality goods at low cost, the concern for quality gave rise to the quality circle movement in the late 1970s and 1980s. However, quality circle programs tended to fail after a period of time as a result of the inability of organisations to change other aspects of their operations. In the 1990s, the concept of total quality management gave rise to large-scale all-embracing programs of change which attempt to alter the entire operational stance of organisations and engage the commitment of all employees to quality.

A major component of modern programs of change has been the introduction of teamwork. First used in the 1960s as part of the quality of work life programs, teamwork became popular in Scandinavia as a way of reorganising work to give workers more control and autonomy in the workplace. The Japanese concept of teamwork is less egalitarian and more concerned with tying the worker more effectively into the production system. Both forms of teamwork can be observed in contemporary programs of change.

More recently, the emerging concept of the learning organisation has attempted to take many of the lessons learned from these programs of organisational change and suggest that organisations, like individuals, are undergoing a continuous process of learning and adaptation. No one program of change can solve all the problems of an organisation because circumstances are always changing. Only organisations that learn from their past mistakes and have established mechanisms for promoting learning will be able to adapt and survive in the long term.

Discussion Questions

1. What is organisational commitment and how does it affect organisational performance?
2. To what extent are the values underlying the OD approach to change in conflict with objectives of efficiency and competitiveness?
3. Can culture be changed? What part can the training practitioner play in the process?
4. Why does the quality approach to change involve such heavy training input?
5. Is teamwork compatible with the Australian workplace?
6. Can organisations learn and how can organisational learning be enhanced?

Chapter 11

Coaching, Counselling and Consulting

Much of this book has been concerned with the provision of training, as though learning is a process that can only take place in a specially constructed learning environment. In fact, much learning takes place outside the context of work: in the family, at school, in the community and so on. Even within the confines of work, most learning takes place on the job without the need for formal training programs (Garavan, 1987). It is the presence of this so-called natural learning that, in part, defines the learning organisation discussed in Chapter 10.

A major source of learning in the workplace is, of course, the manager. The influence of the manager on the general disposition of the employee, not only in regard to learning, is overwhelming. Studies in Australia have shown that it is the way in which employees are treated by their managers that is the key determinant of their commitment, motivation and desire to remain with the organisation (Automotive Industry Council, 1990). It is not surprising therefore that the manager should wield such influence over the processes of employee learning.

The first part of this chapter is concerned with natural learning and, in particular, with those learning processes in which the manager plays a significant role: coaching and counselling. Although usually treated as distinct processes, coaching and counselling share many features in common and may be viewed as extensions of the same basic concept. They are both one-to-one activities; neither coaching nor counselling can be successfully carried out in a group context. They both involve the establishment of a close relationship, beyond that of the usual working relationship, between coach and student, and they both take place outside the formal training environment in the workplace. It is therefore appropriate that both processes are discussed in the same context.

The second part of the chapter is concerned with another one-to-one relationship which is becoming increasingly common in the area of training and development — consulting. Traditionally, Australian organisations have made great use of the services of external consultants in the field of human resources; a practice which has led to the general underdevelopment of the human resources function in many organisations. Frequently, however, training practitioners are called upon to play a consulting role within their own organisations. In both cases, the nature of the client–consultant relationship is a crucial issue. This relationship is the focus for the second part of the chapter.

Origins and Practice of Counselling

Counselling — the process of helping people by talking to them — has a long history in the twentieth century. In the workplace, however, counselling has witnessed a dramatic growth in the last two decades (Novarra, 1986). There are a number of influences that have contributed to the rise in popularity of the counselling movement (Belkin, 1988):

1. **Laboratory psychology** The scientific investigation of the mind began in the late eighteenth century, but flowered in the late nineteenth and early twentieth centuries. It was during this period that the division between cognitive and behaviourist approaches to psychology emerged: see Chapter 3.
2. **Emergence of psychotherapy** Freud and Jung in the twentieth century pioneered the use of clinical techniques to treat people with emotional and nervous disorders. Often, this involved the psychotherapist talking to the client to unlock memories buried in their unconscious.
3. **Mental health reform** The provision of adequate hospitals and treatments for those suffering from mental disorders encouraged research into mental illness and the development of effective cures.
4. **Vocational guidance** Beginning in the United States, the vocational guidance movement has been a strong influence on counselling, involving the application of counselling methods to the problems of career choice.
5. **Humanistic psychology** Perhaps the most powerful influence on the counselling movement has been that of Carl Rogers (see Chapter 3) whose development of non-directive psychotherapy laid the basis for the modern techniques of counselling.

Even a cursory consideration of these influences will reveal that the notions of counselling and psychotherapy are very closely linked. However, it is important to distinguish between the two. Generally, psychotherapy deals with more serious emotional/psychological problems and involves much more intense treatment by the therapist. Counselling is concerned with helping people to identify their problems and do something about them themselves.

Nevertheless, it is clear that counselling and psychotherapy can be viewed as two ends of a continuum. It is the recognition of this fact that has led to demands for the professionalisation of counselling in the workplace. Leaving the provision of counselling to the untrained manager may not be the most appropriate way of helping people cope with their problems at work.

Models of counselling

The fact that counselling and psychotherapy share a common theoretical base in psychology means that there is a wide variety of models for the counselling process. Theories of counselling range from Skinnerian behaviourist approaches, through Freudian psychodynamics, to cognitive and, of course, humanistic approaches.

It is, however, the work of humanist Carl Rogers that has probably had the most pervasive impact on modern counselling technique. Rogers believed in the dignity of the client, and found the conventional psychoanalytic approach tended to devalue and dehumanise the client. His client-centred approach established the base for counselling (Rogers, 1955). In particular, three Rogerian concepts lie at the heart of modern counselling practice (Geldard, 1989).

The first is congruence. The counsellor approaches the client as a natural human being rather than as an expert or therapist. Although the counsellor will be playing a particular role in the relationship with the client, there should be no essential difference between the counsellor as a person and his or her role as counsellor.

The second is empathy. The counsellor needs to put himself or herself in the place of the client and understand the problem from his or her point of view. In this situation, the client directs the counselling process rather than vice versa.

Finally, the counsellor should hold the client in unconditional positive regard. This involves using a non-judgmental approach; not necessarily agreeing with or approving of the client, but not letting personal judgment get in the way of helping the client solve the problem.

Based on these principles, counsellors have developed a number of practical techniques to help clients. These include reflecting what the client says or feels back to them, asking questions to clarify the problem, reframing the problem in a way which is different to the way the client understands the problem, and challenging self-destructive beliefs (SDBs) which are making the client unhappy or disturbed.

The way in which these and other techniques are deployed in a counselling session are illustrated in Figure 11.1 on p 286.

In general, the sequence of a typical counselling session will include the following steps:

- **Introduction** Putting clients at ease and establishing a relationship.
- **Active listening** Letting clients do the talking, while encouraging them to open up by giving verbal and non-verbal cues (nodding, etc).
- **Identifying the problem** Asking relevant questions and clarifying issues.
- **Exploring options and facilitating action** Helping clients to solve the problem themselves.

Figure 11.1 — Process of a counselling session

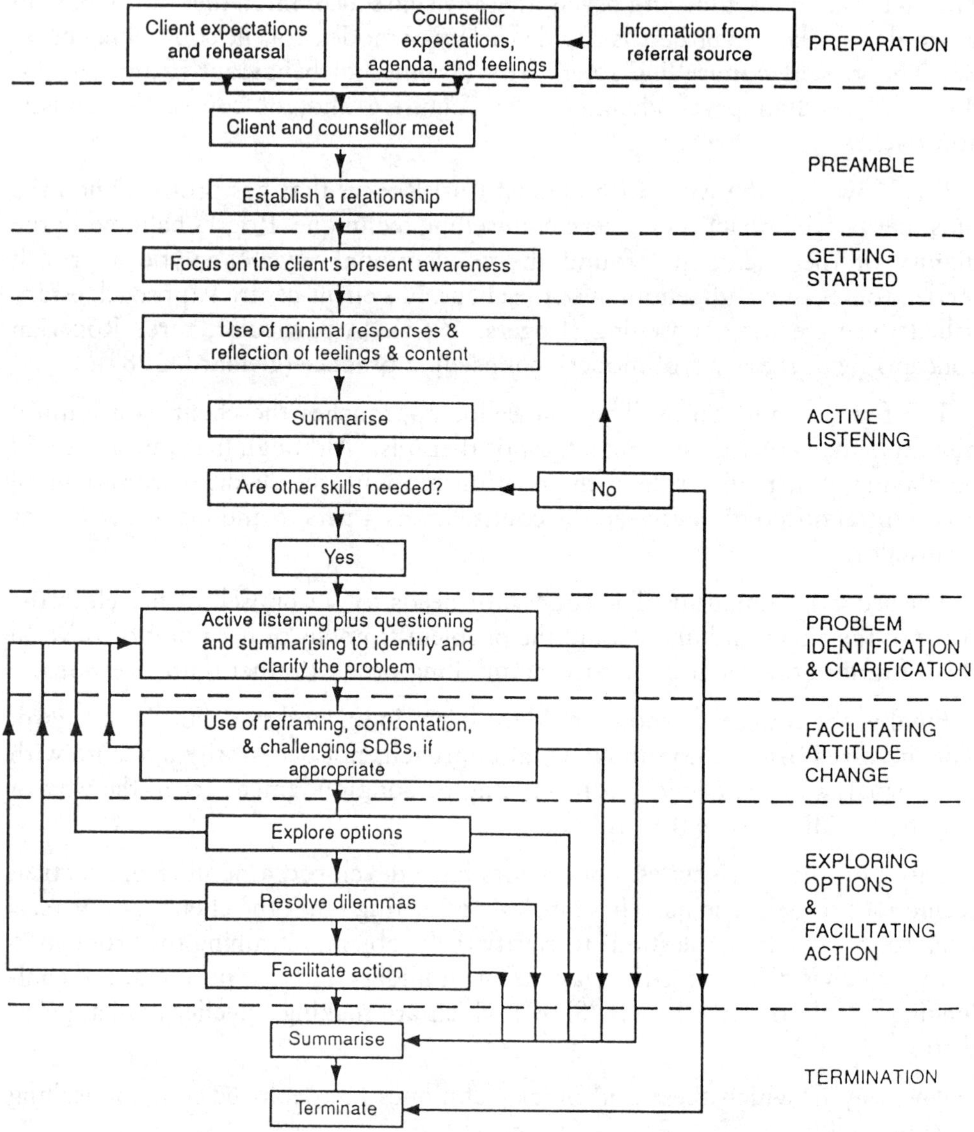

Client expectations and rehearsal → Counsellor expectations, agenda, and feelings ← Information from referral source	PREPARATION
Client and counsellor meet ↓ Establish a relationship	PREAMBLE
Focus on the client's present awareness	GETTING STARTED
Use of minimal responses & reflection of feelings & content ↓ Summarise ↓ Are other skills needed? — No (loop back) / Yes ↓	ACTIVE LISTENING
Active listening plus questioning and summarising to identify and clarify the problem	PROBLEM IDENTIFICATION & CLARIFICATION
Use of reframing, confrontation, & challenging SDBs, if appropriate	FACILITATING ATTITUDE CHANGE
Explore options ↓ Resolve dilemmas ↓ Facilitate action	EXPLORING OPTIONS & FACILITATING ACTION
Summarise ↓ Terminate	TERMINATION

Source: Geldard (1989)

Counselling in the Workplace

The techniques of counselling are used in a number of different settings in the workplace. This section will explore some of the more important of these applications: career counselling, outplacement counselling, employee assistance programs (EAPs) and the possibility of managerial counselling.

Career counselling

Career counselling has developed from the vocational guidance movement mentioned at the beginning of this chapter. While vocational guidance is usually viewed as an activity that takes place with young people, primarily in the school context, career counselling is more clearly a workplace phenomenon, aimed at the development and retention of valued staff.

A number of theories have been developed by organisational psychologists to explain the process of fit between a person and a career. Some use the notion of life stages (Super, 1957) to explain how people's career aspirations change as they progress through life. Others try to relate career choice to early experiences in the family (Roe, 1956). Perhaps the best known career theory is that of Holland, who developed a series of six personality types which can be measured using a specially developed test, the vocational preference inventory. According to Holland, each personality type seeks a work environment appropriate to it. Career dissatisfaction arises if the individuals find themselves working in an inappropriate environment (Holland, 1973).

Theories of careers can help the counsellor guide the individual to make a suitable career choice or overcome career-related problems. Career counselling is a form of employee development. Figure 11.2 below shows how the process of career counselling is an attempt to match the goals of the individual and the organisation. Success in the attempt will benefit both parties. Training and development has a major role to play in the process, as the facilitator of the plans agreed upon at the end of the counselling process.

Figure 11.2 — Elements of career counselling

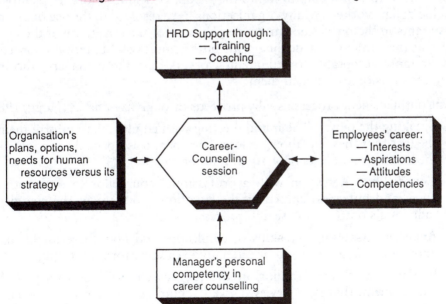

Source: Verlander (1986)

Career counselling is one form of counselling that is not restricted to the one-to-one format normally considered essential for successful counselling. Career planning workshops can be run on a group basis, using a life-planning technique in which strangers from different organisations, or different parts of the same organisation, can explore their long-term plans in a supportive group atmosphere.

Outplacement counselling

One of the key issues for organisations in the 1990s has been downsizing: see Chapter 10. The 1990s has witnessed a massive decline in the numbers employed by large corporations, a trend which shows little prospect of disappearing in the near future (Littler, 1997). Redundancy and retrenchment have become major strategies for competitiveness worldwide, particularly in the manufacturing sector.

However, the effects of downsizing on the morale of the organisation can be devastating; not only for those losing their jobs but also for those left behind who may feel bitter about what has happened to their colleagues (Littler, 1997). As a result, counselling can play an important role in helping all members of an organisation adjust to the reality of retrenchment, and enable the organisation to perform effectively in the post-redundancy period.

In recent years, a number of consulting groups have become involved with outplacement counselling, the most frequently used term to describe the counselling aspects of downsizing. Outplacement counselling can be provided in a number of different ways, from the intensive one-to-one job search services often offered to senior employees, to the group workshops more frequently run for blue-collar workers. Many organisations have resorted to the use of external consultants in the outplacement process because of the sensitivity of the operation and the difficulty of dealing with bitter employees. External counsellors may be more acceptable to redundant workers than the managers who have taken the decision to retrench them.

The outplacement process usually proceeds through five phases (Hogg, 1988):

1. **Breaking the news** The initial meeting with employees to inform them of the fact that they are about to lose their jobs. It is normally conducted by the manager and lasts only 10 minutes or so.
2. **Counselling** A session with a professional counsellor to deal with the anger and bitterness caused by the situation and to focus the energies of individuals onto the job search process.
3. **Analysis** Assessing the skills of employees and how these might match another occupation or job. It often involves some form of testing.
4. **Presentation skills:** Training in the job search skills necessary to find employment; that is, interviewing skills, putting together a resume and so on.
5. **Research:** Finding another job.

The outplacement process is therefore a mixture of counselling, helping employees come to terms with the new situation, and conventional training, equipping them with the skills to find new employment.

Illustration 11.1 — Employee assistance at Pacific Power

> Pacific Power generates electricity for the 5 million inhabitants of New South Wales through a network of power stations located throughout the State. Employing 7000, Pacific Power has always been conscious of the importance of the health and welfare of its workforce for the safe and efficient operation of technically complex power stations.
>
> For this reason, Welfare Officers have been employed in the organisation since 1960. In response to the rising level of concern about the impact of drug and alcohol abuse in the workplace, Pacific Power established an EAP in 1985. Staffed by 4 full-time Employee Assistance Officers (EAOs), the EAP offers a range of services to all employees on a confidential basis.
>
> Employees may be referred to the EAP by their supervisor if a performance problem is identified, or they are free to refer themselves. In either case strict confidentiality is observed with supervisors only informed whether the employee is receiving assistance and if time away from work will be required.
>
> The EAP process involves the initial assessment of the employee's problem by EAOs who are trained to give general counselling. If the employee requires the more specialised help, EAOs will refer them to outside services such as marriage guidance, drug and alcohol agencies, legal advice or personal counselling. The confidentiality guaranteed by the EAP has made the service very popular amongst employees, with EAOs counselling over 2,500 clients per year.
>
> The geographically dispersed nature of Pacific Power's operations means that EAP services cannot be provided at every location, but Occupational Health Nurses at the power stations can refer local employees for counselling.
>
> The EAP also administers the Employee Welfare Fund which provides financial assistance for contributing members and their families in times of distress and hardship. Financed by voluntary contributions of around 20c per week, the Fund is worth over $1m. and is controlled by an elected committee of members.

Employee assistance programs

A more systematic provision of counselling to employees occurs through employee assistance programs (EAPs). Originating in the United States during the 1940s, EAPs were the response of large corporations such as Du Pont, Eastman Kodak and Caterpillar Tractor to the problems posed by alcohol abuse in the work force. Federal legislation in the United States obliging employers to provide programs for the treatment and prevention of alcoholism in the work force led to an explosion of EAPs to the point where there are over 10,000 programs in place and 75 per cent of the *Fortune* 500 operate an EAP (Luthans and Waldersee, 1989).

The different legislative environment of Australia has not provided the same stimulus for the establishment of EAPs as in the United States. Nevertheless, the basis for such an approach certainly exists in this country, which has the highest per capita consumption of alcohol in the English-speaking world and an alcohol abuse problem estimated to cost the economy over $6 billion in lost productivity per year (Mann, 1991). Since 1983 the Industrial Program Service (IPS), based in New South Wales, has worked with counterparts in other states to establish EAPs throughout Australia.

The modern EAP, however, is a broader service than the original anti-alcohol programs of the past. EAPs provide professional assistance, usually in the form of counselling, for a wide variety of problems which may affect an employee's performance at work. These typically include alcohol and drug abuse, family/marital problems, emotional problems and other work-related problems, although the IPS estimates that alcohol and drug abuse problems account for 54 per cent of the problems diagnosed in their clients (IPS, 1990). The services offered by an EAP vary from one organisation to another and in different circumstances, but a general philosophy guides the approach of most programs (Compton, 1988):

1. **The total person** The organisation may only employ the person for 40 hours per week, but the problems they face in non-working hours can have as much of an impact on their performance as those encountered at work.
2. **Work-relatedness** Only problems that impact on work performance are the domain of the EAP.
3. **Reactive strategy** EAPs deal with the problems brought to them by clients rather than attempting to prevent problems.
4. **Professional counselling** Counselling is not conducted by members of management but by trained independent professionals.
5. **Confidentiality** The key to the success of the counselling services of the EAP is the fact that employees can rely upon the complete discretion of the counsellors.

The EAP process will usually follow three basic steps. These steps are illustrated in Figure 11.3 on p 291.

The first stage of the EAP depends on the management skills of observing and diagnosing a problem with an employee. If the problem is beyond the ability of line management to solve, that is, it is not a matter for simple counselling or discipline, then the manager can refer the employee to the EAP. Alternatively, the employee can self-refer. Secondly, the employee receives counselling from the professional staff of the EAP. This may lead to further counselling or to referral for treatment. Finally, the employee receives treatment, if it is appropriate.

Although EAPs involve the provision of counselling services, it is unusual to find them linked to conventional training. The nature of the problems dealt with by EAPs usually precludes a training solution. However, the Ford Motor Company has experimented with a more extended version of the EAP in their American and European operations (Hougham, Thomas and Sisson, 1991). Side by side with the usual services of the EAP, the Ford Employee Development and Assistance Program (EDAP) offers employees company-sponsored training in a range of subject areas, many unconnected with their work. Such non-work related training is viewed by Ford and the unions in the company as a means of developing the wider skills of the work force and securing long-term commitment to the company.

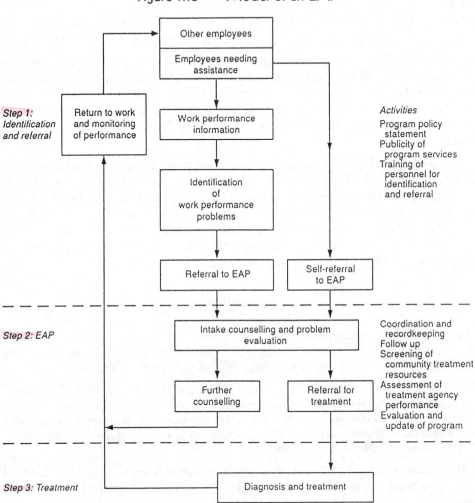

Figure 11.3 — Model of an EAP

Source: Applebaum and Shapiro (1989)

The efficacy of EAPs has proved hard to verify in practice. Corporate claims for high rates of success tend to reflect the numbers who may use the service multiplied by some assumed loss to the company incurred from the types of problems referred. These figures give little or no analysis of the problem-solving rate of the EAPs (Luthans and Waldersee, 1989). It appears that problems of drug and alcohol abuse are not particularly susceptible to this sort of treatment; however, little substantive research has been conducted into the general effectiveness of the EAP.

Managerial counselling

The possibilities for counselling in the corporate environment are limited by the extent to which the manager can fairly be expected to act as a counsellor (Novarra, 1986). The nature of true counselling demands that the onus for problem-solving be located squarely with the client. In the last resort, if the client does not wish to resolve the problem but is prepared to live with it, the counsellor has no mandate to enforce a solution; it is the client's choice.

This may well not be possible in the corporate context. The individual with a problem affecting work performance has no option but to solve the problem or face disciplinary measures. The manager who counsels the employee, no matter how non-directive his or her technique, is inexorably bound into a power relationship with the employee. Counselling is undertaken as a means to an end, namely, the elimination of the problem; the employee has little choice in the matter.

As a result, professional counsellors tend not to regard managerial counselling as 'real' counselling. They argue that the organisation can only provide effective counselling through the services of trained professionals on a confidential basis. Whether or not it is possible for a manager to counsel in this 'pure' form, it is nevertheless the case that the techniques of counselling, active listening, problem clarification and action planning are powerful tools for the development of employees.

Coaching

Coaching is the name generally given to those developmental activities that take place in the workplace setting under the control of the manager. Walker (1992 cited in Gurney, 1995) has defined the role of the coach as follows:

> In the flexible organisation the manager is first and foremost a coach. Coaching narrowly implies training, instructing or guiding, but it is more than that. It is caring, listening, nudging, advising and nurturing others as they strive to achieve results. Good coaching is an essential feature of effective management in a high-performing, flexible organisation.

It is no coincidence that coaching takes its name from the sporting arena. In a sports setting, the coach does not act as a formal trainer but rather as one who aims to improve performance continuously through effective leadership (Stowell, 1988). In the organisation, coaching becomes the day-to-day activity of the manager who uses the workplace to provide learning experiences for employees so that performance is continuously improved.

Generally, the coaching role involves the manager using certain distinct behaviours. The effective coach seems to display supportive behaviours, for example, showing concern and consideration for employees and initiating behaviours such as structured problem-solving discussions, rather than non-supportive behaviours such as aggression and the use of power (Stowell, 1988). Coaching highlights the crucial role of the manager in helping employees to learn at work.

Role of the manager in learning

The concept of the learning organisation was considered in the previous chapter. The creation of the learning organisation involves the nurturing that has been termed 'natural learning' (Garavan, 1987). Natural learning is a process of self-discovery which occurs most frequently outside the contrived settings of formal training and is characterised by:

- consideration being given to all aspects of the individual;
- the assumption that individuals are able to learn for themselves and require only the opportunity to do so;
- individuals accepting full responsibility for their own learning;
- learning being continuous and varied;
- the importance of discovery learning; and
- learning activities being diagnostic rather than prescriptive.

The concept of natural learning therefore mirrors the adult learning principles of Knowles and Rogers: see Chapter 3. The individual is autonomous, and motivated to learn if the conditions are right. It is the creation of the conditions for natural learning that is the key contribution of the manager.

Research into the behaviour of successful manager/coaches has shown that the important variables in effective coaching are (Cooke and Knibbs, 1987):

1. The degree of interest shown by the manager in his or her staff; degree of accessibility to them.
2. The degree of structure that the manager builds into the development process, for example, providing learning opportunities, keeping records, etc.

These two dimensions of managerial performance in the coaching role can form the basis of a grid model. The model is illustrated in Figure 11.4 on p 294. The role played by the manager can vary from the ideal high interest, high structure type to the very poor developer, low interest, low structure type.

The effectiveness of the coaching process therefore depends on the skills of the manager. It is no coincidence that those organisations which report higher levels of investment in employee training and development (the larger organisations) are those which train their managers to develop their staff (Leicester, 1989). Training managers acting as coaches has a multiplier effect on employee development generally.

Quarry and Ash (1996) have shown that coaching has many similarities to on-the-job training. They define five steps in effective coaching:

1. **Determining the need** The determination of the need for coaching usually comes from four situations — the hiring of a new employee, the observation of poor performance, a request for help or consulting with the employee directly.
2. **Explaining** Explaining the task clearly and simply. This is similar to the task analysis associated with on-the-job training.

3. **Demonstrating** After explaining the task, the coach demonstrates exactly how the task is done, with all the resources that are necessary.
4. **Practice** The coach should aim to get the employee to accomplish the task with no assistance or prompting, under the same conditions as he or she will be under on the job.
5. **Feedback** Both during and after the practice step, the coach should give the employee specific feedback on what he or she has done well and less well.

The five steps are illustrated in Figure 11.5 on p 295.

Figure 11.4 — Role of the manager in developing subordinates

Amount of "Interest"	Low ← Amount of "Structure" → High
High	Manager very open and accessible; interested in staff in all areas of activity; keeps close contact at informal level; staff meetings open and democratic (if disorganised); records for staff development are "in the head" or rough notes	Manager provides regular opportunities for review of development needs; identifies/sets up activities to meet needs; systematic induction; open and sensitive to staff and development; meetings positive and participative; procedures and records used constructively in development process
(middle)		Manager provides loose system of staff support and development; encourages training but is not very organised in identifying needs; regular meetings which are quite effective; manager is interested in staff and open to their needs; records kept and used most of the time
Low	Manager seems to take little interest in staff or their development — "I leave it to them"; mainly casual, unplanned contact with subordinates; keeps to procedures reluctantly (if at all); poor records; staff meetings tend to be sterile and normally ineffective	Manager follows procedures rigidly; keeps records, but does not use them to identify development needs; meetings though regular are "one way"; participation not encouraged; sees staff on individual basis to "keep a check on them"; training happens but is routine and unexciting

Source: Cooke and Knibbs (1987)

Figure 11.5 — The five steps to coaching on the job

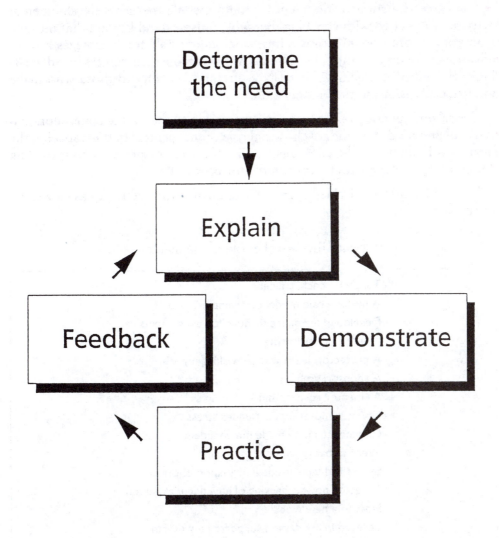

Source: Quarry and Ash (1996)

Mentoring

Although sometimes confused with coaching, mentoring is a very different, and far more extensive, process than coaching. A mentor is an older, more experienced person in the organisation who takes on a younger member of the organisation as a protégé, and through the relationship developed, helps the protégé to advance in his or her career. The role of the mentor is ordinarily considered to be wider than that of the coach or counsellor, and will normally be performed by someone other than the direct superior of the protégé. Often, the role of the mentor is split into two functions.

The career function of the mentor would include the usual developmental activities associated with coaching, but would also extend beyond that into the realm of corporate sponsorship. Thus, mentors not only teach protégés how to advance in the organisation, but also actively promote their careers by advocating their ability and gaining them exposure and visibility to those who make important decisions in the organisation.

The second function of the mentor is more akin to that of the counsellor, and is usually referred to as the psychosocial role of the mentor. In this capacity, the mentor is building up the confidence and self-esteem of protégés by providing counselling, friendship and a role model for behaviour.

Figure 11.6 below provides a summary of the mentor's activities as viewed by the protégé.

Figure 11.6 — The role of the mentor

- Teacher, coach, trainer
- A positive role model or example
- Developed my talent through job assignments
- Opened doors for me
- A protector, learn without risking my job
- A sponsor, visibility
- As mentor rose, so did I
- Counsel, moral support under stress
- Confidence in me made me confident
- Went to bat for me, fought for me
- Bypass red tape, inside information, short-cuts
- Reflected power, backing of an influential person
- Host to a new world
- Believed in my dream, supported my dream
- Represented a more advanced level for which I strove
- Provided me with negative feedback

Source: McKeen and Burke (1989)

The process of mentoring can have benefits for the organisation and the mentor as well as for the protégé. For the protégé, the mentor provides confidential guidance early in his or her career. Because the mentor is not a direct superior, the protégé can approach the mentor with problems it may be impossible to admit to the boss. The experience and influence of the mentor may be able to help clear up problems that would otherwise jeopardise the protégé's career.

Later in one's career, the need for achievement begins to give way to the need to pass on accumulated wisdom and insight to those of another generation (Levinson, 1978). With career horizons limited, a desire to balance achievement needs with nurturing may replace the driving ambition of the younger manager. The mentoring role gives many managers the means to achieve this balance in their professional life.

Effective mentoring programs can lead to much better use of human resources by the organisation. As organisations find it more difficult to recruit seasoned managerial talent in the face of demographic changes, the availability of in-house mentoring will become an important means of developing their own talent (Wright and Werther, 1991). As a result, there has been an explosion of formal mentoring programs in larger organisations in the last few years.

Implementing a mentoring program

Kram (1983) has shown that the mentoring relationship typically follows a four-stage chronology.

1. **Initiation** During the first six to 12 months, the relationship becomes established and both parties adjust to their new roles.
2. **Cultivation** For a period of about two to five years, the mentor relationship is at its most productive.
3. **Separation** As a result of changes in the relationship (tensions) or external conditions (promotion of one party, etc), the relationship ceases to function.
4. **Redefinition**: Protégé and mentor may develop a peer relationship if the feelings engendered by separation can be accommodated.

Some organisations leave the choice of mentor/protégé to chance, providing only a formal policy and encouragement for the mentoring activity (Wright and Werther, 1991). McKeen and Burke (1989) suggest that some of the key elements in the establishment of a formal mentoring program are as follows.

In many cases, the mentor relationship may generate significant emotional strain, as both parties invest considerable energy in the partnership. The intensity of the relationship may result in the souring of relations between mentor and protégé if expectations remain unfulfilled on either side. This may be particularly true in the case of cross-sex mentoring, with the attendant difficulties this may create in a traditional organisational setting. Mentoring programs have become widely established in recent years, to help women counter the effects of the 'glass ceiling' which restricts their progress into management positions. However, issues of power and intent (Coombs, 1997) are often not adequately addressed when these programs are established. Coombs suggests a form of 'mutual mentoring' to overcome these problems, in which each of the partners is a mentor to each other and the mentoring process is brokered between the two mentors for their mutual benefit.

Figure 11.7 — Phases of the mentor relationship

Phase	Definition	Turning points
Initiation	A period of six months to a year during which time the relationship gets started and begins to have importance for both managers.	Fantasies become concrete expectations. Expectations are met; senior manager provides coaching, challenging work, visibility; junior manager provides technical assistance, respect, and desire to be coached. There are opportunities for interaction around work tasks.
Cultivation	A period of two to five years during which time the range of career and psychosocial functions provided expand to a maximum.	Both individuals continue to benefit from the relationship. Opportunities for meaningful and more frequent interaction increase. Emotional bond depends and intimacy increases.
Separation	A period of six months to two years after a significant change in the structural role relationship and/or in the emotional experience of the relationship.	Junior manager no longer wants guidance but rather the opportunity to work more autonomously. Senior manager faces midlife crisis and is less available to provide mentoring functions. Job rotation or promotion limits opportunities for continued interaction; career and psychosocial functions can no longer be provided. Blocked opportunity creates resentment and hostility that disrupts positive interaction.
Redefinition	An indefinite period after the separation phase, during which time the relationship is ended or takes on significantly different characteristics, making it a more peerlike friendship.	Stresses of separation diminish, and new relationships are formed. The mentor relationship is no longer needed in its previous form. Resentment and anger diminish; gratitude and appreciation increase. Peer status is achieved.

Source: Kram (1983)

Illustration 11.2 — Mentoring in the NSW Premier's Department

> State Premier's Departments have the potential to be turned upside down every time a government changes hands. But in the NSW Premier's Department a mentoring program soothed the transition during the Carr Government's first year in office. When the Carr Government was elected to office in 1995, staff within the Premier's Department unexpectedly benefited from an existing mentoring and career development pilot. The program had been established at the beginning of 1995 as part of an affirmative action strategy to boost the numbers of women at senior management levels. Twelve women from middle management were nominated for the program and were teamed up with mentors. Some individual mentors had more than one mentor from senior management, depending on the professional skills they wanted to develop.
>
> The program included six half-day workshops primarily for the mentors which promoted self-directed career development. Consultant Ann Rolfe-Flett of Synergetic Management said: 'They encouraged people to be less dependent on external circumstances,' she said. 'You can't do anything about the wind, but you can trim your sails.' They also helped foster bonds between the mentors. The benefits gained from the program encouraged the mentors to act as informal mentors to other junior employees, establishing informal support networks across the department.
>
> The 1995 NSW election occurred half-way through the program. It delivered a change of government, a new CEO in Bob Carr and a new direction. The Department was split with some functions and staff hived off into a Department of State and Regional Development. The support employees experienced was a completely unexpected outcome of the pilot program, Rolfe-Flett said. The informal networks established as a result of the program supported and reassured individuals during the change. The final workshop featured a session focusing on how people responded to imposed change. It was reassuring for people to learn that, given the upheaval within the Department, what they were feeling was a natural response, Rolfe-Flett said.

Mutual mentoring is characterised by:

- Well-defined program goals which are actively supported at all levels of management.
- Training and development to foster an awareness and understanding of mentoring and its role in career development.
- Creation or modification of organisational structures to foster desired behaviour.
- Design of an appropriate structure for the mentoring relationship.
- Careful selection of mentors and protégés.
- An ongoing program of support and feedback for those involved in mentoring relationships.

It appears that mentor relationships can have a significant positive impact upon the careers of protégés, particularly if they fit into the management culture of the organisation concerned (Whiteley, Dougherty and Dreher, 1991). Nevertheless, the older–younger, mentor–protégé relationship may not be the only relationship that fosters learning in the organisation.

Peer relationships

Of particular importance to members of organisations at all levels and at all stages of their career are relationships with their peers. As with mentoring relationships, peers can provide both career and psychosocial support in the organisation (Kram and Isabella, 1985). In career terms, peers share information and provide feedback to each other. At a psychosocial level, peers can give friendship, emotional support and confirmation. The difference in the relationship between peers and mentors is the lack of the power dimension that inevitably exists in any mentor/protégé relation. The depth of mutuality and trust is potentially far greater than in the conventional mentor relationship.

This depth of trust and mutuality defines a continuum of possible peer relationships. Information peers exist at the low trust end of the continuum, but nevertheless provide an important function in disseminating information of interests to both parties. Collegial peers enjoy a trusting relationship and confide to the extent of providing feedback and support to each other. The most trusting of peer relations is that enjoyed between special peers who are good friends and are willing to disclose aspects of themselves to each other that would otherwise be taboo in a work environment. Naturally, the possibilities for learning increase with the depth of trust existing in the peer relationship.

A further dimension of the peer relationship is the career stage of the peers. As careers progress from the early establishment phase through middle career to late career, the demands on peer relationships change to reflect different concerns. These changes are summarised in Figure 11.8 below.

Figure 11.8 — Dominant themes of peer relationships at successive career stages

Stages	Information peer	Collegial peer	Special peer
Late career	Maintaining knowledge	Assuming consultive role Seeing others as experts	Preparing for retirement Reviewing the past Assessing one's career and life
Middle career	Networking Maintaining visibility	Developing subordinates Passing on wisdom	Threats of obsolescence Reassessment and redirection Work/family conflicts
Advancement	Preparing for advancement Gaining visibility	Gaining recognition Identifying advancement opportunities	Sense of competence and potential Commitment Conformity v individuality Work/family conflicts
Establishment	Learning the ropes Getting the job done	Demonstrating performance Defining a professional role	Sense of competence Commitment Work/family conflicts

Source: Kram and Isabella (1985)

Peer and mentor relationships represent two relationships amongst a relationship constellation (Kram, 1986) in which members of an organisation may be involved for developmental purposes.

Consulting

Consultants are used by organisations to 'fill in the gaps' in corporate expertise. Thus, consulting covers a wide range of fields, from consulting engineers who would be involved in the design and construction of major capital projects, to the smaller consulting firms (often one-person enterprises) typically used in the human resource management context.

Management consulting started in the United States in the early years of the twentieth century (Chickillo and Kleiner, 1990). Booz, Allen and Hamilton was founded in 1914, quickly followed by McKinsey and Company, possibly the best known international management consulting firm in the world. Since World War II, management consulting has flourished, with very few established organisations not employing the services of management consultants at some time in their development. The growth of the market for management consulting has led to its inevitable fragmentation as smaller consulting groups have emerged to challenge the larger companies in particular specialised fields.

As a result, there is a number of consulting groups that specialise in human resource issues, many limiting their operations to perhaps one or two activities within the field. Thus, there are recruitment consultants, remuneration consultants, consultants who specialise in psychological testing, as well as a number of specialist training and development consultants. As a reaction to the emergence of these specialist firms, the larger consulting groups have decentralised their own operations, and most established management consulting firms support specialist HRM and training divisions.

Of course, as discussed earlier in the chapter, organisations do not only employ external consultants. In recent years, internal consultants have flourished in many larger organisations, with training practitioners often having their jobs redefined as internal consultancy. However, the position of the internal consultant as an employee of the organisation is often quite different from that of the external practitioner; a point that will be the focus of later discussion.

Margerison (1988) has defined four different forms of consulting activity. These are based on whether the consultant is external or internal to the organisation, and whether the consultant acts in an advisory or executive role in the relationship with the client. The forms of consulting are summarised in Figure 11.9 on p 302.

Figure 11.9 — Margerison's consulting roles

	External	Internal
Adviser	Role A External consultant advising client	Role B Internal specialist staff advising colleagues
Executive	Role C External project manager directing the client	Role D Internal manager directing subordinates

Source: Margerison (1988)

Role A is the conventional notion of the external consultant who provides special advice to clients for a period of time.

Role B is the full-time executive who can act as a consultant to his or her own colleagues in a coaching and supporting way.

Role C is a more recent consulting role, developed in the construction and computer industries particularly, where a project manager from an outside organisation has responsibility for delivering an assignment but acts as a consultant to the client and a line manager in his or her own organisation.

Role D is a role which has grown rapidly in most organisations over recent years. Today, there are many internal advisers on finance, safety, legal matters and so on.

The client–consultant relationship

The similarity between the roles of the consultant, the counsellor and the coach is the centrality of the one-to-one relationship. In the case of the consultant, the relationship is between the consultant and the client. The nature of the relationship determines the role of the consultant and vice versa. The consultant can play a number of different roles in which the client becomes more or less dependent on the consultant. Champion describes up to nine different roles which the consultant can play, ranging from the hands-on expert who does everything for the client to the counsellor who is concerned with enabling clients to solve the problem for themselves (Champion, Kiel and McLendon, 1990).

In effect, the consultant can play the role either of the content/technical expert, in which the client is put into a dependent role, or of the process facilitator, in which the client is encouraged to solve the problem himself or herself with the consultant in a helping role. The content/process distinction is an important concept in consulting, and defines a continuum along which the various configurations of the client–consultant relationship can be placed. In this sense, content refers to the actual task at hand. Thus, a content-oriented consultant will use technical expertise to produce a solution to the client's problem as the client expresses it. Process refers to the way in which tasks are carried out regardless of content. The process-oriented consultant will therefore focus on developing the relationship with the client, may question the client's understanding of the real problem and aim to help the client find and implement the solution rather than impose a solution (Schein, 1978). The differences between the two orientations are summarised in Figure 11.10 below.

Figure 11.10 — Models for Consulting

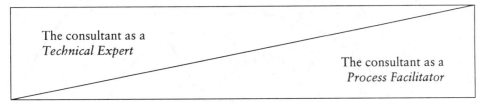

Engineering or purchase models	Clinical or process models
1. The client's statement of the problem is either accepted at face value or verified by the consultant on the basis of his or her technical expertise relative to the problem.	1. The client's statement of the problem is treated as information. The problem is verified jointly by both the client and the consultant.
2. Little time is spent on developing the consultant–client relationship. The connection is generally short-term and problem-oriented.	2. The consultant–client relationship is viewed as an essential ingredient in the process and considerable attention is given to its development.
3. The solution, or prescription, to the problem is generally developed by the consultant and implemented by the client.	3. The major focus of the consultant is to help the client to discover and implement appropriate solutions for himself or herself.
4. The consultant brings technical expertise to bear on the client's problem(s).	4. The consultant is an expert in how to diagnose and facilitate organisational processes.
5. The consultant is primarily concerned with increasing the client's knowledge and skill relative to the stated problem(s).	5. The consultant is primarily concerned with improving the client's diagnostic and problem-solving skills.
6. In general, the client does it for and to the client.	6. In general, the consultant helps the client to do it for and to himself or herself.

Source: Margulies and Rais (1978)

An alternative classification of the client–consultant relationship focuses on the outcomes of consultation and the appropriate behaviour of the consultant. Generally, the consulting process can be viewed as oriented either towards a solution or to a problem (Margerison, 1978). A problem-centred approach will be concerned with finding out more about the problem; a solution-centred approach will focus on the provision of an answer to the problem.

Figure 11.11 — Behavioural models for the consultant

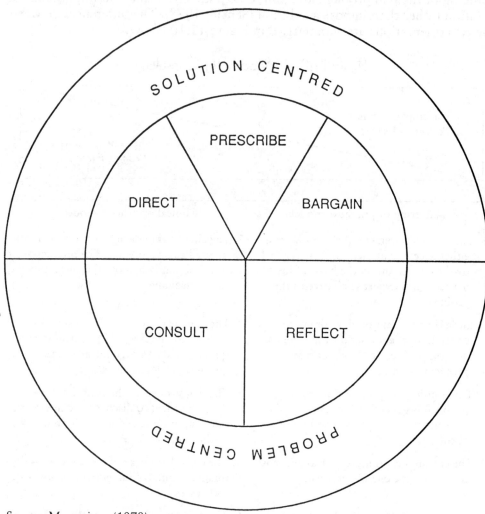

Source: Margerison (1978)

These two approaches involve five possible types of behaviour for the consultant:
1. **Consult** Asking questions or giving information that will indicate problem areas.
2. **Reflect** Reformulating the views of the client and repeating them to indicate understanding.
3. **Direct** Indicating what action needs to be taken.
4. **Prescribe** Recommending a certain course of action.
5. **Bargain** An exchange or negotiated deal.

The two basic approaches are, of course, not mutually exclusive. The consultant may move from one approach to the other, and adopt different behaviours as the relationship with the client develops.

The consulting process

Regardless of the orientation of the client–consultant relationship, it is important that the contract between the two parties is clear to all concerned. Both consultant and client need to be sure what the intended outcomes of the consultancy will be and the nature of the process that will be used to achieve those outcomes. It is in the interest of neither party to produce surprises. As a result, the contracting process between client and consultant can often appear very formal as both parties attempt to minimise the risks associated with the relationship. The consulting process might be broken into three major phases: appraisal, assessment and application.

1. **Appraisal** At this stage, contact is first made between client and consultant. This may occur in a formal sense, with a request from a client, or through informal contact. If the relationship is to develop, the consultant will usually draw up an initial contract stating what he or she intends to do and at what cost. The final part of the appraisal stage occurs when the contract for the consultant's services is negotiated between client and consultant.
2. **Assessment** The first stage in the consulting process involves the analysis of the client's problem. This centres upon the gathering of information in the organisation, and diagnosis based on the data gathered. At this stage, the consultant will usually feed the results of the data gathering back to the client at a formal meeting and seek agreement that the diagnosis is correct.
3. **Application** Based on the diagnosis, the consultant will formulate proposals for the client regarding a recommended course of action. Once the client has made the decision to go ahead with the consultant's proposals, implementation can take place. The final stage in the process is the review of the effectiveness of the action after implementation.

The success of the consulting process depends on the synchronisation of the client's expectations with the actions proposed by the consultant; hence the importance of the formal process of contracting to both parties.

The formal contracting process may, however, not be enough to ensure the success of the client–consultant relationship. There usually needs to be some personal rapport between the parties to engender trust. The process issues of the relationship are often critical to the success of any consulting project. These issues might include whether both parties feel they can work with each other: is the client really committed to the process that the consultant is recommending? Will the client make the necessary resources available to ensure the success of the project (Weisbord, 1984)? The resolution of these personal issues may be of more importance to the long-term success of the project than the formal contracting process.

Illustration 11.3 — Internal consulting in the Australian Public Service

In his address to the 1995 Australian Institute of Training and Development, Edmund Attridge of the Public Service Commission described the growth of internal consulting within the Australian Public Service (APS). For the APS, internal consultants offered a number of advantages over external consultants. In particular, they can be expected to have greater knowledge and familiarity with the organisation's work, culture, values, politics, practices and procedures.

The permanent placement of consultants within the organisation also avoids much of the learning curve associated with hiring in a consultant. It also better places the consultants to participate in long term management of change as opposed to the short term interventions commonly associated with external consultants.

Maintaining professionalism is a particular challenge for an internal consultancy unit in the APS. It means:

- providing an independent and objective judgment that is free of bias;
- fostering creativity and innovation in consultancy work;
- demonstrating a strong client orientation through the quality of services and products provided.

Perhaps the main reason for failure of internal consultancy units is lack of credibility. Credibility in part relates to the ability of people in the unit to promote, to communicate or to represent what they do, including at senior levels. Credibility means keeping up with where the agency and the APS are heading in terms of emerging trends and developments. If, for example, the agency is trying to develop greater teamwork an internal consultant will not be thanked for consultancy solutions that do not involve teamwork.

Absolutely fundamental to the success of internal consultancy is being clear about the business and choosing consultancy assignments which add value to the business. It is best to start with small assignments which have clear measures against which success can be judged. It is best to choose clients who are clear about what they want to achieve and who offer ready access, both to relevant data and to themselves and who can be expected to offer a fair but testing judgment of the work.

The culture of a consultancy unit is very important. The culture needs to be one that fosters creativity, continuous learning, professionalism in approach and teamwork in supporting each other in undertaking assignments. The unit should operate as a business and be constantly concerned with how it can improve its own operations in an ongoing way.

Source: Training and Development in Australia 22:2 7–10

The internal consultant

Although the previous discussion has implicitly equated the consultant with the external provider, the same issues of client–consultant relationships and contracting affect the internal consultant (IC). However, the internal consultant is in a different position from the external one.

In many ways, ICs enjoy a more powerful position than external consultants do. ICs are permanent employees of the organisation for which they consult. This gives ICs a degree of job security which enables them to take more risks because pay is not so dependent on the achievement of specified results. Their knowledge of the organisation and ability to get things done gives ICs a distinct advantage over external consultants, who will often rely on an internal person to supply this information. Continuity of employment with the organisation enables ICs to build on previous successes, and see projects through rather than leaving the organisation as the external consultant is compelled to do.

However, some of these advantages may well work against ICs. Familiarity of organisational members may make it difficult for ICs to maintain the expert credibility that is often accorded to the external consultant. Failures as well as successes are remembered by organisation members. The dependence of ICs on the organisation for their livelihood may make it more difficult for them to implement pure solutions, and they run the risk of having to compromise the integrity of their activities for the sake of acceptability in the organisation (Steele, 1982).

The contradictions in the role of the internal consultant often result in the use by many organisations of both internal and external consultants. Some projects may not be within the capability of the internal consultant to achieve, for organisational reasons as well as lack of expertise. In these cases, the organisation will use the external provider, often in conjunction with the internal consultant to ensure the success of a project.

Summary

This chapter has explored the notion of 'helping' relationships in training and development. Counselling, coaching and consulting focus on the one-to-one relationship between helper and the helped, whether that is between a consultant and client, counsellor and client, mentor and protégé or manager and employee. These one-to-one relationships form an important arena for the development of human resources outside the conventional formal training environment.

Counselling developed from the psychotherapeutic approaches to the treatment of emotional problems in the early twentieth century. The specifically non-directive counselling style finds its origins in the work of Carl Rogers, a founding figure in the development of adult learning theory. Counselling is used with increasing frequency in the workplace to help employees overcome work- or non-work-related problems, and restore their productivity. The chapter explored some of the more common manifestations of counselling in the workplace, including career counselling, outplacement counselling and employee assistance programs. Despite the popularity of the counselling approach, it is doubtful whether managers in a power relationship with employees can effectively counsel others, in the true sense of allowing clients to find their own solutions to problems.

There is a number of other developmental relationships which employees can enjoy with others in the organisation. Chief amongst these, of course, is the relationship between the manager and the employee. The manager plays a crucial role in setting the climate in which effective employee learning can take place.

An increasingly common form of relationship between manager and employee is that of mentoring. The mentor acts not only as a coach but as a sponsor and confidante for the younger employee, who benefits from the wisdom of the more experienced manager. Formal mentoring programs may be difficult to establish, but they appear to enhance the career prospects of those who participate in them. Members of an organisation may also enjoy close relations with their peers, who can provide both support and learning opportunities outside the manager–protégé relationship.

The consultant enjoys a different form of one-to-one relationship with the client. The relationship is defined by a contract that binds both parties to a set of expectations. However, within the contractual relationship, a variety of potential configurations can occur depending on the role of the consultant. The greater the content orientation of the consultant, the higher the level of dependency of the client. Many consultants in the HR area adopt a more process-oriented approach which allows the client to develop his or her own solution to the problem.

Discussion Questions

1. Can a manager be a counsellor?
2. Is counselling a form of employee development?
3. What are the differences between coaching and traditional on-the-job training?
4. What are the difficulties faced by women in a mentoring program?
5. Why are so many Australian organisations dependent on consultants for innovation in the HR area?
6. What are the ethics of the consultant's role?

References

Abrahamson, E (1996) 'Management Fashion', *Academy of Management Review*, 21:1, 254–85

Adler, P (ed) (1992) *Technology and the Future of Work*, Oxford University Press, New York

— and Cole, R (1993) 'Designed for Learning: A Tale of Two Auto Plants', *Sloan Management Review*, Spring: 85–94

Albanese, R (1989) 'Competency-based Management Education', *Journal of Management Development*, 8:2.66–76

Allen Consulting Group (1994) *Successful Reform: Competitive Skills for Australians and Australian Enterprises*, Report to the Australian National Training Authority, Allen Consulting Group, Melbourne

American Assembly of Collegiate Schools of Business (1987) *Outcomes Measurement Project, Phase III, Report*, May

American Society of Training and Development (1997) *Models for Human Performance Improvement: Roles, Competencies and Outputs*, ASTD Press, St Paul, Minnesota

Anderson, J R (1983) *The Architecture of Cognition*, Harvard University Press, Cambridge, Mass

Annett, J and Sparrow, J (1985) 'Transfer of Training: A Review of Research and Practical Implications', *Programmed Learning and Educational Technology*, 22:2, 116–24

Anthony, P D (1990) 'The Paradox of Management Culture or "He Who Leads is Lost"', *Personnel Review*, 19:4, 3–8

Applebaum, E and Batt, R (1994) *The New American Workplace: Transforming Work Systems in the United States*, Cornell University Press, Ithaca

Applebaum, S H and Shapiro, B T (1989) 'The ABCs of EAPs', *Personnel*, July, 42–5

Argyris, C and Schon, D (1976) *Organizational Learning*, Addison-Wesley, Reading, Mass

Arnoff, S (1987) 'Evaluation Issues in the Educational Product Life Cycle' in L S May, C A Moore and S J Zammit, *Evaluating Business and Industry Training*, Kluwer, Boston

Arrow, K (1973) 'Higher Education as a Filter', *Journal of Public Economics*, II, 193–216

Auer, P and Riegler, C (1990) *Post-Taylorism: The Enterprise as a Place of Learning Organizational Change*, Swedish Work Environment Fund and WZB, Sweden

Australian Arbitration and Conciliation Commission (1988) *National Wage Decision*, Print H4000, Australian Conciliation and Arbitration Commission, Melbourne

Australian Bureau of Statistics (1990a) *Employer Training Expenditure Australia, July to September 1989*, AGPS, Canberra

— (1990b) *How Workers Get Their Training Australia, 1989*, AGPS, Canberra

— (1990c) *Projections of the Population of Australia, States and Territories, 1989 – 2031*, AGPS, Canberra

— (1991) *Employer Training Expenditure Australia, July to September 1990*, AGPS, Canberra

— (1994a) *Employer Training Expenditure Australia, July to September 1993*, AGPS, Canberra

— (1994b) *Training and Education Experience Australia, 1993*, AGPS, Canberra

— (1994c) *Employer Training Practices, Australia 1994*, AGPS, Canberra

— (1997) *Employer Training Expenditure Australia, July to September 1996*, AGPS, Canberra

— (1998) *Employer Training Practices, Australia 1997*, AGPS, Canberra

Australian Centre for Industrial Relations Research and Teaching (1995), *Agreements Database and Monitor*, No 5, March

Australian Council of Trade Unions/Trade Development Council (1987) *Australia Reconstructed: ACTU/TDC Mission to Western Europe*, ACTU, Melbourne

Australian Education Council Review Committee (1991) *Young People's Participation in Post-compulsory Education and Training: Report of the AEC Review Committee*, AGPS, Canberra

Australian Education Council/Ministers of Vocational Education, Employment and Training (1992) *Putting General Education Together (The Mayer Report)*, AGPS, Canberra

Australian Manufacturing Council (1990) *The Global Challenge: Australian Manufacturing in the 1990s*, Australian Manufacturing Council, Melbourne

Ausubel, D P (1963) 'A Subsumption Theory of Meaningful Verbal Learning and Retention', *Journal of General Psychology*, 66, 213–24

Automotive Industry Council (1990) *Labour Turnover and Absenteeism: Costs and Causes in the Australian Automotive Industry*, Australian Manufacturing Council, Melbourne

Baker, M (1994) 'Training Down Under: An Overview of the Australian Experience' in R McNabb and K Whitfield (eds), *The Market for Training: International Perspectives on Theory, Methodology and Policy*, Avebury, Aldershot

— and Wooden, M (1992) 'Training in the Australian Labour Market: Evidence from the How Workers Get Their Training Survey', *Australian Bulletin of Labour*, 18, 25–45

— and Wooden, M (1995) *Small and Medium Sized Enterprises and Vocational Education and Training*, Monograph No 1, National Training Markets Research Centre, Adelaide

Banker, R D, Field, J M, Schroeder, R G and Sinha, K K (1996) 'Impact of Work Teams on Manufacturing Performance: A Longitudinal Field Study', *Academy of Management Journal*, 39:4, 867–90

Bandura, A (1969) *Principles of Behavior Modification*, Holt, Rinehart and Winston, New York

— (1977) *Social Learning Theory*, Prentice-Hall, Englewood Cliffs, New Jersey

Bartel, A P and Lichtenberg, F (1987) 'The Comparative Advantage of Educated Workers in Implementing New Technology', *Review of Economics and Statistics*, 66:1, 1–11

Bartlett, F C (1932) *Remembering: A Study of Experimental and Social Psychology*, CUP, Cambridge

Bartz, D E and Calabrese, R L (1991) 'Enhancing Graduate Business School Programmes', *Journal of Management Development*, 10:1, 26–32

Becker, G S (1964) *Human Capital: A Theoretical Analysis with Special Reference to Education*, Columbia University Press, New York

Beckhard, R (1969) *Organization Development*, Addison-Wesley, Reading, Mass

Beer, M, Spector, B, Lawrence, P R, Quinn Mills, D and Walton, R E (1984) *Managing Human Assets*, Free Press, New York

Beggs, J and Chapman, B (1988) 'Labour Turnover Bias in Estimating Wages', *Review of Economics and Statistics*, 70:1, February, 117–23

Belkin, G S (1988) *Introduction to Counseling*, 3rd ed, WCB Publishers, Dubuque, Iowa

Bentley, T J (1988) 'A Guide to Embedded Computer-based Training', *Training and Development in Australia*, 15:1, 19–72

Berger, M (1993) 'A Market-led Training Needs Analysis — Is the Training Needs Analysis Outmoded?', *Industrial and Commercial Training*, 25:1, 26–30

von Bertalanffy, L (1968) *General Systems Theory: Foundations, Developments, Applications*, Brazillier, New York

Billett, S (1993) *Learning is Working When Working is Learning: A Guide to Learning in the Workplace*, Centre for Skill Formation Research and Development, Griffith University

Bishop, J H (1994) *The Incidence and Payoff to Employer Training*, Center for Advanced Human Resource Studies, Working Paper 94-17, Cornell University

Bloom, B S (1956 ed) *Taxonomy of Educational Objectives*, Longman, London

Bloom, N (1988) 'What Do Employee Attitude Surveys Achieve?', *Industrial Marketing Digest*, 13:4, 96–104

Bosworth, D, Wilson, R and Assefa, A (1993) 'The Market for Training: A Human Capital Approach', *International Journal of Manpower*, 14:2,3, 33–46

Boxall, P F, (1996) 'The Strategic HRM Debate and the Resource-Based View of the Firm', *Human Resource Management Journal*, 6:3, 59–75

Boyatzis, R E (1982) *The Competent Manager: A Model for Effective Performance*, Wiley, New York

Bramley, P and Kitson, B (1994) 'Evaluation Training against Business Criteria', *Journal of European Industrial Training*, 18:1, 10–14

Brandenburg, D C (1987) 'Communicating Evaluation Results: The External Evaluator Perspective' in L S May, C A Moore and S J Zammit (eds), *Evaluating Business and Industry Training*, Kluwer, Boston

Braverman, H (1974) *Labor and Monopoly Capitalism: The Degradation of Work in the Twentieth Century*, Monthly Review Press, New York

Brinkerhof, R O (1987) *Achieving Results from Training: How to Evaluate Human Resource Development to Strengthen Programs and Increase Impact*, Jossey Bass, San Francisco

— Brethower, D M, Hluchyj, T and Nowakowski, J R (1983), *Program Evaluation: A Practitioner's Guide for Trainers and Educators*, Kluwer-Nijhoff, Boston

Brown, C, Reich, M, and Stern, D (1993) 'Becoming a High-performance Work Organisation: The Role of Security, Employee Involvement and Training' *International Journal of Human Resource Management*, 4:2, 247–75

Bruner, J S, Goodnow, J J and Austin, G A (1956) *A Study of Thinking*, Wiley, New York

— (1966) *Towards a Theory of Instruction*, Norton, New York

Bureau of Industry Economics (1990) *Manufacturing Investment: Research Report No 3*, AGPS, Canberra

Burleigh, A (1989) *Systematic Identification and Validation of Core Competencies*, Mimeographed, Auckland, New Zealand

Burns, R (1995) *The Adult Learner at Work*, Business and Professional Publishing, Sydney

Business Council of Australia (1990) 'Submission to the Training Costs Review Committee', *Business Council Bulletin*, November, 23–4

Butterworth, P (1995) 'Australia Reconstructed Even More', *Australian Training Review*, March/April, 16–18

Cacioppe, R and Adamson, P (1988) 'Stepping Over the Edge: Outdoor Development for Management Staff', *Human Resource Management Australia*, 26:4, 77–95

Camp, R R, Blanchard, N P and Huszczo, G E (1986) *Toward a More Organizationally Effective Training Strategy and Practice*, Prentice-Hall, Englewood Cliffs, New Jersey

Candy, P and Harris, R (1990) 'Implementing Competency-based Vocational Education: A View from Within', *Journal of Further and Higher Education*, 14:2, 38–57

Cappelli, P (1993) 'Are Skill Requirements Rising?: Evidence from Production and Clerical Jobs', *Industrial and Labor Relations Review*, 46:3, 515–30

— (1994) *Training and Development in Public and Private Policy* (International Library of Management), Dartmouth, Brookfield, USA

— (1995) 'Rethinking Employment', *British Journal of Industrial Relations*, 33:4, 563–602

— and Cascio, W, F (1991) 'Why Some Jobs Command Wage Premiums: A Test of Career Tournament and Internal Labour Market Hypotheses', *Academy of Management Journal*, 34:4, 848–68

Carnevale, A, Meltzer, A S and Gainer, A (1990) *Workplace Basics: The Skills that Employers Really Want*, Jossey-Bass, San Francisco

Carter, E and Gribble, I A (1991) *Work-based Learning — A Discussion Paper*, TAFE National Staff Development Committee

Cattegno, G and Millwood, R (1995) 'Work-based Learning for Managers' in D S Karpin, *Enterprising Nation*, Research Report Volume 1, AGPS, Canberra

Champion, D P, Kiel, D H and McLendon, J A (1990) 'Choosing a Consulting Role', *Training and Development Journal*, 44:2, 66–9

Cher, N (1996) 'Using an Internal Web', *Australian Training Review*, 17, 26–7

Cheren, M (1990) 'Promoting Active Learning in the Workplace' in R M Smith (ed), *Learning to Learn Across the Lifespan*, Jossey-Bass, San Francisco

Chickillo, G P and Kleiner, B H (1990) 'Skills and Roles of Consultants: Training Implications', *Journal of European Industrial Training*, 14:1, 26–30

Child, J and Partridge, B (1982) *Lost Managers: Supervisors in Industry and Society*, Cambridge University Press, England

Clegg, W H (1987) 'Management Training and Evaluation: An Update', *Training and Development Journal*, 41:2, 65–71

Collins, C (ed) (1993a) *Competencies: The Competencies Debate in Australian Education and Training*, Australian College of Education, Canberra

— (1993b) 'Competencies: For and Against', keynote address presented to the *Australian Curriculum Studies Association National Conference*, QUT, Brisbane, 1 July 1993

Collins, R and Hackman, K (1991) *National Survey of Training and Development Practices, July 1991*, CCH–AGSM, Sydney

Commission on the Skills of the American Workforce (1990) *America's Choice: High Skills or Low Wages!*, The National Center on Education and the Economy, Rochester, New York

Compton, R L (1988) 'Who Needs an Employee Assistance Program?', *Human Resource Management Australia*, 26:1, 101–10

Connor, J J (1983) *On The Job Training*, International Human Resources Development Corporation, Boston

Cooke, J and Knibbs, J (1987) 'The Manager's Role in Staff Development', *Journal of European Industrial Training*, 11:1, 5–11

Coombs, L (1997) 'Workplace Mentoring: Learning or Control?' *Transfer*, 2:3, 6–8

Coopers and Lybrand (1985) *A Challenge to Complacency: Changing Attitudes to Training*, Manpower Services Commission, London

Coopey, J and Hartley, J (1991) 'Reconsidering the Case for Organisational Commitment', *Human Resource Management Journal*, 1:3, 18–32

Creedy, J and Whitfield, K (1992) 'Opening the Black Box: Economic Analyses of Internal Labour Markets', *Journal of Industrial Relations*, September, 455–71

Curtain, R (1989) 'How to Identify Skills for Award Restructuring Purposes using a Modified DACUM Technique', unpublished paper given to the *Industry Training for the 1990s Conference* in Sydney, September 1989

— (1990) 'What's Involved in Doing a Skills Review?', *Asia-Pacific HRM*, 28:1, 68–75

— (1994a) 'The Australian Government's Training Reform Agenda: Is It Working?', *Asia-Pacific Journal of Human Resources*, 32:2, 43–56

— (1994b) *The Impact of Industrial Relations on Training: An Analysis of Major Private Sector Awards and Enterprise Bargaining Agreements*, Report prepared for the Business Council of Australia Taskforce on Training, July 1994

— Gough, R and Rimmer, M (1992) *Progress at the Workplace*, National Key Centre in Industrial Relations, Monash University

— and Mathews, J (1990) 'Two Models of Award Restructuring', *Labour and Industry*, 3:1, 58–75

Daly, A, Hitchens, D, and Wagner, K (1985) 'Productivity, Machinery and Skills in a Sample of British and German Manufacturing Plants', *National Institute of Economics Review*, February, 48–61

Davis, R H, Alexander, L T and Yelon, S L (1974) *Learning System Design: An Approach to the Improvement of Instruction*, McGraw Hill, New York

Dawkins, J S (1988) *Industry Training in Australia*, AGPS, Canberra

— (1989) *Improving Australia's Training System*, AGPS, Canberra

— (1991), *The Australian Mission on Management Skills: Volume 1: Report*, AGPS, Canberra

Dawson, P (1991) 'The Historical Emergence and Changing Role of the Industrial Supervisor', *Asia-Pacific HRM*, 29:2, 36–50

Dawson, R P (1993) *Models of Evaluation of Equal Opportunities Training in Local Government with Special Reference to Women*, unpublished PhD thesis, South Bank University, London

— (1995) 'Fill This in Before You Go: Under-utilized Evaluation Sheets', *Journal of European Industrial Training*, 19:2, 3–7

Deal, T E and Kennedy, R H (1982) *Corporate Cultures*, Addison-Wesley, Reading, Mass

Delbridge, R (1995) 'Surviving JIT: Control and Resistance in a Japanese Transplant', *Journal of Management Studies*, 32:6, 803–17

Deming, W E (1982) *Out of the Crisis*, MIT Center for Advanced Engineering Studies, Cambridge, Mass

Denison, D R (1990) *Corporate Culture and Organizational Effectiveness*, John Wiley and Sons, New York

—, E F (1962) *The Sources of Economic Growth in the United States and the Alternatives Before Us*, Committee for Economic Development, New York

Denova, C C (1979) *Test Construction for Evaluation and Training*, American Society for Training and Development Inc, Madison, Wisconsin

Department of Industrial Relations (1993) *Enterprise Bargaining: The First One Thousand Agreements*, AGPS, Canberra

Derry, S J and Murphy, D A (1986) 'Designing Systems that Train Learning Ability: From Theory to Practice', *Review of Educational Research*, 1, 1–39

Dewey, J (1938) *Experience and Education*, Collier Macmillan Publishers, London

Doeringer, P B and Piore, M (1971) *Internal Labor Markets and Manpower Analysis*, Heath, Lexington, Mass

Domberger, S (1989) 'Management Education in Australia: Past, Present and Future', *Corporate Management*, June/July, 89–93

Drago, R (1988) 'Quality Circle Survival: An Exploratory Analysis', *Industrial Relations*, 27:3, 336–51

Dunphy, D (1987) 'The Historical Development of Human Resource Management in Australia', *Human Resource Management Australia*, 25:2, 40–7

— and Stace, D (1990) *Under New Management: Australian Organisations in Transition*, McGraw Hill, Sydney

Dyer, L and Kochan, T A (1995) 'Is There a New HRM? Contemporary Evidence and Future Directions' in B M Downie and M L Coates (eds), *Managing Human Resources in the 1990s and Beyond: Is the Workplace Being Transformed?*, IRC Press, Queens University, Ontario

Dyer, S (1994) 'Kirkpatrick's Mirror', *Journal of European Industrial Training*, 18:5, 31–2

Easterby-Smith, M (1990) 'Creating a Learning Organisation', *Personnel Review*, 19:5, 24–8

Edwards, R (1979) *Contested Terrain: The Transformation of the Workplace in the Twentieth Century*, Basic Books, New York

Employment and Skills Formation Council (1992) *The Australian Vocational Certificate Training System*, AGPS, Canberra

Fayol, H (1949) *General and Industrial Management*, Pitman, London

Fawbert, F (1987) *Using Video in Training. Training Technology Programme (Vol 11)*, Parthenon, Carnforth, UK

Feldman, D C (1989) 'Socialization, Resocialization and Training: Reframing the Research Agenda' in I L Goldstein and Associates (eds), *Training and Development in Organizations*, Jossey-Bass, San Francisco

Ferguson, J and Smith, B (1988) 'Behaviour Modelling: An Overview' *Training and Development in Australia*, 15 (4), 3–8

Field, L (1990) *Skilling Australia*, Longman Cheshire, Melbourne

— with Ford, G W (1995) *Managing Organisational Learning: From Rhetoric to Reality*, Longman Cheshire, Melbourne

Finegold, D, and Soskice, D (1988) 'The Failure of British Training: Analysis and Prescription', *Oxford Review of Economic Policy*, 4, Autumn, 21–53

— (1991) 'Institutional Incentives and Skill Creation: Preconditions for a High Skills Equilibrium' in P Ryan (ed), (1991) *International Comparisons of Vocational Education and Training for Intermediate Skills*, Falmer Press: London

— (1992) 'The Changing International Economy and its Impact on Education and Training', *Oxford Studies in Comparative Education*, 2:2, 57–82

— Schechter, S et al (1995) 'International Models of Management Development: Lessons for Australia' in D S Karpin, *Enterprising Nation*, Research Report Volume 2, AGPS, Canberra

Fiol, C M and Lyles, M A (1985) 'Organizational Learning', *Academy of Management Review*, 10:4, 803–13

Fisher, J C and Podeschi, R L (1989) 'From Lindeman to Knowles: A Change in Vision', *International Journal Of Lifelong Education*, 4, 345–53

Flavell, J H (1979) 'Metacognition and Cognitive Monitoring: A New Area of Psychological Inquiry', *American Psychologist*, 34, 906–11

Fleishman, E A (1972) 'On the Relationship between Abilities, Learning and Human Performance', *American Psychologist*, 27, 1017–32

Ford, G W (1989) 'Conceptual Changes and Innovations in Skill Formation at the Enterprise Level in OECD/CERI', *Technological Change and Human Resources Development: The Service Sector*, OECD, Netherlands

— (1997) 'Journeys of Learning Enterprises — Integrating People, Process and Place', paper presented to the *Australian Human Resources Institute National Convention*, Brisbane, 18–21 May

Forrester, K, Payne, J and Ward K (1995) *Workplace Learning*, Avebury, Aldershot

Foxon, M (1986) 'Evaluation of Training: Art of the Impossible?' *Training Officer*, 22:5, 133–7

Foyster, J (1990) *Getting to Grips with Compentency-based Training*, TAFE National Centre for Research and Development, Adelaide

Fraser, D (1996) *The Training Guarantee: Its Impact and Legacy*, Monitoring and Evaluation Branch, Department of Employment, Education, Training and Youth Affairs, AGPS, Canberra

French, W E and Bell Jr, C H (1990) *Organization Development: Behavioral Science Interventions for Organization Improvement*, 4th ed, Prentice-Hall International, Englewood Cliffs

Gagne, E D (1985) *The Cognitive Psychology of School Learning*, Little Brown and Co, Boston

Gagne, R M, Briggs, L J and Wager, W W (1988) *Principles of Instructional Design*, 3rd ed, Holt, Rinehart and Winston, New York

Galagan, P (1987) 'Computers and Training: Allies or Enemies?' *Training and Development Journal*, 14:4, 73–6

Gallie, D (1991) 'Patterns of Skill Change: Upskilling, Deskilling or the Polarisation of Skills?', *Work, Employment and Society*, 5:3, 319–51

— and White, M (1993) *Employee Commitment and the Skills Revolution*, PSI Publishing, London

Gamble, P R and Messenger, S (1990) 'Preparing Managers for Industry: The Role of Hospitality Management Education', *Journal of European Industrial Training*, 14:3, 13–19

Garavan, T N (1987) 'Promoting Natural Learning Activities within the Organisation', *Journal of European Industrial Training*, 11:7, 18–22

Geldard, D (1989) *Basic Personal Counselling: A Training Manual for Counsellors*, Prentice Hall of Australia, Sydney

Ghiselli, E E (1971) *Explorations in Managerial Talent*, Goodyear Publishing, California

Gilmour, P and Lansbury, R D (1984) *Marginal Manager: The Changing Role of Supervisors in Australia*, University of Queensland Press, St Lucia

Glynn, S, and Gospel, H (1993) 'Britain's Low Skill Equilibrium: A Problem of Demand?', *Industrial Relations Journal*, 24:2, 112–25

Goldstein, I (1986) *Training in Organizations: Needs Assessment, Development and Evaluation*, Brooks/Cole, California

Goldstein, A P and Sorcher, M (1974) *Changing Supervisor Behavior*, Pergamon Press, New York

Goodge, P (1991) 'Development Centres: Guidelines for Decision Makers' *Journal of Management Development*, 10:3, 4–12

Goozee, G (1995) *The Development of TAFE in Australia*, 2nd ed, NCVER, Adelaide

Gospel, H (1994) 'The Survival of Apprenticeship Training in Australia', *Journal of Industrial Relations*, 12:4

— (1995) 'The Decline of Apprenticeship Training in Britain', *Journal of Industrial Relations* 13: 1, 22–44

Gropper, G L (1987) 'A Lesson Based on a Behavioral Approach to Instructional Design' in C M Reigeluth (ed), *Instructional Theories in Action: Lessons Illustrating Selected Theories and Models*, Lawrence Erlbaum Associates, New Jersey

Guest, D E (1987) 'Human Resource Management and Industrial Relations', *Journal of Management Studies*, 24:5, 503–21

— (1990) 'Human Resource Management and the American Dream', *Journal of Management Studies*, 27:4, 377–97

Gurney, R (1995) 'Corporate Coaching — A Preferred Model', *Training and Development in Australia*, 22:3, 3–8

Guthrie, H and Barnett, K (1996) *Training and Enterprise Bargaining; Enterprise-based Approaches to Training*, National Centre for Vocational Education Research, Adelaide

Hager, P, Athanasou, J and Gonczi, A (1994) *Assessment Technical Manual*, AGPS, Canberra

Hall, W C (1995) 'Research in Competency-based Assessment' in W C Hall (ed), *Key Aspects of Competency-based Assessment*, National Centre for Vocational Education Research, Adelaide

Hamblin, A C (1974) *Evaluation and Control of Training*, McGraw Hill, London

Hamel, G and Prahalad, C K (1990) 'The Core Competence of the Corporation', *Harvard Business Review*, May–June, 79–91

Hancock, K and Rawson, D (1993) 'The Metamorphosis of Australian Industrial Relations', *British Journal of Industrial Relations*, 31, 489–513

Handy, C, Gordon, C, Gow, I and Randlesome, C (1988) *Making Managers*, Pitman, London

Hart, F A (1987) 'Computer-Based Training' in R L Craig (ed), *Training and Development Handbook: A Guide to Human Resource Development*, McGraw-Hill, New York

Hartree, A (1986) 'Malcolm Knowles' Theory of Andragogy: A Critique', *International Journal of Lifelong Education*, 3,3, 203–10

Hawthorne, E (1987) *Evaluating Employee Training Programs: A Research-based Guide for Human Resource Managers*, Quorum Books, New York

Hayes, R H and Abernathy, W J (1980) 'Managing Our Way to Economic Decline', *Harvard Business Review*, July/August, 67–77

Hayton, G (1988) *An Introduction to the CODAP Method of Occupational Analysis*, TAFE National Centre for Research and Development, Adelaide

— McIntyre, J, Sweet, R, MacDonald, R, Noble, C, Smith, A and Roberts, P (1996) *Enterprise Training in Australia*, Office of Training and Further Education, Victoria, Melbourne

Hendry, C and Pettigrew, A (1992) 'Patterns of Strategic Change in the Development of Human Resource Management', *British Journal of Management*, 3:3, 137–56

Hermann, G D (1987) *Manual on Occupational Analysis*, Centre for Research in Education and Work, Macquarie University, Sydney

Herzberg, F (1966) *Work and the Nature of Man*, World Publishing Co, Chicago, Ill

Heyes, J and Stuart, M (1996) 'Does Training Matter? Employee Experiences and Attitudes', *Human Resource Management Journal*, 6:3, 7–21

Hirschorn, L (1984) *The Workplace Within: The Psychodynamics of Organizational Life*, MIT Press, Cambridge, Mass

Hitt, M A, Ireland, R D and Hoskisson, R E (1995) *Strategic Management: Competitiveness and Globalisation*, West Publishing Company, Minneapolis/St Paul

Hogg, C (1988) 'Outplacement', IPM Factsheet No 4, *Personnel Management*, 20:4

Holding, D H (1965) *Principles of Training*, Pergamon Press, London

Holland, J (1973) *Making Vocational Choices: A Theory of Careers*, Prentice-Hall, Englewood Cliffs, New Jersey

Holloway, D (1997) 'Work-based Learning in the Tax Office', *Australian Training Review*, 21, 30–31

Hougham, J, Thomas, J and Sisson, K (1991) 'Ford's EDAP Scheme: A Roundtable Discussion', *Human Resource Management Journal*, 1:3, 77–91

Hubbard, G (1990) 'Changing Trends in MBA Education in Australia', *Journal of Management Development*, 9:6, 41–9

Hyman, J (1992) *Training at Work: A Critical Approach*, Routledge, London

Independent Committee of Inquiry into a National Competition Policy (1993) *National Competition Policy* ('The Hilmer report'), AGPS, Canberra

Industrial Program Service, *Annual Report*, 1990–1

Jacques, E (1951) *The Changing Culture of a Factory*, Tavistock Publications, London

Jarvis, P (1983) *Adult and Continuing Education: Theory and Practice*, Croom Helm, London

Johnson, R, (1994) 'Open Learning and Flexible Delivery in Vocational Education', *Australian Training Review*, 11: 13–15

Juran, J M (1962) *Quality Control Handbook*, McGraw Hill, New York

Kamoche, K (1996) 'Strategic Human Resource Management within a Resource-Capability View of the Firm', *Journal of Management Studies*, 33:2, 213–33

Karpin, D S (1995) *Enterprising Nation: Renewing Australia's Managers to Meet the Challenges of the Asia-Pacific Century*, Report of the Industry Taskforce on Leadership and Management Skills, AGPS, Canberra

Kearsley, G (1983) *Computer-based Training*, Addison-Wesley, Reading, Mass

Keep, E (1989) 'Corporate Training Strategies' in J Storey (ed), *New Perspectives on Human Resource Management*, Routledge, London

Kemp, D (1996) 'Training Pathways to Real Jobs', Address to the Australian Council of Social Services, Sydney, 22 May

Kenney, J and Reid, M (1995) *Training Interventions*, 4th ed, Institute of Personnel Development, London

Kim, D (1993) 'The Link between Individual and Organizational Learning', *Sloan Management Review*, Fall: 37–50

Kirkpatrick, D L (1959) 'Techniques for Evaluating Training Programs', *Journal of the American Society for Training and Development*, 13:3–9, 21–6, 14: 13–18, 28–32

— (1975) *Evaluating Training Programs*, American Society for Training and Development Inc, Washington, DC

— (1977) 'Evaluating Training Programs: Evidence versus Proof', *Training and Development Journal*, 31:11, 9–12

— (1983) 'Measuring Training Effectiveness', *Personnel Administrator USA*, November

Knowles, M S (1970) *The Modern Practice of Adult Education: Andragogy versus Pedagogy*, Association, New York

— (1984) *The Adult Learner: A Neglected Species*, 3rd ed, Gulf Publishing, Houston

Kochan, T A and Dyer, L (1993) 'Managing Transformational Change: The Role of Human Resource Professionals', *International Journal of Human Resource Management*, 4:5 69–90

Kohler, W (1925) *The Mentality of Apes*, Routledge and Kegan Paul, London

Kolb, D A (1984) *Experiential Learning: Experience as the Source of Learning and Development*, Prentice-Hall, Englewood Cliffs, New Jersey

Kram, K E (1983) 'Phases of the Mentor Relationship', *Academy of Management Journal*, 26:4, 608–25

— (1986) 'Mentoring in the Workplace' in D T Hall and Associates (eds), *Career Development in Organisations*, Jossey-Bass, San Francisco

— and Isabella, L A (1985) 'Mentoring Alternatives: The Role of Peer Relationships in Career Development', *Academy of Management Journal*, 28:1, 110–32

Laird, D (1986) *Approaches to Training and Development*, 3rd ed, Addison Wesley, Reading, Mass

Lamond, D (1995) 'Karpin on Management: Is that All Managers Should be Doing?', *Journal of the Australian and New Zealand Academy of Management*, 2:1, 21–35

Langford, P (1989) 'The Process of Learning' in P Langford (ed), *Educational Psychology: An Australian Perspective*, Longman Cheshire, Melbourne

Lansbury, R D and Quince, A (1987) 'The Changing Roles of Managerial Employees' in G W Ford, J M Hearn and R D Lansbury (eds), *Australian Labour Relations Readings*, 4th ed, MacMillan, Melbourne

Latham, G P (1989) 'Behavioral Approaches to the Training and Learning Process' in I L Goldstein and Associates (eds), *Training and Development in Organizations*, Jossey-Bass, San Francisco

— and Crandall, S R (1990) 'Organizational and Social Influences Affecting Training Effectiveness' in J E Morrison (ed), *Training for Performance*, Wiley, Chichester

— and Saari, L M (1979) 'The Application of Social Learning Theory to Training Supervisors through Behavior Modeling', *Journal of Applied Psychology*, No 64

Legge, K (1995) *Human Resource Management: Rhetorics and Realities*, Macmillan, London

Leicester, C (1989) 'The Key Role of the Line Manager in Employee Development', *Personnel Management*, 21:3, 53–7

Levine, D I (1993) 'What Do Wages Buy?', *Administrative Science Quarterly*, 38:3, 462–83

Levinson, D J (1978) *The Season of a Man's Life*, Alfred Knopf, New York

Lewin, K (1952) 'Group decision and social change' in G E Swanson, T N Newcombe and R J Lewicki (eds), *Readings in Social Psychology*, Holt, New York

Lewis, P and Thornhill, A (1994) 'The Evaluation of Training: An Organizational Culture Approach', *Journal of European Industrial Training*, 18:8, 25–32

Littler, C R, Dunford, R, Bramble, T and Hede, A (1997) 'The Dynamics of Downsizing in Australia and New Zealand', *Asia-Pacific Journal of Human Resources*, 35:1, 65–79

Locke, E A (1977) 'The Myths of Behavior Modification in Organizations', *Academy of Management Review*, 2: 543–53

— and Latham, G P (1984) *A Theory of Goal Setting and Task Performance*, Prentice-Hall, Englewood Cliffs, N J

Lovell, B R (1980) *Adult Learning*, Croom Helm, London

Lowrie, T (1997) 'BHP Steel, Wollongong, NSW, Certificate of Engineering (Electrical); Graded Tradespersons Training Courses' in E Smith, T Lowrie, J Lobegeier, D Hill and A Bush, *Teaching, Learning and Curriculum: The Effects of Competency-based Training and Recognition of Prior Learning*, project commissioned by ANTARAC, Charles Sturt University, Wagga Wagga

Lundberg, D (1994) *Where are We? Reviewing the Training Reform Agenda*, National Centre for Vocational Education Research, Adelaide

Luthans, F and Waldersee, R (1989) 'What do We Really Know About EAPs?' *Human Resource Management*, 28:3, 385–401

Lynch, L M (ed) (1994) *Training and the Private Sector: International Comparisons*, University of Chicago Press, Chicago

MacDuffie, J P and Krafcik, J F (1988) *The Team Concept: Models for Change and the US Experience*, International Motor Vehicle Program, MIT

MacDuffie, J P and Kochan, T A (1995) 'Do US Firms Invest Less in Human Resources? Training in the World Auto Industry', *Industrial Relations*, 34:2, 147–68

Mager, R F (1975) *Preparing Instructional Objectives*, 2nd ed, Pitman, Belmont

— and Pipe, P (1984) *Analyzing Performance Problems*, 2nd ed, Lake Publishers, California

Maglen, L (1990) 'Challenging the Human Capital Orthodoxy: The Education-Productivity Link Re-examined', *The Economic Record*, December, 281–94

Mann, S (1991) 'Alcohol: Drinking Ourselves to Death', *The Age*, 25 September 1991

Manpower Services Commission (1981) *Glossary of Training Terms*, HMSO, London

Maranto, C and Rogers, R (1984) 'Does Work Experience Increase Productivity? A Test of the On-the-Job Training Hypothesis', *Journal of Human Resources*, 19:3, 341–57

Margerison, C (1978) *Influencing Organizational Change: The Role of the Personnel Specialist*, IPM, London

— (1988) *Managerial Consulting Skills: A Practical Guide*, Gower, Aldershot

Marginson, S (1993) *Education and Public Policy in Australia*, Longman Cheshire, Melbourne

Margulies, N and Rais, A P (1978) *Conceptual Foundations of Organizational Development*, McGraw-Hill, New York

Marsick, V J and Watkins, K E (1990) *Informal and Incidental Learning in the Workplace*, Routledge, London

Mathews, J (1990) *Tools of Change*, Pluto Press, Sydney

— (1993) 'The Industrial Relations of Skill Formation', *International Journal of Human Resource Management*, 4:3, 591–609

— (1994) *Catching the Wave*, Allen and Unwin, Sydney

McClelland, S B (1993) 'Training Needs Assessment: An "Open-Systems" Application', *Journal of European Industrial Training*, 17:1, 12–17

— (1994a) 'Training Needs Assessment Data-gathering Methods: Part 2 — Individual Interviews', *Journal of European Industrial Training*, 18:2, 27–31

— (1994b) 'Training Needs Assessment Data-gathering Methods: Part 3 — Focus Groups', *Journal of European Industrial Training*, 18:3, 29–32

— (1994c) 'Training Needs Assessment Data-gathering Methods: Part 1 — Survey Questionnaires', *Journal of European Industrial Training*, 18:1, 22–6

— Harbaugh, N and Hammett, S (1993) 'Improving Individual and Group Effectiveness', *Journal of Management Development*, 12:3, 48–58

McCloud, P and Siniakis, C (1995) 'Trends in Numbers of Management Students and Managers 1970s–1990s' in D S Karpin, *Enterprising Nation, Research Report Volume 1*, AGPS, Canberra

McCord, A B (1987) 'Job Training' in R L Craig (ed), *Training and Development Handbook: A Guide to Human Resource Development*, McGraw-Hill, New York

McCormick, E J (1979) *Job Analysis*, AMACOM, New York

McDonald, R, Hayton, G, Gonczi, A and Hager, P (1993) *No Small Change: Proposals for a Research and Development Strategy for Vocational Education and Training in Australia*, University of Technology, Sydney

McDonald, S and Heine, A-M (1991) 'Development Centres: Another Window on Performance', *Asia-Pacific HRM*, 29:3, 71–8

McKeen, C A and Burke, R J (1989) 'Mentor Relationships in Organisations: Issues, Strategies and Prospects for Women', *Journal of Management Development*, 8:6, 33–42

McKenzie, P and Long, M (1995) 'Educational Attainment and Participation in Training', paper presented to the Efficiency and Equity in Education Policy Conference, Canberra, 6–7 September, 1995

McGehee, W and Thayer, P W (1961) *Training in Business and Industry*, John Wiley, New York

McGraw, P and Dunford, R (1987) 'The Strategic Use of Quality Circles in Australian Industrial Relations', *Journal of Industrial Relations*, 29:2, 150–68

McGregor, D (1960) *The Human Side of Enterprise*, McGraw-Hill, New York

McLagan, P (1989) *Models for HRD Practice*, ASTD Press, St Paul, Minnesota

McLennan, R (1990) *Managing Organisational Change*, Prentice-Hall, Sydney

Medoff, J L and Abraham, K G (1980) 'Are Those Paid More Really More Productive: The Case of Experience', *Journal of Human Resources*, XVI (Spring), 255–83

— (1981) 'Experience, Performance and Earnings', *Quarterly Journal of Economics*, XCV (December), 703–36

Mezirow, J and Associates (1990) *Fostering Critical Reflection in Adulthood: A Guide to Transformative and Emancipatory Learning*, Jossey-Bass, San Francisco

Midgley, D F (1995) 'The Need for Leadership and Management Skills' in D S Karpin, *Enterprising Nation*, Research Report Volume 1, AGPS, Canberra

Mintzberg, H (1975) 'The Manager's Job: Folklore and Fact', *Harvard Business Review*, 53:4, 49–61

Misko, J (1995) *Transfer: Using Learning in New Contexts*, National Centre for Vocational Education Research, Adelaide

Moore, M L and Dutton, R R (1978) 'Training Needs Analysis: Review and Critique', *Academy of Management Review*, July 1978, 532–45

Morgan, G (1986) *Images of Organization*, Sage, Newbury Park, Ca

Moses, J I and Ritchie, R J (1976) 'Supervisory Relationship Training: A Behavioral Evaluation of a Behavior Modelling Program', *Personnel Psychology*, 29, 351–9

Moses, J L and Byham, W C (1977) *Applying the Assessment Centre Method*, Pergamon Press, Oxford

Moy, J (1991) 'Human Resource Development Practitioner Roles and Competencies: An Analysis of Recent Research', *Asia-Pacific HRM*, 29:4, 7–23

Munchus, G III and McArthur, B (1991) 'Revisiting the Historical Use of the Assessment Centre in Management Selection and Development', *Journal of Management Development*, 10:1, 5–13

Murphy, B P and Swanson, R A (1988) 'Auditing Training and Development', *Journal of European Industrial Training*, 12:2, 13–16

Myburgh, S (1996) 'Online Training', *Australian Training Review* 17, 24–5

Nadler, L and Nadler, Z (1989) *Developing Human Resources*, 3rd ed, Jossey Bass, San Francisco

National Training Board (1991) *National Competency Standards: Policy and Guidelines*, National Training Board, Canberra

National Training Board (1992) *National Competency Standards: Policy and Guidelines*, 2nd ed, National Training Board, Canberra

Nettle, D (1996) 'The Karpin Inquiry and the Role of Management Education in Australia: History Revisited?', *Labour and Industry*, 7:2, 103–21

Nesbit, P and Midgley, D F (1995) 'Management Competencies: A Survey of their Use and Value in Australian Organisations' in D S Karpin, *Enterprising Nation*, Research Report Volume 1, AGPS, Canberra

New South Wales Board of Vocational Education and Training (1994) *Best Practice in Vocational Education and Training* (two volumes), NSW BVET, Sydney

New South Wales Department of Training and Education Co-ordination (1997), *Relationships between Training and Productivity*, Strategic Planning, Resources, Research and Industry Network Services, DTEC, Sydney

Newton, S (1996) The Assessment Process: Integrating into an 'Action Learning' Training Program, paper presented to the NCVER National Conference on Integrating

Assessment: Removing the On-the-Job/Off-the-Job Gap, Perth Hyatt, WA, 4–6 June, 1996

Noonan, P (1996) 'Today's Training System', *Australian Training*, 3:4, 4–7

Noone, L (1991) 'Why I Believe that the Training Guarantee is a Great Leap Backwards Rather Than a Small Step in the Right Direction', *Training and Development in Australia*, 18, 19–20

Novarra, V (1986) 'Can a Manager be a Counsellor?', *Personnel Management*, 18:6, 48–50

Oakland, J S (1989) 'TQM — The New Way to Manage', Proceedings of the Second International Conference on Total Quality Management, IFS Publications, Bedford

OECD (1988) *New Technology in the 1990s — A Socio-Economic Strategy*, Report of a Group of Experts on the Social Aspects of New Technologies, Paris

— (1995) *OECD Observer*, No 193, OECD, Paris

OECD/CERI (1986) *New Technology and Human Resource Development in the Automobile Industry*, OECD, Paris (mimeographed)

— (1988) *Human Resources and Corporate Strategy: Technological Change in Banks and Insurance Companies*, OECD, Paris

Osterman, P (1984) 'Introduction: The Nature and Importance of Internal Labor Markets' in P Osterman (ed), *Internal Labor Markets*, MIT Press, Cambridge, Mass

— (1994) 'How Common is Workplace Transformation and Who Adopts It?', *Industrial and Labor Relations Review*, 47:2, 173–88

— (1995) 'Skill, Training, and Work Organization in American Establishments', *Industrial Relations*, 34:2, 125–46

Ostroff, C and Ford, J K (1989) 'Assessing Training Needs: Critical Levels of Analysis' in I L Goldstein and Associates (eds), *Training and Development in Organizations*, Jossey Bass, San Francisco

Ouchi, W (1981) *Theory Z*, Addison-Wesley, Reading, Mass

Parlett, M and Hamilton, D (1977) 'Evaluation as Illumination' in D Tawney (ed), *Curriculum Education Today*

Pascale, R T and Athos, A G (1981) *The Art of Japanese Management*, Simon and Schuster, New York

Pedler, M (ed) (1983) *Action Learning in Practice*, Gower, Aldershot

— and Boydell, T (1981) *Management Self-Development: Concepts and Practices*, Gower, Aldershot

Peters, T and Waterman, R (1982) *In Search of Excellence: Lessons from America's Best Run Companies*, Harper and Row, New York

Peterson, R and Wilson, W (1992) 'Measuring Customer Satisfaction: Fact and Artifact', *Journal of the Academy of Marketing Science*, 20:1, 61–71

Pettigrew, A, Sparrow, P and Hendry, C (1989) 'The Forces that Trigger Training', *Personnel Management*, December, 28–32

Phillips, J J (1991) *Handbook of Training Evaluation and Measurement Methods*, 2nd ed, Gulf Publishing Company, Houston

Pickett, L (1997) 'Developing the Frontline Manager', *Training and Development in Australia*, 24:1, 18–22

Pollock, J (1991) *The Training Guarantee*, Training Reform Agenda Seminar Series, Canberra

Porter, L W and McKibbin, L E (1988) *Management Education and Development: Drift or Thrust into the 21st Century?*, McGraw Hill, New York

Prais, S, Jarvis, V and Wagner, K (1991) 'Productivity and Vocational Skills in Services in Britain and Germany: Hotels', *National Institute of Economics Review*, November, 52–72

Prien, E P, Goldstein, I L and Macey, W H (1985) 'Needs Assessment: Program and Individual Development', unpublished paper presented to the 89th Convention of the American Psychological Association, Los Angeles, California

Provus, M M (1971) *Discrepancy Evaluation*, McCutchan, Berkeley

Quarry, P and Ash, K (1996) 'The Five Steps to Coaching On The Job' *Training and Development in Australia*, 23:4, 23–4

Railton, K and Milhall, B (1990) 'DACUM — An Approach for Job Redesign and Training Needs Analysis in an Award Restructuring Environment', unpublished paper presented to the Industry Training for the 1990s Conference, Sydney, 1990

Rainbird, H (1994) 'The Changing Role of the Training Function: A Test for the Integration of Human Resource and Business Strategies?', *Human Resource Management Journal*, 5:1, 72–90

Ralph, J (1982) *Inquiry into Management Education Report*, AGPS, Canberra

Ramsay, H (1991) 'Reinventing the Wheel? A Review of the Development and Performance of Employee Involvement', *Human Resource Management Journal*, 1:4, 1–22

Raper, P, Ashton, D, Felstead, A and Storey, J (1997) 'Toward the Learning Organisation? Explaining Current Trends in Training Practice in the UK', *International Journal of Training and Development*, 1:1, 9–21

Rayner P and Hermann, G (1988) 'The Relative Effectiveness of Three Occupational Analysis Methods', *The Vocational Aspect of Education*, 40:106, 47–55

Reich, R (1991) *The Work of Nations: Preparing Ourselves for 21st Century Capitalism*, AA Knopf, New York

Revans, R W (1982) *The Origin and Growth of Action Learning*, Chartwell-Bratt, Bickley, Kent

Robson, M (1982) *Quality Circles: A Practical Guide*, Gower, Aldershot

Roe, A (1956) *The Psychology of Occupations*, John Wiley, New York

Rogers, C R (1955) *Client-centred Therapy*, Houghton Mifflin, Boston

— (1983) *Freedom to Learn for the 80s*, Charles Merrill, Columbus

Romiszowski, A (1981) *Designing Instructional Systems*, Kogan Page, London

— (1984) *Producing Instructional Systems*, Kogan Page, London

Rothwell, W J and Kazanas, H C (1990) 'Planned OJT is Productive OJT', *Training and Development Journal*, 44:10, 53–6

Rumelhart, D E and Norman, D A (1978) 'Accretion, Tuning and Restructuring: Three Modes of Learning' in J W Cotton and R L Klatzky (eds), *Semantic Factors in Cognition*, Lawrence Erlbaum Associates, Hillsdale, New Jersey

Rumsey, D (1992) *The National Alignment of Vocational Education and Training Credentials to the Australian Skills Framework* (The 'Rumsey Report'), VEETAC, Darlinghurst, NSW

— (1994) *Assessment Practical Guide*, AGPS, Canberra

Ryan, P (1991) 'Comparative Research on Vocational Education and Training' in P Ryan (ed), *International Comparisons of Vocational Education and Training*, Falmer Press, London

Rylatt, A (1994) *Learning Unlimited: Practical Strategies and Techniques for Transforming Learning in the Workplace*, Business and Professional Publishing, Sydney

Rylatt, A and Lohan, K (1995) *Creating Training Miracles*, Prentice-Hall, Sydney

Saul, P (1989) 'Employee Surveys — Filling the Gap in Management Information Systems', *Asia-Pacific HRM*, 27:4, 74–86

Savellis, R (1996) 'Australian Industry: Learning to Learn', *Australian Training Review*, 17, 6–8

Savery, L, Dawkins, P and Mazzarol, T (1995) 'Customers' Views of Australian Management: Asia-Pacific Viewpoints' in D S Karpin, *Enterprising Nation, Research Report*, Volume 1, AGPS, Canberra

Schein, E H (1978) 'The Role of the Consultant: Content Expert or Process Facilitator?', *Personnel and Guidance Journal*, 56, 339–43

— (1985) *Organizational Culture and Leadership: A Dynamic View*, Jossey-Bass, San Francisco

— (1988) 'Organizational Socialization', *Sloan Management Review*, Fall, 53–65

Schuler, R S and Jackson, S E (1987) 'Linking Competitive Strategies with Human Resource Management Practices', *Academy of Management Executive*, 1:3, 209–13

Schultz, T (1959) 'Investment in Man: An Economist's View', *The Social Service Review*, 33:2, 109–17

— (1960) 'Capital Formation by Education', *Journal of Political Economy*, 68:6, 571–83

Scriven, M (1967) 'The Methodology of Evaluation in R E Stake' (ed), *Curriculum Evaluation*, AERA Monograph Series on Evaluation, No 1, Rand McNally, Chicago

Seary, R (1993) 'Evaluation: Progressive Workplace Training Evaluation at ICI Botany, NSW', *Australian Training Review*, 9: 4–5

Senge, P M (1990) 'The Leader's Work: Building Learning Organizations', *Sloan Management Review*, Fall, 7–23

— (1990) *The Fifth Discipline: The Art and Practice of the Learning Organization*, Random House, New York

Sewell, G and Wilkinson, B (1992) 'Someone to Watch Over Me: Surveillance, Discipline and the Just-In-Time Labour Process', *Sociology*, 26:2, 271–89

Shiffrin, R M and Schneider, W (1977) 'Controlled and Automatic Information Processing II: Perceptual Learning, Automatic Attending, and a General Theory', *Psychological Review*, 84: 2, 127–90

Shore, L M and Bloom, A J (1986) 'Developing Employees through Coaching and Career Management', *Personnel*, 63,8, quoted in French, W (1990) *Human Resources Management*, Houghton Mifflin, Boston, 362

Short, M, Preston, A and Peetz, D (1993) *The Spread and Impact of Workplace Bargaining: Evidence from the Workplace Bargaining Research Project*, AGPS, Canberra

Shuell, T J (1986) 'Cognitive Conceptions of Learning', *Review of Educational Research*, 4: 411–36

Skinner, B F (1975) 'The Steep and Thorny Way to a Science of Behaviour', *American Psychologist*, No 30

Sloan, J (1994) 'The Market for Training in Australia', Working Paper 131, National Institute of Labour Studies, Flinders University of South Australia

Smith, A (1987) 'Models for Evaluation', unpublished paper given to the Conference on Human Resource Development, Riverina-Murray Institute of Higher Education, July 1987

— (1988) 'Caught in the Middle: Supervisors' Reactions to Organisational Change', unpublished paper given to Australian and New Zealand Association of Management Educators Conference, Perth, November

— (1989) 'Working with Pride: Management and the Process of Change in the British Motor Industry', *Asia-Pacific HRM*, 27:3, 31–40
— (1990) *Supervisory Training in Australia*, School of Commerce, Charles Sturt University, Wagga Wagga
— (1993) 'Australian Training and Development in 1992', *Asia-Pacific Journal of Human Resources*, 31:2, 65-74
— (1997) *Developing a Model of Enterprise Training*, unpublished PhD thesis, University of Tasmania
— Hayton, G, Roberts, P, Thorn, E and Noble, C (1995) *Enterprise Training: The Factors that Affect Demand*, Office of Training and Further Education, Melbourne
Smith, A J and Piper, J A (1990) 'The Tailor Made Training Maze: A Practitioner's Guide to Evaluation', *Journal of European Industrial Training*, 14:8
Smith, B (1986) 'Video and Training: Part I, Some Basics', *Training and Development in Australia*, 13:4, 15–17
— and Delahaye, B (1987) *How To Be an Effective Trainer*, 2nd ed, John Wiley, Sydney
Smith, E (1997) 'Workplace Learning in Apprenticeships: Some Research Results', paper presented to the Learning through Work Conference, Australian Competency Research Centre, Melbourne, May
— Hill, D, Smith, A, Perry, P, Roberts, P, and Bush, A (1996) *The Availability of Competency-based Training in TAFE and Non-TAFE Settings in 1994*, AGPS, Canberra
— Lowrie, T, Lobegeier, J, Hill, D and Bush, A (1997) *Teaching, Learning and Curriculum: The Effects of Competency-based Training and Recognition of Prior Learning*, project commissioned by ANTARAC, Charles Sturt University, Wagga Wagga
— and Keating, J (1997) *Making Sense of Training Reform and Competency-based Training*, Social Science Press, Wentworth Falls
Sparrow, J and Pettigrew, A (1985) 'Britain's Training Problems: The Search for Strategic HRM Approach', *Human Resource Management*, 26:1, 109–27
Spence, M (1974) *Market Signalling: Informational Transfer in Hiring and Related Screening Processes*, Harvard University Press, Cambridge, MA
Stanley, L A (1987) *Guide to Evaluation of Training*, ICPE, Ljubljana, Yugoslavia
State Training Board of Victoria (1997) *Return on Training Investment: Development of Enterprise Frameworks*, Office of Training and Further Education, Melbourne
Storey, J (1989) 'Management Development: A Literature Review and Implications for Further Research Part 1: Conceptualisations and Practices', *Personnel Review*, 18:6, 3–19
— Okazaki-Ward, L, Gow, I, Edwards, P K and Sisson, K (1991) 'Managerial Careers and Management Development: A Comparative Analysis of Britain and Japan', *Human Resource Management Journal*, 1:3, 33–57
Stowell, S J (1988) 'Coaching: A Commitment to Leadership', *Training and Development Journal,* June, 34–8
Strober, M (1990) 'Human Capital Theory: Implications for HR Managers', *Industrial Relations*, 29:2, 214–39
Steedman, H (1993) 'Do Work-force Skills Matter?', *British Journal of Industrial Relations*, 31:2, 285–92
— and Wagner, K (1987) 'A Second Look at Productivity, Machinery and Skills in Britain and Germany', *National Institute Economic Review,* November, 84–95
— and Wagner, K (1989) 'Productivity, Machinery and Skills: Clothing Manufacture in Britain and Germany', *National Institute Economic Review*, May, 40–57

Steele, F (1982) *The Role of the Internal Consultant*, CBI Publishing, Boston, Mass

Storey, J (1992) *Developments in the Management of Human Resources*, Basil Blackwell, Oxford

Stuart, M, (1996) 'The Industrial Relations of Training: A Reconsideration of Training Arrangements', *Industrial Relations Journal*, 27:3, 253–65

Stufflebeam, D L (1983) 'The CIPP Model for program Evaluation' in G Madaus, M Scriven and D L Stufflebeam (eds), *Evaluation Models: Viewpoints on Educational and Human Services Evaluation*, Kluwer-Nijhoff, Boston

— and Webster, W J (1983) 'An Analysis of Alternative Approaches to Evaluation' in G Madaus, M Scriven and D L Stufflebeam (eds), *Evaluation Models: Viewpoints on Educational and Human Services Evaluation*, Kluwer–Nijhoff, Boston

Super, D E (1957) *The Psychology of Careers*, Harper and Row, New York

Sweet, R (1993) *A Client Focussed Vocational Education and Training System*, Dusseldorp Skills Forum, Sydney

— (1994) 'Forging New Connections to the Workplace', paper presented to the *Workplace Learning Conference*, Orange, August

Taylor, F W (1911) *The Principles of Scientific Management*, Harper and Row, New York

Taylor, R (Chair) (1996) *Report of the Review of the ANTA Agreement*, Australian National Training Authority, Brisbane

Teicher, J (1995) 'The Training Guarantee: A Good Idea Gone Wrong' in F Ferrier and C Selby-Smith (eds), *The Economics of Education and Training 1995*, AGPS, Canberra

— and Grauze, A (1996) 'Enterprise Bargaining, Industrial Relations and Training Reforms in Australia', *Australian Bulletin of Labour*, 22:1, 59–80

Tennant, M (1986) 'An Evaluation of Malcolm Knowles' Theory of Adult Learning', *International Journal of Lifelong Education*, 2, 113–22

Thomson, P (1996) *Getting to Grips with Workplace Assessment*, National Centre for Vocational Education Research, Adelaide

— Mathers, R and Quirk, R (1996) *The Grade Debate: Should We Grade Competency-based Assessment?*, National Centre for Vocational Education Research, Adelaide

Thorndike, E L and Woodworth, R S (1901) '(1) The influence of improvement in one mental function upon the efficiency of other functions (2) The estimation of magnitudes (3) Functions involving attention, observation and discrimination', *Psychological Review*, 8, 247–61, 384–95, 553–64

Thurley, K and Wirdenius, H (1973) *Supervision: A Re-appraisal*, Heinemann, London

Tovey, M D (1997) *Training in Australia: Design, Delivery, Evaluation, Management*, Prentice-Hall, Sydney

Training Agency (1989) *Training in Britain: A Study of Funding, Activity and Attitudes*, HMSO, London

Training Costs Review Committee (1991) *Training Costs of Award Restructuring* (The 'Deveson Report'), AGPS, Canberra

Trengrove, W (1997) 'Multiskilling for Nuts and Chips', *Australian Training Review*, 21, 35–6

Trist, E L (1963) *Organizational choice*, Tavistock, London

Turrell, M (1980) *Training Analysis: A Guide to Recognising Training Needs*, MacDonald and Evans, Plymouth

Tuxworth, E (1989) 'Competency-based Education and Training' in J Burke (ed), *Competency based Education and Training*, Falmer Press, London, 10–25

Urwick, L F (1947) *The Elements of Administration*, Pitman, London

United States Congress, Office of Technology Assessment (1990) *Worker Training: Competing in the New International Economy*, OTA-ITE-457, Government Printing Office, Washington D C

Velten, M (1990) 'Training Guarantee Scheme: A Boon or Burden?', *Australian Accountant*, August, 26–9

Verlander, E G (1986) 'Incorporating Career Counselling into Management Development', *Journal of Management Development*, 5:5, 39–45

— (1989) 'Improving University Executive Programs', *Journal of Management Development*, 8:1, 5–19

Walton, R E (1985) 'From Control to Commitment in the Workplace', *Harvard Business Review*, 63:2, March–April

Warr, P, Bird, M and Rackham, N (1970) *Evaluation of Management Training*, Gower, Aldershot

Warren, M W (1979) *Training for Results: A Systems Approach to the Development of Human Resources in Industry*, Addison-Wesley, Reading, Mass

Watson, J B (1915) 'Psychology as the Behaviorist Views It', *Psychology Review*, No 20

Wawn, T, Green, J et al (1995) 'Experienced Insights: Opinions of Australian Managers, Ideals, Strengths and Weaknesses' in D S Karpin, *Enterprising Nation, Research Report Volume 1*, AGPS, Canberra

Weisbord, M R (1984) 'The Organization Development Contract Revisited' *Organisationsentwicklung*, (No) 15–26

Wertheimer, M (1961) *Productive Thinking*, Tavistock Publications, London

Wexley, K N and Latham, G P (1991) *Developing and Training Human Resources in Organizations*, 2nd ed, Harper Collins Publishers, New York

Whiteley, W, Dougherty, T W and Dreher, G F (1991) 'Relationship of Career Mentoring and Socioeconomic Origin to Managers' and Professionals' Early Career Progress', *Academy of Management Journal*, 34:2, 331–51

Wigley, J (1988) 'Evaluating Training: Critical Issues', *Training and Development in Australia*, 15:3, 21–4

Wilkinson, B (1983) *The Shopfloor Politics of New Technology*, Heinemann, London

Williams, B and Hayton, G (1987) *Report of Methods of Occupational and Training Needs Analysis*, TAFE National Centre for Research and Development, Adelaide

Williamson, O E (1975) *Markets and Hierarchies*, Free Press, New York

— (1980) 'The Organization of Work: A Comparative Institutional Assessment', *Journal of Economic Behaviour and Organization*, 1, 5–38

Wils, G (1991) 'Managing Networking — the Design and Dynamics of IMC', *Journal of European Industrial Training*, 15:2, 17–27

Wilson, J and Lilly, M (1996) *Recognition of Prior Learning*, National Centre for Vocational Education Research, Adelaide

Wilson, R (1987) *The Training Technology Programme*, Parthenon, Lancashire, UK

Wolf, A (1993) *Assessment Issues and Problems in Criterion-based Systems*, A Further Education Unit Occasional Paper

Womack, J, Jones, D and Roos, D (1990) *The Machine that Changed the World*, Rawson-Macmillan, New York

Woodruffe, C (1991) 'Competent by Any Other Name', *Personnel Management*, September, 30–3

Wray, D E (1949) 'Marginal Men of Industry', *American Journal of Sociology*, 54: 298–301

Wright, P M and McMahan, G C (1992) 'Theoretical Perspectives for Strategic Human Resource Management,' *Journal of Management*, 18:2, 295–320

Wright, R G and Werther, W B (1991) 'Mentors at Work', *Journal of Management Development*, 10:3, 25–32

Yau, W S L and Sculli, D (1990) 'Managerial Traits and Skills' *Journal of Management Development*, 9:6, 32–7

Zemke, R and Kramlinger, T (1982) *Figuring Things Out: A Trainer's Guide to Needs and Task Analysis*, Addison Wesley, Reading, Mass

Index

References are to pages

Action learning, 244–5
Action research, 263–4
Adult learning, 56–63
Alcan, 73
American Society for Training & Development, 2, 12, 71, 164
Andragogy, 58–61
Apprenticeships, 21, 34–7, 77–8
Assessment
  forms of, 189–91
    diagnostic, 190
    formative, 190
    holistic, 190
    summative, 190
  process of, 191–4
  graded, 193–4
  in the workplace, 195–6
Australian Committee for Training Curriculum (ACTRAC), 26, 30
Australian National Training Authority (ANTA), 20, 21–2, 26, 27, 28, 37, 39, 129, 252
Australian Public Service, 306
Australian Qualifications Framework, 26–7
Australian Standards Framework (ASF), 25
Australian Taxation Office, 55
Australian Vocational Training System, 25
Ausubel, David, 50–1
Award restructuring, 19, 24, 97–8

Bandura, Albert, 46–7, 172–3
Behaviour modelling, 46–7, 172–4
Behavioural objectives, 143–5
Behaviourism, 42–8
BHP Steel, 159
Bloom's Taxonomy, 142–3

Boyatzis, R, 229–30
Braverman, Harry, 90–2
Brinkerhof, R, 202–3
Bruner, Jerome, 49–50, 149
Business games, 241–2
Business schools, 237

Carmichael Report, 25
Case studies, 241
Castlemaine Perkins (XXXX), 99
CD-ROM, 181–2
Charles Sturt University, 107
Classical Management Theory, 226
Coaching, 292–5
Competency inventories, 133–4
Competency standards, 27, 28, 39, 100, 121
Competency-based training (CBT), 25–6, 29–34
  definitions of, 29
  design of, 154–7
  features of, 30–2
  implementation of, 33–4
Computer-based training, 178–82
  CAI, 179–80
  CAL, 180
  CML, 179
Concrete constructions, 135
Conditioning
  classical, 42–3
  operant, 43–6, 147
Consulting, 301–7
  client relationship, 302–5
  internal, 306–7
  process, 305–6
Core competencies, 106
Corporate culture, 265–8
  changing culture, 267–8
  elements of, 266–7
  problems with change, 268

Corporate strategy, 104–7
Cost/Benefit Analysis, 207–8
Counselling, 284–92
  career, 287–8
  managerial, 292
  models of, 285–6
  outplacement, 288–9
Criterion-referenced assessment, 188
Critical Incident Technique, 131–2
Cues, 147

Deming, W Edwards, 269
Declarative knowledge, 54
Design of training programs
  adult learning approach, 151–3
  behaviourist approach, 147–8
  information processing approach, 148–51
Development centres, 246–7
Dewey, John, 56–7
Discovery learning, 50
Discovery strategy, 154
Distance learning, 174–6
Drivers of training, 108–9
Dual system, 87–8

Employee assistance programs, 289–91
Employer Training Expenditure Survey, 7–8
Enterprise bargaining, 99–101
Entry-level training, 34–7
Epiphenomenalism, 45
Evaluation
  criteria, 211–14
  designs, 208–11
  models of, 198–203
  strategic, 214–16
  techniques of, 203–8
  types of, 197–9
Experiential learning, 61–3
Expositive strategy, 152–3

Film, 176
Finegold, David, 88–90, 234–5
Finn Review, 24–5
Flexible delivery, 32
Frontline Management Initiative (FMI), 252–3

Gagne, Robert, 51–2, 145–6, 148–9
General training, 77–8, 80

Gestalt, 48–9
Group for Research in Employment and Training (GREAT), 107, 273
Group training companies, 35

Happiness sheet, 204
Hella Australia, 191
High performance work organisations, 95–7
Holistic assessment, 190
Human Capital Theory, 76–82
  Neo-Human Capital Theory, 84
Human resource development
  definitions, 2–3
  practitioner competencies, 12–13
Human resource management, 101–4
Humanistic learning, 57–8

IBM Australia, 24, 171
ICI Botany, 198
Induction, 166–8
Industrial relations, 97–101
Industry Training Advisory Bodies (ITABs), 28
Informal (Incidental) learning, 71–2
Information processing, 52–5
Internal labour markets, 81–3
Internet, 182–4
Intranets, 184

Job Instruction Technique (JIT), 169

Karpin Committee, 223, 226, 247–50
Key competencies, 25
Kirkpatrick, Donald, 199–201, 218
Knowledge, 153–4
Knowles, Malcolm, 58–61, 151–2
Kohler, Wolfgang, 49
Kolb, David, 61–3

Labour Process Theory, 91–3
Lean production, 94
Learning contract, 59–60
Learning events, 148–9
Learning organisation, 276–80
  adaptation, 277
  building, 277–81
Learning outcomes, 145–6
Lewin, Kurt, 262
  model of change, 263

Manpower Services Commission, 2
Management Charter Initiative, 230
Management competencies, 228–30
Management development
  models of, 234–40
  objectives of, 232–3
  reasons for, 231
  work-based, 239–40
Managers
  education of, 223–5
  numbers of, 223
  roles of, 227–8
  traits of, 227
Master of Business Administration (MBA), 238–9
Mayer Report, 25
Mager, Robert, 143–4
Media, 176–84
Meister, 87–8
Mentoring, 295–9
  implementation of, 297–9
  mutual, 297–90
Metacognition/metamemory, 54
Mezirow, Jack, 72
Moderators of training, 109–11
Motorola, 82, 219
Multimedia, 181–2

National Framework for Recognition of Training (NFROT), 26, 27, 37
National Institute for Economic and Social Research, 85–8
National Training Board, 15, 25, 30
National Training Framework, 26, 27
National Training Reform Agenda, 17, 21–34
Natural learning, 293
NEC Australia, 6
NETTFORCE, 34–5
Norm-referenced assessment, 189
New South Wales Department of Industrial Relations, Employment, Training and Further Education, 270
New South Wales Premier's Department, 299
NUMMI, 279
NZI Insurance, 92

OECD/CERI, 83–5, 280
On-the-Job training, 168–72
Open learning, 174–6
Organisation development, 261–5

Orientation, 166–7
Outcomes evaluation, 199–201
Outdoor management programs, 242–4

Pacific Power, 289
Pavlov, Ivan, 42–3
Peer relationships, 300–1
Performance problem analysis, 117–19
Pirelli Cables, 155
Post-Fordism, 93
Practice
  distributed, 157
  massed, 157
Private training providers, 37–9
  types of, 38–9
Procedural knowledge, 54
Process evaluation, 201–3
Proctor and Gamble, 245
Progressive education, 56–7
Punishment, 44–5

Quality circles, 269–71
Quality of Work Life (QWL), 274
Questionnaires, 204

Ralph Report, 247
Recognition of current competencies, 195
Recognition of prior learning, 31, 194–5
Reinforcement, 44–5
Rogers, Carl, 57–8, 285–6
Role of trainers, 164–6
Role plays, 240–1
Romiszowski, A, 140–1, 153–4, 164

Saturn, 266
Schema, 54
Scientific management, 226
Self-development, 245–6
Self-paced learning, 31–2
Senge, Peter, 277–9
SET, 95–6
Shaping, 45, 147
Skills equilibrium, 88–90
Skinner, B F, 43–6
Smith's Snackfoods, 121
Social learning, 46–7, 171–2
Socialisation, 167–8
Specific training, 77–8, 80–1
Spiral learning, 149–50
Statistical Process Control (SPC), 269
Subsumption, 50

Supervisor, 251–2
Systems approach, 138–42

Technical and Further Education (TAFE), 17, 19, 36–9, 76, 252
Technology, 90–4
Total Quality Management (TQM), 96, 271–3
Toyota Motor Corporation, 94
Traineeships, 21, 25, 34–7
   Career Start, 25, 34
Training and development
   committees, 100
   definitions, 1–4
   environment, 157–8
   importance of, 4–7
   international comparisons of, 10–11
   practitioner, 11–16
Training and Education Experience Survey, 7–8
Training Costs Review Committee, 24
Training Guarantee Scheme, 7, 23–4
Training Needs Analysis (TNA)
   competency-based analysis, 119–22
   individual analysis, 116–17
   occupational analysis, 122–4
   operation analysis, 115–16
   organisation analysis, 115
Training packages, 27, 31
Training Practices Survey, 9–10

Uddevalla (Volvo), 279
User choice, 36, 37

Validation, 197–8
Validity
   external, 213–14
   internal, 212–13
Vestibule training, 172
Video, 176–8
Vocational education and training, 17, 20–1, 85, 87, 88–90

Western Australia Police Force, 175
Watson, J B, 42
Wertheimer, Max, 49
WMC Resources, 211
Woolworths, 233
Workplace learning, 69–74
Workplace trainer competencies, 13–15

Youth unemployment, 18–19

Notes

Notes

Notes

Notes

Notes

Notes

Notes

Notes

Notes

Notes